Joseph Barber Lightfoot

Essays on the Work

Entitled Supernatural Religion

Joseph Barber Lightfoot

Essays on the Work
Entitled Supernatural Religion

ISBN/EAN: 9783337130503

Printed in Europe, USA, Canada, Australia, Japan

Cover: Foto ©Lupo / pixelio.de

More available books at **www.hansebooks.com**

ESSAYS ON THE WORK

ENTITLED

SUPERNATURAL RELIGION

ESSAYS ON THE WORK

ENTITLED

SUPERNATURAL RELIGION

REPRINTED FROM
THE CONTEMPORARY REVIEW.

BY

J. B. LIGHTFOOT, D.D., D.C.L., LL.D.
BISHOP OF DURHAM.

London:
MACMILLAN AND CO.
AND NEW YORK.
1889

All Rights reserved.

PREFACE.

THIS republication of Essays which were written several years ago has no reference to any present controversies. Its justification is the fact that strangers and friends in England and America alike had urged me from time to time to gather them together, that they might be had in a more convenient form, believing that they contained some elements of permanent value which deserved to be rescued from the past numbers of a Review not easily procurable, and thus rendered more accessible to students. I had long resisted these solicitations for reasons which I shall explain presently; but a few months ago, when I was prostrated by sickness and my life was hanging on a slender thread, it became necessary to give a final answer to the advice tendered to me. This volume is the result. The kind offices of my chaplain the Rev. J. R. Harmer, who undertook the troublesome task of verifying the references, correcting the press, and adding the indices, when I was far too ill to attend to such matters myself, have enabled me to bring it out sooner than I had hoped.

When I first took up the book entitled 'Supernatural Religion', I felt, whether rightly or wrongly, that its criticisms were too loose and pretentious, and too full of errors, to produce any permanent effect; and for the most part attacks of this kind on the records of the Divine Life are best left alone. But

I found that a cruel and unjustifiable assault was made on a very dear friend to whom I was attached by the most sacred personal and theological ties; and that the book which contained this attack was from causes which need not be specified obtaining a notoriety unforeseen by me. Thus I was forced to break silence; and, as I advanced with my work, I seemed to see that, though undertaken to redress a personal injustice, it might be made subservient to the wider interests of the truth.

Paper succeeded upon paper, and I had hoped ultimately to cover the whole ground, so far as regards the testimony of the first two centuries to the New Testament Scriptures. But my time was not my own, as I was necessarily interrupted by other literary and professional duties which claimed the first place; and meanwhile I was transferred to another and more arduous sphere of practical work, being thus obliged to postpone indefinitely my intention of giving something like completeness to the work.

In republishing these papers then, the only course open to me, in justice to my adversary as well as to myself, was to reprint them in succession word for word as they appeared, correcting obvious misprints; though in many cases my argument might have been strengthened considerably. Recently discovered documents for instance have established the certainty of the main conclusions respecting Tatian's *Diatessaron*, to which the criticism of the available evidence had led me. Again I have since treated the Ignatian question more fully elsewhere, and satisfied myself on points about which I had expressed indecision in these Essays. On the other hand on one or two minor questions I might have used less confident language.

What shocked me in the book was not the extravagance of the opinions or the divergence from my own views; though I cannot pretend to be indifferent about the veracity of the records which profess to reveal Him, whom I believe to be not only the very Truth, but the very Life. I have often learnt very much even from extreme critics, and have freely acknowledged my obligations; but here was a writer who (to judge from his method) seemed to me, and not to me only[1], where it was a question of weighing probabilities, as is the case in most historical investigations, to choose invariably that alternative, even though the least probable, which would enable him to score a point against his adversary. For the rest I disclaim any personal bias, as against any personal opponent. The author of 'Supernatural Religion', as distinct from the work, is a mere blank to me. I do not even know his name, nor have I attempted to discover it. Whether he is living or dead, I know not. He preferred to write anonymously, and so far as I am concerned, I am glad that it was so; though, speaking for myself, I prefer taking the responsibility of my opinions and statements on important subjects.

In several instances the author either vouchsafed an answer to my criticisms, or altered the form of his statements in a subsequent edition. In all such cases references are scrupulously given in this volume to his later utterances. In most cases my assailant had the last word. He is welcome to it. I am quite willing that careful and impartial critics shall read my statements and his side by side, and judge between us. It is my sole desire, in great things and in small, to be found $\sigma \upsilon \nu \epsilon \rho \gamma \grave{o} \varsigma \ \tau \hat{\eta} \ \mathring{\alpha} \lambda \eta \theta \epsilon \acute{\iota} \alpha$.

[1] See Salmon's *Introduction to the New Testament* p. 9.

BOURNEMOUTH,
May 2, 1889.

TABLE OF CONTENTS.

		PAGE
I.	INTRODUCTION	1—31
II.	THE SILENCE OF EUSEBIUS	32—58
III.	THE IGNATIAN EPISTLES	59—88
IV.	POLYCARP OF SMYRNA	89—141
V.	PAPIAS OF HIERAPOLIS. I.	142—177
VI.	PAPIAS OF HIERAPOLIS. II.	178—216
VII.	THE LATER SCHOOL OF ST JOHN	217—250
VIII.	THE CHURCHES OF GAUL	251—271
IX.	TATIAN'S DIATESSARON	272—288
	DISCOVERIES ILLUSTRATING THE ACTS OF THE APOSTLES	291—302
	INDICES	303—324

SUPERNATURAL RELIGION.

I. INTRODUCTION.

[DECEMBER, 1874]

IF the author of *Supernatural Religion*[1] designed, by withholding his name, to stimulate public curiosity and thus to extend the circulation of his work, he has certainly not been disappointed in his hope. When the rumour once got abroad, that it proceeded from the pen of a learned and venerable prelate, the success of the book was secured. For this rumour indeed there was no foundation in fact. It was promptly and emphatically denied, when accidentally it reached the ears of the supposed author. But meanwhile the report had been efficacious. The reviewers had taken the work in hand and (with one exception) lavished their praises on the critical portions of it. The first edition was exhausted in a few months.

No words can be too strong to condemn the heartless cruelty of this imputation. The venerable prelate, on whom the authorship of this anonymous work was thrust, deserved least of all men to be exposed to such an insult. As an academic teacher and as an ecclesiastical ruler alike, he had distinguished himself by a courageous avowal of his opinions at all costs. For more than a quarter of a century he had lived in the full blaze

---

[1] *Supernatural Religion; An Inquiry into the Reality of Divine Revelation.* Two Vols. Second Edition, 1874. [Subsequent editions are as follows, Third and Fourth Editions (1874), Fifth and Sixth Editions (1875), Third Volume (1877), Complete Edition, in Three Vols. (1879).]

of publicity, and on his fearless integrity no breath of suspicion had ever rested. Yet now, when increasing infirmities obliged him to lay down his office, he was told that his life for years past had been one gigantic lie. The insinuation involved nothing less than this. Throughout those many years, during which the anonymous author, as he himself tells us, had been preparing for the publication of an elaborate and systematic attack upon Christianity, the bishop was preaching Christian doctrine, confirming Christian children, ordaining Christian ministers, without breathing a hint to the world that he felt any misgiving of the truths which he thus avowed and taught. Yet men talked as if, somehow or other, the cause of 'freethinking' had gained great moral support from the conversion of a bishop, though, if the rumour had been true, their new convert had for years past been guilty of the basest fraud of which a man is capable.

And all the while there was absolutely nothing to recommend this identification of the unknown author. The intellectual characteristics of the work present a trenchant contrast to the refined scholarship and cautious logic of this accomplished prelate. Only one point of resemblance could be named. The author shows an acquaintance with the theological critics of the modern Dutch school; and a knowledge of Dutch writers was known, or believed, to have a place among the acquisitions of this omniscient scholar. Truly no reputation is safe, when such a reputation is traduced on these grounds.

I have been assuming however that the work entitled *Supernatural Religion*, which lies before me, is the same work which the reviewers have applauded under this name. But, when I remember that the St Mark of Papias cannot possibly be our St Mark, I feel bound to throw upon this assumption the full light of modern critical principles; and, so tested, it proves to be not only hasty and unwarrantable, but altogether absurd. It is only necessary to compare the statements of highly intellectual reviewers with the work itself; and every unprejudiced mind must be convinced that 'the evidence is fatal to the claims' involved in this identification. Out of five reviews or notices of the work which I have read, only one seems to refer to our *Supernatural Religion*. The other four are plainly dealing with some apocryphal work, bearing the same name and often using the same language, but in its main characteristics quite different from and much more authentic than the volumes before me.

1. It must be observed in the first place, that the reviewers agree in attributing to the work scholarship and criticism of the highest order. 'The author,' writes one, 'is a scientifically trained critic. He has learned to argue and to weigh evidence.' 'The book,' adds a second, 'proceeds from a man of ability, a scholar and a reasoner.' 'His scholarship,' says this same reviewer again, 'is apparent throughout.' 'Along with a wide and minute scholarship,' he writes in yet another place, 'the unknown writer shows great acuteness.' Again a third reviewer, of whose general tone, as well as of his criticisms on the first part of the work, I should wish to speak with the highest respect, praises the writer's 'searching and scholarly criticism.' Lastly a fourth reviewer attributes to the author 'careful and acute scholarship.' This testimony is explicit, and it comes from four different quarters. It is moreover confirmed by the rumour already mentioned, which assigned the work to a bishop who has few rivals among his contemporaries as a scholar and a critic.

Now, since the documents which our author has undertaken to discuss are written almost wholly in the Greek and Latin languages, it may safely be assumed that under the term 'scholarship' the reviewers included an adequate knowledge of these languages. Starting from this as an axiom which will not be disputed, I proceed to inquire what we find in the work itself, which will throw any light on this point.

The example, which I shall take first, relates to a highly important passage of Irenæus[1], containing a reference in some earlier authority, whom this father quotes, to a saying of our

---

[1] Iren. v. 36. 1, 2.

Lord recorded only in St John's Gospel. The passage begins thus:—

'As the elders say, then also shall those deemed worthy of the abode in heaven depart thither; and others shall enjoy the delights of paradise; and others shall possess the splendour of the city; for everywhere the Saviour shall be seen according as they that see Him shall be worthy.'

Then follows the important paragraph which is translated differently by our author[1] and by Dr Westcott[2]. For reasons which will appear immediately, I place the two renderings side by side:—

Westcott.	Supernatural Religion.
'This distinction of dwelling, they taught, exists between those who brought forth a hundred-fold, and those who brought forth sixty-fold, and those who brought forth twenty-fold (Matt. xiii. 8). . . . And it was for this reason the Lord said that *in His Father's House* (ἐν τοῖς τοῦ πατρός) *are many mansions* (John xiv. 2)[3].'	'But there is to be this distinction[4] of dwelling (εἶναι δὲ τὴν διαστολὴν ταύτην τῆς οἰκήσεως) of those bearing fruit the hundred-fold, and of the (bearers of) the sixty-fold, and of the (bearers of) the thirty-fold: of whom some indeed shall be taken up into the heavens, some shall live in Paradise, and some shall inhabit the City, and for that reason (διὰ τοῦτο—*propter hoc*) the Lord declared many mansions to be in the (heavens) of my Father (ἐν τοῖς τοῦ πατρός μου μονὰς εἶναι πολλάς), etc.'

On this extract our author remarks that 'it is impossible for any one who attentively considers the whole of this passage and who makes himself acquainted with the manner in which Irenæus conducts his argument, and interweaves it with texts of Scripture, to doubt that the phrase we are considering is

---

[1] S. R. II. p. 328 sq.
[2] *Canon* p. 63, note 2.
[3] The Greek is Εἶναι δὲ τὴν διαστολὴν ταύτην τῆς οἰκήσεως...καὶ διὰ τοῦτο εἰρηκέναι τὸν Κύριον ἐν τοῖς τοῦ πατρός μου μονὰς εἶναι πολλάς κ.τ.λ.
[4] [Tacitly corrected in ed. 4 (II. p. 328) where the sentence runs: 'But... there is this distinction etc.' See below, p. 56.]

introduced by Irenæus himself, and is in no case a quotation from the work of Papias¹.' As regards the relation of this quotation from the Fourth Gospel to Papias any remarks, which I have to make, must be deferred for the present²; but on the other point I venture to say that any fairly trained schoolboy will feel himself constrained by the rules of Greek grammar to deny what our author considers it 'impossible' even 'to doubt.' He himself is quite unconscious of the difference between the infinitive and the indicative, or in other words between the oblique and the direct narrative; and so he boldly translates εἶναι τὴν διαστολήν as though it were ἔσται (or μέλλει εἶναι) ἡ διαστολή, and εἰρηκέναι τὸν Κύριον as though it were εἴρηκεν ὁ Κύριος. This is just as if a translator from a German original were to persist in ignoring the difference between 'es sey' and 'es ist' and between 'der Herr sage' and 'der Herr sagt.' Yet so unconscious is our author of the real point at issue, that he proceeds to support his view by several other passages in which Irenæus 'interweaves' his own remarks, because they happen to contain the words διὰ τοῦτο, though in every instance the indicative and *not the infinitive* is used. To complete this feat of scholarship he proceeds to charge Dr Westcott with what 'amounts to a falsification of the text³,' because this scholarly writer has inserted the words 'they taught' to show that in the original the sentence containing the reference to St John is in the oblique narrative and therefore reports the words of others⁴. I shall not retort this

¹ [The author's defence is dealt with, pp. 53 sq, 126 sq.]

² [The question is discussed below, p. 142 sq, where the author's subsequent explanation is considered.]

³ [This charge is withdrawn in ed. 4 (II. p. 328 n. 3), but objection is still taken to the words 'they taught' as conveying 'too positive a view of the case.' On the character of this withdrawal see below, p. 53 sq.]

⁴ Our author has already (II. p. 326) accused Tischendorf of 'deliberately falsifying the text by inserting, "say they."' Tischendorf's words are, 'Und deshalb sagen sie habe der Herr den Ausspruch gethan.' He might have spared the 'sagen sie,' because the German idiom 'habe' enables him to express the main fact that the words are not Irenæus' own, without this addition. But he has not altered any idea which the original contains; whereas our author himself has suppressed this all-important fact in his own translation. [On this treatment of Tischen-

charge of 'falsification,' because I do not think that the cause of truth is served by imputing immoral motives to those from whom we differ; and indeed the context shows that our author is altogether blind to the grammatical necessity. But I would venture to ask whether it would not have been more prudent, as well as more seemly, if he had paused before venturing, under the shelter of an anonymous publication, to throw out this imputation of dishonesty against a writer of singular candour and moderation, who has at least given to the world the hostage and the credential of an honoured name. It is necessary to add that our author persists in riveting this grammatical error on himself. He returns to the charge again in two later footnotes[1] and declares himself to have shown 'that it [the reference to the Fourth Gospel] must be referred to Irenæus himself, and that there is no ground for attributing it to the Presbyters at all.' 'Most critics,' he continues, 'admit the uncertainty[2].' As it will be my misfortune hereafter to dispute not a few propositions which 'most critics' are agreed in maintaining, it is somewhat reassuring to find that they are quite indifferent to the most elementary demands of grammar[3].

The passage just discussed has a vital bearing on the main question at issue, the date of the Fourth Gospel. The second example which I shall take, though less important, is not without its value. As in the former instance our author showed his indifference to moods, so here he is equally regardless of tenses. He is discussing the heathen Celsus, who shows an acquaintance with the Evangelical narratives, and whose

dorf see below, pp. 55 sq, 128, 138. The language is modified in ed. 4 (II. p. 326) 'Tischendorf renders the oblique construction of the text by inserting "say they" referring to the Presbyters of Papias,' where the point of grammar is silently conceded.]

The reader may compare S. R. II. p. 100, 'The lightness and inaccuracy with which the "Great African" proceeds is all the better illustrated by the fact, that not only does he accuse Marcion falsely, but he actually defines the motives for which he expunged the passage which never existed etc....he actually repeats the same charge on two other occasions.'

[1] S. R. II. p. 334.
[2] [On the wording of this footnote in ed. 4 see below, p. 58. It is omitted in ed. 6, where see II. p. 333.]
[3] [See further on this subject below, pp. 53 sq, 126 sq.]

date therefore it is not a matter of indifference to ascertain. Origen, in the preface to his refutation of Celsus, distinctly states that this person had been long dead (ἤδη καὶ πάλαι νεκρόν). In his first book again he confesses his ignorance who this Celsus was, but is disposed to identify him with a person of the name known to have flourished about a century before his own time[1]. But at the close of the last book[2], addressing his friend Ambrosius who had sent him the work, and at whose instance he had undertaken the refutation, he writes (or rather, he is represented by our author as writing) as follows:—

'Know, however, that Celsus has promised to write another treatise after this one. . . . If, therefore, he has not fulfilled his promise to write a second book, we may well be satisfied with the eight books in reply to his Discourse. If however, he has commenced and finished this work also, seek it and send it in order that we may answer it also, and confute the false teaching in it etc.[3]'

On the strength of the passage so translated, our author supposes that Origen's impression concerning the date of Celsus had meanwhile been 'considerably modified,' and remarks that he now 'treats him as a contemporary.' Unfortunately however, the tenses, on which everything depends, are freely handled in this translation. Origen does not say, 'Celsus *has promised*,' but 'Celsus *promises*' (ἐπαγγελλόμενον), *i.e.* in the treatise before him, for Origen's knowledge was plainly derived from the book itself. And again, he does not say 'If he *has not fulfilled* his promise to write,' but 'If he *did not write* as he undertook to do' (ἔγραψεν ὑποσχόμενος); nor 'if he *has commenced and finished*,' but 'if he *commenced and finished*' (ἀρξάμενος συνετέλεσε)[4]. Thus Origen's language itself here points to a past epoch, and is in strict accordance with the earlier passages in his work.

These two examples have been chosen, not because they are

---

[1] *c. Cels.* i. 8.
[2] *c. Cels.* viii. 76.
[3] *S. R.* II. p. 231 sq. [So also the Complete Edition (1879) II. p. 229 sq.]
[4] There is also another aorist in the part of the sentence, which our author has not quoted, ἄλλο σύνταγμα... ἐν ᾧ διδάξειν ἐπηγγείλατο.

by any means the worst specimens of our author's Greek, but because in both cases an elaborate argument is wrecked on this rock of grammar. If any reader is curious to see how he can drive his ploughshare through a Greek sentence, he may refer for instance to the translations of Basilides (II. p. 46)[1], or of Valentinus (II. p. 63)[2], or of Philo (II. p. 265 sq)[3]. Or he may draw his inferences from such renderings as ὁ λόγος ἐδήλου, 'Scripture declares[4],' or κατὰ κόρρης προπηλακίζειν[5], 'to inflict a blow on one side;' or from such perversions of meaning as 'did no wrong,' twice repeated[6] as a translation of οὐδὲν ἥμαρτε in an important passage of Papias relating to St Mark, where this Father really means that the Evangelist, though his narrative was not complete, yet 'made no mistake' in what he did record.

Nor does our author's Latin fare any better than his Greek, as may be inferred from the fact that he can translate 'nihil tamen differt credentium fidei,' 'nothing nevertheless differs in the faith of believers[7],' instead of 'it makes no difference to the faith of believers,' thus sacrificing sense and grammar alike[8]. Or it is still better illustrated by the following example:—

| 'Nam ex iis commentatoribus quos habemus, Lucam videtur Marcion elegisse quem caederet.' Tertull. adv. Marc. iv. 2. | 'For of the Commentators whom we possess, Marcion seems (*videtur*) to have selected Luke, which he mutilates.' S. R. II. p. 99[9]. |

Here again tenses and moods are quite indifferent, an imperfect subjunctive being treated as a present indicative;

---

[1] [Tacitly corrected in ed. 6 (II. p. 46).]

[2] [Some of the grammatical errors are corrected in ed. 6 (II. p. 63), where however new mistranslations are introduced, as πολλαχῶς 'in divers parts,' and οὕτω μακαρίζεται...ὅτι ὄψεται τὸν θεόν 'becomes so blessed that he shall see God.']

[3] [τὸ ῥῆμα from 'Reason' becomes 'Word' in ed. 6, but ζητήσαντες still remains 'they who inquire' (II. p. 265).]

[4] II. p. 296 sq. [Corrected in ed. 6.]

[5] II. p. 193. [Corrected in ed. 6.]

[6] I. p. 448, comp. p. 455. [The latter passage is struck out in ed. 6 (see I. p. 455); the former becomes 'committed no error.' See below, p. 163.]

[7] II. p. 384.

[8] [But in ed. 6 (II. p. 384) I see that my translation is tacitly substituted.]

[9] [Defended as a 'paraphrase' (see below, p. 129), but corrected in ed. 6, which also omits the first clause.]

while at the same time our author fails to perceive that the "commentatores" are the Evangelists themselves. His mind seems to be running on the Commentaries of De Wette and Alford, and he has forgotten the Commentaries of Cæsar[1].

Having shown that the author does not possess the elementary knowledge which is indispensable in a critical scholar, I shall not stop to inquire how far he exhibits those higher qualifications of a critic, which are far more rare—whether for instance he has the discriminating tact and nice balance of judgment necessary for such a work, or whether again he realizes how men in actual life do speak and write now, and might be expected to speak and write sixteen or seventeen centuries ago—without which qualifications the most painful study and reproduction of German and Dutch criticism is valueless. These qualifications cannot be weighed or measured, and I must trust to my subsequent investigations to put the reader in possession of data for forming a judgment on these points. At present it will be sufficient to remark that a scholarly writer might at least be expected not to contradict himself on a highly important question of Biblical criticism. Yet this is what our author does. Speaking of the descent of the angel at the pool of Bethesda (John v. 3, 4) in his first part, he writes: 'The passage is not found in the older MSS of the Fourth Gospel, and it was probably a later interpolation[2].' But, having occasion towards the end of his work to refer again to this same passage, he entirely forgets his previously expressed opinion, and is very positive on the other side. 'We must believe,' he writes, 'that this passage did originally belong to the text, and has from an early period been omitted from the

---

[1] [Other errors in translation are given below, p. 129.]

[2] I. p. 113. The last words ran 'certainly a late interpolation' in the first edition (I. p. 103). Thus the passage has undergone revision, and yet the author has not discovered the contradiction. [The author's own explanation of this discrepancy is given below, p. 124. In ed. 6 (I. p. 113) the sentence ends, 'and it is argued that it was probably a later interpolation,' while in the Complete Edition (I. p. 113) it is further qualified 'argued by some.']

MSS on account of the difficulty it presents[1].' And, to make the contradiction more flagrant, he proceeds to give a reason why the disputed words must have formed part of the original text.

It must be evident by this time to any 'impartial mind,' that the *Supernatural Religion* of the reviewers cannot be our *Supernatural Religion*. The higher criticism has taught me that poor foolish Papias, an extreme specimen of 'the most deplorable carelessness and want of critical judgment' displayed by the Fathers on all occasions, cannot possibly have had our St Mark's Gospel before him[2], because he says that his St Mark recorded only 'some' of our Lord's sayings and doings, and did not record them in order (though by the way no one maintains that everything said and done by Christ is recorded in our Second Gospel, or that the events follow in strict chronological sequence); and how then is it possible to resist the conclusion, which is forced upon the mind by the concurrent testimony of so many able reviewers, the leaders of intellectual thought in this critical nineteenth century, to the consummate scholarship of the writer, that they must be referring to a different recension, probably more authentic and certainly far more satisfactory than the book which lies before me?

2. And the difficulty of the popular identification will be found to increase as the investigation proceeds. There is a second point, also, on which our critics are unanimous. Our first reviewer describes the author as 'scrupulously exact in stating the arguments of adversaries.' Our fourth reviewer uses still stronger language: 'The author with excellent candour places before us the materials on which a judgment must rest, with great fulness and perfect impartiality.' The testimony of the other two, though not quite so explicit, tends in the same direction. 'An earnest seeker after truth,' says the second reviewer, 'looking around at all particulars pertaining to his inquiries.' 'The account given in the volume

---

[1] II. p. 421. [The argument in favour of the genuineness is expanded in the Complete Edition (II. pp. 419-423).]
[2] [See below, p. 163 sq.]

we are noticing,' writes the third, 'is a perfect mine of information on this subject, alloyed indeed with no small prejudice, yet so wonderfully faithful and comprehensive that an error may be detected by the light of the writer's own searching and scholarly criticism.'

Now this is not the characteristic of the book before me. The author does indeed single out from time to time the weaker arguments of 'apologetic' writers, and on these he dwells at great length; but their weightier facts and lines of reasoning are altogether ignored by him, though they often occur in the same books and even in the same contexts which he quotes. This charge will, I believe, be abundantly substantiated as I proceed. At present I shall do no more than give a few samples.

Our author charges the Epistle ascribed to Polycarp with an anachronism[1], because, though in an earlier passage St Ignatius is assumed to be dead, 'in chap. xiii he is spoken of as living, and information is requested regarding him "and those who are with him."' Why then does he not notice the answer which he might have found in any common source of information, that when the Latin version (the Greek is wanting here) 'de his qui cum eo sunt' is retranslated into the original language, τοῖς σὺν αὐτῷ, the 'anachronism' altogether disappears[2]? Again, when he devotes more than forty pages to the discussion of Papias[3], why does he not even mention the view maintained by Dr Westcott and others (and certainly suggested by a strict interpretation of Papias' own words), that this father's object in his 'Exposition' was not to construct a new evangelical narrative, but to interpret and illustrate by oral tradition one already lying before him in written documents[4]? This view, if correct, entirely alters the relation of Papias to the written Gospels; and its discussion was a matter of essential importance to the main question at issue. Again,

---

[1] S. R. I. p. 276. [And so throughout all the editions.]
[2] [See below, p. 111.]
[3] I. pp. 444—485.
[4] [The subject is treated at length below, p. 142 sq.]

when he reproduces the Tübingen fallacy respecting 'the strong prejudice' of Hegesippus against St Paul[1], and quotes the often-quoted passage from Stephanus Gobarus, in which this writer refers to the language of Hegesippus condemning the use of the words, 'Eye hath not seen, etc.,' why does he not state that these words were employed by heretical teachers to justify their rites of initiation, and consequently 'apologetic' writers contend that Hegesippus refers to the words, not as used by St Paul, but as misapplied by these heretics? Since, according to the Tübingen interpretation, this single notice contradicts everything else which we know of the opinions of Hegesippus[2], the view of 'apologists' might perhaps have been worth a moment's consideration. And again, in the elaborate examination of Justin Martyr's evangelical quotations[3], in which he had Credner's careful analysis to guide him, and which therefore is quite the most favourable specimen of his critical work, our author frequently refers to Dr Westcott's book to censure it, and many comparatively insignificant points are discussed at great length. Why then does he not once mention Dr Westcott's argument founded on the looseness of Justin Martyr's quotations from the Old Testament, as throwing some light on the degree of accuracy which he might be expected to show in quoting the Gospels[4]? The former Justin supposed to be (as one of the reviewers expresses it) 'almost automatically inspired,' whereas he took a much larger view of the inspiration of the evangelical narratives. A reader fresh from the perusal of *Supernatural Religion* will have his eyes

---

[1] I. p. 441.

[2] [On Hegesippus see below, pp. 34 sq. 42.]

[3] [On Justin Martyr see below, p. 43.]

[4] In I. p. 360, there is a foot-note, 'For the arguments of apologetic criticism the reader may be referred to Canon Westcott's work *On the Canon* pp. 112—139. Dr Westcott does not attempt to deny the fact that Justin's quotations are different from the text of our Gospels; but he accounts for his variations on grounds which are'['seem to us' ed. 6] 'purely imaginary.' I can hardly suppose that our author had read the passage to which he refers. Otherwise the last sentence would doubtless have run thus, 'but he accounts for his variations by arguments which it would give me some trouble to answer.'

opened as to the character of Justin's mind, when he turns to Dr Westcott's book, and finds how Justin interweaves, mis-names, and mis-quotes passages from the Old Testament. It cannot be said that these are unimportant points. In every instance which I have selected these omitted considerations vitally affect the main question at issue.

Our fourth reviewer however uses the words which I have already quoted, 'excellent candour,' 'great fulness,' 'perfect impartiality,' with special reference to the part of the work relating to the authorship and character of the Fourth Gospel, which he describes as 'a piece of keen and solid reasoning.' This is quite decisive. Our author might have had his own grounds for ignoring the arguments of 'apologetic' writers, or he may have been ignorant of them. For reasons which will appear presently, the latter alternative ought probably to be adopted as explaining some omissions. But however this may be, the language of the reviewer is quite inapplicable to the work lying before me. It may be candid in the sense of being honestly meant, but it is not candid in any other sense; and it is the very reverse of full and impartial. The arguments of 'apologetic' writers are systematically ignored in this part of the work. Once or twice indeed he fastens on passages from such writers, that he may make capital of them; but their main arguments remain wholly unnoticed. Why, for instance, when he says of the Fourth Gospel that 'instead of the fierce and intolerant temper of the Son of Thunder, we find a spirit breathing forth nothing but gentleness and love[1],' does he forget to add that 'apologists' have pointed to such passages as 'Ye are of your father the devil,' as a refutation of this statement—passages far more 'intolerant' than anything recorded in the Synoptic Gospels[2]? Why again, when he asserts that 'allusion is undoubtedly made to' St Paul in the words of the Apocalypse, 'them that hold the teaching of Balaam, who taught Balak to cast a stumblingblock before the children of

[1] II. p. 411.
[2] Our author himself refers to this saying for a wholly different purpose later on (II. p. 416).

Israel, to eat things sacrificed to idols[1],' does he forget to mention that St Paul himself uses this same chapter in Jewish history as a warning to those free-thinkers and free-livers, who eat things sacrificed to idols, regardless of the scandal which their conduct might create, and thus, so far from a direct antagonism, there is a substantial agreement between the two Apostles on this point[2]? Why, when he is endeavouring to minimize, if not to deny, the Hebraic[3] character of the Fourth Gospel, does he wholly ignore the investigations of Luthardt and others, which (as 'apologists' venture to think) show that the whole texture of the language in the Fourth Gospel is Hebraic? Why again, when he alludes to 'the minuteness of details[4]' in this Gospel as alleged in defence of its authenticity, is he satisfied with this mere caricature of the 'apologetic' argument? Having set up a man of straw, he has no difficulty in knocking him down. He has only to declare that 'the identification of an eye-witness by details is absurd.' It would have been more to the purpose if he had boldly grappled with such arguments

---

[1] II. p. 408. Our author says, 'It is clear that Paul is referred to in the address to the Church of Ephesus: "And thou didst try them which say that they are Apostles and are not, and didst find them false."' He seems to forget what he himself has said (p. 395), 'No result of criticism rests upon a more secure basis...than the fact that the Apocalypse was written in A.D. 68, 69,' i.e., after St Paul's death. This theory moreover is directly at variance with the one definite fact which we know respecting the personal relations between the two Apostles; namely, that they gave to each other the right hands of fellowship (Gal. ii. 9). It is surprising therefore that this extravagant paradox should have been recently reproduced in an English review of high character.

[2] 1 Cor. x. 7, 8, 14, 21. When the season of persecution arrived, and the constancy of Christians was tested in this very way, St Paul's own principles would require a correspondingly rigid abstinence from even apparent complicity in idolatrous rites. There is every reason therefore to believe that, if St Paul had been living when the Apocalypse was written, he would have expressed himself not less strongly on the same side. On the other hand these early Gnostics who are denounced in the Apocalypse seem, like their successors in the next generation, to have held that a Christian might conform to Gentile practices in these matters to escape persecution. St Paul combats this spirit of license, then in its infancy, in the First Epistle to the Corinthians.

[3] [On the diction of the Fourth Gospel see below, p. 131 sq.]

[4] II. p. 445.

as he might have found in Mr Sanday's book for instance[1]; arguments founded not on the minuteness of details, but on the thorough naturalness with which the incidents develop themselves, on the subtle and inobtrusive traits of character which appear in the speakers, on the local colouring which is inseparably interwoven with the narrative, on the presence of strictly Jewish (as distinguished from Christian) ideas, more especially Messianic ideas, which saturate the speeches, and the like. And, if he could have brought forward any parallel to all this in the literature of the time, or could even have shown a reasonable probability that such a fiction might have been produced in an age which (as we are constantly reminded) was singularly inappreciative and uncritical in such matters, and which certainly has not left any evidence of a genius for realism, for its highest conception of romance-writing does not rise above the stiffness of the Clementines or the extravagance of the Protevangelium —if he could have done this, he would at least have advanced his argument a step[2]. Why again, when he is emphasizing the differences between the Apocalypse and the Fourth Gospel, does he content himself with stating 'that some apologetic writers' are 'satisfied by the analogies which could scarcely fail to exist between two works dealing with a similar (!) theme[3],' without mentioning for the benefit of the reader some of these analogies, as for instance, that our Lord is styled the Word of God in these two writings, and these alone, of the New Testament? He recurs more than once to the doctrine of the Logos, as exhibited in the Gospel, but again he is silent about the presence of this nomenclature in the Apocalypse[4]. Why, when he contrasts the Christology of the Synoptic Gospels with the Christology of St John[5], does he not mention that 'apologists' quote in reply

---

[1] [*The Authorship and Historical Character of the Fourth Gospel* (1872). Macmillans.]

[2] Our author (II. p. 444) speaks of 'the works of imagination of which the world is full, and the singular realism of many of which is recognized by all.' Is this a true description of the world in the early Christian ages? If not, it is nothing to the purpose.

[3] II. p. 389. 'Apologists' lay stress on the *difference* of theme. [See below, p. 131 sq.]

[4] [He does however mention the term elsewhere; see below, p. 123.]

[5] II. p. 468, and elsewhere.

our Lord's words in Matt. xi. 27 sq, 'All things are delivered unto me of my Father; and no man knoweth the Son but the Father; neither knoweth any man the Father, save the Son, and he to whom soever the Son will reveal him. Come unto me, all ye that labour and are heavy laden, and I will give you rest'? This one passage, they assert, covers the characteristic teaching of the Fourth Gospel, and hitherto they have not been answered. Again, our author says very positively that 'the Synoptics clearly represent the ministry of Jesus as having been limited to a single year, and his preaching is confined to Galilee and Jerusalem, where his career culminates at the fatal Passover;' thus contrasting with the Fourth Gospel, which 'distributes the teaching of Jesus between Galilee, Samaria, and Jerusalem, makes it extend at least over three years, and refers to three Passovers spent by Jesus at Jerusalem[1].' Why then does he not add that 'apologetic' writers refer to such passages as Matt. xxiii. 37 (comp. Luke xiii. 34), 'O, Jerusalem, Jerusalem, ...*how often* would I have gathered thy children together'? Here the expression 'how often,' it is contended, obliges us to postulate other visits, probably several visits, to Jerusalem, which are not recorded in the Synoptic Gospels themselves. And it may be suggested also that the twice-repeated notice of time in the context of St Luke, 'I do cures *to-day and to-morrow, and the third day* I shall be perfected,' 'I must walk *to-day and to-morrow and the day following*,' points to the very duration of our Lord's ministry, as indicated by the Fourth Gospel[2]. If so, the coincidence is the more remarkable, because it does not appear that St Luke himself, while recording these prophetic words, was aware of their full historical import. But whatever may be thought of this last point, the contention of 'apologetic' writers is that here, as elsewhere, the Fourth Gospel supplies the key to historical difficulties in the Synoptic narratives, which are not unlocked in the course of those narratives themselves, and this fact increases their confidence in its value as an authentic record[3].

[1] II. p. 451.

[2] [These passages are added without comment in the Complete Edition in a note on II. p. 453.]

[3] [On this point see below, p. 131.]

I. INTRODUCTION.

Again: he refers several times to the Paschal controversy of the second century as bearing on the authorship of the Fourth Gospel. On one occasion he devotes two whole pages to it[1]. Why then does he not mention that 'apologetic' writers altogether deny what he states to be absolutely certain; maintaining on the contrary that the Christian Passover, celebrated by the Asiatic Churches on the 14th Nisan, commemorated not the Institution of the Lord's Supper, but, as it naturally would, the Sacrifice on the Cross, and asserting that the main dispute between the Asiatic and Roman Churches had reference to the question whether the commemoration should take place always on the 14th Nisan (irrespective of the day of the week) or always on a Friday? Thus, they claim the Paschal controversy as a witness on their own side. This view may be right or wrong; but inasmuch as any person might read the unusually full account of the controversy in Eusebius from beginning to end, without a suspicion that the alternative of the 14th or 15th Nisan, as the day of the Crucifixion, entered into the dispute at all, the *onus probandi* rests with our author, and his stout assertions were certainly needed to supply the place of arguments[2].

The same reticence or ignorance respecting the arguments of 'apologetic' writers is noticeable also when he deals with the historical and geographical allusions in the Fourth Gospel. If by any chance he condescends to discuss a question, he takes care to fasten on the least likely solution of 'apologists' (*e. g.* the identification of Sychar and Shechem)[3], omitting altogether to

---

[1] II. p. 472 sq; comp. pp. 186 sq, 271. [The statement stands unchanged in the Complete Edition (II. p. 474 sq).]

[2] [See further, p. 99 sq.]

[3] II. p. 421. Travellers and 'apologists' alike now more commonly identify Sychar with the village bearing the Arabic name Askar. This fact is not mentioned by our author. He says moreover, 'It is admitted' ['evident' ed. 6] 'that there was no such place [as Sychar, Συχάρ], and apologetic ingenuity is severely taxed to explain the difficulty.' This is altogether untrue. Others besides 'apologists' point to passages in the Talmud which speak of 'the well of Suchar (or Sochar, or Sichar);' see Neubauer *La Géographie du Talmud* p. 169 sq. Our author refers in his note to an article by Delitzsch *Zeitschr. f. Luth. Theol.* 1856 p. 240 sq.

notice others[1]. But as a rule, he betrays no knowledge whatever of his adversaries' arguments. One instance will suffice to illustrate his mode of procedure. Referring to the interpretation of Siloam as 'sent,' in John ix. 7, he stigmatizes this as 'a distinct error,' because the word signifies 'a spring, a fountain, a flow of water;' and he adds that 'a foreigner with a slight knowledge of the language is misled by the superficial analogy of sound[2].' Does he not know (his Gesenius will teach him this) that Siloam signifies a fountain, or rather, an aqueduct, a conduit, like the Latin *emissarium*, because it is derived from the Hebrew *shalach* 'to send'? and if he does know it, why has he left his readers entirely in the dark on this subject? As the word is much disguised in its Greek dress (*Siloam* for *Shiloach*), the knowledge of its derivation is not unimportant, and 'apologists' claim to have this item of evidence transferred to their side of the account. Any one disposed to retaliate upon our author for his habitual reticence would find in these volumes, ready made for his purpose, a large assortment of convenient phrases ranging from 'discreet reserve' to 'wilful and deliberate evasion.' I do not intend to yield to this temptation. But the reader will have drawn his own conclusions from this recklessness of assault in one whose own armour is gaping at every joint.

But indeed, when he does stoop to notice the arguments of 'apologetic' writers, he is not always successful in apprehending their meaning.

Thus he writes of the unnamed disciple, the assumed author of the Fourth Gospel:—

'The assumption that the disciple thus indicated is John, rests principally on the fact that whilst the author mentions the other Apostles, he seems studiously to avoid directly naming John, and also that he only once[3] distinguishes John the Baptist by the ap-

He cannot have read the article, for these Talmudic references are its main purport.

[1] [The whole question of Sychar is treated at length below, p. 133 sq, where also the author's explanation of his meaning is given.]

[2] II. p. 419. [This whole section is struck out in the Complete Edition (see II. p. 417), but the error survived ed. 6 (II. p. 419).]

[3] ['never once' ed. 6 (II. p. 424).]

pellation ὁ βαπτιστής, whilst he carefully distinguishes the two disciples of the name of Judas, and always speaks of the Apostle Peter as 'Simon Peter,' or 'Peter,' or but rarely as 'Simon' only. Without pausing to consider the slightness of this evidence, etc.[1]'

Now the fact is, that the Fourth Evangelist never once distinguishes this John as 'the Baptist,' though such is his common designation in the other Gospels; and the only person, in whom the omission would be natural, is his namesake John the son of Zebedee. Hence 'apologists' lay great stress on this fact, as an evidence all the more valuable, because it lies below the surface, and they urge with force, that this subtle indication of authorship is inconceivable as the literary device of a forger in the second century. We cannot wonder, however, if our author considers this evidence so slight that he will not even pause upon it, when he has altogether distorted it by a mis-statement of fact. But it is instructive to trace his error to its source. Turning to Credner, to whom the author gives a reference in a footnote, I find this writer stating that the Fourth Evangelist

'Has not found it necessary to distinguish John the Baptist from the Apostle John his namesake *even so much as once* (auch nur ein einziges Mal) by the addition ὁ βαπτιστής[2].'

So then our author has stumbled over that little word 'nur,' and his German has gone the way of his Greek and his Latin[3]. But the error is instructive from another point of view. This argument happens to be a commonplace of 'apologists.' How comes it then, that he was not set right by one or other of these many writers, even if he could not construe Credner's German? Clearly this cannot be the work which the reviewers credit with an 'exhaustive' knowledge of the

[1] II. p. 423 sq.
[2] Credner *Einl.* I. p. 210 '...hat er es nicht für nöthig gefunden, den Täufer Johannes von dem gleichnamigen Apostel Johannes auch nur ein einziges Mal durch den Zusatz ὁ βαπ- τιστής zu unterscheiden (i. 6, 15, 19, 26, 28, 29, 32, 35, 41; iii. 23, 24, 25, 26, 27; iv. 1; v. 33, 36; x. 40, 41).'
[3] [For the author's own explanation of this error see below, p. 124 sq.]

literature of the subject. I may be asked indeed to explain how, on this theory of mistaken identity which I here put forward, the work reviewed by the critics came to be displaced by the work before me, so that no traces of the original remain. But this I altogether decline to do, and I plead authority for refusing. 'The merely negative evidence that our actual [*Supernatural Religion*] is not the work described by [the Reviewers] is sufficient for our purpose[1].'

3. But the argument is strengthened when we come to consider a third point. 'The author's discussions,' writes our first reviewer, 'are conducted in a judicial method.' 'He has the critical faculty in union with a calm spirit.' 'Calm and judicial in tone,' is the verdict of our second reviewer. The opinion of our third and fourth reviewers on this part may be gathered not so much from what they say as from what they leave unsaid. A fifth reviewer however, who seems certainly to have had our *Supernatural Religion* before him, holds different language. He rebukes the author—with wonderful gentleness, considering the gravity of the offence—for 'now and then losing patience.'

Now whether calmness of tone can be said to distinguish a work which bristles with such epithets as 'monstrous,' 'impossible,' 'audacious,' 'preposterous,' 'absurd;' whether the habit of reiterating as axiomatic truths what at the very best are highly precarious hypotheses—as, for instance, that Papias did not refer to our St Mark's Gospel—does not savour more of the vehemence of the advocate than of the impartiality of the judge, I must ask the reader to decide for himself. But of the highly discreditable practice of imputing corrupt motives to those who differ from us there cannot be two opinions. We have already seen how a righteous nemesis has overtaken our author, and he has covered himself with confusion, while recklessly flinging a charge of 'falsification' at another. Unfortunately however that passage does not stand alone. I will not take up the reader's time with illustrations of a practice, of

[1] *S. R.* I. p. 459.

which we have seen more than enough already. But there is one example which is sufficiently instructive to deserve quoting. Dr Westcott writes of Basilides as follows:—

'At the same time, he appealed to the authority of Glaucias, who, as well as St Mark, was "an interpreter of St Peter[1]."'

The inverted commas are given here as they appear in Dr Westcott's book. It need hardly be said that Dr Westcott is simply illustrating the statement of Basilides that Glaucias was an interpreter of St Peter by the similar statement of Papias and others that St Mark was an interpreter of the same apostle—a very innocent piece of information, one would suppose. On this passage however our author remarks:—

'Now we have here again an illustration of the same misleading system which we have already condemned, and shall further refer to, in the introduction after 'Glaucias' of the words '*who as well as St Mark was* an interpreter of St Peter.' The words in italics are the gratuitous addition of Canon Westcott himself, and can only have been inserted for one of two purposes: (I) to assert the fact that Glaucias was actually an interpreter of Peter, as tradition represented Mark to be; or (II) to insinuate to unlearned readers that Basilides himself acknowledged Mark as well as Glaucias as the interpreter of Peter. We can hardly suppose the first to have been the intention, and we regret to be forced back upon the second, and infer that the temptation to weaken the inferences from the appeal of Basilides to the uncanonical Glaucias, by coupling with it the allusion to Mark, was [unconsciously, no doubt] too strong for the apologist[2].'

Dr Westcott's honour may safely be left to take care of itself. It stands far too high to be touched by insinuations like

---

[1] *Canon* p. 264. The words of Clement (*Strom.* vii. 17) to which Dr Westcott refers, are: Καθάπερ ὁ Βασιλείδης, κἂν Γλαυκίαν ἐπιγράφηται διδάσκαλον, ὡς αὐχοῦσιν αὐτοί, τὸν Πέτρου ἑρμηνέα.

[2] *S. R.* II. p. 44 sq. The words which I have enclosed in brackets were inserted in the Second Edition. A frank withdrawal would have been worth something; but this insertion only aggravates the offence. [After having been partly re-written in ed. 6 (II. p. 44), the whole section is cut out in the Complete Edition (see II. p. 44).]

these. I only call attention to the fact that our author has removed Dr Westcott's inverted commas[1], and then founded on the passage so manipulated a charge of unfair dealing, which could only be sustained in their absence, and which even then no one but himself would have thought of. I will not retort upon our author the charge of 'deliberate falsification,' which he so freely levels at others, for I do not believe that he had any such intention. The lesson suggested by this highly characteristic passage is of another kind. It exemplifies the elaborate looseness which pervades the critical portion of this book. It illustrates the author's inability to look at things in a straightforward way. It emphasizes more especially the suspicious temper of the work, which makes it, as even a favourable reviewer has said, 'painfully sceptical'—a temper which must necessarily vitiate all the processes of criticism, and which, if freely humoured elsewhere, would render life intolerable and history impossible[2].

It is difficult to see what end the author proposed to attain by all this literary browbeating. In the course of my examination I shall be constrained to adopt many a view which has been denounced beforehand as impossible and absurd; and I shall give my reasons for doing so. If by an 'apologist'[3] is meant one who knows that he owes everything which is best and truest in himself to the teaching of Christianity—not the Christless Christianity which alone our author would spare, the works with the mainspring broken, but the Christianity of the Apostles and Evangelists—who believes that its doctrines, its sanctions, and its hopes, are truths of the highest moment to the wellbeing of mankind, and who, knowing and believing all this, is ready to use in its defence such abilities as he has, then a man may be proud to take even the lowest place among the ranks of 'apologists,' and to brave any insinuations of dishonesty which an anonymous critic may fling at him.

[1] [For the author's explanation of his language see below, p. 123 sq.]

[2] [This point is reverted to below, pp. 134, 137 sq.]

[3] [Our author's explanation of the term is given below, p. 134.]

There is however another more subtle mode of intimidation which plays an important part in these volumes. Long lists of references are given in the notes, to modern critics who (as the reader would infer from the mode of reference) support the views mentioned or adopted by the author in the text. I have verified these references in one or two cases, and have found that several writers, at all events, do not hold the opinions to which their names are attached[1]. But, under any circumstances, these lists will not fetter the judgment of any thoughtful mind. It is strange indeed, that a writer who denounces so strongly the influence of authority as represented by tradition, should be anxious to impose on his readers another less honourable yoke. There is at least a presumption (though in individual cases it may prove false on examination) that the historical sense of seventeen or eighteen centuries is larger and truer than the critical insight of a section of men in one late half century. The idols of our cave never present themselves in a more alluring form than when they appear as the 'spirit of the age.' It is comparatively easy to resist the fallacies of past times, but it is most difficult to escape the infection of the intellectual atmosphere in which we live. I ask myself, for instance, whether one who lived in the age of the rabbis would have been altogether right in resigning himself to the immediate current of intellectual thought, because he saw, or seemed to see, that it was setting strongly in one direction.

This comparison is not without its use. Here were men eminently learned, painstaking, minute; eminently ingenious also, and in a certain sense, eminently critical. In accumulating and assorting facts—such facts as lay within their reach— and in the general thoroughness of their work, the rabbis of Jewish exegesis might well bear comparison with the rabbis of neologian criticism. They reigned supreme in their own circles for a time; their work has not been without its fruits; many useful suggestions have gone to swell the intellectual and moral inheritance of later ages; but their characteristic

[1] [One such list is dealt with in full, p. 65 sq.]

teaching, which they themselves would have regarded as their chief claim to immortality, has long since been consigned to oblivion. It might be minute and searching, but it was conceived in a false vein; it was essentially unhistorical, and therefore it could not live. The modern negative school of criticism seems to me to be equally perverse and unreal, though in a different way; and therefore I anticipate for it the same fate.

Mr Matthew Arnold, alluding to an eccentric work of rationalizing tendencies written by an English scholar, and using M. Renan as his mouthpiece, expresses the opinion that 'an extravagance of this sort could never have come from Germany where there is a great force of critical opinion controlling a learned man's vagaries, and keeping him straight[1].' I confess that my experiences of the critical literature of Germany have not been so fortunate. It would be difficult, I think, to find among English scholars any parallel to the mass of absurdities, which several intelligent and very learned German critics have conspired to heap upon two simple names in the Philippian Epistle, Euodia and Syntyche; first, Baur suggesting that the pivot of the Epistle, which has a conciliatory tendency, is the mention of Clement, a mythical or almost mythical person, who represents the union of the Petrine and Pauline parties in the Church[2]; then Schwegler, carrying the theory a step further, and declaring that the two names, Euodia and Syntyche, actually represent these two parties, while the true yoke-fellow is St Peter himself[3]; then Volkmar, improving the occasion, and showing that this fact is indicated in their very names, Euodia or 'Rightway,' and Syntyche or 'Consort,' denoting respectively the orthodoxy of the one party and the incorporation of the other[4]; lastly, Hitzig lamenting that interpreters of the New Testament are not more thoroughly imbued with the language and spirit of the Old, and maintain-

---

[1] *Essays in Criticism* p. 57.
[2] *Paulus* p. 469 sq (1st ed.).
[3] *Nachapost. Zeitalter* II. p. 135.
[4] *Theolog. Jahrb.* xv. p. 311 sq, xvi. p. 147 sq.

ing that these two names are reproductions of the patriarchs Asher and Gad—their sex having been changed in the transition from one language to another—and represent the Greek and Roman elements in the Church, while the Epistle to the Philippians itself is a plagiarism from the Agricola of Tacitus[1]. When therefore I find our author supporting some of his more important judgments by the authority of 'Hitzig, Volkmar and others,' or of 'Volkmar and others[2],' I have my own opinion of the weight which such names should carry with them[3].

It is not however against the eccentricities of individuals, except so far as these can be charged to a vicious atmosphere and training, that I would rest the chief stress of my complaint. The whole tone and spirit of the school in its excess of scepticism must, I venture to think, be fatal to the ends of true criticism. A reviewer of *Supernatural Religion* compares the author's handling of the reconstructive efforts of certain conservative critics regarding the Fourth Gospel to Sir G. C. Lewis's objections to Niebuhr's 'equally arbitrary reconstruction of early Roman history.' From one point of view this comparison is instructive. We have no means of testing the value of that eminent writer's negative criticisms of early Roman history. But where additional knowledge has enabled us to apply a test to his opinions, as, for instance, respecting the interpretation of the Egyptian hieroglyphic language, we find that his scepticism led him signally astray.

---

[1] *Zur Kritik Paulinischer Briefe.* Leipzig, 1870. The author's conclusions are supported by an appeal to the Hebrew, Arabic, Syriac, and Armenian languages. The learning of this curious pamphlet keeps pace with its absurdity. If the reader is disposed to think that this writer must be laughing in his sleeve at the methods of the modern school to which he belongs, he is checked by the obviously serious tone of the whole discussion. Indeed it is altogether in keeping with Hitzig's critical discoveries elsewhere. To this same critic we owe the suggestion, that the name of the fabulist Æsop is derived from Solomon's "*hyssop* that springeth out of the wall," 1 Kings iv. 33: *Die Sprüche Salomo's* p. xvi sq.

[2] *e.g.* respecting the date of the book of Judith, on which depends the authenticity of Clement's Epistle (I. p. 222), the date of Celsus (II. p. 228), etc.

[3] [See further, p. 141.]

It seems to be assumed that, because the sceptical spirit has its proper function in scientific inquiry (though even here its excesses will often impede progress), therefore its exercise is equally useful and equally free from danger in the domain of criticism. A moment's reflection however will show that the cases are wholly different. In whatever relates to morals and history—in short, to human life in all its developments—where mathematical or scientific demonstration is impossible, and where consequently everything depends on the even balance of the judicial faculties, scepticism must be at least as fatal to the truth as credulity.

The author of *Supernatural Religion* proposes to himself the task of demonstrating that the miraculous element in Christianity is a delusion. The work is divided into three parts. The first part undertakes to prove that miracles are not only highly improbable, but antecedently incredible, so that no amount of testimony can overcome the objections to them. As a subsidiary aim, he endeavours to show that the sort of evidence, which, under the most favourable circumstances, we should be likely to obtain in the early Christian ages, ought not to inspire confidence. The second and third parts are occupied in examining the actual witnesses themselves, that is, the four Gospels; the second being devoted to the Synoptists, and the third to St John. The main contention is that the four Gospels are entirely devoid of evidence sufficient to satisfy us of their date and authorship, considering the momentous import of their contents. These portions of the work therefore are chiefly occupied in examining the external testimonies to the authenticity and genuineness of the Gospels. In the case of St John the internal character of the document is likewise subjected to examination.

Obviously, if the author has established his conclusions in the first part, the second and third are altogether superfluous[1]. It is somewhat strange therefore, that more than three-fourths

---

[1] [Our author objects to this conclusion; see below, p. 138 sq.]

of the whole work should be devoted to this needless task. Impressed, as it would seem, by the elaboration of these portions, reviewers have singled them out for special praise, even when they have condemned the first as unsatisfactory. With this estimate of their value I find myself altogether unable to agree; and in the articles which will follow I hope to give my reasons for dissenting. Regarded as a handbook of the critical fallacies of the modern destructive school, *Supernatural Religion* well deserves examination.

For this reason I shall hereafter occupy myself solely with the two latter portions of the work, and more especially with the external evidences of the Gospels; but there is one point, affecting the main question at issue, which it is impossible to pass over in silence. Anyone who, with the arguments of the first part fresh in his memory, will turn to the final chapter, in which the author gives a confession of faith, must be struck with the startling dislocation between the principles from which the work starts and the manifesto with which it concludes. Our author has eliminated, as he believes, the miraculous or supernatural element from the Gospel. He will have nothing to say to 'Ecclesiastical Christianity,' by which strange phrase is meant the Christianity of the Apostles and Evangelists. He will not even hear of a future life with its hopes and fears[1]. He will purge the Gospel of all 'dogmas,' and will present it as an ethical system alone. The extreme beauty, I might almost say the absolute perfection, of Christ's moral teaching[2] he not only allows, but insists upon. 'Morality,' he adds, 'was the essence of his system; theology was an after-thought[3].' And yet almost in the same breath he adopts as his 'two fundamental principles, Love to God and love to man.' He commends a 'morality based upon the earnest and intelligent acceptance of Divine Law, and perfect recognition of the brotherhood of man,' as 'the highest conceivable by humanity[4].' He speaks of the 'purity of heart which alone "sees God[5]."' He enforces

[1] II. p. 484.
[2] II. p. 487 sq.
[3] II. p. 486.
[4] II. p. 487 sq.
[5] II. p. 489.

the necessity of 'rising to higher conceptions of an infinitely wise and beneficent Being . . . . whose laws of wondrous comprehensiveness and perfection we ever perceive in operation around us [1].' All this is well said, but is it consistent? This universal 'brotherhood of man,' what is it but a 'dogma' of the most comprehensive application? This 'Love to God' springing from the apprehension of a 'wondrous perfection,' and the recognition of an 'infinitely wise and beneficent Being,'— in short, this belief in a Heavenly Father, which on any showing was the fundamental axiom of our Lord's teaching, and which our author thus accepts as a cardinal article in his own creed, —what is it but a theological proposition of the most overwhelming import, before which all other 'dogmas' sink into insignificance?

And what room, we are forced to ask, has he left for such a dogma? In the first portion of the work our author has been careful not to define his position. He has studiously avoided committing himself to a belief in a universal Father or a moral Governor, or even in a Personal God. If he had done so, he would have tied his hands at once. Very much of the reasoning which he brings forward against the miraculous element in Christianity in answer to Dr Mozley and Dean Mansel falls to the ground when this proposition is assumed. His arguments prove nothing, because they prove too much: for they are equally efficacious, or equally inefficacious, against the doctrine of a Divine providence or of human responsibility, as they are against the resurrection of Christ. The truth is, that when our author closes his work, he cannot face the conclusions to which his premises would inevitably lead him. They are too startling for himself, as well as for his readers, in their naked deformity; and with a noble inconsistency he clutches at these 'dogmas' to save himself from sinking into the abyss of moral scepticism.

Mr J. S. Mill's inexorable logic may not be without its use, as holding up the mirror to such inconsistency. On his own narrow premises this eminent logician builds up his own

[1] *S. R.* II. p. 490.

narrow conclusions with remorseless rigour. Our author in his first part adopts this same narrow basis, and truly enough finds no resting-place for Christianity upon it, as indeed there is none for any theory of a providential government. But at the conclusion he tacitly and (as it would seem) quite unconsciously assumes a much wider standing-ground. If he had not done so, he himself would have been edged off his footing, and hurled down the precipice. A whole pack of 'pursuing wolves'[1] is upon him, far more ravenous than any which beset the path of the believers in revelation; and he has left himself no shelter. If he had commenced by defining what he meant by 'Nature' and 'Supernatural,' he might have avoided this inconsistency, though he must have sacrificed much of his argument to save his creed. As it is, he has unconsciously juggled with two senses of Nature. Nature in the first part, where he is arguing against miracles, is the aggregate of external phenomena—the same Nature against which Mr Mill prefers his terrible indictment for its cruelty and injustice. But Nature in the concluding chapter involves the idea of a moral Governor and a beneficent Father; and this idea can only be introduced by opening flood-gates of thought which refuse to be closed just at the moment when it is necessary to bar the admission of the miraculous. Our author has ranged himself unconsciously with the 'intuitive philosophers,' of whom Mr Mill speaks so scornfully. He has appealed, though he does not seem to be aware of it, to the inner consciousness of man, to the instincts and cravings of humanity, to interpret and supplement the teachings of external Nature; and he is altogether unaware how large a concession he has made to believers in revelation by so doing.

Even though we should close our eyes to all other considerations, it is vain to ignore the inevitable moral consequences which flow from this mode of reasoning; for they are becoming every day more apparent. The demand is made that we should abandon our Christianity on grounds which logically involve the abandonment of any belief in the providential

[1] *S. R.* I. p. xiv.

government of the world and in the moral responsibility of man. Young men are apt to be far more logical than their elders. Older persons are taught by long experience to distrust the adequacy of their premises: consciously or unconsciously they supplement the narrow conclusions of their logic by larger lessons learnt from human life or from their own heart. But generally speaking, the young man has no such distrust. His teacher has appealed to Nature, and to Nature he shall go. The teacher becomes frightened, struggles to retrace his steps, and speaks of 'an infinitely wise and beneficent Being'; but the pupil insolently points out how

> Nature, red in tooth and claw,
> With ravin, shrieks against his creed.

The teacher urges, 'All that is consistent with wise and omnipotent Law is prospered and brought to perfection[1]:' and the pupil replies: 'You have limited my horizon to this life, and in this life the facts do not verify your statement.' The teacher says, Believe that you—you personally—'are eternally cared for and governed by an omnipresent immutable power for which nothing is too great, nothing too insignificant[2].' The pupil says: 'My Christianity did show me how this was possible; but with my Christianity I have cast it away as a delusion. I could not stop short at this point consistently with the principles you have laid down for my guidance. I have done as you told me to do; I have "ratified the fiat which maintains the order of Nature[3]," and I find Nature wholly

> Careless of the single life.

I will therefore please myself henceforth.' The teacher speaks of 'the purity which alone sees God;'. and to him the expression has a real meaning, for his mind is unconsciously saturated with ideas which he has certainly not learnt from his adopted philosophy: but to the pupil it has lost its articulate utterance, and is no better than sounding brass or a tinkling cymbal. Hence the pupil, having thrown off his Christianity, too often

---

[1] II. p. 492.   [2] II. p. 492.   [3] II. p. 492.

follows out the principles of his teacher to their logical conclusions, and divests himself also of moral restraints, except so far as it may be convenient or necessary for him to submit to them. Happily this has not been the case hitherto in the large majority of instances. The permanence of habits formed in a nobler school of teaching, the abiding presence of a loftier ideal not derived from this new philosophy, and (we may add also) the voice of an inward witness whose authority is denied, but whose warnings nevertheless compel a hearing, all tend to raise the level of men's conduct above their principles. The full moral consequences of the teaching would only then be seen, if ever a generation should grow up, moulded altogether under its influences.

II. The Silence of Eusebius.

[January, 1875.]

'IT is very important,' says the author of *Supernatural Religion*, when commencing his critical investigations, 'that the silence of early writers should receive as much attention as any supposed allusions to the Gospels[1].' In the present article I shall act upon this suggestion. In one province more especially, relating to the external evidences for the Gospels, silence occupies a prominent place. This mysterious oracle will be interrogated, and, unless I am mistaken, the response elicited will not be at all ambiguous.

To Eusebius we are indebted for almost all that we know of the lost ecclesiastical literature of the second century. This literature was very considerable. The Expositions of Papias, in five books, and the Ecclesiastical History of Hegesippus, likewise in five books, must have been full of important matter bearing on our subject. The very numerous works of Melito and Claudius Apollinaris, of which Eusebius has preserved imperfect lists[2], ranged over the wide domain of theology, of morals, of exegesis, of apologetics, of ecclesiastical order; and here again a flood of light would probably have been poured on

---

[1] i. p. 212. The references throughout this article are given to the fourth edition. But, with the single exception which I shall have occasion to notice at the close, I have not observed any alterations from the second, with which I have compared it in all the passages here quoted.

[2] Euseb. *H. E.* iv. 26, 27.

the history of the Canon, if time had spared these precious documents of Christian antiquity. Even the extant writings of the second century, however important they may be from other points of view, give a very inadequate idea of the relation of their respective authors to the Canonical writings. In the case of Justin Martyr for instance, it is not from his Apologies or from his Dialogue with Trypho that we should expect to obtain the fullest and most direct information on this point. In works like these, addressed to Heathens and Jews, who attributed no authority to the writings of Apostles and Evangelists, and for whom the names of the writers would have no meaning, we are not surprised that he refers to those writings for the most part anonymously and with reserve. On the other hand, if his treatise against Marcion (to take a single instance) had been preserved, we should probably have been placed in a position to estimate with tolerable accuracy his relation to the Canonical writings. But in the absence of all this valuable literature, the notices in Eusebius assume the utmost importance, and it is of primary moment to the correctness of our result that we should rightly interpret his language. Above all, it is incumbent on us not to assume that his silence means exactly what we wish it to mean. Eusebius made it his business to record notices throwing light on the history of the Canon. The first care of the critic therefore should be to inquire with what aims and under what limitations he executed this portion of his work.

Now, our author is eloquent on the silence of Eusebius. His fundamental assumption is that where Eusebius does not mention a reference to or quotation from any Canonical book in any writer of whom he may be speaking, there the writer in question was himself silent. This indeed is only the application of a general principle which seems to have taken possession of our author's mind. The argument from silence is courageously and extensively applied throughout these volumes. It is unnecessary to accumulate instances, where 'knows nothing' is substituted for 'says nothing,' as if the two were convertible terms; for such instances are countless. But in the case of

Eusebius the application of the principle takes a wider sweep. Not only is it maintained that A knows nothing of B, because he says nothing of B; but it is further assumed that A knows nothing of B, because C does not say that A says anything of B. This is obviously an assumption which men would not adopt in common life or in ordinary history; still less is it one to which a competent jury would listen for a moment: and therefore a prudent man may well hesitate before adopting it.

With what unflinching boldness our author asserts his position, will appear from the following passages:—

Of Hegesippus he writes[1]:—

'The care with which Eusebius searches for every trace of the use of the books of the New Testament in early writers, and his anxiety to produce any evidence concerning their authenticity, render his silence upon the subject almost as important as his distinct utterance when speaking of such a man as Hegesippus.'

And again[2]:—

'It is certain that Eusebius, who quotes with so much care the testimony of Papias, a man of whom he speaks disparagingly, regarding the Gospels *and the Apocalypse*[3], would not have neglected to have availed himself of the evidence of Hegesippus, for whom he has so much respect, had that writer furnished him with any opportunity.'

[1] *S. R.* I. p. 432.

[2] I. p. 433 sq. I must leave it to others to reconcile the statement respecting the Apocalypse in the text with another which I find elsewhere in this work (I. p. 483): 'Andrew, a Cappadocian bishop of the fifth century, mentions that Papias, amongst others of the Fathers, considered the Apocalypse inspired. *No reference is made to this by Eusebius;* but although, from his Millenarian tendencies, it is very probable that Papias regarded the Apocalypse with peculiar veneration as a prophetic book, *this evidence is too vague and isolated to be of much value.*' The difficulty is increased when we compare these two passages with a third (II. p. 335): 'Andrew of Cæsarea, in the preface to his Commentary on the Apocalypse, mentions that Papias maintained 'the credibility' (τὸ ἀξιόπιστον) of that book, or in other words, its Apostolic origin. . . . Apologists *admit the genuineness of this statement*, nay, claim it as undoubted evidence of the acquaintance of Papias with the Apocalypse. . . . Now *he must therefore have recognised the book as the work of the Apostle John.*' The italics, I ought to say, are my own, in all the three passages quoted.

[3] ['regarding the composition of the first two Gospels' ed. 6 (I. p. 433). The error is acknowledged in the preface to that edition (p. xxi).]

II. THE SILENCE OF EUSEBIUS.

And again[1]:—'As Hegesippus does not[2] mention any Canonical work of the New Testament etc.' And in the second volume he returns to the subject[3]:—

'It is certain that, had he (Hegesippus) mentioned[4] our Gospels, and we may say particularly the Fourth, the fact would have been recorded by Eusebius.'

Similarly he says of Papias[5]:—

'Eusebius, who never fails to enumerate[6] the works of the New Testament to which the Fathers refer, does not pretend[7] that Papias knew either the Third or Fourth Gospels.'

And again, in a later passage[8]:—

'Had he (Papias) expressed any recognition[9] of the Fourth Gospel, Eusebius would certainly have mentioned the fact, and this silence of Papias is strong presumptive evidence against the Johannine Gospel.'

And a little lower down[10]:—

'The presumption therefore naturally is that, as Eusebius did not mention the fact, he did not find any reference to the Fourth Gospel in the work of Papias[11].'

So again, our author writes of Dionysius of Corinth[12]:—

'No quotation from, or allusion to, any writing of the New Testament occurs in any of the fragments of the Epistles still extant; nor does Eusebius make mention of any such reference in the Epistles which have perished[13], which he certainly would not have omitted to do had they contained any.'

---

[1] I. p. 435.
[2] ['so far as we know' inserted in ed. 6.]
[3] II. p. 320.
[4] ['said anything interesting about' Complete Edition (II. p. 318).]
[5] I. p. 488.
[6] ['to state what the Fathers say about' ed. 6. On the ambiguity of this expression see below, p. 183 sq.
[7] ['mention' ed. 6.]
[8] II. p. 322.
[9] ['said anything regarding the composition or authorship' ed. 6.]
[10] II. p. 323.
[11] [So also ed. 6. In the Complete Edition (II. p. 321) the sentence ends 'did not find anything regarding the Fourth Gospel in the work of Papias, and that Papias was not acquainted with it.']
[12] II. p. 164.
[13] [In ed. 6 the sentence ends here.]

And lower down[1]:—

'It is certain that had Dionysius mentioned[2] books of the New Testament, Eusebius would, as usual, have stated the fact.'

This indeed is the fundamental assumption which lies at the basis of his reasoning; and the reader will not need to be reminded how much of the argument falls to pieces, if this basis should prove to be unsound. A wise master-builder would therefore have looked to his foundations first, and assured himself of their strength, before he piled up his fabric to this height. This however our author has altogether neglected to do. If only a small portion of the time which has been spent on amassing references to modern German and Dutch critics had been bestowed on investigating what Eusebius himself says and what he leaves unsaid, the result, it can hardly be doubted, would have been very different.

Of this principle and its wide application, as we have seen, the author has no misgivings. He declares himself absolutely certain about it. It is with him *articulus stantis aut cadentis critices*. We shall therefore do well to test its value, because, quite independently of the consequences directly flowing from it, it will serve roughly to gauge his trustworthiness as a guide in other departments of criticism, where, from the nature of the case, no test can be applied. In the land of the unverifiable there are no efficient critical police. When a writer expatiates amidst conjectural quotations from conjectural apocryphal Gospels, he is beyond the reach of refutation. But in the present case, as it so happens, verification is possible, at least to a limited extent; and it is important to avail ourselves of the opportunity.

In the first place then, Eusebius himself tells us what method he intends to pursue respecting the Canon of Scripture. After enumerating the writings bearing the name of St Peter, as follows;—(1) The First Epistle, which is received by all, and was quoted by the ancients as beyond dispute ; (2) The Second

---

[1] II. p. 166.

[2] ['said anything about' ed. 6. The whole sentence is omitted in the Complete Edition.]

Epistle, which tradition had not stamped in the same way as Canonical (ἐνδιάθηκον, 'included in the Testament'), but which nevertheless, appearing useful to many, had been studied (ἐσπουδάσθη) with the other Scriptures; (3) The Acts, Gospel, Preaching, and Apocalypse of Peter, which four works he rejects as altogether unauthenticated and discredited—he continues[1]:—

'But, as my history proceeds, I will take care (προὔργου ποιήσομαι), along with the successions (of the bishops), to indicate what Church writers (who flourished) from time to time have made use of any of the disputed books (ἀντιλεγομένων), and what has been said by them concerning the Canonical (ἐνδιαθήκων) and acknowledged Scriptures, and anything that (they have said) concerning those which do not belong to this class. Well, then, the books bearing the name of Peter, of which I recognise (ἔγνων) one Epistle only as genuine and acknowledged among the elders of former days (πάλαι), are those just enumerated (τοσαῦτα). But the fourteen Epistles of Paul are obvious and manifest (πρόδηλοι καὶ σαφεῖς). Yet it is not right to be ignorant of the fact that some persons have rejected the Epistle to the Hebrews, saying that it was disputed by the Church of the Romans as not being Paul's. And I will set before (my readers) on the proper occasions (κατὰ καιρὸν) what has been said concerning this (Epistle) also by those who lived before our time (τοῖς πρὸ ἡμῶν).'

He then mentions the Acts of Paul, which he 'had not received as handed down among the undisputed books,' and the Shepherd of Hermas, which 'had been spoken against by some' and therefore 'could have no place among the acknowledged books,' though it had been read in churches and was used by some of the most ancient writers. And he concludes:—

[1] Euseb. *H. E.* iii. 3. The important words are τίνες τῶν κατὰ χρόνους ἐκκλησιαστικῶν συγγραφέων ὁποίαις κέχρηνται τῶν ἀντιλεγομένων, τίνα τε περὶ τῶν ἐνδιαθήκων καὶ ὁμολογουμένων γραφῶν καὶ ὅσα περὶ τῶν μὴ τοιούτων αὐτοῖς εἴρηται. The words spaced will show the two different modes of treatment; (1) The mention of references or testimonies in the case of the disputed writings only; (2) The record of anecdotes in the case of acknowledged and disputed writings alike. The double relative in the first clause, τίνες ...ὁποίαις, is incapable of literal translation in English; but this does not affect the question. The two modes are well illustrated in the case of Irenæus. Eusebius gives from this Father *testimonies* to the Epistle to the Hebrews etc., and *anecdotes* respecting the Gospel and Apocalypse alike.

'Let this suffice as a statement (εἰς παράστασιν . . . εἰρήσθω) of those Divine writings which are unquestionable, and those which are not acknowledged among all.'

This statement, though not so clear on minor points as we could wish, is thoroughly sensible and quite intelligible in its main lines. It shows an appreciation of the conditions of the problem. Above all, it is essentially straightforward. It certainly does not evince the precision of a lawyer, but neither on the other hand does it at all justify the unqualified denunciations of the uncritical character of Eusebius in which our author indulges. The exact limits of the Canon were not settled when Eusebius wrote. With regard to the main body of the writings included in our New Testament there was absolutely no question; but there existed a margin of *antilegomena* or disputed books, about which differences of opinion existed, or had existed. Eusebius therefore proposes to treat these two classes of writings in two different ways. This is the cardinal point of the passage. Of the antilegomena he pledges himself to record when any ancient writer *employs* any book belonging to their class (τίνες ὁποίαις κέχρηνται); but as regards the undisputed Canonical books he only professes to mention them, when such a writer has something to *tell about them* (τίνα περὶ τῶν ἐνδιαθήκων εἴρηται). Any *anecdote* of interest respecting them, as also respecting the others (τῶν μὴ τοιούτων), will be recorded. But in their case he nowhere leads us to expect that he will allude to mere *quotations*, however numerous and however precise[1].

This statement is inserted after the record of the martyrdom of St Peter and St Paul, and has immediate and special reference to their writings. The Shepherd of Hermas is only mentioned incidentally, because (as Eusebius himself intimates) the author was supposed to be named in the Epistle to the Romans. But the occasion serves as an opportunity for the historian to lay down the general principles on which he intends to act. Somewhat later, when he arrives at the history of the

[1] [Quoted by *S. R.* ed. 6, p. xiv. below, p. 178 sq.] For his criticism upon this Essay see

II. THE SILENCE OF EUSEBIUS.

last years of St John, he is led to speak of the writings of this Apostle also; and as St John's Gospel completes the tetrad of Evangelical narratives, he inserts at this point his account of the Four Gospels. This account concludes as follows[1]:—

'Thus much (ταῦτα) we ourselves (have to say) concerning these (the Four Gospels); but we will endeavour more particularly (οἰκειότερον) on the proper occasions (κατὰ καιρὸν) by quoting the ancient writers to set forth what has been said by anyone else (τοῖς ἄλλοις) also concerning them. Now, of the writings of John, the first (former, προτέρα) of his Epistles also is acknowledged as beyond question alike among our contemporaries (τοῖς νῦν) and among the ancients, while the remaining two are disputed. But respecting the Apocalypse opinions are drawn in opposite directions, even to the present day, among most men (τοῖς πολλοῖς). Howbeit it also shall receive its judgment (ἐπίκρισιν) at a proper season from the testimonies of the ancients.'

After this follows the well-known passage in which he sums up the results at which he has arrived respecting the Canon. With this passage, important as it is in itself, I need not trouble my readers.

Here again it will be seen that the same distinction as before is observed. Of the Gospels the historian will only record anecdotes concerning them. On the other hand, in the case of the Apocalypse mere references and quotations will be mentioned, because they afford important data for arriving at a decision concerning its Canonical authority.

Hitherto we have discovered no foundation for the superstructure which our author builds on the silence of Eusebius. But the real question, after all, is not what this historian professes to do, but what he actually does. The original prospectus is of small moment compared with the actual balance-sheet, and in this case time has spared us the means of instituting an audit to a limited extent. With Papias and Hegesippus and Dionysius of Corinth, any one is free to indulge in sweeping assertions with little fear of conviction; for we know nothing, or next to nothing, of these writers, except what Eusebius himself has

[1] *H. E.* iii. 24.

told us. But Eusebius has also dealt with other ancient writings in relation to the Canon, as, for instance, those of Clement of Rome, of Ignatius, of Polycarp, of Irenæus, and others; and, as these writings are still extant, we can compare their actual contents with his notices. Here a definite issue is raised. If our author's principle will stand this test, there is a very strong presumption in its favour; if it will not, then it is worthless.

Let us take first the Epistle of CLEMENT OF ROME. This Epistle contains several references to Evangelical narratives—whether oral or written, whether our Canonical Gospels or not, it is unnecessary for the present to discuss[1]. It comprises a chapter relating to the labours and martyrdom of St Peter and St Paul[2]. It also, as our author himself allows (accepting the statement of Tischendorf), 'here and there . . . makes use of passages from Pauline Epistles[3].' It does more than this; it mentions definitely and by name St Paul's First Epistle to the Corinthians, alluding to the parties which called themselves after Paul and Cephas and Apollos[4]. Of all this Eusebius says not a word. He simply remarks that Clement, by

'putting forward (παραθείς) many thoughts of the (Epistle) to the Hebrews, and even employing some passages from it word for word (αὐτολεξεί), shows most clearly that the document (σύγγραμμα) was not recent (when he wrote)[5].'

This is strictly true, as far as it goes; the passages are too

---

[1] See Lardner *Credibility* II. p. 35 sq (1835). For the sake of economising space I shall refer from time to time to this work, in which the testimonies of ancient writers are collected and translated, so that they are accessible to English readers. Any one, whose ideas have been confused by reading *Supernatural Religion*, cannot fail to obtain a clearer view of the real state of the case by referring to this book. It must be remembered, however, that recent discovery has added to the amount of evidence, more especially in reference to the Fourth Gospel.

I refer, of course, to the quotations in the Gnostic fragments preserved by Hippolytus, and in the Clementine Homilies.

[2] Clem. Rom. 5.

[3] S. R. I. p. 223.

[4] Clem. Rom. 47. 'Take up the Epistle of the blessed Paul the Apostle. What first did he write to you in the beginning of the Gospel? Of a truth he gave injunctions to you in the Spirit (πνευματικῶς) concerning himself and Cephas and Apollos, because even then ye had made parties (προσκλίσεις).'

[5] Euseb. *H. E.* iii. 37.

many and too close to leave any doubt about their source; but the Epistle to the Hebrews is not directly named, as the Epistle to the Corinthians is.

The IGNATIAN EPISTLES deserve to be considered next. The question of their genuineness does not affect the present inquiry; for the seven letters contained in what is commonly called the Short Greek recension, whether spurious or not, were confessedly the same which Eusebius read; and to these I refer. For the sake of convenience I shall call the writer Ignatius, without prejudging the question of authorship. Ignatius then presents some striking coincidences with our Synoptic Gospels (whether taken thence or not, I need not at present stop to inquire), *e.g.* 'Be thou wise as a serpent in all things, and harmless always as a dove[1],' 'The tree is manifest by its fruit[2],' 'He that receiveth, let him receive[3].' He likewise echoes the language of St John, *e.g.* 'It (the Spirit) knoweth whence it cometh and whither it goeth[4],' 'Jesus Christ ......in all things pleased Him that sent Him[5],' with other expressions. He also refers to the examples of St Peter and St Paul[6]. He describes the Apostle of the Gentiles as 'making mention of' the Ephesians 'in every part of his letter' (or 'in every letter[7]'). These letters moreover contain several passages which are indisputable reminiscences of St Paul's Epistles[8]. Yet of all this Eusebius says not a word. All the information which he gives respecting the relation of Ignatius to the Canon is contained in this one sentence[9]:—

'Writing to the Smyrnæans, he has employed expressions (taken) I know not whence, recording as follows concerning Christ:—

"And I myself know and believe that He exists in the flesh after the resurrection. And when He came to Peter and those with him (πρὸς τοὺς περὶ Πέτρον), He said unto them, 'Take hold, feel me, and see that I am not an incorporeal spirit' [literally,

[1] *Polyc.* 2; comp. Matt. x. 16.
[2] *Ephes.* 14; comp. Matt. xii. 33.
[3] *Smyrn.* 6; comp. Matt. xix. 12.
[4] *Philad.* 7; comp. John iii. 8.
[5] *Magn.* 8; comp. John viii. 29.
[6] *Rom.* 4.
[7] *Ephes.* 12.
[8] See Lardner II. p. 78 sq for the testimonies in Ignatius generally.
[9] Euseb. *H. E.* iii. 36.

'demon,' δαιμόνιον ἀσώματον]; and immediately they touched Him, and believed."'

It should be added that, though Eusebius does not know the source of this reference, Jerome states that it came from the Gospel of the Hebrews[1].

Now let us suppose that these Epistles were no longer extant, and that we interpreted the silence of Eusebius on the same principle which our author applies to Papias and Hegesippus and Dionysius of Corinth. 'Here,' we should say, 'is clearly a Judaising Christian—an Ebionite of the deepest hue. He recognises St Peter as his great authority. He altogether ignores St Paul. He knows nothing of our Canonical Gospels, and he uses exclusively the Gospel of the Hebrews. Thus we have a new confirmation of the Tübingen theory respecting the origin of the Christian Church. The thing is obvious to any impartial mind. Apologetic writers must indeed be driven to straits if they attempt to impugn this result.' It so happens that this estimate of Ignatius would be hopelessly wrong. He appeals to St Paul as his great example[2]. His Christology is wholly unlike the Ebionite, for he distinctly declares the perfect deity as well as the perfect humanity of Christ[3]. And he denounces the Judaisers at length and by name[4]. What then is the value of a principle which, when applied in a simple case, leads to conclusions diametrically opposed to historical facts?

From Ignatius we pass to POLYCARP. Here again the genuineness of the Epistle bearing this Father's name does not affect the question; for it is confessedly the same document which Eusebius had before him. In Polycarp's Epistle[5] also there are several coincidences with our Gospels. There is a hardly disputable embodiment of words occurring in the Acts. There are two or three references to St Paul by name. Once he is directly mentioned as writing to the Philippians. There

[1] *De Vir. Illustr.* c. 16.
[2] *Ephes.* 12; comp. *Rom.* 4.
[3] *Ephes.* 7; comp. *Ephes.* 1, *Polyc.* 3, *Rom.* 6 etc.
[4] *Magn.* 8—10; comp. *Philad.* 6.
[5] See Lardner II. p. 99 sq for the passages.

II. THE SILENCE OF EUSEBIUS.   43

are obvious quotations from or reminiscences of Romans, 1, 2 Corinthians, Galatians, Ephesians, 1 Thessalonians, 1, 2 Timothy, not to mention other more doubtful coincidences. Of all this again Eusebius 'knows nothing.' So far as regards the Canon, he does not think it necessary to say more than that 'Polycarp in his aforesaid (δηλωθείσῃ) writing (γραφῇ) to the Philippians, which is in circulation (φερομένῃ) to the present day, has used certain testimonies from the First (former) Epistle of Peter[1].' Here again, we might say, is a Judaiser, the very counterpart of Papias. This inference indeed would be partially, though only partially, corrected by the fact that Eusebius in an earlier place[2], to illustrate his account of Ignatius, quotes from Polycarp's Epistle a passage in which St Paul's name happens to be mentioned. But this mention (so far as regards the matter before us) is purely accidental; and the sentence relating to the Canon entirely ignores the Apostle of the Gentiles, with whose thoughts and language nevertheless this Epistle is saturated.

When we turn from Polycarp to JUSTIN MARTYR, the phenomena are similar. This Father introduces into his extant writings a large number of Evangelical passages. A few of these coincide exactly with our Canonical Gospels; a much larger number have so close a resemblance that, without referring to the actual text of our Gospels, the variations would not be detected by an ordinary reader. Justin Martyr professes to derive these sayings and doings from written documents, which he styles *Memoirs of the Apostles,* and which (he tells his heathen readers) 'are called Gospels[3].' His expressions and arguments moreover in some passages recall the language of St Paul's Epistles[4]. Of all this again Eusebius 'knows nothing.' So far as regards the Canon of the New Testament, he contents himself with stating that Justin 'has made mention (μέμνηται) of the Apocalypse of John, clearly saying that it is (the work) of the Apostle[5].'

His mode of dealing with THEOPHILUS OF ANTIOCH is still

[1] *H. E.* iv. 14. [2] *H. E.* iii. 36. [3] 1. *Apol.* 66.
[4] See Semisch *Justin Martyr* I.   [5] *H. E.* iv. 18.

more instructive. Among the writings of this Father, he mentions one work addressed *To Autolycus*, and another *Against the Heresy of Hermogenes*[1]. The first is extant: not so the other. In the extant work Theophilus introduces the unmistakeable language of Romans, 1, 2 Corinthians, Ephesians, Philippians, 1 Timothy, Titus, not to mention points of resemblance with other Apostolic Epistles which can hardly have been accidental[2]. He has one or two coincidences with the Synoptic Gospels, and, what is more important, he quotes the beginning of the Fourth Gospel by name, as follows[3]:—

'Whence the Holy Scriptures and all the inspired men (πνευματοφόροι) teach us, one of whom, John, says, "In the beginning was the Word, and the Word was with God," showing that at the first (ἐν πρώτοις) God was alone, and the Word in Him. Then he says, "And the Word was God; all things were made by Him, and without Him was not anything made."'

This quotation is direct and precise. Indeed even the most suspicious and sceptical critics have not questioned the adequacy of the reference[4]. It is moreover the more conspicuous, because it is the one solitary instance in which Theophilus quotes directly and by name any book of the New Testament. Here again Eusebius is altogether silent. But of the treatise no longer extant he writes, that in it 'he (Theophilus) has used testimonies from the Apocalypse of John[5].' This is all the information which he vouchsafes respecting the relation of Theophilus to the Canon.

One example more must suffice. IRENÆUS[6] in his extant work on heresies quotes the Acts again and again, and directly ascribes it to St Luke. He likewise cites twelve out of the thirteen Epistles of St Paul, the exception being the short letter to Philemon. These twelve he directly ascribes to the Apostle in one place or another, and with the exception of 1 Timothy and Titus he gives the names of the persons addressed; so that the identification is complete. The list of

---

[1] *H. E.* iv. 24. [2] Lardner II. p. 208 sq. [3] *Ad Autol.* ii. 22.
[4] *S. R.* II. p. 474. [5] *H. E.* iv. 24. [6] Lardner II. p. 175 sq.

references to St Paul's Epistles alone occupies two octavo pages of three columns each in the index to Stieren's *Irenæus*. Yet of all this Eusebius 'knows nothing.' In a previous chapter indeed he happens to have quoted a passage from Irenæus, relating to the succession of the Roman bishops, in which this Father states that Linus is mentioned by St Paul 'in the Epistle to Timothy[1];' but the passage relating to the Canon contains no hint that Irenæus recognised the existence of any one of St Paul's Epistles; and from first to last there is no mention of the Acts. The language of Eusebius here is highly characteristic as illustrating his purpose and method. He commences the chapter by referring back to his original design, as follows[2]:—

'Since, at the commencement of our treatise, we have made a promise, saying that we should adduce at the proper opportunities the utterances of the ancient elders and writers of the Church, in which they have handed down in writing the traditions that reached them concerning the Canonical (ἐνδιαθήκων) writings, and Irenæus was one of these, let me now adduce his notices also, and first those relating to the sacred Gospels, as follows.'

He then quotes a short passage from the third book, giving the circumstances under which the Four Gospels were written. Then follow two quotations from the well-known passage in the fifth book, in which Irenæus mentions the date and authorship of the Apocalypse, and refers to the number of the beast. Eusebius then proceeds:—

'This is the account given by the above-named writer respecting the Apocalypse also. And he has made mention too of the First Epistle of John, adducing very many testimonies out of it; and likewise also of the First (former) Epistle of Peter. And he not only knows, but even receives the writing of the 'Shepherd,' saying, 'Well then spake the writing' [or 'scripture,' ἡ γραφή] 'which says, "First of all believe that God is One, even He that created all things;"' and so forth.'

This is all the information respecting the Canon of the New

---

[1] *H. E.* v. 6.   [2] *H. E.* v. 8.

Testament which he adduces from the great work of Irenæus. In a much later passage[1], however, he has occasion to name other works of this Father no longer extant; and of one of these he remarks that in it 'he mentions the Epistle to the Hebrews, and the so-called Wisdom of Solomon, adducing certain passages from them.'

From these examples, combined with his own prefatory statements, we feel justified in laying down the following canons as ruling the procedure of Eusebius:—

(1) His main object was to give such information as might assist in forming correct views respecting the Canon of Scripture.

(2) This being so, he was indifferent to any quotations or references which went towards establishing the canonicity of those books which had never been disputed in the Church. Even when the quotation was direct and by name, it had no value for him.

(3) To this class belonged (i) the Four Gospels; (ii) the Acts; (iii) the thirteen Epistles of St Paul.

(4) As regards these, he contents himself with preserving any anecdotes which he may have found illustrating the circumstances under which they were written, *e.g.* the notices of St Matthew and St Mark in Papias, and of the Four Gospels in Irenæus.

(5) The Catholic Epistles lie on the border-land between the *Homologumena* and the *Antilegomena*, between the universally acknowledged and the disputed books. Of the Epistles of St John for instance, the First belonged to the one class, the Second and Third to the other. Of the Epistles of St Peter again, the First was acknowledged, the Second disputed. The Catholic Epistles in fact occupy an exceptional position.

Respecting his treatment of this section of the Canon he is not explicit in his opening statement, and we have to infer it from his subsequent procedure. As this however is uniform, we seem able to determine with tolerable certainty the principle on

[1] *H. E.* v. 26.

II. THE SILENCE OF EUSEBIUS.

which he acts. He subjects all the books belonging to this section to the same law. For instance, he mentions any references to 1 John and 1 Peter (*e.g.* in Papias, Polycarp, and Irenæus), though in the Church no doubt was ever entertained about their genuineness and authority. He may have thought that this mention would conduce to a just estimate of the meaning of silence in the case of disputed Epistles, as 2 Peter and 2, 3 John.

(6) The Epistle to the Hebrews and the Apocalypse still remain to be considered. Their claim to a place in the Canon is, or has been, disputed: and therefore he records every decisive notice respecting either of them, *e.g.* the quotations from the Epistle to the Hebrews in Clement of Rome and Irenæus, and the notices of the Apocalypse in Justin and Melito[1] and Apollonius[2], and Theophilus and Irenæus. So too, he records any testimony, direct or indirect, bearing the other way, *e.g.* that the Roman presbyter Gaius mentions only thirteen Epistles of St Paul, 'not reckoning the Epistle to the Hebrews with the rest[3].'

(7) With regard to the books which lie altogether outside the Canon, but which were treated as Scripture, or quasi-scripture, by any earlier Church writer, he makes it his business to record the fact. Thus he mentions the one quotation in Irenæus from the Shepherd of Hermas; he states that Hegesippus employs the Gospel according to the Hebrews; he records that Clement of Alexandria in the *Stromateis* has made use of the Epistles of Barnabas and Clement, and in the *Hypotyposeis* has commented on the Epistle of Barnabas and the so-called Apocalypse of Peter[4].

It will have appeared from the above account, if I mistake not, that his treatment of this subject is essentially frank. There is no indication of a desire to make out a case for those writings which he and his contemporaries received as Canonical, against those which they rejected. The Shepherd of Hermas is

[1] *H. E.* iv. 26.
[2] *H. E.* v. 18.
[3] *H. E.* vi. 20.
[4] *H. E.* vi. 13, 14.

somewhere about two-thirds the length of the whole body of the thirteen Epistles of St Paul. He singles out the one isolated passage from Hermas in Irenæus, though it is quoted anonymously; and he says nothing about the quotations from St Paul, though they exceed two hundred in number, and are very frequently cited by name.

It is necessary however, not only to investigate his principles, but also to ascertain how far his application of these principles can be depended upon. And here the facts justify us in laying down the following rules for our guidance:—

(i) As regards the anecdotes containing information relating to the books of the New Testament he restricts himself to the narrowest limits which justice to his subject will allow. His treatment of Irenæus makes this point clear. Though he gives the principal passage in this author relating to the Four Gospels[1], he omits to mention others which contain interesting statements directly or indirectly affecting the question, e.g. that St John wrote his Gospel to counteract the errors of Cerinthus and the Nicolaitans[2]. Thus too, when he quotes a few lines alluding to the unanimous tradition of the Asiatic elders who were acquainted with St John[3], he omits the context, from which we find that this tradition had an important bearing on the authenticity of the Fourth Gospel, for it declared that Christ's ministry extended much beyond a single year, thus confirming the obvious chronology of the Fourth Gospel against the apparent chronology of the Synoptists.

(ii) As regards the quotations and references the case stands thus. When Eusebius speaks of 'testimonies' in any ancient writer taken from a Scriptural book, we cannot indeed be sure that the quotations were direct and by name (this was certainly not the case in some), but we may fairly assume that they were definite enough, or numerous enough, or both, to satisfy even a sceptical critic of the modern school. This is the case, for instance, with the quotations from the Epistle to the

---

[1] Iren. iii. 1. 1.
[2] Iren. iii. 11. 1.
[3] Iren. ii. 25, cited in Euseb. *H. E.* iii. 23.

Hebrews in Clement of Rome, and those from the First Epistle of St Peter in Polycarp. *In no instance which we can test does Eusebius give a doubtful testimony.* On the other hand he omits several which might fairly be alleged, and have been alleged by modern writers, as, for instance, the coincidence with 1 John in Polycarp[1]. He may have passed them over through inadvertence, or he may not have considered them decisive.

I am quite aware that our author states the case differently; but I am unable to reconcile his language with the facts. He writes as follows[2]:—

'He (Eusebius) states however, that Papias "made use of testimonies from the First Epistle of John, and likewise from that of Peter." As Eusebius, however, does not quote the passages from Papias, we must remain in doubt whether he did not, as elsewhere, assume from some similarity of wording that the passages were quotations from these Epistles, whilst in reality they might not be. Eusebius made a similar statement with regard to a supposed quotation in the so-called Epistle of Polycarp[5] upon very insufficient grounds[3].'

For the statement 'as elsewhere' our author has given no authority, and I am not aware of any.

The note to which the number in the text[5] refers is 'Ad Phil. vii.; Euseb. *H. E.* iv. 14.'

I cannot help thinking there is some confusion here. The passage of Eusebius to which our author refers in this note relates how Polycarp 'has employed certain testimonies from the First (former) Epistle of Peter.' The chapter of Polycarp, to which he refers, contains a reference to the First Epistle of St John, which has been alleged by modern writers, but is not alleged by Eusebius. This same chapter, it is true, contains the words 'Watch unto prayer,' which present a coincidence with 1 Pet. iv. 7. But no one would lay any stress on this one

[1] Polyc. *Phil.* 7.
[2] *S. R.* I. p. 483.
[3] [The author's mode of dealing with this passage in his later editions is commented upon below, p. 191 sq.

In the Complete Edition (1879) the words 'as elsewhere' still remain. The last sentence however, which survived ed. 6, is at length withdrawn, and with it the offending note.]

expression: the strong and unquestionable coincidences are elsewhere. Moreover our author speaks of a single 'supposed quotation,' whereas the quotations from 1 Peter in Polycarp are numerous. Thus in c. 1 we have 'In whom, not having seen, ye believe, and believing ye rejoice with joy unspeakable and full of glory,' from 1 Pet. i. 8: in c. 2, 'Girding up your loins,' from 1 Pet. i. 13 (comp. Ephes. vi. 14); 'Having believed on Him that raised up our Lord Jesus Christ from the dead and gave Him glory,' from 1 Pet. i. 21; 'Not rendering evil for evil, or railing for railing,' from 1 Pet. iii. 9: in c. 5, 'Every lust warreth against the Spirit,' from 1 Pet. ii. 11: in c. 8, 'Who bore our sins with His own body ($\tau\hat{\varphi}$ ἰδίῳ σώματι) on the tree,' from 1 Pet. ii. 24; 'Who did no sin, neither was guile found in His mouth,' from 1 Pet. ii. 22: in c. 10, 'Lovers of the brotherhood,' from 1 Pet. ii. 17; 'Be ye all subject one to another,' from 1 Pet. v. 5; 'Having your conversation unblamable among the Gentiles, that from your good works both ye may receive praise, and the Lord may not be evil spoken of in you,' from 1 Pet. ii. 12 (comp. iv. 14 in the received text). I am quite at a loss to conceive how any one can speak of these numerous and close coincidences as 'very insufficient grounds.' And though our author elsewhere, as, for instance, in the quotations from the Fourth Gospel in Tatian and in the Clementine Homilies[1], has resisted evidence which (I venture to think) would satisfy any jury of competent critics, yet I cannot suppose that he would hold out against such an array of passages as we have here, and I must therefore believe that he has overlooked the facts. I venture to say again that, in these references to early writers relating to the Canon, Eusebius (where we are able to test him) *never overstates the case.* I emphasize this assertion, because I trust some one will point out my error if I am wrong. If I am not shown to be wrong, I shall make use of the fact hereafter[2].

This investigation will have thrown some light upon the author's sweeping assertions with respect to the arbitrary

[1] *S. R.* II. pp. 374—379, 336—341.   [2] [On this matter see below, p. 191 sq.]

action which he supposes to have presided over the formation of the Canon, and still more on his unqualified denunciations of the uncritical spirit of Eusebius. But such was not my immediate purpose.

Hypotheses non fingimus. We have built no airy castles of criticism on arbitrary *à priori* assumptions as to what the silence of Eusebius must mean. We have put the man himself in the witness-box; we have confronted him with facts, and cross-examined him; thus we have elicited from him his principles and mode of action. I may perhaps have fallen into some errors of detail, though I have endeavoured to avoid them, but the main conclusions are, I believe, irrefragable. If they are not, I shall be obliged to any one who will point out the fallacy in my reasoning; and I pledge myself to make open retractation, when I resume these papers in a subsequent number. If they are, then the reader will not fail to see how large a part of the argument in *Supernatural Religion* has crumbled to pieces.

Our author is quite alive to the value of a system of 'positively enunciating[1].' 'A good strong assertion,' he says, 'becomes a powerful argument, since few readers have the means of verifying its correctness[2].' His own assertions, which I quoted at the outset of this investigation, are certainly not wanting in strength, and I have taken the liberty of verifying them. Any English reader may do the same. Eusebius is translated, and so are the Ante-Nicene Fathers.

I now venture on a statement which might have seemed a paradox if it had preceded this investigation, but which, coming at its close, will, if I mistake not, commend itself as a sober deduction from facts. *The silence of Eusebius respecting early witnesses to the Fourth Gospel is an evidence in its favour.* Its Apostolic authorship had never been questioned by any Church writer from the beginning, so far as Eusebius was aware, and therefore it was superfluous to call witnesses. It was not excused, because it had not been accused. In short, the silence

[1] *S. R.* II. p. 62.   [2] *S. R.* II. p. 66.

of Eusebius here means the very opposite to that which our author assumes it to mean.

If any one demurs to this inference, let him try, on any other hypothesis, to answer the following questions:—

(1) How is it that, while Eusebius alleges repeated testimonies to the Epistle to the Hebrews, he is silent from first to last about the universally acknowledged Epistles of St Paul, such as Romans, 1, 2 Corinthians, and Galatians?

(2) How is it that he does not mention the precise and direct testimony in Theophilus to the Gospel of St John, while he does mention a reference in this same author to the Apocalypse?

And this explanation of the silence of Eusebius, while it is demanded by his own language and practice, alone accords with the known facts relating to the reception of the Fourth Gospel in the second century. Its theology is stamped on the teaching of orthodox apologists; its authority is quoted for the speculative tenets of the manifold Gnostic sects, Basilideans, Valentinians, Ophites; its narrative is employed even by a Judaising writer like the author of the Clementines. The phenomena which confront us in the last quarter of the second century are inexplicable, except on the supposition that the Gospel had had a long previous history. How else are we to account for such facts as that the text already exhibits a number of various readings, such as the alternative of 'only begotten God' for 'the only begotten Son' in i. 18, and 'six' for 'five' in iv. 18, or the interpolation of the descent of the angel in v. 3, 4; that legends and traditions have grown up respecting its origin, such as we find in Clement of Alexandria and in the Muratorian fragment[1]; that perverse mystical interpretations, wholly foreign to the simple meaning of the text, have already encrusted it, such as we meet with in the commentary of Heracleon? How is it that ecclesiastical writers far and wide receive it without misgiving at this epoch—Irenæus in Gaul, Tertullian in Africa, Clement in Alexandria, Theophilus at Antioch, the anonymous

[1] [See below, p. 188 sq.]

Muratorian writer perhaps in Rome? that they not only receive it, but assume its reception from the beginning? that they never betray a consciousness that any Church or Churchman had ever questioned it? The history of the first three-quarters of the second century is necessarily obscure owing to the paucity of remains. A flood of light is suddenly poured in during the remaining years of the century. Our author is content to grope in the obscurity: any phantoms may be conjured up here; but the moment the light is let in, he closes his eyes and can see nothing. He refuses altogether to discuss Irenæus, though Irenæus was a disciple of Polycarp, and Polycarp was a disciple of St John. Even if it be granted that the opinion of Irenæus, as an isolated individual, is not worth much, yet the wide-spread and traditional belief which underlies his whole language and thoughts is a consideration of the highest moment: and Irenæus is only one among many witnesses. The author's treatment of the external evidences to the Fourth Gospel is wholly vitiated by his ignoring the combined force of such facts as these. A man might with just as much reason assert that a sturdy oak sapling must have sprung up overnight, because circumstances had prevented him from witnessing its continuous growth.

The author of *Supernatural Religion* was kind enough to send me an early copy of his fourth edition, and I sincerely thank him for his courtesy. Unfortunately it arrived too late for me to make any use of it in my previous article. With one exception however, I have not noticed that my criticisms are affected by any changes which may have been made. But this single exception is highly important. A reader, with only the fourth edition before him, would be wholly at a loss to understand my criticism, and therefore some explanation is necessary.

In my former article[1] I pointed out that the author had founded a charge of 'falsification' against Dr Westcott on a grammatical error of his own. He had treated the infinitive and indicative moods as the same for practical purposes; he had confused the oblique with the direct narrative; he had

---

[1] [See above, pp. 3 sq, 5 sq.]

maintained that the passage in question (containing a reference to St John) was Irenæus' own, whereas the grammar showed that Irenæus was repeating the words of others; and consequently, he had wrongly accused Dr Tischendorf and Dr Westcott, because in their translations they had brought out the fact that the words did not belong to Irenæus himself.

I place the new note relating to Dr Westcott side by side with the old[1]:—

FOURTH EDITION.	EARLIER EDITIONS.
'Having just observed that a note in this place, in previous editions, has been understood as an accusation against Dr Westcott of deliberate falsification of the text of Irenæus, we at once withdraw it with unfeigned regret that the expressions used could bear an interpretation so far from our intention. *We desired simply to object to the insertion of "they taught"* (*On the Canon* p. 61, note 2), without some indication, in the absence of the original text, that these words were merely supplementary and conjectural. The source *of the indirect passage* is, of course, matter of argument, and we make it so; but it seems to us that the introduction of specific words like these, without explanation of any kind, conveys to the general reader too positive a view of the case. We may perhaps be permitted to say that we fully recognise Dr Westcott's sincere love of truth, and feel the most genuine respect for his character.'	'Canon Westcott, who quotes this passage in a note (*On the Canon* p. 61, note 2), translates here, "This distinction of dwelling, they taught, exists" etc. The introduction of "they taught" here is most unwarrantable; and being inserted, without a word of explanation or mark showing its addition by the translator, in a passage *upon whose interpretation there is difference of opinion*, and whose origin is in dispute, it amounts to a falsification of the text. Dr Westcott neither gives the Greek nor the ancient Latin version for comparison.'

[1] II. p. 328. In the quotations which follow, I have italicised some portions to show the difference of interpretation in the earlier and later editions.

II. THE SILENCE OF EUSEBIUS.

Considering the gravity of his accusation, I think that our author might have been more explicit in his retractation. He might have stated that he not only retracted his charge against Dr Westcott, but also withdrew his own interpretation of the passage. He might have confessed that, having in his earlier editions assumed the words to be Irenæus' own, he had found out his mistake[1]; that accordingly he acknowledged the passage to be oblique; that therefore, after all, Dr Westcott was right and he was wrong; and that the only question with him now was how best to break the force of the true interpretation, in its bearing on the authenticity of the fourth Gospel.

The reader will not find in this fourth edition, from beginning to end, the slightest intimation of all this. He is left with the impression that the author regrets having used a strong expression respecting Dr Westcott, but that otherwise his opinion is unchanged. Whether I have or have not rightly interpreted the facts, will be seen from a juxtaposition of passages from the fourth and earlier editions.

FOURTH EDITION.	EARLIER EDITIONS.
'Now, in the quotation from Irenæus given in this passage, *Tischendorf renders the oblique construction* by inserting "say they," referring to the Presbyters of Papias; and, as he does not give the original, he should at least have indicated that these words are supplementary. We shall endeavour[2]' etc.	'Now in the quotation from Irenæus given in this passage, *Tischendorf deliberately falsifies the text* by inserting "say they;" and, as he does not give the original, the great majority of readers could never detect how he thus adroitly contrives to strengthen his argument. As regards the whole statement of the case, we must affirm that it misrepresents the facts. We shall endeavour' etc.

Lower down he mentions how Irenæus 'continues with a quotation from Isaiah his own train of reasoning,' adding in the early editions—'and it might just as well be affirmed that

---

[1] I see that it was pointed out in the *Inquirer* of Nov. 7th [1874].

[2] [*S. R.* (ed. 4) II. p. 326.]

Irenæus found the quotation from the Prophet in Papias as that which we are considering¹.' As the reference to Isaiah is in the indicative, whereas the clause under consideration is in the infinitive, this was equivalent to saying that the one mood is just as good as the other, where it is a question of the direct or oblique narrative. This last sentence is tacitly removed in the fourth edition.

In the translation of the infinitive εἶναι δὲ τὴν διαστολὴν we notice this difference :—

FOURTH EDITION.	EARLIER EDITIONS.
'But .... there is this distinction.'	'But there is to be this distinction.'

The translation of the passage containing these oblique infinitives is followed by the author's comment, which is altered thus :—

FOURTH EDITION.	EARLIER EDITIONS.
'Now it is impossible for anyone who attentively considers the whole of this passage, and who makes himself acquainted with the manner in which Irenæus conducts his argument, and interweaves it *with quotations, to assert that the phrase we are considering* must have been taken from a book referred to three chapters earlier, and *was not introduced by Irenæus from some other source.*'	'Now it is impossible for anyone who attentively considers the whole of this passage, and who makes himself acquainted with the manner in which Irenæus conducts his argument, and interweaves it *with texts of Scripture, to doubt that the phrase we are considering is introduced by Irenæus himself,* and is in no case a quotation from the work of Papias.'

Here the author has tacitly withdrawn an interpretation which a few weeks before he declared to be beyond the reach of doubt, and has substituted a wholly different one for it. He then proceeds :—

FOURTH EDITION.	EARLIER EDITIONS.
'In the passage from the commencement of the second paragraph Irenæus enlarges upon,	'The passage from the commencement of the second paragraph (§ 2) is an enlargement

¹ [*S. R.* (ed. 2) II. p. 327.]

and illustrates, what "the Presbyters say" regarding the blessedness of the Saints, *by quoting the view held* as to the distinction between those bearing fruit thirty-fold, sixty-fold, and one hundred-fold, and *the interpretation given of the saying* regarding "many mansions."'

or comment on what the Presbyters say regarding the blessedness of the Saints, and Irenæus illustrates the distinction between those bearing fruit thirty-fold, sixty-fold, and one hundred-fold, so often represented in the Gospel, *by the saying* regarding "many mansions" being prepared in Heaven.'

After this our author, in the earlier editions, quotes a number of passages from Irenæus to support his view that the words in question are direct and not oblique, because they happen to begin with διὰ τοῦτο. It is unfortunate that not one of them is in the infinitive mood, and therefore they afford no illustration of the point at issue.

'These,' he there adds, ' are *all direct quotations by Irenæus*, as is *most certainly* that which we are considering, which is introduced in precisely the same way. That this is the case is further *shown* etc. . . . and it is rendered *quite certain* by the fact that' etc.

All these false parallels are withdrawn in the fourth edition, and the sentence is rewritten. We are now told that '*the source of his* (Irenæus') *quotation is quite indefinite, and may simply be the exegesis of his own day*'.' So then it was a quotation after all, and the old interpretation, though declared to be 'most certain' and 'quite certain' in two consecutive sentences, silently vanishes to make room for the new. But why does the author allow himself to spend nine octavo pages over the discussion of this one passage, freely altering sentence after sentence to obliterate all traces of his error, without any intimation to the reader? Had not the public a right to expect more distinctness of statement, considering that the author had been led by this error to libel the character of more than one writer? Must not anyone reading the apology to Dr Westcott, contained in the note quoted above, necessarily carry off a wholly false impression of the facts?

[1] [*S. R.* II. p. 330.]

I add one other passage for comparison:—

FOURTH EDITION.	EARLIER EDITIONS.
'We have disposed of his alternative that the quotation being by "the Presbyters" was more ancient even than Papias, by showing that it *may be referred to Irenæus himself quoting probably from contemporaries*, and that there is no ground for attributing it to the Presbyters at all[1].'	'We have disposed of his alternative that the quotation, being by "the Presbyters," was more ancient even than Papias, by showing that it *must be attributed to Irenæus himself*, and that there is no ground for attributing it to the Presbyters at all.'

Surely this writer might have paused before indulging so freely in charges of 'discreet reserve,' of 'disingenuousness,' of 'wilful and deliberate evasion,' and the like.

[1] [*S. R.* II. p. 334. See above, p. 6.]

III. THE IGNATIAN EPISTLES.

[FEBRUARY, 1875.]

THE letters bearing the name of Ignatius[1], with which we are immediately concerned, profess to have been written by the saint as he was passing through Asia Minor on his way to martyrdom. If their representations be true, he was condemned at Antioch, and sent to Rome to suffer death in the amphitheatre by exposure to the wild beasts. The exact year of the martyrdom is uncertain, but the limits of possibility are not very wide. The earlier date assigned is about A.D. 107, and the later about A.D. 116. These letters, with a single exception, are written to different Churches of Asia Minor (including one addressed more especially to Polycarp, Bishop of Smyrna). The exceptional letter is sent to the Roman Church, apprising the Christians of the metropolis that his arrival among them may soon be expected, declaring his eagerness for martyrdom, and intreating them not to interpose and rescue him from his fate. His language supposes that there were at this time members of the Roman Church sufficiently influential to obtain either a pardon or a commutation of his sentence. The letters to the Asiatic Churches have a more general reference. They contain exhortations, friendly greetings, warnings against internal divisions and against heretical doctrines. With some of these Churches

---

[1] [The Essay on the Ignatian Epistles represents the writer's views at the time when it was written. In the course of the Essay he has stated that at one time he had entertained misgivings about the seven Vossian letters. His maturer opinions establishing their genuineness will be found in his volumes on the *Apostolic Fathers* Part II. S. Ignatius, S. Polycarp, 1885 (London, Macmillan and Co.), to which he refers his readers.]

he had been brought in personal contact; with others he was acquainted only through their delegates.

Of the three forms in which the Ignatian letters have been handed down to us, one may be dismissed from our consideration at once. The Long Recension, preserved both in the Greek original and in a Latin translation, may be regarded as universally condemned. In the early part of the last century an eccentric critic, whose Arian sympathies it seemed to favour, endeavoured to resuscitate its credit, and one or two others, at long intervals, have followed in his wake; but practically it may be regarded as dead. It abounds in anachronisms of fact or diction; its language diverges widely from the Ignatian quotations in the writers of the first five centuries. Our author places its date in the sixth century, with Ussher; I should myself ascribe it to the latter half of the fourth century. This however is a matter of little consequence. Only, before passing on, I would enter a protest against the argument of our author that, because the Ignatian letters were thus interpolated 'in the sixth century,' therefore 'this very fact increases the probability of much earlier interpolation also[1].' I am unable to follow this reasoning. I venture to think that we cannot argue back from the sixth, or even the fourth century, to the second; that this later forgery must not be allowed to throw any shadow of suspicion on the earlier Ignatian letters; and that the question of a prior interpolation must be decided by independent evidence.

The two other forms of the Ignatian letters may be described briefly as follows:—

(1) The first comprises the seven letters which Eusebius had before him, and in the same form in which he read them— to the Ephesians, Magnesians, Trallians, Romans, Philadelphians, Smyrnæans, and Polycarp. It is true that other Epistles confessedly spurious are attached to them in the MSS; but these (as will appear presently) do not properly belong to this collection, and were added subsequently. This collection is

[1] *S. R.* I. p. 263.

preserved not only in the original Greek, but also in Latin and Armenian versions. Fragments also are extant of Coptic and Syriac versions, from which last, and not from the original Greek, the Armenian was translated. The discovery of these epistles, first of all by Ussher in the Latin translation, and then by Isaac Voss in the Greek original, about the middle of the seventeenth century, was the death-blow to the Long Recension. Ussher's dissertations had the honour of giving it the happy despatch. It is usual to call this recension, which thus superseded the other, the Short Greek; but this term is for obvious reasons objectionable, and I shall designate these Epistles the *Vossian*.

(2) The second is extant only in a Syriac dress, and contains three of the Epistles alone—to Polycarp, to the Ephesians, and to the Romans—in a still shorter form. These Syriac Epistles were discovered among the Nitrian MSS in the British Museum, and published by Cureton in 1845. I shall therefore call these the *Curetonian* Epistles.

Cureton's discovery stirred up the Ignatian dispute anew. It was soon fanned into flames by the controversy between Bunsen and Baur, and is raging still. The two questions are these: (1) Whether the Vossian or the Curetonian Epistles are prior in time; in other words, whether the Vossian Epistles were expanded from the Curetonian by interpolation, or whether the Curetonian were reduced from the Vossian by excision and abridgment; and (2) when this question has been disposed of, whether the prior of these two recensions can be regarded as genuine or not.

The question respecting the Ignatian letters has, from the nature of the case, never been discussed exclusively on its own merits. The pure light of criticism has been crossed by the shadows of controversial prepossession on both sides. From the era of the Reformation onward, the dispute between Episcopacy and Presbyterianism has darkened the investigation; in our own age the controversies respecting the Canon of Scripture and the early history of Christianity have interfered with equally injurious effects. Besides these two main questions which are affected by the Ignatian letters, other subjects indirectly involved have aided the strife and confusion. The antagonism between Papal and Protestant writers materially affected the discussion in the sixteenth century, and the antagonism between Arianism and Catholicity in the eighteenth. But the disturbing influence of these indirect questions, though not inconsiderable at the time, has not been lasting.

In the present paper I shall not attempt to treat of the Ignatian question as a whole. It will simply be my business to analyse the statements and discuss the arguments of the author of *Supernatural Religion* relating to this subject. I propose, when I resume these papers again, to say something of the Apostolic Fathers in reference to early Christian belief and to the New Testament Canon; and this cannot be done with any effect until the way has been so far cleared as to indicate the extent to which we can employ the Ignatian letters as valid testimony.

The Ignatian question is the most perplexing which confronts the student of earlier Christian history. The literature is voluminous; the considerations involved are very wide, very varied, and very intricate. A writer therefore may well be pardoned if he betrays a want of familiarity with this subject. But in this case the reader naturally expects that the opinions at which he has arrived will be stated with some diffidence.

The author of *Supernatural Religion* has no hesitation on the subject. 'The whole of the Ignatian literature,' he writes, 'is a mass of falsification and fraud[1].' 'It is not possible,' he says, 'even if the Epistle [to the Smyrnæans] were genuine, which it is not, to base any such conclusion upon these words[2].' And again:—

'We must, however, go much further, and assert that none of the Epistles have any value as evidence for an earlier period than the end of the second, or beginning of the third, century, even if they possess any value at all[3].'

And immediately afterwards:—

[1] I. p. 269.   [2] I. p. 270.   [3] I. p. 274.

'We have just seen that the martyr-journey of Ignatius to Rome is, for cogent reasons, declared to be wholly fabulous, and the Epistles purporting to be written during that journey must be held to be spurious[1].'

The reader is naturally led to think that a writer would not use such very decided language unless he had obtained a thorough mastery of his subject; and when he finds the notes thronged with references to the most recondite sources of information, he at once credits the author with an 'exhaustive' knowledge of the literature bearing upon it. It becomes important therefore to inquire whether the writer shows that accurate acquaintance with the subject, which justifies us in attaching weight to his dicta, as distinguished from his arguments.

I will take first of all a passage which sweeps the field of the Ignatian controversy, and therefore will serve well as a test. The author writes as follows:—

'The strongest internal, as well as other evidence, into which space forbids our going in detail, has led the majority of critics to recognise the Syriac Version as the most genuine form of the letters of Ignatius extant, and this is admitted by most[2] of those who nevertheless deny the authenticity of any of the Epistles[3].'

No statement could be more erroneous, as a summary of the results of the Ignatian controversy since the publication of the Syriac Epistles, than this. Those who maintain the genuineness of the Ignatian Epistles, in one or other of the two forms, may be said to be almost evenly divided on this question of priority. While Cureton and Bunsen and Ritschl and Ewald and Weiss accept the Curetonian letters, Uhlhorn and Denzinger and Petermann and Hefele and Jacobson and Zahn still adhere to the Vossian. But this is a trifling error compared with what follows. The misstatement in the last clause of the sentence will, I venture to think, surprise anyone who is at all familiar with the literature of the Ignatian controversy. Those, who

[1] I. p. 274.
[2] ['many' ed. 6 (I. p. 264); the reading 'most' is explained in the preface to that edition (p. xxvi) as a misprint.]
[3] I. p. 263 sq.

'deny the authenticity of any of the Epistles,' almost universally maintain the priority of the Vossian Epistles, and regard the Curetonian as later excerpts. This is the case, for instance, with Baur[1] and Zeller[2] and Hilgenfeld[3] and Merx[4] and Scholten[5]. It was reserved for a critic like Volkmar[6] to entertain a different opinion; but, so far as I have observed, he stands alone among those who have paid any real attention to the Ignatian question. Indeed, it will be apparent that this position was forced upon critics of the negative school. If the Ignatian letters, in either form, are allowed to be genuine, the Tübingen views of early Christian history fall to the ground. It was therefore a matter of life and death to this school to condemn them wholly. Now the seven Vossian Epistles are clearly very early[7]; and, if the Curetonian should be accepted as the progenitors of the Vossian, the date is pushed so far back that no sufficient ground remains for denying their genuineness. Hence, when Bunsen forced the question on the notice of his countrymen by advocating the Curetonian letters as the original work of Ignatius, Baur instinctively felt the gravity of the occasion, and at once took up the gauntlet. He condemned the Curetonian Epistles as mere excerpts from the Vossian; and in this he has been followed almost without exception by those who advocate his views of early Christian history. The case of Lipsius is especially instructive, as illustrating this point. Having at one time maintained the priority and genuineness of the Curetonian letters, he has lately, if I rightly understand him, retracted his former opinion on both questions alike[8].

But how has our author ventured to make this broad state-

---

[1] *Die Ignatianischen Briefe etc., Eine Streitschrift gegen Herrn Bunsen*, Tübingen, 1848.

[2] *Apostelgeschichte* p. 51. He declares himself 'ganz einverstanden' with Baur's view.

[3] *Apostol. Väter* p. 189; *Zeitschrift* (1874) p. 96 sq.

[4] *Meletemata Ignatiana* (1861).

[5] *Die ält. Zeugn.* p. 50.

[6] *Evangelien* (1870) p. 636.

[7] Volkmar himself, in the passage to which the last note refers, supposes that the seven Epistles date about A.D. 170.

[8] For the earlier opinion of Lipsius, see *Aechtheit d. Syr. Recens. d. Ign. Briefe* p. 159; for his later opinion, *Hilgenfeld's Zeitschrift* (1874), p. 211 sq.

ment, when his own notes elsewhere contain references to nearly all the writers whom I have named as belonging to this last category, and even to the very passages in which they express the opposite opinion? To throw some light on this point, I will analyse the author's general statement of the course of opinion on this subject given in an earlier passage. He writes as follows:—

'These three Syriac Epistles have been subjected to the severest scrutiny, and many of the ablest critics have pronounced them to be the only authentic Epistles of Ignatius, whilst others, who do not admit that even these are genuine letters emanating from Ignatius, still prefer them to the version of seven Greek Epistles, and consider them the most ancient form of the letters which we possess[1]. As early as the sixteenth century however, the strongest doubts were expressed regarding the authenticity of any of the Epistles ascribed to Ignatius. The Magdeburg Centuriators first attacked them, and Calvin declared [p. 260] them to be spurious[1], an opinion fully shared by Chemnitz, Dallæus, and others, and similar doubts, more or less definite, were expressed throughout the seventeenth century[2], and onward to comparatively recent times[3], although the means of forming a judgment were not then so complete as now. That the Epistles were interpolated there was no doubt. Fuller examination and more comprehensive knowledge of the subject have confirmed earlier doubts, and a large mass of critics recognise that the authenticity of none of these Epistles can be established, and that they can only be considered later and spurious compositions[4].'

The first note [1] on p. 259 is as follows:—

'Bunsen, *Ignatius v. Ant. u. s. Zeit*, 1847; *Die drei ächt. u. d. vier unächt. Br. des Ignat.*, 1847; Bleek, *Einl. N. T.*, p. 145; Böhringer, *K. G. in Biograph.*, 2 Aufl., p. 16; Cureton, *The Ancient Syriac Version of Eps. of St Ignatius*, etc., 1845; *Vindiciæ Ignat.*, 1846, *Corpus Ignatianum*, 1849; Ewald, *Gesch. d. V. Isr.*, vii. p. 313; Lipsius, *Aechtheit d. Syr. Recens. d. Ign. Br.* in *Illgen's Zeitschr. f. hist. Theol.*, 1856, H. i., 1857, *Abhandl. d. deutsche-morgenl. Gesellschaft.* i. 5, 1859, p. 7; Milman, *Hist. of Chr.*, ii. p. 102; Ritschl, *Entst. altk. Kirche*, p. 403, anm.; Weiss, *Reuter's Repertorium*, Sept. 1852.' [The rest of the note touches another point, and need not be quoted.]

These references, it will be observed, are given to illustrate more immediately, though perhaps not solely, the statement that writers 'who do not admit that even these [the Curetonian Epistles] are genuine letters emanating from Ignatius, still prefer them to the version of seven Greek Epistles, and consider them the most ancient form of the letters which we possess.' The reader therefore will hardly be prepared to hear that not one of these nine writers condemns the Ignatian letters as spurious. Bleek[1] alone leaves the matter in some uncertainty, while inclining to Bunsen's view; the other eight distinctly maintain the genuineness of the Curetonian letters[2].

As regards the names which follow in the text, it must be remembered that the Magdeburg Centuriators and Calvin wrote long before the discovery of the Vossian letters. The Ignatian Epistles therefore were weighted with all the anachronisms and impossibilities which condemn the Long Recension in the judgment of modern critics of all schools. The criticisms of Calvin more especially refer chiefly to those passages which are found in the Long Recension alone. The clause which follows contains a direct misstatement. Chemnitz did not fully share the opinion that they were spurious; on the contrary he quotes them several times as authoritative; but he says that they 'seem to have been altered in many places to strengthen the position of the Papal power etc.[3]'

The note [(2)] on p. 260 runs as follows:—

'By Bochartus, Aubertin, Blondel, Basnage, Casaubon, Cocus, Humfrey, Rivetus, Salmasius, Socinus (Faustus), Parker, Petau, etc., etc.; cf. Jacobson, *Patr. Apost.*, i. p. xxv; Cureton, *Vindiciæ Ignatianæ*, 1846, appendix.'

Here neither alphabetical nor chronological order is observed. Nor is it easy to see why an Englishman R. Cook, Vicar of Leeds, should be Cocus, while a foreigner, Petavius, is Petau. These however are small matters. It is of more consequence to

---

[1] p. 142 (ed. 1862).
[2] The references in the case of Lipsius are to his earlier works, where he still maintains the priority and genuineness of the Curetonian letters.
[3] See Pearson's *Vindiciæ Ignatianæ* p. 28 (ed. Churton).

observe that the author has here mixed up together writers who lived before and after the discovery of the Vossian Epistles, though this is the really critical epoch in the history of the Ignatian controversy. But the most important point of all is the purpose for which they are quoted. 'Similar doubts' could only, I think, be interpreted from the context as doubts 'regarding the authenticity of any of the Epistles ascribed to Ignatius.' The facts however are these[1]. Bochart condemns the Ignatian Epistle to the Romans on account of the mention of 'leopards,' of which I shall speak hereafter, but says nothing about the rest, though probably he would have condemned them also. Aubertin, Blondel, Basnage, R. Parker, and Saumaise, reject all. Humfrey (1584) considers that they have been interpolated and mutilated, but he believes them genuine in the main. Cook (1614) pronounces them 'either supposititious or shamefully corrupted.' F. Socinus (A.D. 1624) denounces corruptions and anachronisms, but so far as I can see, does not question a nucleus of genuine matter. Casaubon (A.D. 1615), so far from rejecting them altogether, promises to defend the antiquity of some of the Epistles with new arguments. Rivet explains that Calvin's objections apply not to Ignatius himself but to the corrupters of Ignatius, and himself accepts the Vossian Epistles as genuine[2]. Petau, before the discovery of the Vossian letters, had expressed the opinion that there were interpolations in the then known Epistles, and afterwards on reading the Vossian letters, declared it to be a *prudens et justa suspicio* that these are the genuine work of Ignatius.

The next note[(3)] p. 260 is as follows:—

[Wotton, *Præf. Clem. R. Epp.*, 1718]; J. Owen, *Enquiry into original nature, etc., Evang. Church: Works*, ed. Russel, 1826, vol. xx. p. 147; Oudin, *Comm. de Script. Eccles. etc.* 1722, p. 88;

[1] The reader will find the opinions of these writers given in Jacobson's *Patres Apostolici* I. p. xxvii; or more fully in Pearson's *Vindiciæ Ignatianæ* p. 27 sq, from whom Russel's excerpts, reprinted by Jacobson, are taken.

[2] [In his preface to ed. 6 (p. xxxiii) our author admits his error in the case of Rivet, whose name is struck out from the note on I. p. 260 in that edition.]

Lampe, *Comm. analyt. ex Evang. Joan.*, 1724, i. p. 184; Lardner, *Credibility, etc., Works*, ii. p. 68 f.; Beausobre, *Hist. Crit. de Manichée, etc.*, 1734, i. p. 378, note 3; Ernesti, *N. Theol. Biblioth.*, 1761, ii. p. 489; [Mosheim, *de Rebus Christ.*, p. 159 f.]; Weismann, *Introd. in Memorab. Eccles.*, 1745, p. 137; Heumann, *Conspect. Reipub. Lit.*, 1763, p. 492; Schroeckh, *Chr. Kirchengesch.*, 1775, ii. p. 341; Griesbach, *Opuscula Academ.*, 1824, i. p. 26; Rosenmüller, *Hist. Interpr. Libr. Sacr. in Eccles.*, 1795, i. p. 116; Semler, *Paraphr. in Epist. ii. Petri*, 1784, Præf.; Kestner, *Comm. de Eusebii H. E. condit.*, 1816, p. 63; Henke, *Allg. Gesch. chr. Kirche*, 1818, i. p. 96; Neander, *K. G.* 1843, ii. p. 1140 [cf. i. p. 357, anm. 1]; Baumgarten-Crusius. *Lehrb. chr. Dogmengesch.*, 1832, p. 83, cf. *Comp. chr. Dogmengesch.*, 1840, p. 79; [*Niedner, Gesch. chr. K.*, p. 196; Thiersch, *Die K. im ap. Zeit*, p. 322; Hagenbach, *K. G.*, i. p. 115 f.]; cf. Cureton, *Vind. Ign. append.*; Ziegler, *Versuch ein. prag. Gesch. d. kirchl. Verfassungs-formen*, u. s. w., 1798, p. 16; J. E. C. Schmidt, *Versuch üb. d. gedopp. Recens. d. Br. S. Ignat.* in *Henke's Mag. f. Rel. Phil.*, u. s. w. [1795; cf. *Biblioth. f. Krit.*, u. s. w., *N. T.*, i. p. 463 ff., *Urspr. kath. Kirche*, II. i. p. 1 f.]; *H'buch Chr. K. G.*, i. p. 200.

The brackets are not the author's, but my own.

This is doubtless one of those exhibitions of learning which have made such a deep impression on the reviewers. Certainly, as it stands, this note suggests a thorough acquaintance with all the by-paths of the Ignatian literature, and seems to represent the gleanings of many years' reading. It is important to observe however, that every one of these references, except those which I have included in brackets, is given in the appendix to Cureton's *Vindiciæ Ignatianæ*, where the passages are quoted in full. Thus two-thirds of this elaborate note might have been compiled in ten minutes. Our author has here and there transposed the order of the quotations, and confused it by so doing, for it is chronological in Cureton. But what purpose was served by thus importing into his notes a mass of borrowed and unsorted references? And, if he thought fit to do so, why was the key-reference to Cureton buried among the rest, so that it stands in immediate connection with some additional references on which it has no bearing?

III. THE IGNATIAN EPISTLES. 69

Moreover, several of the writers mentioned in this note express opinions directly opposed to that for which they are quoted. Wotton, for instance[1], defends the genuineness of the Vossian Epistles very decidedly, and at some length, against Whiston, whose Arianism led him to prefer the Long Recension. Weismann declares that 'the authenticity and genuineness of the Epistles have been demonstrated clearly and solidly' by Pearson and others, so that no valid objections remain affecting the main question. Thiersch again, who wrote after the publication of Cureton's work, uses the three Syriac Epistles as genuine, his only doubt being whether he ought not to accept the Vossian Epistles and to regard the Curetonian as excerpts. Of the rest a considerable number, as for instance, Lardner, Beausobre, Schroeckh, Griesbach, Kestner, Neander, and Baumgarten-Crusius, with different degrees of certainty or uncertainty, pronounce themselves in favour of a genuine nucleus[2].

The next note [4], which I need not quote in full, is almost as unfortunate. References to twenty authorities are there given, as belonging to the 'large mass of critics' who recognise that the Ignatian Epistles 'can only be considered later and spurious compositions.' Of these Bleek (already cited in a previous note) expresses no definite opinion. Gfrörer declares that the substratum (*Grundlage*) of the seven Epistles is genuine, though 'it appears as if later hands had introduced interpolations into both recensions' (he is speaking of the Long Recension and the Vossian). Harless avows that he must 'decidedly reject with the most considerable critics of older and more recent times' the opinion maintained by certain persons that the Epistles are 'altogether spurious,' and proceeds to treat a passage as genuine because it stands in the Vossian

---

[1] See Jacobson *Patres Apostolici* I. p. xlvi, where the passage is given.

[2] [Our author (ed. 6, p. xxxv sq) falls foul of my criticism of his references. It is contrary to my purpose to reopen the question, but I confidently leave it to those who will examine the passages for themselves to say whether he is justified in his inferences. He however 'gives up' Wotton and Weismann.]

letters as well as in the Long Recension[1]. Schliemann also says that 'the external testimonies oblige him to recognise a genuine substratum,' though he is not satisfied with either existing recension. All these critics, it should be observed, wrote before the discovery of the Curetonian letters. Of the others, Hase commits himself to no opinion; and Lechler, while stating that the seven Epistles left on his mind an impression unfavourable to their genuineness, and inclining to Baur's view that the Curetonian letters are excerpts from the others, nevertheless adds, that he cannot boast of having arrived at a decided conviction of the spuriousness of the Ignatian letters. One or two of the remaining references in this note I have been unable to verify; but, judging from the names, I should expect that the rest would be found good for the purpose for which they are quoted by our author.

I am sorry to have delayed my readers with an investigation which—if I may venture to adopt a phrase, for which I am not myself responsible—'scarcely rises above the correction of an exercise[2].' But these notes form a very appreciable and imposing part of the work, and their effect on its reception has been far from inconsiderable, as the language of the reviewers will show. It was therefore important to take a sample and test its value. I trust that I may be spared the necessity of a future investigation of the same kind. If it has wearied my readers, it has necessarily been tenfold more irksome to myself. Ordinary errors, such as must occur in any writer, might well have been passed over; but the character of the notes in *Supernatural Religion* is quite unique, so far as my experience goes, in works of any critical pretensions.

In the remainder of the discussion our author seems to depend almost entirely on Cureton's preface to his *Ancient Syriac Version*, to which indeed he makes due acknowledgment from time to time. Notwithstanding the references to other later writers which crowd the notes already mentioned, they

---

[1] p. xxxiv (Reprint of 1858). 1875, p. 9.
[2] *Fortnightly Review*, January,

appear (with the single exception of Volkmar) to have exercised no influence on his discussion of the main question. One highly important omission is significant. There is no mention, from first to last, of the Armenian version. Now it happens that this version (so far as regards the documentary evidence) has been felt to be the key to the position, and around it the battle has raged fiercely since its publication. One who (like our author) maintains the priority of the Curetonian letters, was especially bound to give it some consideration, for it furnishes the most formidable argument to his opponents. This version was given to the world by Petermann in 1849, the same year in which Cureton's later work, the *Corpus Ignatianum*, appeared, and therefore was unknown to him[1]. Its bearing occupies a more or less prominent place in all, or nearly all, the writers who have specially discussed the Ignatian question during the last quarter of a century. This is true of Lipsius and Weiss and Hilgenfeld and Uhlhorn, whom he cites, not less than of Merx and Denzinger and Zahn, whom he neglects to cite. The facts established by Petermann and others are these;—(1) This Armenian version, which contains the seven Vossian Epistles together with other confessedly spurious letters, was translated from a previous Syriac version. Indeed fragments of this version were published by Cureton himself, as a sort of appendix to the Curetonian letters, in the *Corpus Ignatianum*, though he failed to see their significance. (2) This Syriac version conformed so closely to the Syriac of the Curetonian letters that they cannot have been independent. Either therefore the Curetonian letters were excerpts from this complete version, or this version was founded upon and enlarged from the pre-existing Curetonian letters by translating and adding the supplementary letters and parts of letters from the Greek. The former may be the right solution, but the latter is *a priori* more probable; and therefore a discussion which, while assuming the priority of the Curetonian letters, ignores this version altogether,

[1] He mentions an earlier edition of this Version printed at Constantinople in 1783, but had not seen it; *Corp. Ign.* p. xvi.

has omitted a vital problem of which it was bound to give an account.

I have no wish to depreciate the labours of Cureton. Whether his own view be ultimately adopted as correct or not, he has rendered inestimable service to the Ignatian literature. But our author has followed him in his most untenable positions, which those who have since studied the subject, whether agreeing with Cureton on the main question or not, have been obliged to abandon. Thus he writes:—

'Seven Epistles have been selected out of fifteen extant, all equally purporting to be by Ignatius, simply because only that number were mentioned by Eusebius[1].'

And again:—

'It is a total mistake to suppose that the seven Epistles mentioned by Eusebius have been transmitted to us in any special way. These Epistles are mixed up in the Medicean and corresponding ancient Latin MSS with the other eight Epistles, universally pronounced to be spurious, without distinction of any kind, and all have equal honour[2].'

with more to the same effect.

This attempt to confound the seven Epistles mentioned by Eusebius with the other confessedly spurious Epistles, as if they presented themselves to us with the same credentials, ignores all the important facts bearing on the question. (1) Theodoret, a century after Eusebius, betrays no knowledge of any other Epistles, and there is no distinct trace of the use of the confessedly spurious Epistles till late in the sixth century at the earliest. (2) The confessedly spurious Epistles differ widely in style from the seven Epistles, and betray the same hand which interpolated the seven Epistles. In other words, they clearly formed part of the Long Recension in the first instance. (3) They abound in anachronisms which point to an age later than Eusebius, as the date of their composition. (4) It is not strictly true that the seven Epistles are mixed up with the confessedly spurious Epistles. In the Greek and Latin MSS

[1] I. p. 264. [2] I. p. 265.

III. THE IGNATIAN EPISTLES. 73

as also in the Armenian version, the spurious Epistles come after the others[1]; and this circumstance, combined with the facts already mentioned, plainly shows that they were a later addition, borrowed from the Long Recension to complete the body of Ignatian letters.

Indeed our author seems hardly able to touch this question at any point without being betrayed into some statement which is either erroneous or misleading. Thus, summing up the external evidence, he writes:—

'It is a fact, therefore, that up to the second half of the fourth century no quotation ascribed to Ignatius, except one by Eusebius, exists, which is not found in the three short Syriac letters[2].'

In this short statement three corrections are necessary. (1) Our author has altogether overlooked one quotation in Eusebius from *Ephes.* 19, because it happens not to be in the Ecclesiastical History, though it is given in Cureton's *Corpus Ignatianum*[3]. (2) Of the two quotations in the Ecclesiastical History, the one which he here reckons as found in the Syriac Epistles is not found in those Epistles in the form in which Eusebius quotes it. The quotation in Eusebius contains several words which appear in the Vossian Epistles, but not in the Curetonian; and as the absence of these words produces one of those abruptnesses which are characteristic of the Curetonian letters, the fact is really important for the question under discussion[4]. (3) Though Eusebius only directly quotes two passages in his Ecclesiastical History, yet he gives a number of particulars respecting the

---

[1] The Roman Epistle indeed has been separated from its companions, and is embedded in the Martyrology which stands at the end of this collection in the Latin Version, where doubtless it stood also in the Greek, before the мs of this latter was mutilated. Otherwise the Vossian Epistles come together, and are followed by the confessedly spurious Epistles in the Greek and Latin мss. In the Armenian all the Vossian Epistles are together, and the confessedly spurious Epistles follow. See Zahn *Ignatius von Antiochien* p. 111.

[2] I. p. 262.

[3] p. 164.

[4] Ign. *Rom.* 5, where the words ἐγὼ γινώσκω νῦν ἄρχομαι μαθητὴς εἶναι are found in Eusebius as in the Vossian Epistles, but are wanting in the Curetonian. There are other smaller differences.

places of writing, the persons named, etc., which are more valuable for purposes of identification than many quotations.

Our author's misstatement however does not in this instance affect the main question under discussion. The fact remains true, when all these corrections are made, that the quotations in the second and third centuries are confined to passages which occur both in the Curetonian and in the Vossian Epistles, and therefore afford no indication in favour of either recension as against the other. The testimony of Eusebius in the fourth century first differentiates them.

Hitherto our author has not adduced any arguments which affect the genuineness of the Ignatian Epistles as a whole. His reasons, even on his own showing, are valid only so far as to give a preference to the Curetonian letters as against the Vossian. When therefore he declares the whole of the Ignatian literature to be 'a mass of falsification and fraud[1],' we are naturally led to inquire into the grounds on which he makes this very confident and sweeping assertion. These grounds we find to be twofold.

(1) In the first place he conceives the incidents, as represented in the Epistles, to be altogether incredible. Thus he says[2]:—

'The writer describes the circumstances of his journey as follows:—" From Syria even unto Rome I fight with wild beasts, by sea and by land, by night and day; being bound amongst ten leopards, which are the band of soldiers: who even when good is done to them render evil." Now if this account be in the least degree true, how is it possible to suppose that the martyr could have found means to write so many long epistles, entering minutely into dogmatic teaching, and expressing the most deliberate and advanced views regarding ecclesiastical government?'

And again:—

'It is impossible to suppose that soldiers such as the quotation above describes would allow a prisoner, condemned to wild beasts for professing Christianity, deliberately to write long epistles at every stage of his journey, promulgating the very doctrines for

[1] *S. R.* i. p. 269.   [2] *S. R.* i. p. 267.

which he was condemned. And not only this, but on his way to martyrdom, he has, according to the epistles, perfect freedom to see his friends. He receives the bishops, deacons, and members of various Christian communities, who come with greetings to him, and devoted followers accompany him on his journey. All this without hindrance from the "ten leopards," of whose cruelty he complains, and without persecution or harm to those who so openly declare themselves his friends and fellow-believers. The whole story is absolutely incredible.'

To this objection, plausible as it may appear at first sight, a complete answer is afforded by what is known of Roman procedure in other cases[1]. As a matter of fact, Christian prisoners during the early centuries were not uncommonly treated by the authorities with this same laxity and indulgence which is here accorded to Ignatius. An excited populace or a stern magistrate might insist on the condemnation of a Christian; a victim must be sacrificed to the wrath of the gods, or to the majesty of the law; a human life must be 'butcher'd to make a Roman holiday;' but the treatment of the prisoners meanwhile, even after condemnation, was, except in rare instances, the reverse of harsh. St Paul himself preaches the Gospel apparently with almost as much effect through the long years of his imprisonment as when he was at large. During his voyage he moves about like the rest of his fellow-travellers; when he arrives at Rome, he is still treated with great consideration. He writes letters freely, receives visits from his friends, communicates with churches and individuals as he desires, though the chain is on his wrist and the soldier at his side all the while. Even at a much later date, when the growth of the Christian Church may have created an alarm among statesmen and magistrates which certainly cannot have existed in the age of Ignatius, we

---

[1] This objection is well discussed by Zahn *Ignatius von Antiochien* p. 278 sq (1873), where our author's arguments are answered by anticipation substantially as I have answered them in the text. I venture to call attention to this work (which does not appear yet to have attracted the notice of English writers) as the most important contribution to the Ignatian literature which has appeared since Cureton's publications introduced a new era in the controversy. Zahn defends the genuineness of the Vossian Epistles.

see the same leniency of treatment, and (what is more important) the same opportunities of disseminating their opinions accorded to the prisoners. Thus Saturus and Perpetua, the African martyrs, who suffered under Severus[1] (apparently in the year 202 or 203), are allowed writing materials, with which they record the extant history of their sufferings; and they too are visited in prison by Christian deacons, as well as by their own friends. They owed this liberty partly to the humanity of the chief officers; partly to gratuities bestowed by their friends on the gaolers[2]. Even after the lapse of another half-century, when Decius seriously contemplated the extermination of Christianity, we are surprised to find the amount of communication still kept up with the prisoners in their dungeons. The Cyprianic correspondence reveals to us the confessors and martyrs writing letters to their friends, visited by large numbers of people, even receiving the rites of the Church in their prisons at the hands of Christian priests.

But the most powerful testimony is derived from the representations of a heathen writer. The Christian career of Peregrinus must have fallen within the reign of Antoninus Pius (A.D. 138—161). Thus it is not very far removed, in point of time, from the age of Ignatius. This Peregrinus is represented by Lucian, writing immediately after his death (A.D. 165), as being incarcerated for his profession of Christianity, and the satirist thus describes the prison scene[3]:—

'When he was imprisoned, the Christians, regarding it as a great calamity, left no stone unturned in the attempt to rescue him. Then, when they found this impossible, they looked after his wants in every other respect with unremitting zeal (οὐ παρέργως ἀλλὰ σὺν σπουδῇ). And from early dawn old women, widows, and orphan children, might be seen waiting about the doors of the prison; while their officers (οἱ ἐν τέλει αὐτῶν) succeeded, by bribing the keepers, in

---

[1] Ruinart *Acta Martyrum Sincera* p. 134 sq. (Ratisbon, 1859).

[2] Ruinart p. 141. 'Praepositus carceris, qui nos magni facere coepit... multos fratres ad nos admittebat, ut et nos et illi invicem refrigeraremus,' p 144. 'Tribunus... jussit illos humanius haberi, ut fratribus ejus et ceteris facultas fieret introeundi et refrigerandi cum eis.'

[3] *De Morte Peregr.* 12.

III. THE IGNATIAN EPISTLES.

passing the night inside with him. Then various meals were brought in, and religious discourses were held between them, and this excellent Peregrinus (for he still bore this name) was entitled a new Socrates by them. Moreover, there came from certain cities in Asia deputies sent by the Christian communities to assist and advise and console the man. Indeed they show incredible despatch, when any matter of the kind is undertaken as a public concern; for, in short, they spare nothing. And so large sums of money came to Peregrinus at that time from them, on the plea of his fetters, and he made no inconsiderable revenue out of it.'

The singular correspondence in this narrative with the account of Ignatius, combined with some striking coincidences of expression[1], have led to the opinion that Lucian was acquainted with the Ignatian history, if not with the Ignatian letters. For this view there is much to be said; and, if it be true, the bearing of the fact on the genuineness of the Ignatian literature is important, since Lucian was born in Syria somewhere about A.D. 120, and lived much in Asia Minor. At all events it is conclusive for the matter in hand, as showing that Christian prisoners were treated in the very way described in these epistles. The reception of delegates and the freedom of correspondence, which have been the chief stumbling-blocks to modern criticism in the Ignatian letters, appear quite as prominently in the heathen satirist's account of Peregrinus[2].

[1] See Zahn *Ignatius* p. 527. Lucian says of Peregrinus (now no longer a Christian, but a Cynic), c. 41, φασὶ δὲ πάσαις σχεδὸν ταῖς ἐνδόξοις πόλεσιν ἐπιστολὰς διαπέμψαι αὐτόν, διαθήκας τινὰς καὶ παραινέσεις καὶ νόμους· καί τινας ἐπὶ τούτῳ πρεσβευτὰς τῶν ἑταίρων ἐχειροτόνησε νεκραγγέλους καὶ νερτεροδρόμους προσαγορεύσας. This description exactly corresponds to the letters and delegates of Ignatius. See especially Polyc. 7, χειροτονῆσαί τινα ...... ὃς δυνήσεται θεοδρόμος καλεῖσθαι. The Christian bystanders reported that a dove had been seen to issue from the body of Polycarp when he was martyred at the stake (*Martyr. Polyc.* c. 16). Similarly Lucian represents himself as spreading a report, which was taken up and believed by the Cynic's disciples, that a vulture was seen to rise from the pyre of Peregrinus when he consigned himself to a voluntary death by burning. It would seem that the satirist here is laughing at the credulity of these simple Christians, with whose history he appears to have had at least a superficial acquaintance.

[2] As a corollary to this argument, our author says that the Epistles themselves bear none of the marks of composition under such circumstances.

In the light of these facts the language of Ignatius becomes quite intelligible. He was placed under the custody of a maniple of soldiers. These ten men would relieve guard in turns, the prisoner being always bound to one or other of them day and night, according to the well-known Roman usage, as illustrated by the case of St Paul. The martyr finds his guards fierce and intractable as leopards. His fight with wild beasts, he intimates, is not confined to the arena of the Flavian amphitheatre; it has been going on continuously ever since he left Antioch. His friends manage to secure him indulgences by offering bribes, but the soldiers are exorbitant and irritating in the extreme[1]. The more they receive, the more they exact. Their demands keep pace with his exigencies. All this is natural, and it fully explains the language here ascribed to Ignatius. A prisoner smarting under such treatment naturally dwells on the dark side of the picture, without thinking how a critic, writing in his study centuries afterwards, will interpret his fragmentary and impulsive utterances. In short, we must treat Ignatius as a man, and not as an automaton. Men will not talk mechanically, as critics would have them talk.

(2) Having declared 'the whole story' to be 'absolutely incredible,' on the grounds which I have just considered, our author continues[2]:—

It is sufficient to reply that even the Vossian Epistles are more abrupt than the letters written by St Paul, when chained to a soldier. The abruptness of the Curetonian Epistles is still greater—indeed so great as to render them almost unintelligible in parts. I write this notwithstanding that our author, following Cureton, has expressed a different opinion respecting the style of the Curetonian letters.

Our author speaks also of the length of the letters. The Curetonian Letters occupy five large octavo pages in Cureton's translation, p. 227. Even the seven Vossian Letters might have been dictated in almost as many hours; and it would be strange indeed if, by bribe or entreaty, Ignatius could not have secured this indulgence from one or other of his guards during a journey which must have occupied months rather than weeks. He also describes the Epistles as purporting to be written 'at every stage of his journey.' 'Every stage' must be interpreted 'two stages,' for all the Seven Vossian Epistles profess to have been written either at Smyrna or at Troas.

[1] This, as more than one writer has pointed out, seems to be the meaning of οἱ καὶ εὐεργετούμενοι χείρους γίνονται, Ign. *Rom.* 5.

[2] *S. R.* I. p. 268.

'This conclusion, irresistible in itself, is, however, confirmed by facts arrived at from a totally different point of view. It has been demonstrated that Ignatius was not sent to Rome at all, but suffered martyrdom in Antioch itself on the 20th December, A.D. 115[?], when he was condemned to be cast to wild beasts in the amphitheatre, in consequence of the fanatical excitement produced by the earthquake which took place on the 13th of that month[4].'

The two foot-notes contain no justification of this very positive statement, though so much depends upon it; but the reader is there furnished with a number of references to modern critics. These references have been analysed by Dr Westcott[1], with results very similar to those which my analysis of the author's previous notes has yielded. In some cases the writers express opinions directly opposed to that for which they are quoted; in others they incline to views irreconcilable with it; and in others they suspend judgment. When the references are sifted, the sole residuum on which our author rests his assurance is found to be a hypothesis of Volkmar[2], built upon a statement of John Malalas, which I shall now proceed to examine. The words of John Malalas are—

'The same king Trajan was residing in the same city (Antioch) when the visitation of God (*i.e.* the earthquake) occurred. And at that time the holy Ignatius, the bishop of the city of Antioch, was martyred (or bore testimony, ἐμαρτύρησε) before him (ἐπὶ αὐτοῦ); for he was exasperated against him, because he reviled him[3].'

The earthquake is stated by Malalas to have occurred on the 13th of December, A.D. 115. On these statements, combined with the fact that the day dedicated to St Ignatius at a later age was the 20th of December[4], Volkmar builds his theory. It will be observed that the cause of the martyr's death, as laid down by Volkmar, receives no countenance from the story of

---

[1] *A Few Words on Supernatural Religion* p. xx sq, a preface to the fourth edition of Dr Westcott's *History of the Canon*, but published separately.

[2] *Handbuch der Einleitung in die Apokryphen* i. pp. 49 sq, 121 sq.

[3] p. 276 (ed. Bonn.).

[4] In St Chrysostom's age it appears to have been kept at quite a different time of the year—in June; see Zahn, p. 53.

Malalas, who gives a wholly different reason—the irritating language used to the emperor.

Now this John Malalas lived not earlier than the latter half of the sixth century, and possibly much later. His date therefore constitutes no claim to a hearing. His statement moreover is directly opposed to the concurrent testimony of the four or five preceding centuries, which, without a dissentient voice, declare that Ignatius suffered at Rome. This is the case with all the writers and interpolators of the Ignatian letters, of whom the earliest is generally placed, even by those critics who deny their genuineness, about the middle or in the latter half of the second century. It is the case with two distinct martyrologies[1], which, agreeing in little else, are united in sending the martyr to Rome to die. It is the case necessarily with all those Fathers who quote the Ignatian letters in any form as genuine, amongst whom are Irenæus and Origen and Eusebius and Athanasius. It is the case with Chrysostom, who, on the day of the martyr's festival, pronounces at Antioch an elaborate panegyric on his illustrious predecessor in the see[2]. It is the case with several other writers also, whom I need not enumerate, all prior to Malalas.

But John Malalas, it is said, lived at Antioch. So did Chrysostom some two centuries at least before him. So did Evagrius, who, if the earliest date of Malalas be adopted, was his contemporary, and who, together with all preceding authorities, places the martyrdom of Ignatius in Rome. If therefore the testimony of Malalas deserves to be preferred to this cloud of witnesses, it must be because he approves himself elsewhere as a sober and trustworthy writer.

As a matter of fact however, his notices of early Christian history are, almost without exception, demonstrably false or palpably fabulous[3]. In the very paragraph which succeeds the

---

[1] The one first published by Ruinart from a Colbert ms, and the other by Dressel from a Vatican ms. The remaining Martyrologies, those of the Metaphrast, of the Bollandists, and of the Armenian version, have no independent value, being compacted from these two.

[2] The authorities for these statements will be found in Cureton's *Corpus Ignatianum* p. 158 sq.

[3] See Lipsius *Ueber das Verhältniss des Textes der drei Syrischen Briefe etc.* p. 7.

sentence quoted, he relates how Trajan had five Christian women burnt alive; the emperor then mingled their ashes with the metal from which the vessels used for the baths were cast; the bathers were seized with swooning-fits in consequence; the vessels were again melted up; and out of the same metal were erected five pillars in honour of the five martyrs by the emperor's orders. These pillars, adds Malalas, stand in the bath to the present day. As if this were not enough, he goes on to relate how Trajan made a furnace and ordered any Christians, who desired, to throw themselves into it—an injunction which was obeyed by many. Nor when he leaves the domain of hagiology for that of chronology, is this author any more trustworthy. For instance, he states that Manes first propounded his doctrine in the reign of Nerva, and that Marcion still further disseminated the Manichean heresy under Hadrian[1]. An anachronism of a century or more is nothing to him.

We have seen by this time what authority suffices, in our author's judgment, to 'demonstrate' a fact; and no more is necessary for my purpose. But it may be worth while adding that the error of Malalas is capable of easy explanation. He has probably misinterpreted some earlier authority, whose language lent itself to misinterpretation. The words μαρτυρεῖν, μαρτυρία, which were afterwards used especially of martyrdom, had in the earlier ages a wider sense, including other modes of witnessing to the faith: the expression ἐπὶ Τραιανοῦ again is ambiguous and might denote either 'during the reign of Trajan,' or 'in the presence of Trajan.' A blundering writer like Malalas might have stumbled over either expression[2].

The objections of our author have thus been met and answered; and difficulties which admit of this easy explanation cannot, I venture to think, be held to have any real weight against even a small amount of external testimony in favour of the Epistles. The external testimony however is considerable in this case[3].

[1] pp. 268, 279 (ed. Bonn.).
[2] The former explanation is suggested by Lipsius, l.c.; the latter by Zahn, p. 67.
[3] The testimonies to which I refer in this paragraph will be found in Cureton's *Corpus Ignatianum* p. 158 sq. [The question of the credibility of

The Epistle of Polycarp, which purports to have been written so soon after this journey of Ignatius through Asia Minor that the circumstances of the martyr's death were not fully known there, speaks of his letters in language which is entirely applicable to the existing documents. Our author indeed declares this Epistle also to be spurious. But Irenæus, the pupil of Polycarp, bears testimony to the existence of such an Epistle; and I pledge myself to answer in a subsequent paper the objections urged against its genuineness by our author and others[1]. Besides this, Irenæus, writing about A.D. 180—190, quotes a characteristic and distinctive passage from the Epistle to the Romans, not indeed mentioning Ignatius by name, but introducing the quotation as the words of a member of the Christian brotherhood. And again, in the first half of the next century Origen cites two passages from these letters, ascribing them directly to Ignatius. I say nothing of the later and more explicit references and quotations of Eusebius, important as these are in themselves. Our author indeed seems to consider this amount of testimony very insufficient. But even if we set Polycarp aside, it would hardly be rash to say that the external evidence for at least two-thirds of the remains of classical antiquity is inferior. We Christians are constantly told that we must expect to have our records tested by the same standards which are applied to other writings. This is exactly what we desire, and what we do not get. It is not easy to imagine the havoc which would ensue, if the critical principles of the Tübingen school and their admirers were let loose on the classical literature of Greece and Rome.

External testimony therefore leaves a very strong presumption in favour of the genuineness of the Ignatian letters in one form or other; and before rejecting them entirely, we are bound to show that internal evidence furnishes really substantial and valid objections to their authenticity. It is not sufficient, for instance, to allege that the saint's desire for martyrdom, as

Malalas, and of the meaning of ἐπὶ Τραϊανοῦ, is treated more fully in my *Apostolic Fathers*, Part II. S. Ignatius,

S. Polycarp, II. pp. 437—447 (ed. 2).]
[1] [This pledge is fulfilled below, p. 93 sq.]

exhibited in these Epistles, is extravagant, because we have ample testimony for believing that such extravagance (whether commendable or not) was highly characteristic of the faith and zeal of the early Christians when tried by persecution. Nor again, is it of any avail to produce some eccentricities of thought or language, because there is no *a priori* reason why St Ignatius should not have indulged in such eccentricities.

Unless therefore really solid objections can be urged, we are bound by all ordinary laws of literary evidence to accept as genuine at all events the shortest form in which these Epistles are presented to us. In other words, the Curetonian letters at least must be received. And as these satisfy all the quotations and references of the second and third centuries (though not those of Eusebius in the first half of the fourth), perhaps not more is required by the external testimony. Against the genuineness of these it may be presumed that our author has advanced what he considered the strongest arguments which the case admits; and I have answered them. I am quite aware that other objections have been alleged by other critics; but it will be sufficient here to express a conviction that these have no real force against even the slightest external testimony, and to undertake to meet them if they are reproduced. Thus all the supposed anachronisms have failed. Bochart, for instance, was bold enough to maintain that the Ignatian Epistle to the Romans could not have been written before the time of Constantine the Great, because 'leopards' are mentioned in it, and the word was not known until this late age. In reply to Bochart, Pearson and others showed conclusively, by appealing (among other documents) to the contemporary Acts of Martyrdom of Perpetua and Felicitas (who suffered when Geta was Cæsar, about A.D. 202), that 'leopards' were so called more than a century at least before Constantine, while they gave good reasons for believing that the word was in use much earlier. I am able to carry the direct evidence half a century farther back. The word occurs in an early treatise of Galen (written about the middle of the second century), without any indication that it was then a new or unusual term. This passage, which (so far as I am aware) has been hitherto overlooked, carries the use back to within some forty years, or less, of the professed date of the Ignatian letters; and it must be regarded as a mere accident that no earlier occurrence has been noticed in the scanty remains of Greek and Roman literature which bridge over the interval. Of the institution of episcopacy again, it is sufficient to say that its prevalence in Asia Minor at this time, whatever may have been the case elsewhere, can only be denied by rejecting a large amount of direct and indirect evidence on this side of the question, and by substituting in its place a mere hypothesis which rests on no basis of historical fact.

On the other hand, the Epistles themselves are stamped with an individuality of character which is a strong testimony to their genuineness. The intensity of feeling and the ruggedness of expression seem to bespeak a real living man. On this point however it is impossible to dwell here; anyone who will take the pains to read these Epistles continuously will be in a better position to form a judgment on this evidence of style, than if he had been plied with many arguments.

But if the Curetonian letters are the genuine work of Ignatius, what must we say of the Vossian? Were the additional portions, which are contained in the latter but wanting in the former, also written by the saint, or are they later interpolations and additions? This is a much more difficult question.

As a first step towards answering this question, we may observe that there is one very strong reason for believing that the Vossian letters cannot have been written after the middle of the second century. The argument from silence has been so often abused, that one is almost afraid to employ it at all. Yet here it seems to have a real value. The writer of these letters, whoever he was, is evidently an orthodox Catholic Christian, and at the same time a strong controversialist. It is therefore a striking fact that he is altogether silent on the main controversies which agitated the Church, and more especially the Church of Asia Minor, in the middle and latter half of the second century. There is not a word about Montanism or about the Paschal controversy. It is difficult to believe that such a writer could have kept clear of these 'burning' questions, if he had lived in the midst of them. Even though his sense of historical propriety might have preserved him from language involving a positive anachronism, he would have taken a distinct side, and would have made his meaning clear by indirect means. Again, there is nothing at all bearing on the great Gnostic heresies of this age. The doctrines of the Marcionites, of the Valentinians, even of the Basilideans, (though Basilides flourished under Hadrian), are not touched. On the contrary, the writer several times uses language which an orthodox churchman, writing in the second half of the second century or later, would almost certainly have avoided. Among other expressions he salutes the Church of the Trallians 'in the *pleroma*' —an expression which could not escape the taint of heresy when once Valentinus had promulgated his system, of which the pleroma was the centre. Nor again, is it likely that such a writer would have indulged in expressions which, however innocent in themselves, would seem very distinctly to countenance the Gnostic doctrine of the inherent evil of matter, as for instance, where he says that he has not in him any 'matter-loving ($\phi\iota\lambda\delta\upsilon\lambda o\nu$) fire (of passion)[1],' and the like. The bearing of these facts has (so far as I remember) been overlooked, and yet it is highly important.

Having regard to these and similar phenomena, I do not see how it is reasonable to date the Vossian Epistles after the middle of the second century. But still it does not follow that they are genuine; and elsewhere I had acquiesced in the earlier opinion of Lipsius, who ascribed them to an interpolator writing about A.D. 140[2]. Now however I am obliged

---

[1] Ign. *Rom.* 7. In the Syriac version the expression is watered down (perhaps to get rid of the Gnostic colouring), and becomes 'fire for another love;' and similarly in the Long Greek $\phi\iota\lambda o\hat{\upsilon}\nu$ $\tau\iota$ is substituted for $\phi\iota\lambda\delta\upsilon\lambda o\nu$.

Compare *Rom.* 6, 'neque per materiam seducatis,' a passage which is found in the Latin translation, but has accidentally dropped out, or been intentionally omitted, from the Greek.

[2] *e.g. Philippians* p. 232 sq.

to confess that I have grave and increasing doubts whether, after all, they are not the genuine utterances of Ignatius himself. The following reasons weigh heavily in this scale. (1) Petermann's investigations, which have been already mentioned, respecting the Armenian version and its relation to a pre-existing Syriac version, throw a new light on the Curetonian letters. When it is known that there existed a complete version of the Vossian letters in this language, the theory that the Curetonian letters are excerpts becomes at least highly plausible, since the two sets of Syriac letters were certainly not independent the one of the other. (2) Notwithstanding Cureton's assertions, which our author has endorsed, the abruptness of the Curetonian letters is very perplexing in some parts. Subsequent writers, even while maintaining their genuineness, have recognised this difficulty, and endeavoured to explain it. It is far from easy, for instance, to conceive that the Ephesian letter could have ended as it is made to end in this recension. (3) Though the Vossian letters introduce many historical circumstances respecting the journey of Ignatius, the condition of the Church of Antioch, and the persons visiting or visited by him, no contradictions have yet been made out; but, on the contrary, the several notices fit in one with another in a way which at all events shows more care and ingenuity than might be expected in a falsifier. (4) All the supposed anachronisms to which objection has been taken in these Epistles fail on closer investigation. More especially stress has been laid on the fact that this writer describes Christ as God's 'eternal Logos, not having proceeded from Silence[1];' and objectors have urged that this expression is intended as a refutation of the Valentinian doctrine. Pearson thought it sufficient to reply that the Valentinians did not represent the Logos as an emanation from Silence, but from an intermediate Æon ; and when the treatise of Hippolytus was discovered, an answer seemed to be furnished by the fact that Silence held a conspicuous place in the tenets of the earlier sect of Simonians,

---

[1] Ign. *Magn.* 8. ὅς ἐστιν αὐτοῦ λόγος [ἀΐδιος, οὐκ] ἀπὸ σιγῆς προελθών.

and the Ignatian expression was explained as a reference to their teaching. But fresh materials for the correction of the Ignatian text, which Cureton and Petermann have placed in our hands, seem to show very clearly (though these editors have overlooked the importance of the facts) that in the original form of the passage the words 'eternal' and 'not' were wanting; so that the expression stood, 'Who is His Logos, having proceeded from Silence.' They are omitted in the Armenian version and in the passage as cited by Severus of Antioch[1]; while the paraphrase of the Long Recension seems to point in the same direction, though this is more doubtful. Severus more especially comments on the quotation, so that his reading is absolutely certain. Such a combination of early authorities is very strong evidence in favour of the omission. Moreover it is difficult to explain how the words, if genuine, should have been omitted; whereas their insertion, if they were no part of the original text, is easily accounted for. In the middle of the fourth century, Marcellus of Ancyra expressed his Sabellianism in almost identical language[2]; he spoke of Christ as the Logos issuing from Silence; and there was every temptation with orthodox scribes to save the reputation of St Ignatius from complicity in heretical opinions, and at the same time to deprive Marcellus of the support of his great name. I call attention to these facts, both because they have been overlooked, and because the passage in question has furnished their main argument to those who charge these Epistles with anachronisms.

Of the character of these Epistles, it must suffice here to say that the writer at all events was thoroughly acquainted with the manner and teaching of St Ignatius. As regards the substance, they contain many extragavances of sentiment and teaching, more especially relating to the episcopal office, from which the Curetonian letters are free and which one would not willingly believe written by the saint himself. But it remains

[1] Cureton's *Corp. Ign.* p. 245.
[2] Euseb. *Eccl. Theol.* ii. 9, etc.

See on this subject a paper in the *Journal of Philology*, No. ii. p. 51 sq.

a question, whether such considerations ought to outweigh the arguments on the other side. At all events it cannot be shown that they exhibit any different type of doctrine, though the mode of representation may seem exaggerated. As regards style, the Curetonian letters are more rugged and forcible than the Vossian; but as selected excerpts, they might perhaps be expected to exhibit these features prominently.

For the reasons given I shall, unless I am shown to be wrong, treat the Curetonian letters as the work of the genuine Ignatius, while the Vossian letters will be accepted as valid testimony at all events for the middle of the second century. The question of the genuineness of the latter will be waived. I fear that my indecision on this point will contrast disadvantageously with the certainty which is expressed by the author of *Supernatural Religion*. If so, I am sorry, but I cannot help it.

IV. POLYCARP OF SMYRNA.

[MAY, 1875.]

POLYCARP, Bishop of Smyrna, is the most important person in the history of the Christian Church during the ages immediately succeeding the Apostles. In the eyes of his own and the next generations, Clement of Rome appears to have held a more prominent position, if we may judge from the legendary stories which have gathered about his name; but for ourselves the interest which attaches to Polycarp is far greater. This importance he owes to his peculiar position, rather than to any marked greatness or originality of character. Two long lives —those of St John and of Polycarp—span the period which elapsed between the personal ministry of our Lord and the great Christian teachers living at the close of the second century. Polycarp was the disciple of St John, and Irenæus was the disciple of Polycarp. We know enough of St John's teaching, if the books ascribed to him in our Canon are accepted as genuine. We are fully acquainted with the tenets of Irenæus, and of these we may say generally that on all the most important points they conform to the theological standard which has satisfied the Christian Church ever since. But of the intermediate period between the close of the first century and the close of the second, the notices are sparse, the literature is scanty and fragmentary. Hence modern criticism has busied itself with hypothetical reconstructions of Christian history during this interval. It has been maintained that the greater part of the writings of our Canon were unknown and unwritten at the beginning of this period. It has been supposed that there was a complete discontinuity in the career of the Christian Church throughout the world. The person of Polycarp is a standing protest against any such surmises. Unless Irenæus was entirely mistaken as to the teaching of his master, unless the extant Epistle ascribed to Polycarp is altogether spurious, these views must fall to the ground. It is indispensable for the advocates of the Tübingen theory respecting the origin of the Christian Church and the Scriptural Canon to make good both these positions alike. Otherwise it can have no standing ground. My object in the following investigations is to show that neither position is tenable.

Polycarp was born more than thirty years before the close of the first century, and he survived to the latter half of the second. The date of his birth may be fixed with some degree of certainty as A.D. 69 or 70. At all events it cannot have been later than this. At the time of his martyrdom, which is now ascertained to have taken place A.D. 155 or 156[1], he declared that he had served Christ eighty-six years[2]; and, if this expression be explained as referring to the whole period of his life (which is the more probable supposition), we are carried back to the date which I have just given.

Thus Polycarp was born on the eve of a great crisis, which was fraught with momentous consequences to the Church at large, and which more especially made itself felt in the Christian congregations of his own country, proconsular Asia. The fall of Jerusalem occurred in the autumn of the year 70. But at the final assault the Christians were no longer among the besieged. The impending war had been taken as the signal for their departure from the doomed city. The greater number had retired beyond the Jordan, and founded Christian colonies in Pella and the neighbourhood. But the natural leaders of the

---

[1] See below, p. 103 sq.
[2] *Mart. Polyc.* 9. ὀγδοήκοντα καὶ ἓξ ἔτη ἔχω δουλεύων αὐτῷ. This expression is somewhat ambiguous in itself, and for ἔχω δουλεύων Eusebius reads δουλεύω.

Church—the surviving Apostles and personal disciples of Christ—had sought a home elsewhere. From this time forward it is neither to Jerusalem nor to Pella, but to proconsular Asia, and more especially to Ephesus as its metropolis, that we must look for the continuance of the original type of Apostolic doctrine and practice. At the epoch of the catastrophe we find the Apostle John for a short time living in exile—whether voluntary or constrained, it is unnecessary to inquire—in the island of Patmos. Soon after this he takes up his abode at Ephesus, which seems to have been his headquarters during the remainder of his long life[1]. And John was not alone in choosing Asia Minor as his new home. More especially the companions of his early youth seem to have been attracted to this neighbourhood. Of two brother Apostles and fellow-countrymen of Bethsaida this is distinctly recorded. Andrew, the brother of Simon Peter, appears in company with John in these later years, according to an account which seems at least so far trustworthy[2]. The presence of Philip, the special friend of Andrew[3], in these parts is recorded on still better authority[4]. Philip himself died at Hierapolis in Phrygia; but one of his three daughters was buried at Ephesus, where perhaps he had resided at an earlier date. Among other personal disciples of Christ, not otherwise known to us, who dwelt in these districts of Asia Minor, Aristion and a second John are mentioned, with whom Papias, the friend of Polycarp, had conversed[5].

Among these influences Polycarp was brought up. His own words, to which I have already alluded, seem to show that he was born of Christian parentage. At all events he must have been a believer from early childhood. If his parents were Christians,

[1] Papias in Euseb. *H. E.* iii. 39; Iren. ii. 22. 5 (and elsewhere); Polycrates in Euseb. *H. E.* v. 24; Clem. Alex. *Quis div. salv.* 42 (p. 958); Apollonius in Euseb. *H. E.* v. 18.

[2] *Muratorian Fragment* p. 33, ed. Tregelles (written about A.D. 170—180).

[3] John i. 44, xii. 21 sq.

[4] Papias in Euseb. *H. E.* iii. 39; Polycrates in Euseb. *H. E.* iii. 31, v. 24; Caius (Hippolytus?) in Euseb. *H. E.* iii. 30. I have given reasons for believing that the Philip who lived at Hierapolis was the Apostle and not the Evangelist in *Colossians* p. 45 sq.

[5] Papias, *l. c.*

they probably received their first lessons in the Gospel from the teachers of an earlier date—from St Paul who had planted the Churches of Asia Minor, or from St Peter who appears to have watered them[1], or from the immediate disciples of one or other of these two Apostles. But during the childhood and youth of Polycarp himself the influence of St John was paramount. Irenæus reports (and there is no reason for questioning the truth of his statement) that St John survived to the reign of Trajan[2], who ascended the imperial throne A.D. 98. Thus Polycarp would be about thirty years old at the time of St John's death. When therefore Irenæus relates that he was appointed bishop in Smyrna 'by Apostles[3],' the statement involves no chronological difficulty, even though we interpret the term 'bishop' in its more restricted sense, and not as a synonyme for presbyter, according to its earlier meaning. Later writers say distinctly that he was appointed to the episcopal office by St John[4].

At all events, he appears as Bishop of Smyrna in the early years of the second century. When Ignatius passes through Asia Minor on his way to martyrdom, he halts at Smyrna, where he is received by Polycarp. At a later stage in his journey he writes to his friend. The tone of his letter is altogether such as might be expected from an old man writing to a younger, who nevertheless held a position of great responsibility, and had shown himself worthy of the trust. After expressing his thankfulness for their meeting, and commending his friend's steadfast faith, which was 'founded as on an immovable rock,' he proceeds:—

Vindicate thine office in all diligence, whether in things carnal or in things spiritual. Have a care for unity, than which nothing is better. Sustain all men, even as the Lord sustaineth thee. Suffer all men in love, as also thou doest. Give thyself to unceasing prayer. Ask for more wisdom than thou hast. Keep watch, and preserve a wakeful spirit. . . . Be thou wise as the serpent in all things, and harmless always as the dove. . . . The time requireth thee, as pilots

---

[1] 1 Pet. i. 1.
[2] Iren. iii. 3. 4.
[3] Iren. ii. 22. 5, iii. 3. 4.
[4] *e.g.* Tertull. *de Præscr. Hær.* 32.

require winds, or as a storm-tossed mariner a haven, so that it may find God. . . . Be sober, as God's athlete. . . . Stand firm as an anvil under the stroke of the hammer. It becomes a great athlete to endure blows and to conquer. . . . Show thyself more zealous than thou art. . . . Let nothing be done without thy consent, neither do thou anything without God's consent, as indeed thou doest not[1].

The close of the letter is addressed mainly to the Smyrnæans, enforcing their reciprocal obligations towards their bishop.

This letter, if the additional matter in the Vossian Epistles may be trusted, was written from Troas, when the martyr was on the point of embarking for Neapolis[2]. The next stage of his journey would bring him to Philippi, where he halted. Thence he proceeded by the great Egnatian road across the continent to the Hadriatic, on his way to Rome.

Shortly after this, Polycarp himself addresses a letter to the Philippians. He had been especially invited by his correspondents to write to them, but he had also a reason of his own for doing so. During this season of the year, when winter had closed the high seas for navigation, all news from Rome must travel through Macedonia to Asia Minor. At Smyrna they had not yet received tidings of the fate of Ignatius; and he hoped to get early information from his correspondents, who were some stages nearer to Rome where, as Polycarp assumed, his friend had already suffered martyrdom[3].

This was the occasion of the letter, which for various reasons possesses the highest interest as a document of early Christian literature, though far from remarkable in itself.

Its most important feature is the profuseness of quotation from the Apostolic writings. Of a Canon of the New Testament, strictly so called, it is not probable that Polycarp knew anything[4]. This idea was necessarily, as Dr Westcott has shown, the growth of time. But of the writings which are

[1] Ign. *Polyc.* 1—4.
[2] *ib.* § 8.
[3] Polyc. *Phil.* 13. See below, p. 111 sq.
[4] This supposition is quite consistent with his using certain writings as authoritative. Thus he appeals to the *Oracles of the Lord* (§ 7), and he treats St Paul as incomparably greater than himself or others like him (§ 3).

included in our Canon he shows a wide knowledge and an ample appreciation. In this respect he may not unprofitably be compared with Clement of Rome. Clement of Rome, there is good reason to believe, was a Hellenist Jew[1]; he must have been brought up in a familiar acquaintance with the Old Testament Scriptures. On the other hand Polycarp, as we have already seen, was probably the son of Christian parents; at all events he was educated from his earliest childhood in the knowledge of the Gospel; he had grown up in the society of Apostles and Apostolic men. This contrast of education makes itself apparent in the writings of the two Fathers. Though there are clear indications in Clement that he was acquainted with many of the Apostolic Epistles, yet his quotations are chiefly taken from the Old Testament. Again and again he cites continuous passages, and argues from them at length. But with Polycarp the case is different. The New Testament has exchanged places with the Old, at least so far as practical use is concerned. Notwithstanding its brevity, Polycarp's Epistle contains decisive coincidences with or references to between thirty and forty passages in the New Testament[2]. On the other hand, with the single exception of four words from the apocryphal book of Tobit[3], there is no quotation taken immediately from the Old Testament. Elsewhere indeed he cites the words of Ps. iv. 4, but these are evidently quoted

---

[1] The question of the Jewish or Gentile origin of Clement has been much disputed. My chief reason for the view adopted in the text is the fact that he shows not only an extensive knowledge of the Old Testament, but also an acquaintance with the traditional teaching of the Jews. I find the name borne by a Jew in a sepulchral inscription (Orell. *Inscr.* 2899): D. M. CLEMETI . CAESARVM . N . N . SERVO . CASTELLARIO . AQVAE . CLAVDIAE . FECIT . CLAVDIA . SABBATHIS . ET . SIBI . ET . SVIS. If a conjecture may be hazarded, I venture to think that our Clement was a freedman or the son of a freedman in the household of Flavius Clemens, the cousin of Domitian, whom the Emperor put to death for his profession of Christianity. It is a curious fact, that Clement of Alexandria bears the name *T. Flavius Clemens*. He also was probably descended from some dependent belonging to the household of one or other of the Flavian princes.

[2] Lardner *Credibility* Pt. II. c. vi.

[3] *Phil.* § 10. 'Eleemosyna de morte liberat,' from Tobit iv. 10, xii. 9.

from St Paul, and not directly from the Psalmist, as his context shows[1].

Not less remarkable than the number of his quotations from the New Testament is their wide range. Of the Evangelical references I shall have occasion to speak in a subsequent article. Besides these there is a strong coincidence with the Acts which can hardly be accidental[2]; and there are passages or expressions taken from most of the Apostolic Epistles. Among the latter the most decisive examples frequently refer to those very Epistles which modern criticism has striven to discredit. It cannot reasonably be questioned for instance, that Polycarp was acquainted with the Epistle to the Ephesians and with the two Epistles to Timothy. Of the indisputable references to the First Epistle of St Peter I have already spoken in a former paper[3].

But the most important fact, in its bearing on recent controversy, is the relation of the writer to St Paul. According to the hypothesis of the Tübingen school, there was a personal antagonism between St Paul and St John, and an irreconcilable feud between their respective schools. It is therefore with special interest that we look to see what the most eminent scholar of the beloved disciple says about the Apostle of the Gentiles. Now St Paul occupies quite the most prominent place in Polycarp's Epistle. This prominence is partly explained by the fact that he is writing to a Church of St Paul's founding, but this explanation does not detract from its value. St Paul is the only Apostle who is mentioned by name; his writings are the only Apostolic writings which are referred to by name; of his thirteen Epistles, there are probable references to as many as eleven[4]; there are direct appeals to his example

---

[1] *Phil.* § 12. 'Ut his scripturis dictum est; *Irascimini, et nolite peccare, et Sol non occidat super iracundiam vestram*,' evidently taken from Ephes. iv. 26.

[2] *ib.* § 1. ὃν ἤγειρεν ὁ Θεὸς λύσας τὰς ὠδῖνας τοῦ ᾅδου, from Acts ii. 24.

[3] [See above, p. 49 sq.]

[4] The unrepresented Epistles are Titus and Philemon. The reference to Colossians is uncertain; and in one or two other cases the coincidence is not so close as to remove all possibility of doubt.

and his teaching alike: there is even an apology on the writer's part for the presumption of seeming to set himself up as a rival to the Apostle by writing to a Church to whom he had addressed an Epistle[1]. Altogether the testimony to the respect in which St Paul is held by the writer is as complete as language can make it. If therefore the Epistle be accepted as genuine, the position of the Tübingen school must be abandoned.

From considering the phenomena of the extant Epistle, we pass by a natural transition to the second point which I proposed to investigate, the traditions of the author's teaching.

Polycarp was no longer a young man, when his Epistle was written. But he lived on to see a new generation grow up from infancy to mature age afterwards; and as the companion of Apostles and the depositary of the Apostolic tradition, his influence increased with his increasing years. Before he died, even unbelievers had come to regard him as the 'Father of the Christians.'

Of his later years a glimpse is afforded to us in the record of an eye-witness. Among the disciples of his old age were two youths, companions for the time, but destined to stand far apart in after life—

'Like cliffs that had been rent asunder;'

the elder, Florinus, who became famous afterwards as a heretical leader; the younger, Irenæus, who stood forward as the great champion of orthodoxy. The following is the remonstrance addressed by Irenæus to his former associate after his defection:—

These opinions, Florinus, that I may speak without harshness, are not of sound judgment; these opinions are not in harmony with the Church, but involve those adopting them in the greatest impiety; these opinions even the heretics outside the pale of the Church have never ventured to broach; these opinions the elders before us, who also were disciples of the Apostles, did not hand down to thee. For I saw thee, when I was still a boy ($\pi\alpha\hat{\imath}\varsigma$ ὢν ἔτι), in Lower Asia in

[1] *Phil.* § 3.

company with Polycarp, while thou wast faring prosperously in the royal court, and endeavouring to stand well with him. For I distinctly remember (διαμνημονεύω) the incidents of that time better than events of recent occurrence; for the lessons received in childhood (ἐκ παίδων), growing with the growth of the soul, become identified with it; so that I can describe the very place in which the blessed Polycarp used to sit when he discoursed, and his goings out and his comings in, and his manner of life, and his personal appearance, and the discourses which he held before the people, and how he would describe his intercourse with John and with the rest who had seen the Lord, and how he would relate their words. And whatsoever things he had heard from them about the Lord, and about his miracles, and about his teaching, Polycarp, as having received them from eye-witnesses of the life of the Word[1], would relate altogether in accordance with the Scriptures. To these (discourses) I used to listen at the time with attention by God's mercy which was bestowed upon me, noting them down, not on paper, but in my heart; and by the grace of God, I constantly ruminate upon them faithfully (γνησίως). And I can testify in the sight of God, that if the blessed and Apostolic elder had heard anything of this kind, he would have cried out, and stopped his ears, and said after his wont, 'O good God, for what times hast Thou kept me, that I should endure such things?' and would even have fled from the place where he was sitting or standing when he heard such words. And indeed, this can be shown from his letters which he wrote either to the neighbouring Churches for their confirmation, or to certain of the brethren for their warning and exhortation[2].

Unfortunately the chronological notices are not sufficiently precise to enable us to fix the date either of this intercourse with Polycarp, or of the letter to Florinus in which Irenæus records it. In the year 155 or 156 Polycarp died; in the year 177 Irenæus became Bishop of Lyons. Putting these two facts together, we may perhaps assume that Irenæus must have been a pupil of Polycarp somewhere between A.D. 135—150. The mention of the 'royal court' seems at first sight to suggest the

---

[1] τῶν αὐτοπτῶν τῆς ζωῆς τοῦ Λόγου. I would gladly translate this 'the eye-witnesses of the Word of Life' (comp. 1 John i. 1), as it is commonly taken; but I cannot get this out of the Greek order. Possibly there is an accidental transposition in the common text. The Syriac translator has 'those who saw with their eyes the living Word.'

[2] Euseb. *H. E.* v. 20.

hope of a more precise solution; but even if this notice be taken to imply the presence of the Emperor for the time being in Asia Minor, our information respecting the movements of Hadrian and his successors is too scanty to afford ground for any safe inference[1].

Of the later career of Florinus, we are informed that he was at one time a presbyter of the Roman Church; that he afterwards fell away, and taught his heresy in the metropolis; that in consequence Irenæus addressed to him this letter from which I have given the extract, and which was also entitled 'On Monarchy' or 'Showing that God is not the author of evil' (ποιητὴν κακῶν)—this being the special heresy of Florinus; and that afterwards, apparently by a rebound, he lapsed into Valentinianism, on which occasion Irenæus wrote his treatise on the Ogdoad[2]. As the treatise of Irenæus on the Ogdoad can hardly have been written later than his extant work on Heresies, in which Valentinianism is so fully discussed as to render any such

[1] Dodwell and Grabe explain the reference by a visit of Hadrian to Asia, which the former places A.D. 122, and the latter A.D. 129 (Grabe *Proleg.* sect. 1); but both these dates seem too early, even if there were no other objections. Massuet (*Diss. in Iren.* ii. sect. 2) considers that the expression does not imply the presence of the imperial court in Asia, but signifies merely that Florinus was a courtier in high favour with the Emperor. But Irenæus could hardly have expressed himself so, if he had meant nothing more than this. The succeeding Emperor, Antoninus Pius (A.D. 138 —161), spent his time almost entirely in Italy. Capitolinus says of him: 'Nec ullas expeditiones obiit, nisi quod ad agros suos profectus et ad Campaniam,' *Vit. Anton.* 7. He appears however to have gone to Egypt and Syria in the later years of his reign (Aristid. *Op.* i. p. 453, ed. Dind.), and the account of John Malalas would seem to imply that he visited Asia Minor on his return (p. 280, ed. Bonn.). But M. Waddington (*Vie du Rhéteur Ælius Aristide* p. 259 sq) shows that he was still at Antioch in the early part of the year 155; so that this visit, if it really took place, is too late for our purpose.

As no known visit of a reigning Emperor will suit, I venture to offer a conjecture. About the year 136, T. Aurelius Fulvus was proconsul of Asia (Waddington *Fastes des provinces Asiatiques* p. 724). Within two or three years from his proconsulate he was raised to the imperial throne, and is known as Antoninus Pius. Florinus may have belonged to his suite, and Irenæus in after years might well call the proconsul's retinue, in a loose way, the 'royal court' by anticipation. This explanation gives a visit of sufficient length, and otherwise fits in with the circumstances.

[2] Euseb. *H. E.* v. 15, 20.

partial treatment superfluous, and which dates from the episcopate of Eleutherius (A.D. 177—190), we are led to the conclusion that the letter to Florinus was one of the earliest writings of this Father.

Thus we are left without any means of ascertaining the exact age of Irenæus when he sat at the feet of Polycarp. But beyond this uncertainty his testimony is as explicit as could well be desired. All experience, if I mistake not, bears out his statement respecting the vividness of the memory during this period of life. In a recent trial, the most fatal blot in the evidence was the inability of a pretender to give any information respecting the games and studies, the companions, the familiar haunts, of the school and college days of the person with whom he identified himself. It is the penalty which mature age pays for clearer ideas and higher powers of generalisation, that the recollection of facts becomes comparatively blurred. Very often an old man will relate with perfect distinctness the incidents of his youth and early manhood, while a haze will rest over much of the intervening period. Those who have listened to a Sedgwick after a lapse of sixty or seventy years repeating anecdotes of the 'statesmen' in his native dale, or describing the circumstances under which he first heard the news of the battle of Trafalgar, will be able to realize the vividness of the stories which the aged Polycarp would tell to his youthful pupil of his intercourse with the last surviving Apostle—the memory of the narrator being quickened and the interest of the hearer intensified, in this case, by the conviction that they were brought face to face with facts such as the world had never seen before.

One incident more is recorded of this veteran preacher of the Gospel. In the closing years of his life he undertook a journey to Rome, where he conferred with the bishop, Anicetus. The main subject of this conference was the time of celebrating the Passion. Polycarp pleaded the practice of St John and the other Apostles with whom he had conversed, for observing the actual day of the Jewish Passover, without respect to the day of the week. On the other hand, Anicetus could point to the fact that his predecessors, at least as far back as Xystus, who succeeded to the see soon after the beginning of the century, had always kept the anniversary of the Passion on a Friday and that of the Resurrection on a Sunday, thus making the day of the month give place to the day of the week. Neither convinced the other, but they parted good friends. This difference of usage did not interfere with the most perfect cordiality; and, as a sign of this, Anicetus allowed Polycarp to celebrate the Eucharist in his stead[1]. About forty years later, when the Paschal controversy was revived, and Victor, a successor of Anicetus, excommunicated the Asiatic Churches, Irenæus, though himself an observer of the Western usage, wrote to remonstrate with Victor on this harsh and tyrannical measure. An extract from his letter is preserved by Eusebius, in which these incidents respecting his old master are recorded[2]. Irenæus insists strongly on the fact that "the harmony of the faith" has never been disturbed hitherto by any such diversities of usage.

To this visit to Rome Irenæus makes another reference in his extant work against Heresies. The perfect confidence with which he appeals to the continuity of the Apostolic tradition, and to the testimony of Polycarp as the principal link in the chain, gives a peculiar significance to this passage, and no apology is needed for quoting it at length. After speaking of the succession of the Roman bishops, through whom the true doctrine has been handed down to his own generation without interruption, he adds—

And (so it was with) Polycarp also, who not only was taught by Apostles, and lived in familiar intercourse (συναναστραφείς) with many that had seen Christ, but also received his appointment in Asia from Apostles, as Bishop in the Church of Smyrna, whom we too have seen in our youth (ἐν τῇ πρώτῃ ἡμῶν ἡλικίᾳ), for he survived long, and departed this life at a very great age, by a glorious and most notable martyrdom, having ever taught these very things, which he had learnt from the Apostles, which the Church hands down, and which alone are true. To these testimony is borne by all

---

[1] This at least seems to be the most probable meaning of παρεχώρησε τὴν εὐχαριστίαν.

[2] Euseb. *H. E.* v. 24.

the Churches in Asia, and by the successors of Polycarp up to the present time, who was a much more trustworthy and safer witness of the truth than Valentinus and Marcion, and all such wrong-minded men. He also, when on a visit to Rome in the days of Anicetus, converted many to the Church of God from following the aforenamed heretics, by preaching that he had received from the Apostles this doctrine, and this only, which was handed down by the Church, as the truth. And there are those who have heard him tell how John, the disciple of the Lord, when he went to take a bath in Ephesus, and saw Cerinthus within, rushed away from the room without bathing, with the words, 'Let us flee, lest the room should indeed fall in, for Cerinthus, the enemy of the truth, is within.' Yea, and Polycarp himself also on one occasion, when Marcion confronted him and said, 'Dost thou recognize me?' answered, 'I recognize the firstborn of Satan.' Such care did the Apostles and their disciples take not to hold any communication, even by word, with any of those who falsify the truth, as Paul also said, 'A man that is a heretic after a first and second admonition, avoid; knowing that such an one is perverted and sinneth, being self-condemned.' Moreover, there is an Epistle of Polycarp addressed to the Philippians, which is most adequate (ἱκανωτάτη), and from which both his manner of life and his preaching of the truth may be learnt by those who desire to learn and are anxious for their own salvation. And again, the Church in Ephesus, which was founded by Paul, and where John survived till the times of Trajan, is a true witness of the tradition of the Apostles[1].

I have given these important extracts at length because they speak for themselves. If I mistake not, they will be more convincing than many arguments. It is impossible to doubt the sincerity of Irenæus, when he thus explicitly and repeatedly maintains that the doctrines which he holds and teaches are the same which Polycarp had held and taught before him. On the other hand, a school of critics which has arisen in the present generation maintains that Irenæus was mistaken from beginning to end; that, instead of this continuity in the teaching and history of the Church, there had been a violent dislocation; that St John, as an Apostle of the Circumcision, must have had a deep-rooted aversion to the doctrine and work of St Paul; and

[1] Iren. iii. 3. 4.

that Polycarp, as a disciple of St John, must have shared that aversion, and cannot therefore have recognized the authority of the Apostle of the Gentiles.

It is difficult to believe that those who hold this theory have seriously faced the historical difficulties which it involves, or have attempted to realize any combination of circumstances by which this revolution could have been brought about in such a manner as to escape the notice of the next succeeding generations. I shall probably have occasion hereafter to speak of the solidarity of the Church at this epoch. At present it is sufficient to say that the direct personal testimony of Irenæus respecting Polycarp is by no means the only, or even the greatest, impediment to this theory. He constantly appeals to the Asiatic elders, the disciples and followers of the Apostles, in confirmation of his statement. Among the Christian teachers of proconsular Asia who immediately succeeded Polycarp, are two famous names, Melito of Sardis and Claudius Apollinaris of Hierapolis. They must already have reached middle life before Polycarp's martyrdom. They were not merely practical workers, but voluminous writers also. The lists of their works handed down to us comprise the widest range of topics; they handle questions of Christian ethics, of Scriptural interpretation, of controversial divinity, of ecclesiastical order, of theological metaphysics. Was there then any possibility of a mistake here? To us the history of the Church during the second century is obscure, because all this voluminous literature, except a few meagre fragments, has been blotted out. But to the contemporaries and successors of Irenæus it was legible enough. 'Who does not know,' exclaims his own pupil Hippolytus, 'the books of Irenæus and Melito and the rest, which declare Christ to be God and man[1]?'

This mission of peace to Rome must have been one of the latest acts of the old man's life. The accession of Anicetus to the see of Rome is variously dated; but the earliest year is about A.D. 150, and an eminent recent critic, who has paid special attention to the subject, places it between A.D. 154 and

---

[1] Quoted anonymously in Euseb. *H. E.* v. 28.

IV. POLYCARP OF SMYRNA.

A.D. 156[1]. In the year 155, or 156 at the latest, Polycarp fell a martyr.

The details of his martyrdom are recorded in a contemporary document, which takes the form of a letter from the Church of Smyrna, addressed more immediately to the Church of Philomelium but challenging at the same time a wider circulation[2]. The simplicity with which the narrators record omens and occurrences easily explicable in themselves, but invested by their surcharged feelings with a miraculous character, is highly natural. The whole narrative is eminently touching and instructive; but the details have little or no bearing on my immediate purpose. It is sufficient to say that Polycarp had retired into the country to escape persecution; that the populace, not satisfied with the victims already sacrificed to their fury, demanded the life of Polycarp, as the 'father of the Christians;' that his hiding-place was betrayed by a boy in his service, under the influence of torture; that the magistrates urged him to save his life by submitting to the usual tests, by pronouncing the formula, 'Cæsar is Lord,' or offering sacrifice, or swearing by the fortune of the Emperor, or reviling Christ; that he declared himself unable to blaspheme a Master whom he had served for eighty-six years, and from whom he had received no wrong; and that consequently he was burnt at the stake, Jews and Heathens vying with each other in feeding the flames. The games were already past; otherwise he would have been condemned to the wild beasts—the usual punishment for such contumacy.

Polycarp was martyred during the proconsulship of Statius Quadratus. The commonly received date of his death is A.D. 166 or 167, as given in the Chronicon of Eusebius. Quite recently however, M. Waddington has subjected the proconsular *fasti* of Asia Minor to a fresh and rigorous scrutiny[3]. This

---

[1] Lipsius *Chronologie der Römischen Bischöfe* p. 263.

[2] See Jacobson's *Patres Apostolici* ii. p. 604.

[3] See his *Mémoire sur la Chronologie de la Vie du Rhéteur Ælius Aristide* in the *Mémoires de l'Académie des Inscriptions* xxvi. p. 202 sq; and his *Fastes des provinces Asiatiques* in Le Bas and Waddington's *Voyage Archéologique en Grèce et en Asie Mineure*.

Statius Quadratus is mentioned by the orator Aristides; and by an investigation of the chronology of Aristides' life, with the aid of newly-discovered inscriptions, M. Waddington arrives at the result that Quadratus was proconsul in 154, 155; and, as Polycarp was martyred in the early months of the year, his martyrdom must be dated A.D. 155. This result is accepted by M. Renan[1], and substantially also by Hilgenfeld and Lipsius[2], who however (for reasons into which it is unnecessary to enter here) postpones the martyrdom to the following year, A.D. 156. M. Waddington's arguments seem conclusive, and this rectification of date removes some stumbling-blocks. The relations between St John and Polycarp for instance, as reported by Irenæus and others, no longer present any difficulty, when the period during which the lives of the two overlap each other is thus extended. The author of *Supernatural Religion* very excusably adopts the received date of Polycarp's martyrdom, being unaware, as it would seem, of these recent investigations.

In this account of Polycarp, I have assumed the genuineness of the Epistle ascribed to him; but the author of *Supernatural Religion* has taken his side with those writers who condemn it as spurious, and I am therefore obliged to give reasons for this confidence.

So far as regards external testimony, it must be confessed that the Epistle of Polycarp presents itself with credentials of exceptional value. The instances are very rare indeed where a work of antiquity can claim the direct testimony of a pupil of the writer to whom it is ascribed. The statement of Irenæus respecting the authorship of this Epistle is explicit; and indeed, as the reference is not denied either by the author of *Supernatural Religion* or by other critics, like Lipsius and Hilgenfeld, who nevertheless condemn the Epistle as spurious, I am saved all trouble in establishing its adequacy. Our author indeed is content to set it aside, because 'the testimony of Irenæus is not

---

[1] *L'Antechrist* p. 566.
[2] Lipsius in the *Zeitsch. f. Wissensch. Theol.* xvii. p. 188 (1874); Hilgenfeld *ib.* p. 325 sq.

IV. POLYCARP OF SMYRNA. 105

... entitled to much weight, inasmuch as his intercourse with Polycarp was evidently confined to a short period of his extreme youth, and we have no reason to suppose that he had any subsequent communication with him[1].' I do not see how the notice of Irenæus justifies the statement that the period was short; but the passage has been given above, and the reader may judge for himself. Nor does it seem probable, considering that the communications between Asia Minor and southern Gaul were close and frequent, that the pupil should altogether have lost sight of the master whom he revered, when he migrated to his new and distant home in the west. But, even though all this be granted, the fact still remains, that the testimony is exceptionally good and would in ordinary cases be regarded as quite decisive. I do not say that it is impossible Irenæus could have been mistaken; there is always risk of error in human testimony; but I maintain that, unless we are required to apply a wholly different standard of evidence here from that which is held satisfactory in other cases, we approach this Epistle with a very strong guarantee of its authenticity, which can only be invalidated by solid and convincing proofs, and against which hypothetical combinations and ingenious surmises are powerless[2]. Whether the objections adduced by the impugners of this Epistle are of this character, the reader will see presently.

From the external we turn to the internal evidence. We are asked to believe that this letter was forged on the confines of the age of Irenæus and Clement of Alexandria. But can anything be more unlike the ecclesiastical literature of this later generation, whether we regard the use of the New Testament, or the notices of ecclesiastical order, or the statements of theological doctrine? The Evangelical quotations are still given (as in Clement of Rome) with the formula, 'The Lord said;' the passages from the Apostolic Epistles are still, for the

---

[1] *S. R.* I. p. 276.
[2] It should be mentioned also that we have another exceptional guarantee in the fact that Polycarp's Epistle was read in the Church of Asia; Jerome *Vir. Ill.* 17, 'Usque hodie in Asiae conventu legitur.'

most part, indirect and anonymous. Though two or three chapters are devoted to injunctions respecting the ministry of the Church, there is not an allusion to episcopacy from beginning to end. Though the writer's ideas of the Person of Christ practically leave nothing to be desired, yet these ideas are still held in solution, and have not yet crystallized into the dogmatic forms which characterize the later generation. And from first to last this Epistle is silent upon those questions which interested the Church in the second half of the second century. Of Montanism, of the Paschal controversy, of the developed Gnostic heresies of this period, it says nothing. A supposed reference to Marcion I shall have to discuss presently. For the moment it is sufficient to say that an allusion so vague and pointless as this would be must certainly have missed its aim.

But this argument from internal evidence gains strength when considered from another point of view. The only intelligible theory—indeed, so far as I remember, the only attempt at a theory—offered to account for this Epistle by those who deny its genuineness or its integrity, connects it closely with the Ignatian letters. If forged, it was forged by the same hand which wrote the seven Vossian Epistles; if interpolated, it was interpolated by the person who expanded the three genuine Epistles into the seven. According to either hypothesis, the object was to recommend the Ignatian forgery on the authority of a great name; the motive betrays itself in the thirteenth chapter, where Polycarp is represented as sending several of the Ignatian Epistles to the Philippians along with his own letter. This theory is at all events intelligible; and, so far as I can see, it is the only rational theory of which the case admits.

Let us ask then, whether there is any improbability in the circumstances, as here represented. Ignatius had stayed at Philippi on his way to martyrdom; the Philippians had been deeply impressed by their intercourse with him; writing to Polycarp afterwards, they had requested him to send them a copy of the martyr's letter or letters to him; he complies with the request, and appends also copies of other letters written by

Ignatius, which he happened to have in his possession. Is this at all unnatural? Suppose on the other hand, that the letter of Polycarp had contained no such reference to Ignatius and his Epistles, would it not have been regarded as a highly suspicious circumstance, that, writing to the Philippians so soon after Ignatius had visited both Churches, Polycarp should have said nothing about so remarkable a man? When I see how this argument from silence is worked in other cases, I cannot doubt that it would have been plied here as a formidable objection either to the truth of the Ignatian story, or to the genuineness of Polycarp's Epistle, or to both. My conclusion is that this notice proves nothing either way, when it stands alone. If the other contents of the Polycarpian Epistle are questionable, then it enforces our misgivings. If not, then this use of the notice is only another illustration of the over-suspicious temperament of modern criticism, which, as I ventured to suggest in an earlier paper, must be as fatal to calm and reasonable judgment in matters of early Christian history, as it is manifestly in matters of common life. The question therefore is narrowed to this issue, whether the Epistle of Polycarp bears evidence in its style and diction or in its modes of thought or in any other way, that it was written by the same hand which penned the Ignatian letters.

And here I venture to say that, however we test these documents, the contrast is very striking; more striking in fact than we should have expected to find between two Christian writers who wrote about the same time and were personally acquainted with each other. I will apply some of these tests.

1. The stress which Ignatius lays on episcopacy as the keystone of ecclesiastical order and the guarantee of theological orthodoxy, is well known. Indeed it is often supposed that the Ignatian Letters were written for this express purpose. In Polycarp's Epistle on the other hand, as I have already said, there is no mention of episcopacy. He speaks at length about the duties of the presbyters, of the deacons, of the widows, and others, but the bishop is entirely ignored. More especially he

directs the younger men to be obedient to 'the presbyters and deacons, as to God and Christ,' but nothing is said about obedience to the bishop[1]. At a later point he has occasion to speak of an offence committed by one Valens, a presbyter, but here again there is the same silence. All this is quite intelligible, if the letter is genuine, on the supposition either that there was a vacancy in the Philippian bishopric at this time, or, as seems more probable, that the ecclesiastical organization there was not yet fully developed; but it is, so far as I can see, quite inconceivable that a forger whose object was to recommend episcopacy should have pictured a state of things so damaging to his main purpose. The supposed forger indeed shows himself throughout quite indifferent on this subject. There is every reason for believing that Polycarp was Bishop of Smyrna at this time; yet in the heading of the letter he does not assert his title, but writes merely, 'Polycarp and the presbyters with him.'

2. If we turn from ecclesiastical organization to doctrinal statement, the contrast still remains. We meet with no such strong expressions as are found in the Ignatian letters; Polycarp never speaks of 'the blood of God,' 'the passion of my God,' 'Jesus Christ our God,' and the like. Even in the commoner modes of designating our Lord, a difference is perceptible. Thus the favourite mode of expression with Ignatius is 'Jesus Christ' simply, which occurs nearly a hundred times; whereas in Polycarp it is only found twice (one passage being a quotation). On the other hand, the usual expression in Polycarp is 'Our Lord Jesus Christ,' which apparently occurs only twice in the Ignatian Epistles, and in both instances with various readings. Again the combination 'God and Christ,' occurring three times in Polycarp, does not appear once in the Ignatian letters[2].

---

[1] *Phil.* § 5.

[2] I believe that the facts stated in the text are strictly correct; but I may have overlooked some passages. At all events a careful reader will, if I mistake not, observe a marked difference in the ordinary theological language of the two writers.

3. The divergence of the two writers as regards Scriptural quotations is still more remarkable. Though the seven Ignatian letters are together at least five times as long as the Epistle of Polycarp, the quotations from the Apostolic Epistles in the latter are many times more numerous, as well as more precise, than in the former. Whole passages in Polycarp are made up of such quotations strung together, while in Ignatius they are very rare, being for the most part epigrammatic adaptations and isolated coincidences of language or thought. Nor indeed is their range coextensive. Thus the Epistle of Polycarp, as I pointed out in a former article[1], is pervaded with the language of St Peter's First Epistle, but in the Ignatian letters there is no trace of its use[2].

4. But this divergence only forms part of a still broader and more decisive contrast. The profuseness of quotation in Polycarp's Epistle arises from a want of originality. The writer reproduces the thoughts and words of others, because his mind is essentially receptive and not creative. He is altogether wanting in independence of thought. On the other hand, the Ignatian letters are remarkable for their individuality. Of all early Christian writings they are pre-eminent in this respect. They are full of idiomatic expressions, quaint images, unexpected turns of thought and language. They exhibit their characteristic ideas, which obviously have a high value for the writer, for he recurs to them again and again, but which the reader often finds it extremely difficult to grasp, owing to their singularity.

I venture to think that any one who will carefully consider these contrasts—more especially the last, as extending over the whole field—must be struck with the impossibility of the theory which makes this letter part of the assumed Ignatian forgeries. This hypothesis requires us to believe that a very uncritical age produced a literary fiction, which, for subtlety and natural-

---

[1] [See above, p. 49 sq.]

[2] Ign. *Magn.* 13 is given by Lardner (p. 88) as a coincidence with 1 Pet. v. 5. But the expression in question, 'to be subject one to another,' occurs also in Ephes. v. 21, even if any stress could be laid on the occurrence of these few obvious words.

ness of execution, leaves the most skilful forgeries of the nineteenth century far behind.

And the hypothesis of interpolation is encumbered with difficulties of the same kind, and hardly less considerable. This hypothesis was shaped and developed by Ritschl[1], whose theory has been accepted by some later writers. He supposes that the greater part of the Epistle is the genuine production of the person whose name it bears, written however, not immediately after the death of Ignatius, but in the later years of Polycarp's long life. The three passages which relate to Ignatius, together with other parts which he defines, he supposes to have been interpolated by the same forger who amplified the three genuine letters of the martyr of Antioch into the seven of the Vossian collection. But if any one will take the passages which Ritschl has struck out as interpolated, he will find that the general style is the same; that individual expressions, more especially theological expressions, are the same; that the quotations are from the same range of books, as in the other parts, extending even to coincidences of expression with the Epistle of Clement of Rome; and that altogether there is nothing to separate one part from another, except the *a priori* assumption that the references to Ignatius must be unhistorical. I do not know whether these facts have been pointed out before, and I cannot do more here than hint at lines of investigation which any one may follow up for himself. But when the phenomena are fully recognized, I venture to think that the difficulties in Ritschl's theory will be felt to be many times greater than those which it is framed to remove.

Of the general character of the Epistle, as affecting the question of its genuineness, the author of *Supernatural Religion* has said nothing. But he has reproduced special objections which have been urged by previous writers; and to these I wish to call attention, because they are very good, and not unfavourable, illustrations of the style of criticism which is in vogue with the negative school.

[1] *Altkatholische Kirche* p. 584 sq (ed. 2).

IV. POLYCARP OF SMYRNA.

1. Our author writes in the first place:—

We have just seen that the martyr-journey of Ignatius to Rome is, for cogent reasons, declared to be wholly fabulous, and the epistles purporting to be written during that journey must be held to be spurious. The Epistle of Polycarp, however, not only refers to the martyr-journey (c. ix), but to the Ignatian Epistles which are inauthentic (c. xiii), and the manifest inference is that it also is spurious.

Of the fabulous character of the martyr-journey I have already disposed in my previous article on the Ignatian letters[1]. For the present I reserve what I have to say concerning the assumed reference to the 'inauthentic' Epistles, as this objection will reappear again.

2. Our author on a later page urges that—

In the Epistle itself, there are many anachronisms. In ch. ix the 'blessed Ignatius' is referred to as already a considerable time dead, and he is held up with Zosimus and Rufus, and also with Paul and the rest of the Apostles, as examples of patience: men who have not run in vain, but are with the Lord; but in ch. xiii he is spoken of as living, and information is requested regarding him, 'and those who are with him.'

To this objection I had already supplied the answer[2] which has been given many times before, and which, as it seemed to me, the author ought in fairness to have noticed. I had pointed out that we have only the Latin version here, and that the present tense is obviously due to the translator. The original would naturally be τῶν σὺν αὐτῷ, which the translator, being obliged to supply a substantive verb, has carelessly rendered 'his qui cum eo *sunt*.' If any one will consider what has been just said about the general character of the Epistle, he will see that this is the only reasonable explanation of the fact, whether we regard the work as genuine or not. If it is not genuine, the forger has executed his task with consummate skill and appreciation; and yet here he is charged with a piece of bungling

---

[1] [See above, p. 63 sq.]   [2] [See above, p. 11.]

which a schoolboy would have avoided. It is not merely an anachronism, but a self-contradiction of the most patent kind. The writer, on this hypothesis, has not made up his mind whether Ignatius is or is not supposed to be dead at the time, and he represents the fact differently in two different parts[1].

But our author apparently is quite unaware that οἱ σὺν αὐτῷ might mean equally well, 'those who *were* with him,' and 'those who *are* with him.' At least I cannot attach any other meaning to his reply, in which he retorts upon me my own words used elsewhere, and speaks of my argument as being 'wrecked upon this rock of grammar[2].' If so, I can only refer him to Thucydides or any Greek historian, where he will find scores of similar instances. I need hardly say that the expression itself is quite neutral as regards time, meaning nothing more than 'his companions,' and that the tense must be supplied according to the context or the known circumstances of the case. But I am not sorry that our author has fallen into this error, for it has led me to investigate the usage of Polycarp and his translator, and has thus elicited the following facts:—(1) Unless he departed from his ordinary usage, Polycarp would have employed the short expression οἱ σὺν αὐτῷ or οἱ μετ' αὐτοῦ in such a case. Thus he has οἱ σὺν αὐτῷ in the opening paragraph, and τοῖς ἐξ ὑμῶν in c. 9, with other similar instances. (2) The translator, if he had the words τοῖς σὺν αὐτῷ before him, would almost certainly supply the substantive verb, as he has done in the opening, 'qui cum eo *sunt* presbyteri;' in c. 3, 'illis qui tunc *erant* hominibus,' and 'quae *est* in Deo;' in c. 9, 'qui ex vobis *sunt*;' and probably also in c. 12, 'qui *sunt* sub coelo' (the Greek is wanting in this last passage). (3) The translator, in supplying the verb, was as likely as not to give the wrong tense. In fact, in the only other passage in the Epistle where it was possible to make a mistake, he has gone wrong on

---

[1] Ritschl (*l. c.* p. 586), though himself condemning the thirteenth chapter as an interpolation, treats this objection as worthless, and says very decidedly that the corresponding Greek must have been τῶν μετ' αὐτοῦ.

[2] *Fortnightly Review*, January, 1875, p. 14.

this very point; he has translated ἦν καὶ εἴδετε ... ἐν ἄλλοις τοῖς ἐξ ὑμῶν mechanically by a present tense, 'quam et vidistis ... in aliis qui ex vobis *sunt*,' though the persons are mentioned in connection with St Ignatius and St Paul, and though it is distinctly stated immediately afterwards that they *all* were dead, having, as we may infer from the context, ended their life by martyrdom. In fact, he has made the very same blunder which I ascribe to him here.

This objection therefore may be set aside for ever. But the notices which I have been considering suggest another reflection. Is the historical position which the writer of this letter takes up at all like the invention of a forger? Would he have thought of placing himself at the moment of time when Ignatius is supposed to have been martyred, but when the report of the circumstances had not yet reached Smyrna? If he had chosen this moment, would he not have made it clear, instead of leaving his readers to infer it by piecing together notices which are scattered through the Epistle—notices moreover, which, though entirely consistent with each other, are so far from obvious that his translator has been led astray by them, and that modern critics have woven out of them these entanglements which it has taken me so much time to unravel?

3. But our author proceeds:—

Moreover, although thus spoken of as alive, the writer already knows of his Epistles, and refers, in the plural, to those written by him 'to us, and all the rest which we have by us.' The reference here, it will be observed, is not only to the Epistles to the Smyrnæans and to Polycarp himself, but to other spurious epistles which are not included in the Syriac version.

I have already shown that Ignatius is not spoken of as alive; but, if he had been alive, I do not see why Polycarp should not have known of his Epistles, seeing that of the seven Vossian letters four claim to have been written from Smyrna, when the saint was in some sense Polycarp's guest, and two to have been written to Smyrna. Therefore of the seven Epistles, supposing them to be genuine, Polycarp would almost necessarily have been acquainted with six.

By the 'other spurious Epistles,' which the Epistle of Polycarp is supposed to recognize, I presume that our author means the four of the Vossian collection, which have no place in the Syriac. If so, I would reply that, supposing the three Syriac Epistles to represent the only genuine letters *extant*, these Epistles themselves bear testimony to the fact that Ignatius wrote several others besides; for in one passage in these Syriac Epistles (*Rom.* 4) the martyr says, 'I write to *all the Churches* and charge *all men*.' And again, when Polycarp writes, τὰς ἐπιστολὰς Ἰγνατίου τὰς πεμφθείσας ἡμῖν ὑπ' αὐτοῦ it is sufficient to advert to the fact that, like the Latin *epistolae*, the plural ἐπιστολαὶ is frequently used convertibly with the singular ἐπιστολή for a single letter[1], and indeed appears to be so used in an earlier passage by Polycarp himself of St Paul's Epistle to the Philippians[2]; so that the notice is satisfied by the single Epistle to Polycarp which is included in the Syriac letters, and does not necessarily imply also the Epistle to the Smyrnæans which has no place there. But of this passage generally I would say, that though it may be a question whether the language does not favour the genuineness of the Vossian letters, as against the Curetonian, it cannot be taken to impugn the genuineness of the Epistle of Polycarp itself, authenticated, as this Epistle is, by Irenæus, and exhibiting, as we have seen, every mark of genuineness in itself.

4. Our author then continues:—

Dallæus pointed out long ago, that ch. xiii abruptly interrupts the conclusion of the Epistle.

In what sense this chapter can be said to interrupt the conclusion it is difficult to say. It occupies exactly the place which would naturally be assigned to such personal matters; for it follows upon the main purport of the letter, while it immediately

---

[1] I have collected several instances in *Philippians* p. 138 sq. [See also below, p. 189.]
[2] Polyc. *Phil.* § 3.

precedes the recommendation of the bearer and the final salutation. On the same showing the conclusion of the greater number of St Paul's Epistles is 'abruptly interrupted.'

5. The next argument is of another kind:—

The writer vehemently denounces, as already widely spread, the Gnostic heresy and other forms of false doctrine which did not exist until the time of Marcion, to whom and to whose followers he refers in unmistakable terms. An expression is used in ch. vii in speaking of these heretics, which Polycarp is reported by Irenæus to have actually applied to Marcion in person, during his stay in Rome about A.D. 160. He is said to have called Marcion the 'first-born of Satan,' ($\pi\rho\omega\tau\acute{o}\tau o\kappa o s\ \tau o\hat{v}\ \Sigma a\tau a\nu\hat{a}$), and the same term is employed in this epistle with regard to every one who holds such false doctrines. The development of these heresies, therefore, implies a date for the composition of the Epistle, at earliest, after the middle of the second century, a date which is further confirmed by other circumstances.

I will take the latter part of this statement first, correcting however one or two errors of detail. M. Waddington's investigations, to which I have already alluded[1], oblige us to place Polycarp's visit to Rome some few years before 160, since his death is fixed at A.D. 155 or 156. Again, Irenæus does not state that the interview between Polycarp and Marcion took place at Rome. It may have taken place there, but it may have occurred at an earlier date in Asia Minor, of which region Marcion was a native[2]. These however are not very important matters. The point of the indictment lies in the fact that about A.D. 140, earlier or later, Polycarp is reported to have applied the expression 'first-born of Satan' to Marcion, while in the Epistle, purporting to have been written many years before, he appears as using this same expression of other Gnostic teachers. This argument is a good illustration of the reasons which satisfy

---

[1] [See above, pp. 98, 103 sq.]

[2] The words of Irenæus are, καὶ αὐτὸς δὲ ὁ Πολύκαρπος Μαρκίωνί ποτε εἰς ὄψιν αὐτῷ ἐλθόντι κ.τ.λ. Zahn (*Ignatius* p. 496) remarks on this that the ποτέ refers us to another point of time than the sojourn of Polycarp in Rome mentioned in the preceding sentence. I could not feel sure of this; but it separates this incident from the others, and leaves the time indeterminate.

even men like Lipsius and Hilgenfeld. To any ordinary judicial mind, I imagine, this coincidence, so far as it goes, would appear to point to Polycarp as the author of the Epistle; for the two facts come to us on independent authority—the one from oral tradition through Irenæus, the other in a written document older than Irenæus. Or, if the one statement arose out of the other, the converse relation of that which this hypothesis assumes is much more probable. Irenæus, as he tells us in the context, was acquainted with the Epistle, and it is quite possible that in repeating the story of Polycarp's interview with Marcion he inadvertently imported into it the expression which he had read in the Epistle. But the independence of the two is far more probable. As a fact, men do repeat the same expressions again and again, and this throughout long periods of their lives. Such forms of speech arise out of their idiosyncrasies, and so become part of them. This is a matter of common experience, and in the case of Polycarp we happen to be informed incidentally that he had a habit of repeating favourite expressions. Irenæus, in a passage already quoted, mentions his exclamation, 'O good God,' as one of these[1].

Our author however declares that the passage in the Epistle which contains this expression is directly aimed at Marcion and his followers; and, inasmuch as Marcion can hardly have promulgated his heresy before A.D. 130—140 at the earliest, this fact, if it be a fact, condemns as spurious a work which professes to have been written some years before. But is there anything really characteristic of Marcion in the description? Our author does not explain himself, nor can I find anything which really justifies the statement in the writers to whom I am referred in his footnote. I turn therefore to the words themselves—

> For every one who doth not confess that Jesus Christ has come in the flesh, is antichrist; and whosoever doth not confess the testimony of the cross, is of the devil; and whosoever perverteth the oracles of the Lord to (serve) his own lusts, and saith that there is neither resurrection nor judgment, this man is a first-born of Satan[2].

[1] In the *Letter to Florinus*, quoted above, p. 96 sq.   [2] Polyc. *Phil.* § 7.

To illustrate the relation of these denunciations to Marcionite doctrine, I will suppose a parallel. I take up a book written by a Nonconformist, and I find in it an attack (I am not concerned with the truth or falsehood of the opinions attacked) on the doctrines of episcopal succession, of sacramental grace, of baptismal regeneration, and the like. It is wholly silent about claims to Papal domination, about infallibility, about purgatory and indulgences, about the worship of the Virgin or of the Saints. Am I justified in concluding that the writer is 'referring in unmistakable terms' to the Church of Rome, because the Church of Rome, in common with the majority of Churches, holds the doctrines attacked? Would not any reasonable man draw the very opposite inference, and conclude that the writer cannot mean the Church of Rome, because there is absolute silence about the distinctive tenets of that Church?

So it is here. Marcion, in common with almost all Gnostic sects, held some views which are here attacked. But Marcion had also doctrines of his own, sharp, trenchant, and startling. Marcion taught that the God of the New Testament was a distinct being from the God of the Old, whom he identified with the God of Nature; that these two Gods were not only distinct but antagonistic; that there was an irreconcilable, internecine feud between them; and that Jesus Christ came from the good God to rescue men from the God of Nature and of the Jews. This was the head and front of his offending; and consequently a common charge against him with orthodox writers is that he 'blasphemes God[1].' Of this there is not a hint in Polycarp's denunciation. Again, Marcion rejected the authority of the Twelve, denouncing them as false Apostles, and he confined his Canon to St Paul's Epistles and to a Pauline Gospel. Again, Marcion prohibited marriage, and even refused to baptize married persons. On these points also Polycarp is silent.

But indeed the case against this hypothesis is much stronger than would appear from the illustration which I have used.

---

[1] *e.g.* Iren. i. 27. 2, 3; iii. 12. 12.

Not only is there nothing specially characteristic of Marcion in the heresy or heresies denounced by Polycarp, not only were the doctrines condemned held by divers other teachers besides, but some of the charges are quite inapplicable to him. The passage in question denounces three forms of heretical teaching, which may or may not have been combined in one sect. Of these the first, 'Whosoever doth not confess that Jesus Christ has come in the flesh,' is capable of many interpretations. It may refer, for instance, to the separationism of Cerinthus, who maintained that the spiritual Being Christ descended on the man Jesus after the baptism, and left Him before the crucifixion, so that, while Jesus suffered, Christ remained impassible[1]; or it may describe the pure docetism, which maintained that our Lord's body was a mere phantom body, so that His birth and life and death alike were only apparent, and not real[2]; or it may have some reference different from either. I cannot myself doubt that the expression is borrowed from the First Epistle of St John, and there it seems to refer to Cerinthus, the contemporary of the Apostle[3]; but Polycarp may have used it with a much wider reference. Under any circumstances, though it would no doubt apply to Marcion, who held strong docetic views, it would apply to almost every sect of Gnostics besides. The same may be said of the second position attacked, 'Whoso-

---

[1] Iren. i. 26. 1.

[2] This seems to be the form of heresy attacked in the Ignatian letters: *Magn.* 11; *Trall.* 9; *Smyrn.* 1.

[3] 1 John iv. 2, 3, 'Every spirit that confesseth Jesus Christ come (ἐληλυθότα) in the flesh is of God; and every spirit that confesseth not Jesus is not of God.' I cannot refrain from expressing the suspicion that the correct reading in this second clause may be λύει, 'divideth' or 'dissolveth,' instead of μὴ ὁμολογεῖ, 'confesseth not.' It is the reading of the old Latin, of Irenæus, of Tertullian, and of Origen; and Socrates (*H. E.* vii. 32) says that it was found 'in the old copies.' Though the passages of Irenæus and Origen are only extant in Latin versions, yet the contexts clearly show that the authors themselves so read it. It is difficult to conceive that the very simple μὴ ὁμολογεῖ would be altered into λύει, whereas the converse change would be easy. At all events λύει must represent a very early gloss, dating probably from a time when the original reference of St John was obvious; and it well describes the Christology of Cerinthus. See the application in Irenæus, iii. 16, 8 'Sententia eorum homicidialis ... *Comminuens et per multa dividens* Filium Dei; quos ... Ioannes in praedicta epistola fugere eos praecepit dicens' etc.

ever doth not confess the testimony of the cross,' which might include not only divers Gnostic sects, but many others as well. But the case is wholly different with the third, 'Whosoever perverteth the oracles of the Lord to (serve) his own lusts, and saith that there is neither resurrection nor judgment.' To this type of error, and this only, the description 'first-born of Satan' is applied in the text, and of this I venture to say that it is altogether inapplicable to Marcion. No doubt Marcion, like every other heretical teacher of the second century, or indeed of any century, did 'pervert the oracles of the Lord' by his tortuous interpretations; but he did not pervert them 'to his own lusts.' The high moral character of Marcion was un-impeachable, and is recognized by the orthodox writers of the second century; the worst charge which they bring against him is disappointed ambition. He was an ascetic of the most uncompromising and rigorous type. I cannot but regard it as a significant fact that when Scholten wishes to fasten this denunciation on Marcion, he stops short at 'pervert the oracles of the Lord,' and takes no account of the concluding words 'to his own lusts,' though these contain the very sting of the accusation[1]. Obviously the allusion here is to that antinomian license which many early Gnostic teachers managed to extract from the spiritual teaching of the Gospel. We find germs of this immoral doctrine a full half century before the professed date of Polycarp's Epistle, in the incipient Gnosticism which St Paul rebukes at Corinth[2]. We have still clearer indications of it in the Pastoral Epistles; and when we reach the epoch of the Apocalypse, which our author himself places somewhere in the year 68 or 69, the evil is almost full blown[3]. This interpretation becomes more evident when we consider the expression in the light of the accompanying clause, where the same persons are described as saying that there was 'no resurrection nor judgment.' This can hardly mean anything else than that they denied the doctrine of a future retribution, and

---

[1] *Die ältesten Zeugnisse* p. 41. sq, etc.
[2] *e.g.* 1 Cor. vi. 12—18, viii. 1
[3] Rev. ii. 6, 14, 15, 20, 24.

so broke loose from the moral restraints imposed by fear of consequences. Here again, they had their forerunners in those licentious speculators belonging to the Christian community at Corinth who maintained that 'there is no resurrection of the dead[1],' and whose Epicurean lives were a logical consequence of their Epicurean doctrine. And here, too, the Pastoral Epistles supply a pertinent illustration. If we are at a loss to conceive how they could have extracted such a doctrine out of 'the oracles of the Lord,' the difficulty is explained by the parallel case of Hymenæus and Philetus, who taught that 'the resurrection had already taken place[2],' or in other words, that all such terms must be understood in a metaphorical sense as applying to the spiritual change, the new birth or resuscitation of the believer in the present world[3]. Thus everything hangs together. But such teaching is altogether foreign to Marcion. He did indeed deny the resurrection of the flesh, and the future body of the redeemed[4]. This was a necessary tenet of all Gnostics, who held the inherent malignity of matter. In this sense only he denied a resurrection; and he did not deny a judgment at all. Holding, like the Catholic Christian, that men would be rewarded or punished hereafter according to their deeds in this life, he was obliged to recognize a judgment in some form or other. His Supreme God indeed, whom he represented as pure beneficence, could not be a judge or an avenger, but he got over the difficulty by assigning the work of judging and punishing to the Demiurge[5]. To revert to my illustration, this is as though our Nonconformist writer threw out a charge of Erastianism against the anonymous body of Christians whom he was attacking, and whom nevertheless it was sought to identify with the Church of Rome.

---

[1] 1 Cor. xv. 12.
[2] 2 Tim. ii. 18.
[3] Iren. ii. 31. 2; Tertull. *de Resurr. Carn.* 19.
[4] Iren. i. 27. 3, Tertull. *adv. Marc.* v. 10, *de Præscr. Hær.* 33.
[5] See Neander *Church History* ii. p. 147; and to the references there given add Iren. iii. 25. 2 'Alterum quidem *judicare* et alterum quidem salvare dixerunt,' and sect. 3, 'Marcion igitur ipse dividens Deum in duo, alterum quidem bonum et alterum *judicialem* dicens,' with the context.

6. The next argument is of a wholly different kind:—

The writer evidently assumes a position in the Church to which Polycarp could only have attained in the latter part of his life, and of which we first have evidence about A.D. 160, when he was deputed to Rome for the Paschal discussion.

This argument will not appeal to Englishmen with any power, when they remember that the ablest and most powerful Prime Minister whom constitutional England has seen assumed the reins of government at the early age of twenty-four. But Polycarp was not a young man at this time. M. Waddington's investigations here again stand us in good stead. If we take the earlier date of the martyrdom of Ignatius, Polycarp was now in his fortieth year at least; if the later date, he was close upon fifty. He had been a disciple, apparently a favourite disciple, of the aged Apostle St John. He was specially commended by Ignatius, who doubtless had spoken of him to the Philippians. History does not point to any person after the death of Ignatius whose reputation stood nearly so high among his contemporaries. So far as any inference can be drawn from silence, he was now the one prominent man in the Church. What wonder then that the Philippians should have asked him to write to them? To this request, I suppose, our author refers when he speaks of the writer 'assuming a position in the Church;' for there is nothing else to justify it. On his own part Polycarp writes with singular modesty. He associates his presbyters with himself in the opening address; he says that he should not have ventured to write as he does, if he had not received a request from the Philippians; he even deprecates any assumption of superiority[1].

7. But our author continues:—

And throughout, the Epistle depicts the developed organization of that period.

---

[1] I might add also that it is directly stated in the account of his martyrdom (§ 13), that he was treated with every honour, καὶ πρὸ τῆς πολιᾶς, 'even before his grey hairs,' as the words run in Eusebius, *H. E.* iv. 15. The common texts substitute καὶ πρὸ τῆς μαρτυρίας.

This argument must, I think, strike any one who has read the Epistle as surprising. There is, as I have said already, no reference to episcopacy from beginning to end[1]; and in this respect it presents the strongest contrast to writings of the age of Irenæus, to which it is here supposed to belong. Irenæus and his contemporaries are so familiar with episcopacy as a traditional institution, that they are not aware of any period when it was not universal; and more especially when they are dealing with heretics, they appeal to the episcopate as the depositary of the orthodox and Apostolic tradition in matters of doctrine and practice. The absence of all such language in Polycarp's Epistle is a strong testimony to its early date.

8. Lastly, another argument is alleged:—

Hilgenfeld has pointed out another indication of the same date, in the injunction 'Pray for the kings' (Orate pro regibus), which, in 1 Peter ii. 17, is 'Honour the king' (τὸν βασιλέα τιμᾶτε), which accords with the period after Antoninus Pius had elevated Marcus Aurelius to joint sovereignty (A.D. 147), or better still, with that in which Marcus Aurelius appointed Lucius Verus his colleague, A.D. 161.

Here we have only to ask why *Orate pro regibus* should be translated 'Pray for *the* kings,' rather than 'Pray for kings,' and the ghost of a divided sovereignty vanishes before the spell. There is no reason whatever for supposing that the expression has anything more than a general reference. Even if the words had stood in the original ὑπὲρ τῶν βασιλέων and not ὑπὲρ βασιλέων, the presence of the article would not, according to ordinary Greek usage, necessarily limit the reference to any particular sovereigns. But there is very good reason for believing that the definite article had no place in the original. The writer of this Epistle elsewhere shows acquaintance with the First Epistle to Timothy. Thus in one place (§ 4), he combines two passages which occur in close proximity in that Epistle; 'The love of money is the source of all troubles (1 Tim. vi. 10): knowing therefore that we brought nothing into the

---

[1] Hilgenfeld (*Apost. Väter* p. 273) evidently feels this difficulty, and apologizes for it.

world, neither are we able to carry anything out (1 Tim. vi. 7), let us arm ourselves' etc. Hence it becomes highly probable that he has derived this injunction also from the same Epistle; 'I exhort first of all, that supplications, prayers, intercessions, thanksgivings, be made for all men; for kings, and for all that are in authority' (ii. 2)[1], where it is $ὑπὲρ βασιλέων$. After his manner, Polycarp combines this with other expressions that he finds in the Evangelical and Apostolical writings (Ephes. vi. 18, Matt. v. 44, Phil. iii. 18), and gives the widest possible range to his injunction; 'Pray for all the saints; pray also for kings and potentates and princes, and for them that persecute and hate you, and for the enemies of the cross, etc.' We may therefore bid farewell to Marcus Aurelius and Lucius Verus.

Our author at the outset speaks of 'some critics who affirm the authenticity of the Epistle attributed to him [Polycarp], but who certainly do not justify their conclusion by any arguments nor attempt to refute adverse reasons.' He himself passes over in silence all answers which have been given to the objections alleged by him. Doubtless he considered them unworthy of notice. I have endeavoured to supply this lacuna in his work; and the reader will judge for himself on which side the weight of argument lies.

The author of *Supernatural Religion* in his Reply, which appeared in the January number of the *Fortnightly Review*, pointed out two inaccuracies in my first article. In adverting to his silence respecting the occurrence of the Logos in the Apocalypse[2], I ought to have confined my remark to the portion of his work in which he is contrasting the doctrinal teaching of this book with that of the Apocalypse, where especially some mention of it was to be expected. He has elsewhere alluded, as his references show, to the occurrence of the term in the Apocalypse. The other point relates to the passage in which he charges Dr Westcott with insinuating in an underhand way what he knew not to be true respecting Basilides. While commenting

---

[1] This reference to 1 Tim. ii. 2 is pointed out in Jacobson's note.

[2] See above, p. 15 sq.

on his omission of Dr Westcott's inverted commas in the extract which I gave[1], I overlooked the fact that he had just before quoted Dr Westcott's text correctly, as it stands in Dr Westcott's book. Though I find it still more difficult to understand how he could have brought this most unwarrantable charge when the fact of Dr Westcott's inverted commas was distinctly before him, I am not the less bound to plead guilty of an oversight, which I think I can explain to myself but which I shall not attempt to excuse, and to accept the retort of looseness, which he throws back upon me.

For the rest, I could not desire a more complete vindication of my criticisms than that which is furnished by the author's reply.

I cannot, for instance, take any blame to myself for not foreseeing the misprints which our author pleads, because they must have baffled far higher powers of divination than mine. Thus I found[2] the author stating that the fourth Evangelist 'only once distinguishes John the Baptist by the appellation ὁ βαπτιστής[3],' whereas, as a matter of fact, he never does so; and comparing the whole sentence with a passage in Credner[4], to which the author refers in his footnote, I found that it presented a close parallel, as the reader will see:—

Während der Verfasser die beiden Apostel gleiches Namens, Judas, sorgfältig unterscheidet (vergl. 14, 22), den Ap. Thomas näher bezeichnet (11, 16; 20, 24; 21, 2) und den Apostel Petrus, nur Simon Petrus, oder Petrus, nie Simon allein nennt (s. § 96, Nr. 3.), hat er es nicht für nöthig gefunden, den Täufer Johannes von dem gleichnamigen Apostel Johannes *auch nur ein einziges Mal* durch den Zusatz ὁ βαπτιστής zu unterscheiden (1, 6. 15. 19. 26, etc.).	He [the author] *only once* distinguishes John the Baptist by the appellation ὁ βαπτιστής, whilst he carefully distinguishes the two disciples of the name of Judas, and always speaks of the Apostle Peter as 'Simon Peter,' or 'Peter,' but rarely as 'Simon' only.

[1] See above, p. 20.
[2] See above, p. 17 sq.
[3] S. R. I. p. 423.
[4] Credner *Einleitung* p. 209 sq.

Seeing that the two passages corresponded so closely[1] the one to the other (the clauses however being transposed), I imagined that I had traced his error to its source in the correspondence of the two particular expressions which I have italicized, and that he must have stumbled over Credner's 'auch nur ein einziges Mal.' He has more than once gone wrong elsewhere in matters of fact relating to the New Testament. Thus he has stated that the saying about the first being last and the last first occurs in St Matthew alone of the Synoptic Gospels, though it appears also in St Mark (x. 31) and (with an unimportant variation) in St Luke (xiii. 30)[2]. Thus again, he can remember 'no instance whatever' where a New Testament writer 'claims to have himself performed a miracle[3],' though St Paul twice speaks of his exercising this power as a recognized and patent fact[4]. This explanation of his mistake therefore seemed to me to be tolerably evident. I could not have foreseen that, where the author wrote '*never* once,' the printer printed '*only* once.' This error runs through all the four editions.

But the other clerical error which our author pleads was still further removed from the possibility of detection. I had called attention[5] to the fact that, in the earlier part of his book, our

---

[1] The author, in his reply, calls attention to the fact that the language of the other writers to whom he gives references in his footnote is too clear to be misunderstood.

[2] I do not think I can have misapprehended our author's meaning, but it is best to give his own words: 'Now even Tischendorf does not pretend that this [a saying cited in the Epistle of Barnabas] is a quotation of Matt. xx. 16, "Thus the last shall be first, and the first last" (οὕτως ἔσονται οἱ ἔσχατοι πρῶτοι καὶ οἱ πρῶτοι ἔσχατοι), the sense of which is quite different. The application of the saying in this place in the first Synoptic Gospel is evidently quite false, and depends merely on the ring of words and not of ideas. Strange to say, *it is not found in either of the other Gospels;* but, like the famous phrase which we have been considering, it nevertheless appears twice quite irrelevantly, in two places of the first Gospel. In xix. 30, it is quoted again with slight variation: "But many first shall be last, and last first,"' etc. *S. R.* I. p. 247. The italics are my own.

[3] *S. R.* I. p. 200 sq.

[4] Rom. xv. 19; 2 Cor. xii. 12. The point to be observed is, that St Paul treats the fact of his working miracles as a matter of course, to which a passing reference is sufficient.

[5] [See above, p. 9.]

author had written respecting the descent of the angel at Bethesda (John v. 3, 4)—

> This passage is not found in the older MSS of the fourth Gospel, and it was probably a later interpolation[1].

whereas towards the end of his second volume he had declared that the passage was genuine; and I had pointed out that the last words stood 'certainly a late interpolation' in the first edition, so that the passage had undergone revision, while yet the contradiction had been suffered to remain.

In justice to our author, I will give his reply in his own words:—

> The words 'it is argued that' were accidentally omitted from vol. i. p. 113, line 19, and the sentence should read, 'and it is argued that it was probably a later interpolation[2].'

To this the following note is appended:—

> I altered 'certainly' to 'probably' in the second edition, as Dr Lightfoot points out, in order to avoid the possibility of exaggeration, but my mind was so impressed with the certainty that I had clearly shown I was merely, for the sake of fairness, reporting the critical judgment of others, that I did not perceive the absence of the words given above.

This omission runs through four editions.

But more perplexing still is the author's use of language.

The reader will already have heard enough of the passage in Irenæus, where this Father quotes some earlier authority or authorities who refer to the fourth Gospel; but I am compelled to allude to it again. In my first article I had accused the author of ignoring the distinction between the infinitive and indicative—between the oblique and direct narrative—and maintaining, in defiance of grammar, that the words might very well be Irenæus' own[3]. In my second article I pointed out that whole sentences were tacitly altered or re-written or omitted in the fourth edition, and that (as I unhesitatingly inferred) he had found out his mistake[4]. I have read over the passage

---

[1] *S. R.* i. p. 113.
[2] *Fortnightly Review*, January, 1875, p. 9 sq.
[3] [See above, p. 3 sq.]
[4] See above, p. 53 sq.

carefully again in its earlier form in the light of the explanation which the author gives in his reply, and I cannot put any different interpretation on his language. It seems to me distinctly to aim at proving two things: (1) That there is no reason for thinking that the passage is oblique at all, or that Irenæus is giving anything else besides his own opinion (pp. 326—331); and (2) That, even supposing it to be oblique, there is no ground for identifying the authorities quoted with the presbyters of Papias (pp. 331—334). With this last question I have not concerned myself hitherto. It will come under discussion in a later article, when I shall have occasion to treat of Papias[1]. It was to the first point alone that my remarks referred. The author however says in his reply that his meaning was the same throughout, that he knew all the while Irenæus must be quoting from some one else, and that he 'did what was possible to attract attention to the actual indirect construction[2].' Why then did he translate the oblique construction as if it were direct? Why, after quoting as parallels a number of direct sentences in Irenæus containing quotations, did he add, 'These are all direct quotations by Irenæus, as is most certainly that which we are now considering, which is introduced in precisely the same way[3]?' Why in his fourth edition, in which he first introduces a recognition of the oblique construction, did he withdraw all these supposed parallels, which, if his opinion was unchanged, still remained as good for his purpose (whatever that purpose might be) as they had ever been? Further discussion on this point would obviously be wasted. I can only ask any reader who is

[1] [See below, p. 194 sq.]

[2] *Fortnightly Review*, l. c. p. 5. The author states that he 'actually inserted in the text the opening words, εἶναι δὲ τὴν διαστολὴν ταύτην τῆς οἰκήσεως, for the express purpose of showing the construction.' The impression however which his own language left on my mind was quite different. It suggested that he inserted the words not for this purpose, but for quite another, namely, to show that there was nothing corresponding to Tischendorf's 'they say,' or Dr Westcott's 'they taught,' in the original, and so to justify his charge of 'falsification.' If the reader will refer to the context, and more especially to note 4 on p. 328 of the second volume of *Supernatural Religion* (in the editions before the fourth), he will see what strong justification I had for taking this view.

[3] *S. R.* II. p. 330.

interested in this matter to refer to the book itself, and more especially to compare the fourth[1] with the earlier editions, that he may judge for himself whether any other interpretation, except that which I and others besides myself[2] have put upon his words, was natural. The author has declared his meaning, but I could only judge by his language.

I now proceed to notice some other of the chief points in our author's reply; and perhaps it may be convenient in doing so to follow the order adopted in my original article to which it is a rejoinder.

1. In the first place then, the author is annoyed that I spoke disparagingly of his scholarship[3]; and in reply he says that the criticism in which I have indulged 'scarcely rises above the correction of an exercise or the conjugation of a verb[4].' I cannot help thinking this language unfortunate from his own point of view; but let that pass. If the reader will have the goodness to refer back to my article, he will find that, so far from occupying the main part of it on points of scholarship which have no bearing on the questions under discussion, as the author seems to hint, I have taken up about two-thirds of a page only[5] with such matters. In the other instances which I have selected, his errors directly affect the argument

---

[1] I ought to add that these alterations do not appear to have been made in all copies of the fourth edition. I am informed by a correspondent that in his copy the whole passage stands as in the earlier editions.

[2] *Inquirer*, Nov. 7, 1874. 'Elsewhere a blunder on the part of the writer is made the occasion of a grave charge against Dr Tischendorf and Canon Westcott. They are accused of deliberately falsifying etc. ... His own translation however overlooks the important fact that at the critical point in question Irenæus passes from the direct to the indirect speech. This is made obvious by the employment of the infinitive in place of the indicative. The English language affords no means of indicating this change except by the introduction of some such phrases as those employed by Tischendorf and Westcott, which simply denote the transition to be *obliqua oratio*. To neglect this is to throw the whole passage into confusion; and the writer's attempt to fasten a suspicion of dishonesty on the critics whose views he is combating recoils in the shape of a suggestion of imperfect scholarship upon himself.'

This occurs in a highly favourable review of the book.

[3] See above, p. 3 sq.

[4] *Fortnightly Review*, l. c. p. 9.

[5] [Corresponding to about a page in this reprint, pp. 7, 8 'These two examples...Commentaries of Cæsar.']

for the time being at some vital point. It would have been possible to multiply examples, if examples had been needed. I might have quoted, for instance, such renderings as καταβὰς περιπατείτω, 'come down let him walk about¹;' or 'Ἰοῦστά τις ἐν ἡμῖν ἐστι Συροφοινίκισσα, τὸ γένος Χανανῖτις, ἧς τὸ θυγάτριον κ.τ.λ. 'Justa, who is amongst us, a Syrophœnician, a Canaanite by race, whose daughter' etc.² Both these renderings survive to the fourth edition.

I must not however pass over the line of defence which our author takes, though only a few words will be necessary. I do not see that he has gained anything by sheltering himself behind others, when he is obviously in the wrong. Not a legion of Tischendorfs, for instance, can make ἐπαγγελλόμενον signify 'has promised³,' though it is due to Tischendorf to add that notwithstanding his loose translation he has seen through the meaning of Origen's words, and has not fastened an error upon himself by a false interpretation, as our author has done. And in other cases, where our author takes upon himself the responsibility of his renderings, his explanations are more significant than the renderings themselves. Scholars will judge whether a scholar, having translated *quem caederet*⁴, 'whom he mutilates,' could have brought himself to defend it as a 'paraphrase⁵.' I am not at all afraid that dispassionate judges hereafter will charge me with having unduly depreciated his scholarship.

But our author evidently thinks that the point was not worth establishing at all. I cannot agree with him. I feel sure that, if he had been dealing with some indifferent matter, as for instance some question of classical literature, he would not have received any more lenient treatment from independent reviewers; and I do not see why the greater importance of the subject should be pleaded as a claim for immunity from critical

---

¹ *S. R.* I. p. 336. [Tacitly corrected in ed. 6.]

² *S. R.* II. p. 23. [Tacitly corrected in ed. 6.]

³ *Fortnightly Review, l. c.* p. 7 sq. I need not stop to inquire whether Tischendorf's 'nicht geschrieben hat' conveys exactly the same idea which is conveyed in English, 'has not written,' as our author assumes in his reply.

⁴ [See above, p. 8.]

⁵ *Fortnightly Review, l. c.* p. 9, note.

examination. It does not seem to me to be a light matter that an author assuming, as the author of *Supernatural Religion* does, a tone of lofty superiority over those whom he criticizes, should betray an ignorance of the very grammar of criticism. But in the present case there was an additional reason why attention should be called to these defects. It was necessary to correct a wholly false estimate of the author's scholarship with which reviewers had familiarized the public, and to divest the work of a prestige to which it was not entitled.

2. In the next place I ventured to dispute the attribute of impartiality with which the work entitled *Supernatural Religion* had been credited. And here I would say that my quarrel was much more with the author's reviewers than with the author himself. I can understand how he should omit to entertain the other side of the question with perfect sincerity. It appeared from the book itself, and it has become still more plain from the author's Reply, that he regards 'apologists' as persons from whom he has nothing to learn, and with whose arguments therefore he need not for the most part concern himself. But the fact remains that the reader has had an *ex parte* statement presented to him, while he has been assured that the whole case is laid before him.

Of this one-sided representation I adduced several instances. To these our author demurs in his reply. As regards Polycarp, I believe that the present article has entirely justified my allegation. Of Papias, Hegesippus, and Justin, I shall have occasion to speak in subsequent articles. At present it will be sufficient to challenge attention to what Dr Westcott has written on the last-mentioned writer, and ask readers to judge for themselves whether our author has laid the case impartially before them.

Several of my examples had reference to the Gospel of St John. Of these our author has taken exception more especially to three.

As regards the first, I have no complaint to make, because he has quoted my own words, and I am well content that they should tell their own tale. If our author considers the argument 'unsound in itself, and irrelevant to the direct purpose of the work[1],' I venture to think that discerning readers will take a different view. I had directed attention[2] to certain passages in the Synoptic Gospels (Matt. xxiii. 37; Luke xiii. 34) as implying other visits to Jerusalem which these Gospels do not themselves record, and therefore as refuting the hypothesis that our Lord's ministry was only of a single year's duration, and was exercised wholly in Galilee and the neighbourhood until the closing visit to Jerusalem—a hypothesis which rests solely on the arbitrary assumption that the record in the Synoptists is complete and continuous. Thus the supposed difficulty in St John's narrative on this fundamental point of history disappears. In fact the Synoptists give no continuous chronology in the history of our Lord's ministry between the baptism and the passion; the incidents were selected in the first instance (we may suppose) for purposes of catechetical instruction, and are massed together sometimes by connection of subject, sometimes (though incidentally) by sequence of time. In St John, on the other hand, the successive festivals at Jerusalem are the vertebræ of the chronological backbone, which is altogether wanting to the account of Christ's ministry in the Synoptists. We cannot indeed be sure even here that the vertebræ are absolutely continuous; many festivals may have been omitted; the ministry of Christ may have extended over a much longer period, as indeed Irenæus asserts that it did[3]; but the three passovers bear testimony to a duration of between two and three years at the least.

The second point has reference to the diction of the fourth Gospel, as compared with the Apocalypse[4]. Here I am glad to find that there is less difference of opinion between us than I had imagined. If our author does not greatly differ from

[1] *Fortnightly Review*, l.c. p. 18.
[2] [See above, p. 16 sq.]
[3] Iren. ii. 22. 5. The passover of the Passion cannot have been later than A.D. 36, because before the next passover Pilate had been superseded. This is the only *terminus ad quem*, so far as I am aware, which is absolutely decisive; and it would allow of a ministry of eight years. The probability is that it was actually much shorter, but it is only a probability.
[4] [See above, p. 14 sq.]

Luthardt's estimate of the language, neither do I[1]. On the other hand, I did not deny, and (so far as I am aware) nobody has denied, that there is a marked difference between the Apocalypse and the Gospel, in respect of diction; only it is contended that two very potent influences must be taken into account which will explain this difference. In the first place, the subjects of the two books stand widely apart. The apocalyptic purport of the one book necessarily tinges its diction and imagery with a very strong Hebraic colouring, which we should not expect to find in a historical narrative. Secondly, a wide interval of time separates the two works. The Apocalypse was written, according to the view which our author represents 'as universally accepted by all competent critics,' about A.D. 68, 69[2]. It marks the close of what we may call the *Hebraic* period of St John's life—*i.e.*, the period which (so far as we can gather alike from the notices and from the silence of history) he had spent chiefly in the East and among Aramaic-speaking peoples. The Gospel on the other hand, according to all tradition, dates from the last years of the Apostle's life, or, in other words, it was written (or more probably dictated) at the end of the *Hellenic* period, after an interval of twenty or thirty years, during which St John had lived at Ephesus, a great centre of Greek civilization. Our author appears to be astonished that Luthardt should describe the 'errors' in the Apocalypse as not arising out of ignorance, but as 'intentional emancipations from the rules of grammar.' Yet it stands to reason, I think, that this must be so with some of the most glaring examples at all events. A moment's

---

[1] I am afraid however that our author would not agree with me in regarding it as plainly the language of a man accustomed to think in Hebrew. He himself says (*S. R.* II. p. 413), 'Its Hebraisms are not on the whole greater than was almost invariably the case with Hellenic Greek.' Though the word is printed 'Hellenic,' not only in the four editions, but likewise in the author's own extract in the *Fortnightly Review* (p. 19), I infer from the context, that it ought to be read 'Hellenistic,' [which word is tacitly substituted in ed. 6]. By 'Hellenic' would be meant the common language, as ordinarily spoken by the mass of the Greeks, and as distinguished from a literary dialect like the Attic; by 'Hellenistic,' the language of Hellenists, *i.e.*, Greek-speaking Jews. The two things are quite different.

[2] *S. R.* II. p. 395.

reflection will show that one who could write ἀπὸ ὁ ὤν, κ.τ.λ. 'from He that is,' etc. (Rev. i. 4), in sheer ignorance that ἀπὸ does not take a nominative case, would be incapable of writing any two or three consecutive verses of the Apocalypse. The book, after all allowance made for solecisms, shows a very considerable command of the Greek vocabulary, and (what is more important) a familiarity with the intricacies of the very intricate syntax of this language.

On the third point, to which our author devotes between three and four pages, more explanation is required. I had remarked[1] on the manner in which our author deals with the name 'Sychar' in the fourth Gospel, and had complained that he only discusses the theory of its identification with Shechem, omitting to mention more probable solutions. To this remark I had appended the following note:

Travellers and 'apologists' alike now more commonly identify Sychar with the village bearing the Arabic name Askar. This fact is not mentioned by our author. He says moreover, 'It is admitted that there was no such place [as Sychar, Συχάρ], and apologetic ingenuity is severely taxed to explain the difficulty.' *This is altogether untrue.* Others besides 'apologists' point to passages in the Talmud which speak of 'the well of Suchar (or Sochar, or Sichar);' see Neubauer, 'La Geographie du Talmud,' p. 169 sq. Our author refers in his note to an article by Delitzsch ('Zeitschr. f. Luth. Theol.' 1856, p. 240 sq). *He cannot have read the article, for these Talmudic references are its main purport.*

Our author in his reply quotes this note, and italicizes the passages as they are printed here. I am glad that he has done so, for I wish especially to call attention to the connection between the two. He adds that 'an apology is surely due to the readers of the *Contemporary Review,*' and, as he implies, to himself, 'for this style of criticism,' to which he says that he is not accustomed[2].

I am not sorry that this rejoinder has obliged me to rescue from the obscurity of a footnote a fact of real importance in its bearing on the historical character of the fourth Gospel. As for

---

[1] [See above, p. 17 sq.] [2] *Fortnightly Review,* l. c. p. 20.

apologizing, I will most certainly apologize, if he wishes it. But I must explain myself first. I am surprised that this demand should be made by the same person who penned certain sentences in *Supernatural Religion*. I am not a little perplexed to understand what canons of controversial etiquette he would lay down; for, while I have merely accused him, in somewhat blunt language, of great carelessness, he has not scrupled to charge others with 'wilful and deliberate evasion,' with 'unpardonable calculation upon the ignorance of his readers,' with 'a deliberate falsification,' with 'disingenuousness[1]' and other grave moral offences of the same kind. Now I have been brought up in the belief that offences of this class are incomparably more heinous than the worst scholarship or the grossest inaccuracy; and I am therefore obliged to ask whether he is not imposing far stricter rules on others than he is prepared to observe himself, when he objects to what I have said. Nevertheless I will apologize; but I cannot do so without reluctance, for he is asking me to withdraw an explanation which seemed to me to place his mode of proceeding in the most favourable light, and to substitute for it another which I should not have ventured to suggest. When I saw in his text the unqualified statement, 'It is admitted that there was no such place[2],' and found in one of his footnotes on the same page a reference to an article by an eminent Hebraist devoted to showing that such a place is mentioned several times in the Talmud, I could draw no other conclusion than that he had not read the article in question, or (as I might have added), having read it, had forgotten its contents. The manner in which references are given elsewhere in this work, as I have shown in my article on the Ignatian Epistles, seemed to justify this inference. His own explanation however is quite different:—

My statement is, that it is admitted that there was no such place

---

[1] *S. R.* I. p. 469; II. pp. 56, 59, 73, 326. [The last reference should be omitted: the words had been already withdrawn (ed. 4) before this Essay was written; but the language in the other references remains unaltered through six editions, and is only slightly modified in the Complete Edition.]

[2] [*S. R.* II. p. 421; and so ed. 6. The Complete Edition substitutes 'evident' for 'admitted.']

as Sychar—I ought to have added, 'except by apologists, who never admit anything'—but I thought that in saying, 'and apologetic ingenuity is severely taxed to explain the difficulty,' I had sufficiently excepted apologists, and indicated that many assertions and conjectures are advanced by them for that purpose.

Certainly this qualifying sentence needed to be added; for no reader could have supposed that the author intended his broad statement to be understood with this all-important reservation. Unfortunately however this explanation is not confined to 'apologists.' As I pointed out, it is adopted by M. Neubauer also, who (unless I much mistake his position) would altogether disclaim being considered an apologist, but who nevertheless, being an honest man, sets down his honest opinion, without considering whether it will or will not tend to establish the credibility of the Evangelist.

But after all, the really important question for the reader is not what this or that person thinks on this question, but what are the facts. And here I venture to say that, when our author speaks of 'assertions and conjectures' in reference to Delitzsch's article, such language is quite misleading. The points which the Talmudical passages quoted by him establish are these:—

(1) A place called 'Suchar,' or 'Sychar,' is mentioned in the Talmud. Our author speaks of 'some vague references in the Talmud to a somewhat similar, but not identical, name.' But the fact is, that the word Συχάρ, if written in Hebrew letters, would naturally take one or other of the two forms which we find in the Talmud, סוכר (Suchar) or סיכר (Sychar). In other words, the transliteration is as exact as it could be. It would no doubt be possible to read the former word 'Socher,' and the latter 'Sicher,' because the vowels are indeterminate within these limits. But so far as identity was possible, we have it here.

(2) The Talmudical passages speak not only of 'Sychar,' but of 'Ayin-Sychar,' *i.e.*, 'the Well of Sychar.'

(3) The 'Well of Sychar' which they mention is in a corn-growing country. This is clear from the incident which leads

to the mention of the place in the two principal Talmudical passages where it appears, *Baba Kamma* 82b, *Menachoth* 64b. It is there stated that on one occasion, when the lands in the neighbourhood of Jerusalem were laid waste by war, and no one knew whence the two loaves of the Pentecostal offering, the first-fruits of the wheat harvest, could be procured, they were obliged ultimately to bring them from 'the valley of the Well of Sychar.' Now the country which was the scene of the interview with the Samaritan woman is remarkable in this respect—'one mass of corn, unbroken by boundary or hedge'[1]—as it is described by a modern traveller; and indeed the prospect before Him suggests to our Lord, as we may well suppose, the image which occurs in the conversation with the disciples immediately following—'Lift up your eyes, and look on the fields; for they are white already to harvest[2].' It is true that the Talmudical passages do not fix the locality of their 'Ayin-Sychar;' but all the circumstances agree. It was just from such a country as this (neither too near nor too far distant for the notices) that the Pentecostal loaves would be likely to be procured in such an emergency.

The reader will draw his own conclusions. He will judge for himself whether the unqualified statement, 'It is admitted that there was no such place as Sychar,' is or is not misleading. He will form his own opinion whether a writer, who deliberately ignores these facts, because they are brought forward by 'apologists who never admit anything,' is likely to form an impartial judgment.

The identification of Sychar with Askar, to which recent opinion has been tending, is a question of less importance. Notwithstanding the difficulty respecting the initial *Ain* in the latter word, an identification which has commended itself to Oriental scholars like Ewald and Delitzsch and Neubauer can hardly be pronounced impossible. I venture to suggest that the initial *Ain* of 'Askar' may be explained by supposing the word to be a contraction for *Ayin-Sychar*, the 'Well of Sychar.'

---

[1] Stanley *Sinai and Palestine* p. 229.   [2] John iv. 35.

This corruption of the original name into a genuine Arabic word would furnish another example of a process which is common where one language is superposed upon another, *e.g.*, Charter-House for Chartreuse.

3. The third point to which I called attention[1] was the author's practice of charging those from whom he disagreed with dishonesty. This seemed to me to be a very grave offence, which deserved to be condemned by all men alike, whatever their opinions might be. And in the present instance I considered that the author was especially bound to abstain from such charges, because he had thought fit to shelter himself (as he was otherwise justified in doing) under an anonyme. Moreover, the offence was aggravated by the fact that one of the writers whom he had especially selected for this mode of attack was distinguished for his moderation of tone, and for his generous appreciation of the position and arguments of his adversaries.

This is our author's reply—

Dr Lightfoot says, and says rightly, that 'Dr Westcott's honour may safely be left to take care of itself.' It would have been much better to have left it to take care of itself, indeed, than trouble it by such advocacy. If anything could check just or generous expression, it would be the tone adopted by Dr Lightfoot; but nevertheless, I again say, in the most unreserved manner, that neither in this instance, nor in any other, have I had the most distant intention of attributing 'corrupt motives' to a man like Dr Westcott, whose single-mindedness I recognize, and for whose earnest character I feel genuine respect. The utmost that I have at any time intended to point out is that, utterly possessed as he is by orthodox views in general, and on the Canon in particular, he sees facts, I consider, through a dogmatic medium, and unconsciously imparts his own peculiar colouring to statements which should be more impartially made[2].

I am well content to bear this blame when I have elicited this explanation. A great wrong had been done, and I wished to see it redressed. But who could have supposed that this was

[1] [See above, p. 20 sq.]   [2] *Fortnightly Review*, l.c. p. 13.

our author's meaning? Who could have imagined that he had all along felt a 'genuine respect' for the single-mindedness of one whom he accused of 'discreet reserve,' of 'unworthy suppression of the truth,' of 'clever evasion,' of 'ignorant ingenuity or apologetic partiality,' of 'disingenuousness,' of 'what amounts to falsification,' and the like, and whom in the very passage which has called forth this explanation he had charged with yielding to a 'temptation' which was 'too strong for the apologist,' and 'insinuating to unlearned readers' what he knew to be untrue respecting Basilides? This unfortunate use of language, I contend, is no trifling matter where the honour of another is concerned; and, instead of his rebuke, I claim his thanks for enabling him to explain expressions which could only be understood in one way by his readers, and which have so grievously misrepresented his true meaning.

I trust also that our author wishes us to interpret the charges which he has brought against Tischendorf[1] in the same liberal spirit. I certainly consider that Tischendorf took an unfortunate step when he deserted his proper work, for which he was eminently fitted, and came forward as an apologist; and, if our author had satisfied himself with attacking the weak points of his apologetic armour, there would have been no ground for complaint, and on some points I should have agreed with him. But I certainly supposed that 'deliberate falsification' meant 'deliberate falsification.' I imagined, as ordinary readers would imagine, that these words involved a charge of conscious dishonesty. I am content to believe now that they were intended to impute to him an unconscious bias.

In our author's observations on my criticism of his general argument, there is one point which seems to call for observation. Of all my remarks, the one sentence which I should least have expected to incur his displeasure, is the following:—

> Obviously, if the author has established his conclusions in the first part, the second and third are altogether superfluous[2].

I fancied that, in saying this, I was only translating his own

---

[1] [See above, pp. 5, 55, 128.]   [2] [See above, p. 26.]

opinion into other words. I imagined that he himself wished the second and third parts to be regarded as a work of supererogation. Was I altogether without ground for this belief? I turn to the concluding paragraph of the first part, and I find these words:—

Those who have formed any adequate conception of the amount of testimony which would be requisite in order to establish the reality of occurrences in violation of the order of nature, which is based upon universal and invariable experience, must recognize that, *even if the earliest asserted origin of our four Gospels could be established upon the most irrefragable grounds*, the testimony of the writers—men of like ignorance with their contemporaries, men of like passions with ourselves—*would be utterly incompetent to prove the reality of miracles*[1].

What does this mean, except that even though it should be necessary to concede every point against which the author is contending in the second and third parts, still the belief in the Gospel miracles is irrational? Is the language which I have used at all stronger than our author's own on this point? But I am glad to have elicited from him an expression of opinion that the question is not foreclosed by the arguments in the first part[2].

---

[1] *S. R.* I. p. 210. The italics are mine.

[2] Towards the close of his Reply the author makes some remarks on a 'Personal God,' in which he accuses me of misunderstanding him. It may be so, but then I venture to think that he does not quite understand himself, as he certainly does not understand me. I do not remember that he has anywhere defined the terms 'Personal' and 'Anthropomorphic,' as applied to Deity; and without definition, so many various conceptions may be included under the terms as to entangle a discussion hopelessly. No educated Christian, I imagine, believes in an anthropomorphic Deity in the sense in which this anthropomorphism is condemned in the noble passage of Xenophanes which he quotes in the first part of his work. In another sense, our author himself in his concluding chapter betrays his anthropomorphism; for he attributes to the Divine Being wisdom and beneficence and forethought, which are conceptions derived by man from the study of himself. Indeed, I do not see how it is possible to conceive of Deity except through some sort of anthropomorphism in this wider sense of the term, and certainly our author has not disengaged himself from it.

In spite of our author's repudiation in his reply, I boldly claim the writer of the concluding chapter of *Supernatural Religion* as a believer in a Personal God, in the only sense in

For some expressions in his concluding paragraph I sincerely thank the author, though I find it difficult to reconcile them with either the tone or the substance of the preceding reply. I trust that I have already relieved him from the apprehension that I should confine myself to 'desultory efforts.' I had hoped that some of the topics in my first article might have been laid aside for ever, but his reply has compelled me to revert to them. He does me no more than justice when he credits me with earnestness. I am indeed in earnest, as I believe him to be. But it seems to me that the motives for earnestness are necessarily more intense in my case than in his; for (to say nothing else), as I read history, the morality of the coming generations of Englishmen is very largely dependent on the answers which they give to the questions at issue between us. As he has withheld his name, he has deprived me of the pleasure of reciprocating any expression of personal respect. Thus he has placed me at a great disadvantage. I know nothing of the man, and can speak only of the book. Of the book I would wish to say that one who has taken so much pains to regulate his personal belief is so far entitled to every consideration. And, if this had been all, I should have entertained and expressed the highest respect for him, however faulty his processes might appear to me, and however dangerous his results. But, when I observed that the author, not content with ignoring the facts and reasonings, went on to impugn the honesty of his opponents; when I noticed that again and again the arguments on one side of the question were carefully arrayed, while the arguments on the other side were altogether omitted; when I perceived that he denied the authenticity of every work, and questioned the applicability of every reference, which made against him; when in short I saw that, however sincere the writer's personal convictions might be,

which I understand Personality as applied to the Divine Being. He distinctly attributes will and mind to the Divine Being, and this is the very idea of personality, as I conceive the term. He not only commits himself to a belief in a Personal God, but also in a wise and beneficent Personal God who cares for man. On the other hand, the writer of the first part of the work seemed to me to use arguments which were inconsistent with these beliefs.

the critical portion of the work was stamped throughout with the character of an advocate's *ex parte* statement, I felt that he had forfeited any claim to special forbearance. For the rest, I do not wish to be unjust to the book, and I am sorry if, while attempting to correct an exceedingly false estimate, I have seemed to any one to be so; but I do not see any good in paying empty and formal compliments which do not come from the heart, and I cannot consent to tamper with truths which seem to me of the highest moment. Still, I should be sorry to think that so much energetic work had been thrown away. If the publication of this book shall have had the effect of attracting serious attention to these most momentous subjects, it will have achieved an important result. But I would wish to add one caution. No good will ever come from merely working on the lines of modern theorists. Perhaps the reader will forgive me if I add a few words of explanation, for I do not wish to be misunderstood. I should be most ungrateful if, in speaking of German writers, I used the language of mere depreciation. If there is any recent theologian from whom I have learnt more than from another, it is the German Neander. Nor can I limit my obligations to men of this stamp. All diligent students of early Christian history must have derived the greatest advantage on special points from the conscientious research, and frequently also from the acute analysis, even of writers of the most extreme school. But it is high time that the incubus of fascinating speculations should be shaken off, and that Englishmen should learn to exercise their judicial faculty independently. Any one who will take the pains to read Irenæus through carefully, endeavouring to enter into his historical position in all its bearings, striving to realize what he and his contemporaries actually thought about the writings of the New Testament and what grounds they had for thinking it, and, above all, resisting the temptation to read in modern theories between the lines, will be in a more favourable position for judging rightly of the early history of the Canon than if he had studied all the monographs which have issued from the German press during the last half century.

V.—PAPIAS OF HIERAPOLIS.

[AUGUST, 1875.]

TWO names stand out prominently in the Churches of proconsular Asia during the age immediately succeeding the Apostles—Polycarp of Smyrna, and Papias of Hierapolis. Having given an account of Polycarp in my last article, I purpose now to examine the notices relating to Papias. These two fathers are closely connected together in the earliest tradition. Papias, writes Irenæus, was 'a hearer of John and a companion of Polycarp[1].' On the latter point we may frankly accept the evidence of Irenæus. A pupil of Polycarp, at all events, was not likely to be misinformed here. But to the former part of the statement objections have been raised in ancient and modern times alike; and it will be my business in the course of this investigation to inquire into its credibility. Yet, even if Papias was not a personal disciple of St John, still his age and country place him in more or less close connection with the traditions of this Apostle; and it is this fact which gives importance to his position and teaching.

Papias wrote a work entitled, 'Exposition of Oracles of the Lord,' in five books, of which a few scanty fragments and notices are preserved, chiefly by Irenæus and Eusebius. The object and contents of this work will be discussed hereafter; but it is necessary to quote at once an extract which Eusebius has preserved from the preface, since our estimate of the date and posi-

---

[1] Iren. v. 33. 4 'Ιωάννου μὲν ἀκουστής, Πολυκάρπου δὲ ἑταῖρος γεγονώς.

tion of Papias will depend largely on the interpretation of its meaning.

Papias then, addressing (as it would appear) some friend to whom the work was dedicated, explains its plan and purpose as follows[1]:—

But I will not scruple also to give a place for you along with my interpretations to everything that I learnt carefully and remembered carefully in time past from the elders, guaranteeing their truth. For, unlike the many, I did not take pleasure in those who have so very much to say (τοῖς τὰ πολλὰ λέγουσιν), but in those who teach the truth; nor in those who relate foreign commandments, but in those [who record] such as were given from the Lord to the Faith, and are derived from the Truth itself. And again, on any occasion when a person came [in my way] who had been a follower of the elders (εἰ δέ που καὶ παρηκολουθηκώς τις τοῖς πρεσβυτέροις ἔλθοι), I would inquire about the discourses of the elders—what was said by Andrew, or by Peter, or by Philip, or by Thomas or James, or by John or Matthew or any other of the Lord's disciples, and what Aristion and the Elder John, the disciples of the Lord, say. For I did not think that I could get so much profit from the contents of books as from the utterances of a living and abiding voice (οὐ γὰρ τὰ ἐκ τῶν βιβλίων τοσοῦτόν με ὠφελεῖν ὑπελάμβανον, ὅσον τὰ παρὰ ζώσης φωνῆς καὶ μενούσης.)

This passage is introduced by Eusebius with the remark that, though Irenæus calls Papias a hearer of John,

Yet Papias himself, in the preface to his discourses, certainly does not declare that he himself was a hearer and eye-witness of the holy Apostles, but he shows, by the language which he uses, that he received the matters of the faith from those who were their friends.

Then follows the extract which I have given; after which Eusebius resumes:—

Here it is important to observe, that he twice mentions the name of John. The former of these he puts in the same list with

---

[1] Euseb. *H. E.* iii. 39 Οὐκ ὀκνήσω δέ σοι καὶ ὅσα ποτὲ παρὰ τῶν πρεσβυτέρων καλῶς ἔμαθον καὶ καλῶς ἐμνημόνευσα συγκατατάξαι [v. l. συντάξαι] ταῖς ἑρμηνείαις, διαβεβαιούμενος ὑπὲρ αὐτῶν ἀληθειαν, κ. τ. λ. This same reference will hold for all the notices from Eusebius which are quoted in this article, unless otherwise stated.

Peter and James and Matthew and the rest of the Apostles, clearly intending the Evangelist; but the second John he mentions after an interval (διαστείλας τὸν λόγον), and places among others outside the number of the Apostles, putting Aristion before him, and he distinctly calls him an 'elder;' so that by these facts the account of those is proved to be true who have stated that two persons in Asia had the same name, and that there were two tombs in Ephesus, each of which, even to the present time, bears the name of John.

Then, after speculating on the possibility that this second John was the author of the Apocalypse, he continues:—

Papias avows that he has received the sayings of the Apostles from those who had been their followers (τῶν αὐτοῖς παρηκολουθηκότων), but says that he himself was an immediate hearer of Aristion and the Elder John. Certainly he mentions them many times in his writings, and records their traditions.

The justice of this criticism has been disputed by many recent writers, who maintain that the same John, the son of Zebedee, is meant in both passages. But I cannot myself doubt that Eusebius was right in his interpretation, and I am glad for once to find myself entirely agreed with the author of *Supernatural Religion*. It will be observed that John is the only name mentioned twice, and that at its second occurrence the person bearing it is distinguished as the 'elder' or 'presbyter,' this designation being put in an emphatic position before the proper name. We must therefore accept the distinction between John the Apostle and John the Presbyter, though the concession may not be free from inconvenience, as introducing an element of possible confusion.

But it does not therefore follow that the statement of Irenæus was incorrect. Though this passage in the preface of Papias lends no support to the belief that he was a personal disciple of John the son of Zebedee, yet it is quite consistent with such a belief. Irenæus does not state that he derived his knowledge from this preface, or indeed from any part of the work. Having listened again and again to Polycarp while describing the sayings and doings of John the Apostle[1],

[1] See above, p. 96 sq.

he had other sources of information which were closed to Eusebius. Nor indeed is there any chronological or other difficulty in supposing that he may have derived the fact from direct intercourse with Papias himself. But the possibility still remains that he was guilty of this confusion which Eusebius lays to his charge; and the value of his testimony on this point is seriously diminished thereby.

It will have been noticed that in the above extract Papias professes to derive the traditions of 'the elders,' with which he illustrated his expositions, from two different sources. He refers *first*, to those sayings which he had heard from their own lips, and *secondly*, to those which he had collected at second-hand from their immediate followers. What class of persons he intends to include under the designation of 'elders' he makes clear by the names which follow. The category would include not only Apostles like Andrew and Peter, but also other personal disciples of Christ, such as Aristion and the second John. In other words, the term with him is a synonyme for the Fathers of the Church in the first generation. This meaning is entirely accordant with the usage of the same title elsewhere. Thus Irenæus employs it to describe the generation to which Papias himself belonged[1]. Thus again, in the next age, Irenæus in turn is so designated by Hippolytus[2]. And, when we descend as low as Eusebius, we find him using the term so as to include even writers later than Irenæus, who nevertheless, from their comparative antiquity, were to him and his generation authorities as regards the traditions and usages of the Church[3]. Nor indeed did Papias himself invent this usage. In the Epistle to the Hebrews for instance, we read that 'the elders obtained a good report[4]'; where the meaning is defined by the list which follows, including Old Testament worthies from Abel to 'Samuel and the prophets.' Thus this

---

[1] *Hær.* iv. 27. 1, 3; iv. 30. 1; iv. 31. 1; v. 5. 1; v. 33. 3; v. 36. 1, 2.

[2] *Ref. Hær.* vi. 42, 55, 'The blessed elder Irenæus.' Clement of Alexandria uses the same phrase of Pantænus; Euseb. *H. E.* vi. 14.

[3] *H. E.* iii. 3; v. 8; vi. 13.

[4] Heb. xi. 2.

sense of 'elders' in early Christian writers corresponds very nearly to our own usage of 'fathers,' when we speak of the Fathers of the Church, the Fathers of the Reformation, the Pilgrim Fathers, and the like.

Thus employed therefore, the term 'presbyters' or 'elders' denotes not office, but authority and antiquity[1]. It is equivalent to 'the ancient' or 'primitive worthies[2].' But at its last occurrence in the extract of Papias, where it is applied to the second John, this is apparently not the case. Here it seems to be an official title, designating a member of the order of the presbyterate. Though modern critics have stumbled over this two-fold sense of the word πρεσβύτερος in the same context, it would create no difficulty to the contemporaries of Papias, to whom 'the Presbyter John' must have been a common mode of designation in contradistinction to 'the Apostle John,' and to whom therefore the proper meaning would at once suggest itself. Instances are not wanting elsewhere in which this word is used with two senses, official and non-official, in the same passage[3].

Of the elders with whom Papias was personally acquainted, we can only name with certainty Aristion and the Presbyter John; but as regards these Eusebius is explicit. To them the Apostle John may perhaps be added, as we have seen, on the authority of Irenæus. Beyond these three names we have no authority for extending the list, though there is a possibility that in very early life he may have met with others, more especially Andrew and Philip, who are known to have lived in

---

[1] Weiffenbach *Das Papias-Fragment* (Giessen, 1874) has advocated at great length the view that Papias uses the term as a title of office throughout, p. 34 sq; but he has not succeeded in convincing subsequent writers. His conclusions are opposed by Hilgenfeld *Papias von Hierapolis* p. 245 sq (in his *Zeitschrift*, 1875), and by Leimbach *Das Papias-Fragment* p. 63 sq. Weiffenbach supposes that the elders are distinguished from the Apostles and personal disciples whose sayings Papias sets himself to collect. This view demands such a violent wresting of the grammatical connection in the passage of *Papias* that it is not likely to find much favour.

[2] In illustration of this use, it may be mentioned that in the Letter of the Gallican Churches (Euseb. *H. E.* v. 1) the term is applied to the Zacharias of Luke i. 5 sq.

[3] 1 Tim. v. 1, 2, 17, 19.

these parts. But, however this may be, it seems to follow from the words of his preface that his direct intercourse with these elders or personal disciples of the Lord had not been great. It was probably confined to the earlier part of his life, before he had any thought of writing his book; and the information thence derived was in consequence casual and fragmentary. When he set himself to collect traditions for this special purpose, he was dependent on secondary evidence, on the information collected from scholars and followers of these primitive elders.

We are now in a position to investigate the age of Papias; but, as a preliminary to this investigation, it is necessary to say something about the authority for the one definite date which is recorded in connection with him. In my article on Polycarp, I pointed out that recent investigations had pushed the date of this father's martyrdom several years farther back, and that some chronological difficulties attaching to the commonly received date had thus been removed[1]. A similar difficulty meets us in the case of Papias; and it disappears in like manner, as I hope to show, before the light of criticism. The *Chronicon Paschale*, which was compiled in the first half of the seventh century[2], represents Papias as martyred at Pergamum about the same time when Polycarp suffered at Smyrna, and places the event in the year 164. If this statement were true, we could hardly date his birth before A.D. 80, and even then he would have lived to a very advanced age. But there is a certain difficulty[3] in supposing that one born at this late date should have been directly acquainted with so many personal disciples of our Lord. No earlier writer however mentions the date, or even the fact, of the martyrdom—not even Eusebius, who has much to say both about Papias and about the martyrologies of this epoch; and this absence of confirmation renders the statement highly suspicious.

---

[1] See above, p. 103 sq.

[2] See Clinton, *Fast. Rom.* II. p. 835.

[3] This difficulty however cannot be regarded as serious. At the last (the sixtieth) anniversary of the battle of Waterloo, the *Times* gave the names of no fewer than seventy-six Waterloo officers as still living.

I believe that I have traced the error to its source, which indeed is not very far to seek. The juxtaposition of the passage in this Chronicle with the corresponding passage in the History of Eusebius [1] will, if I mistake not, tell its own tale.

CHRONICON PASCHALE.	EUSEBIUS.
In the 133rd year of the Ascension of the Lord *very severe persecutions having dismayed* (ἀνασοβησάντων) *Asia*, many were *martyred*, among whom *Polycarp* . . .	At this time *very severe persecutions having disturbed* (ἀναθορυβησάντων) *Asia*, *Polycarp* is perfected by *martyrdom* . . . and in the same writing concerning him were attached other martyrdoms . . . and next in order (ἑξῆς) memoirs of *others* (ἄλλων) also, who were martyred *in Pergamum*, a city of Asia, *are extant* (φέρεται), Carpus and PAPYLUS, and a woman Agathonice. . . .
and *in Pergamum others* (ἕτεροι), among whom was PAPIAS and many others (ἄλλοι), whose martyrdoms *are extant* (φέρονται) also in writing. . . .	
Justin, a philosopher of the word received among us (τοῦ καθ' ἡμᾶς λόγου), *having presented a second book in defence of the doctrines received among us* to Marcus Aurelius and Antoninus Verus, the emperors, *is decorated* not long after *with the divine* crown of *martyrdom, Crescens* accusing (?) him.	And at the same time with these (κατὰ τούτους) *Justin* also, who was mentioned shortly before by us, *having presented a second book in defence of the doctrines received among us* to the aforementioned rulers, *is decorated with divine martyrdom*, a philosopher *Crescens* . . . having hatched the plot against him, etc.

The sequence of events, and the correspondence of individual phrases, alike show that the compiler of this Chronicle derived his information from the History of Eusebius[2]. But either he or his transcriber has substituted a well known name, *Papias*, for a more obscure name, *Papylus*. If the last letters of the word were blurred or blotted in his copy of Eusebius, nothing would

---

[1] *Chron. Pasch.* p. 481 sq (ed. Bonn.); Euseb. *H. E.* iv. 15.

[2] There is no indication that the author of this Chronicle used any other document in this part besides the History of Eusebius and the extant Martyrology of Polycarp which Eusebius here quotes.

V. PAPIAS OF HIERAPOLIS. 149

be more natural than such a change. It is only necessary to write the two names in uncials, ΠΑΠΙΑΣ ΠΑΠΥΛΟΣ, to judge of its likelihood[1]. This explanation indeed is so obvious, when the passages are placed side by side, that one can only feel surprised at its not having been pointed out before. Thus the martyrdom of Papias, with its chronological perplexities (such as they are), disappears from history; and we may dismiss the argument of the author of *Supernatural Religion*, that 'a writer who suffered martyrdom under Marcus Aurelius (c. A.D. 165) can scarcely have been a hearer of the Apostles[2].'

Thus we are left to infer the date of Papias entirely from the notices of his friends and contemporaries; but these will assist us to a very fair approximation. (1) He was a hearer of at least two personal disciples of Christ, Aristion and the Presbyter John. If we suppose that they were among the youngest disciples of our Lord, and lived to old age, we shall be doing no violence to probability. Obviously there were in their case exceptional circumstances which rendered intercourse with them possible. If so, they may have been born about A.D. 10 or later, and have died about A.D. 90 or later. In this case their intercourse with Papias may be referred to the years A.D. 85—95, or thereabouts. (2) He was acquainted with the daughters of Philip, who dwelt with their father at Hierapolis, where they died in old age. Whether this Philip was the Apostle, as the earliest writers affirm, or the Evangelist, as others suppose[3], is a question of little moment for my immediate purpose—the date of Papias. In the latter case these daughters would be the same who are mentioned at the time of St Paul's last visit to Jerusalem, A.D. 58, apparently as already grown up to womanhood[4]. On the former supposition they would belong to the same

---

[1] The martyrdom of Papias is combined with that of Polycarp in the Syriac Epitome of the *Chronicon* of Eusebius (p. 216, ed. Schöne). The source of the error is doubtless the same in both cases.

[2] *S. R.* I. p. 448.

[3] I had taken the latter view in an article on Papias which I wrote for the *Contemporary Review* some years before these Essays; but I think now that the Apostle is meant, as the most ancient testimony points to him. I have given my reasons for this change of opinion in *Colossians* p. 45 sq.

[4] Acts xxi. 9.

generation, and probably would be about the same age. As a very rough approximation, we may place their birth about A.D. 30, and their death about A.D. 100—110. (3) Papias is called by Irenæus a 'companion' of Polycarp, whose life (as we saw) extended from A.D. 69 to A.D. 155[1]. The word admits a certain latitude as regards date, though it suggests something approaching to equality in age. But on the whole the notices affecting his relations to Polycarp suggest that he was rather the older man of the two. At all events Eusebius discusses him immediately after Ignatius and Quadratus and Clement, *i.e.* in connection with the fathers who flourished in the reign of Trajan or before; while the notice of Polycarp is deferred till a much later point in the history, where it occurs in close proximity with Justin Martyr[2]. This arrangement indicates at all events that Eusebius had no knowledge of his having been martyred at the same time with Polycarp, or indeed of his surviving to so late a date. Otherwise he would naturally have inserted his account of him in this place. If it is necessary to put the result of these incidental notices in any definite form, we may say that Papias was probably born about A.D. 60—70.

But his work was evidently written at a much later date. He speaks of his personal intercourse with the elders, as a thing of the remote past[3]. He did not write till false interpretations of the Evangelical records had had time to increase and multiply. We should probably not be wrong if we deferred its publication till the years A.D. 130—140, or even later. Our author places it at least as late as the middle of the second century[4].

[1] See above, p. 90.

[2] The chapter relating to Papias is the thirty-ninth of the third book; those relating to Polycarp are the fourteenth and fifteenth of the fourth book, where they interpose between chapters assigned to Justin Martyr and events connected with him.

[3] It is true that he uses the present tense once, ἅ τε 'Αριστίων καὶ ὁ πρεσβύτερος 'Ιωάννης...λέγουσιν [see above, p. 143], and hence it has been inferred that these two persons were still living when the inquiries were instituted. But this would involve a chronological difficulty; and the tense should probably be regarded as a historic present introduced for the sake of variety.

[4] *S. R.* I. p. 444, 'About the middle of the second century.' Elsewhere (II. p. 320) he speaks of Papias as ' flourishing in the second half of the second century.'

The opinions of a Christian writer who lived and wrote at this early date, and had conversed with these first disciples, are not without importance, even though his own mental calibre may have been small. But the speculations of the Tübingen school have invested them with a fictitious interest. Was he, or was he not, as these critics affirm, a Judaic Christian of strongly Ebionite tendencies? The arguments which have been urged in defence of this position are as follows:—

1. In the first place we are reminded that he was a millenarian. The Chiliastic teaching of his work is the subject of severe comment with Eusebius, who accuses him of misinterpreting figurative sayings in the Apostolic writings and assigning to them a literal sense. This tendency appears also in the one passage which Irenæus quotes from Papias. But the answer to this is decisive. Chiliasm is the rule, not the exception, with the Christian writers of the second century; and it appears combined with views the very opposite of Ebionite. It is found in Justin Martyr, in Irenæus, in Tertullian[1]. It is found even in the unknown author of the epistle bearing the name of Barnabas[2], which is stamped with the most uncompromising and unreasoning antagonism to everything Judaic.

2. A second argument is built on the fact that Eusebius does not mention his quoting St Paul's Epistles or other Pauline writings of the Canon. I have already disposed of this argument in an earlier paper on the 'Silence of Eusebius[3].' I have shown that Papias might have quoted St Paul many times, and by name, while nevertheless Eusebius would not have recorded the fact, because it was not required by his principles or consistent with his practice to do so. I have shown that this interpretation of the silence of Eusebius in other cases, where we are able to test it, would lead to results demonstrably and hopelessly wrong. I have pointed out for instance, that it would most certainly conduct us to the conclusion that the

---

[1] Justin Martyr *Dial.* 51 sq (p. 271 sq), 80 sq (p. 307); Irenæus *Hær.* v. 31 sq; Tertullian *adv. Marc.* iii. 24, *de Resurr. Carn.* 24.
[2] *Ep. Barn.* § 15.
[3] See above, p. 32 sq.

152   ON SUPERNATURAL RELIGION.

writer of the Ignatian Epistles was an Ebionite—a conclusion diametrically opposed to the known facts of the case[1].

3. Lastly, it is argued that Papias was an Ebionite, because he quoted the Gospel according to the Hebrews. In the first place, however, the premiss is highly questionable. Eusebius does not say, as in other cases, that Papias 'uses' this Gospel, or that he 'sets down facts from' it[2], but he writes that Papias relates 'a story about a woman accused of many sins before the Lord' (doubtless the same which is found in our copies of St John's Gospel, vii. 53—viii. 11), and he adds 'which the Gospel according to the Hebrews contains[3].' This does not imply that Papias derived it thence, but only that Eusebius found it there. Papias may have obtained it, like the other stories to which Eusebius alludes, 'from oral tradition' (ἐκ παραδόσεως ἀγράφου). But, even if it were directly derived thence, the conclusion does not follow from the premiss. The Gospel according to the Hebrews is quoted both by Clement of Alexandria and by Origen, though these two fathers accepted our four Gospels alone as canonical[4]. It may even be quoted, as Jerome asserts that it is, and as the author himself believes[5], by the writer of

---

[1] See above, p. 41 sq.

[2] These are the expressions employed elsewhere of this Gospel; *H. E.* iii. 25, 27; iv. 22.

[3] *H. E.* iii. 39 ἦν τὸ κατ' Ἑβραίους εὐαγγέλιον περιέχει.

[4] Clem. *Strom.* ii. 9 (p. 453). Our author says, 'Clement of Alexandria quotes it [the Gospel according to the Hebrews] with quite the same respect as the other Gospels' (*S. R.* I. p. 422). He cannot have remembered, when he wrote this, that Clement elsewhere refuses authority to a saying in an Apocryphal Gospel because 'we do not find it in the four Gospels handed down to us' (*Strom.* iii. 13, p. 553). 'Origen,' writes our author again, 'frequently made use of the Gospel according to the Hebrews' (*l. c.*). Yes; but Origen draws an absolute line of demarcation between our four Gospels and the rest. He even illustrates the relation of these Canonical Gospels to the Apocryphal by that of the true prophets to the false under the Jewish dispensation. *Hom. I. in Luc.* (III. p. 932). Any reader unacquainted with the facts would carry away a wholly false impression from our author's account of the use made of the Gospel according to the Hebrews.

[5] *S. R.* I. pp. 272 sq, 332 sq. The fact that Eusebius did not know the source of this quotation (*H. E.* iii. 36), though he was well acquainted with the Gospel according to the Hebrews, seems to me to render this very doubtful.

V. PAPIAS OF HIERAPOLIS. 153

the Ignatian letters, a most determined anti-Ebionite. If Papias had cited the Gospel according to the Hebrews only once, Eusebius would have mentioned the fact, because he made it his business to record these exceptional phenomena; whereas he would have passed over any number of quotations from the Canonical Gospels in silence.

As all these supposed tokens of Ebionite tendencies have failed, we are led to inquire whether any light is thrown on this question from other quarters.

And here his name is not altogether unimportant. Papias was bishop of Hierapolis, and apparently a native of this place. At all events he seems to have lived there from youth; for his acquaintance with the daughters of Philip, who resided in this city, must have belonged to the earlier period of his life. Now Papias was a designation of the Hierapolitan Zeus[1]; and owing to its association with this god, it appears to have been a favourite name with the people of Hierapolis and the neighbourhood. It occurs several times in coins and inscriptions belonging to this city and district[2]. In one instance we read of a 'Papias, who is also Diogenes,' this latter name 'Zeus-begotten' being apparently regarded as a rough synonyme for the Phrygian word[3]. We find mention also in Galen of a physician belonging to the neighbouring city of Laodicea, who bore this name[4]. Altogether it points to a heathen rather than a Jewish origin.

But more important than his name, from which the inference, though probable, is still precarious[5], are his friendships and associations. Papias, we are told, was a companion of Polycarp[6]. The opinions of Polycarp have been considered in a previous article[7]; and it has there been shown that the

---

[1] Boeckh *Corp. Inscr.* 3817, Παπίᾳ Διῒ σωτῆρι.

[2] Boeckh 3930, 3912a App.: Mionnet IV. p. 301.

[3] Boeckh 3817.

[4] Galen *Op.* XII. p. 799 (ed. Kühn).

[5] One Rabbi Papias is mentioned in the Mishna *Shekalim* iv. 7; *Edaioth* vii. 6. I owe these references to Zunz *Namen der Juden* p. 16.

[6] See above, p. 142.

[7] See above, p. 89 sq.

hypothesis of Ebionite leanings in his case is not only unsupported, but cannot be maintained except by an entire disregard of the evidence, which is of different kinds, and all leads to the opposite conclusion. As regards Papias therefore, it is reasonable to infer, in the absence of direct evidence, that his views were, at all events, in general accordance with his friend's. Moreover, the five books of Papias were read by Irenæus and by Eusebius, as well as by later writers; and, being occupied in interpretation, they must have contained ample evidence of the author's opinions on the main points which distinguished the Ebionite from the Catholic—the view of the Mosaic law, the estimate of the Apostle Paul, the conception of the person of Christ. It is therefore important to observe that Irenæus quotes him with the highest respect, as an orthodox writer and a trustworthy channel of Apostolic tradition. Eusebius again, though he is repelled by his millennarianism, calling him 'a man of very mean capacity,' and evidently seeking to disparage him in every way, has yet no charge to bring against him on these most important points of all. And this estimate of him remains to the last. Anastasius of Sinai for instance, who wrote in the latter half of the sixth century, and who is rigidly and scrupulously orthodox, according to the standard of orthodoxy which had been created by five General Councils, had the work of Papias in his hands. He mentions the author by name twice; and on both occasions he uses epithets expressive of the highest admiration. Papias is to him 'the great,' 'the illustrious[1].'

But indeed Eusebius has left one direct indication of the opinions of Papias, which is not insignificant. He tells us that Papias 'employed testimonies from the First Epistle of John.' How far this involves a recognition of the Fourth Gospel I shall

---

[1] ὁ πάνυ, ὁ πολύς. The first passage will be found in the original Greek in Routh *Rel. Sacr.* I. p. 15 (comp. Migne *Patr. Græc.* lxxxix. p. 860, where only the Latin 'clarissimus' is given); the second in Migne *ib.* p. 961 (comp. Routh *l. c.* p. 16, where again only the Latin 'celebris' is given).

have to consider hereafter. At present it is sufficient to say that this Epistle belongs to the class of writings in our Canon which is the most directly opposed to Ebionism.

It may be said indeed, that Papias was foolish and credulous. But unhappily foolishness and credulity are not characteristic of any one form of Christian belief—or unbelief either.

The work of Papias, as we saw, was entitled, 'Exposition of Oracles of the Lord,' or (more strictly), 'of Dominical Oracles[1].' But what was its nature and purport? Shall we understand the word 'exposition' to mean 'enarration,' or 'explanation'? Was the author's main object to construct a new Evangelical narrative, or to interpret and explain one or more already in circulation? This is a vital point in its bearing on the relation of Papias to our Canonical Gospels. Our author, ignoring what Dr Westcott and others have said on this subject, tacitly assumes the former alternative without attempting to discuss the question. Yet, if this assumption is wrong, a very substantial part of his argument is gone.

The following passage will illustrate the attitude of the author of *Supernatural Religion* towards this question:—

This work was less based on written records of the teaching of Jesus than on that which Papias had been able to collect from tradition, which he considered more authentic, for, like his contemporary Hegesippus, Papias avowedly prefers tradition to any written works with which he was acquainted[2].

I venture to ask in passing, where our author obtained his information that Hegesippus 'avowedly prefers tradition to any written works with which he was acquainted.' Certainly not from any fragments or notices of this writer which have been hitherto published.

[1] Whether the first word should be singular or plural, 'Exposition' (ἐξήγησις) or 'Expositions' (ἐξηγήσεις), I need not stop to inquire. The important points are (1) that Papias uses λογίων, not λόγων—'oracles,' not 'words' or 'sayings'; (2) that he has κυριακῶν λογίων, not λογίων τοῦ Κυρίου— 'Dominical Oracles,' not 'Oracles of the Lord.' I shall have occasion hereafter to call attention to both these facts, which are significant, as they give a much wider range to his subject-matter than if he had used the alternative expressions.

[2] S. R. I. p. 434 sq.

After quoting the extract from the preface of Papias which has been given above, our author resumes:—

It is clear from this that, even if Papias knew any of our Gospels, he attached little or no value to them, and that he knew absolutely nothing of Canonical Scriptures of the New Testament. His work was evidently intended to furnish a more complete collection of the discourses of Jesus from oral tradition than any previously existing, with his own expositions; and this is plainly indicated by his own words, and by the title of his work, Λογίων κυριακῶν ἐξήγησις[1].

'The natural and only reasonable course,' he adds in a note, 'is to believe the express declaration of Papias, more especially as it is made, in this instance, as a prefatory statement of his belief.' He has appealed to Cæsar, and to Cæsar he shall go.

What then is the natural interpretation of the title 'Exposition of Oracles of' (or 'relating to') 'the Lord'? Would any one, without a preconceived theory, imagine that 'exposition' here meant anything else but explanation or interpretation? It is possible indeed, that the original word ἐξήγησις might, in other connections, be used in reference to a narrative, but its common and obvious sense is the same which it bears when adopted into English as 'exegesis.' In other words, it expresses the idea of a commentary on some text. The expression has an exact parallel, for instance, in the language of Eusebius when, speaking of Dionysius of Corinth, he says that this writer introduces into his letter to the Church of Amastris 'expositions of Divine Scriptures' (γραφῶν θείων ἐξηγήσεις), or when he says that Irenæus quotes a certain 'Apostolic elder' and gives his 'expositions of Divine Scriptures' (the same expression as before)[2]. It is used more than once in this sense, and it is not used in any other, as we shall see presently, by Irenæus[3].

---

[1] So again, I. p. 484 sq, 'Whatever books Papias knew, however, it is certain, from his own express declaration, that he ascribed little importance to them, and preferred tradition as a more reliable source of information regarding Evangelical history,' etc. See also II. p. 320 sq.

[2] *H. E.* iv. 23, v. 8.

[3] See below, p. 160.

Moreover Anastasius of Sinai distinctly styles Papias an 'exegete,' meaning thereby, as his context shows, an 'interpreter' of the Holy Scriptures[1].

'The title of his work' therefore does not 'indicate' anything of the kind which our author assumes it to indicate[2]. It does not suggest a more authentic narrative, but a more correct interpretation of an existing narrative. And the same inference is suggested still more strongly, when from the title we turn to the words of the preface; '*But* I will not scruple *also* to give a place *along with my interpretations* (συγκατατάξαι ταῖς ἑρμηνείαις) to all that I learnt carefully and remembered carefully in time past from the elders.' Here the sense of 'exegesis' in the title is explained by the use of the unambiguous word 'interpretations.' But this is not the most important point. The interpretations must have been interpretations of something. Of what then? Certainly not of the oral traditions, for the interpretations are presupposed, and the oral traditions are mentioned subsequently, being introduced to illustrate the interpretations. The words which I have italicised leave no doubt about this. The 'also,' which (by the way) our author omits, has no significance otherwise. The expression 'along with the interpretations' is capable only of one meaning. In other words, the only account which can be given of the passage, consistently with logic and grammar, demands the following sequence:—(1) The text, of which something was doubtless said in the preceding passage, for it is assumed in the extract itself. (2) The interpretations which explained the text, and which were the main object of the work. (3) The oral traditions, which, as the language here shows, were subordinate to the interpretations, and which Papias mentions in a slightly apologetic tone. These oral traditions had obviously a strong attraction for Papias; he introduced them

---

[1] The references will be found above, p. 154.

[2] The proper word, if the work had been what our author supposes, was not ἐξήγησις but διήγησις, which Eusebius uses several times of the anecdotes related by Papias; *H. E.* iii. 39.

frequently to confirm and illustrate his explanations. But only the most violent wresting of language can make them the text or basis of these interpretations[1].

A good example of the method thus adopted by Papias and explained in his preface is accidentally preserved by Irenæus[2]. This father is discoursing on the millennial reign of Christ. His starting point is the saying of our Lord at the last supper, 'I will not drink henceforth of the fruit of this vine, until that day when I drink it new with you in my Father's kingdom.' (Matt. xxvi. 29.) He takes the words literally, and argues that they must imply a terrestrial kingdom, since only men of flesh can drink the fruit of the vine. He confirms this view by appealing to two other sayings of Christ recorded in the Gospels—the one the promise of a recompense in the resurrection of the just to those who call the poor and maimed and lame and blind to their feast (Luke xiv. 13, 14); the other the assurance that those who have forsaken houses or lands for Christ's sake shall receive a hundredfold now *in this present time* (Matt. xix. 29; Mark x. 29, 30; Luke xviii. 30)[3], which last expression, he maintains, can only be satisfied by an earthly reign of Christ. He then attempts to show that the promises to the patriarchs also require the same solution, since hitherto

---

[1] This attempt has recently been made by Weiffenbach *Das Papias-Fragment* p. 16 sq; and it is chiefly valuable as a testimony to the real significance of the words, which can only be set aside by such violent treatment. Weiffenbach is obliged to perform two acts of violence on the sentence: (1) He supposes that there is an anacoluthon, and that the καὶ ὅσα ποτέ here is answered by the words εἰ δέ που καὶ παρηκολουθηκώς, which occur several lines below. (2) He interprets ταῖς ἑρμηνείαις 'the interpretations belonging to them.' Each of these by itself is harsh and unnatural in the extreme; and the combination of the two may be safely pronounced impossible. Even if his grammatical treatment could be allowed, the fact will still remain that the *interpretations are presupposed*. Weiffenbach's constructions of this passage are justly rejected by the two writers who have written on the subject since his essay appeared, Hilgenfeld and Leimbach.

[2] *Hær.* v. 33. 1 sq.

[3] It may be observed in passing, as an illustration of the looseness of early quotations, that this passage, as given by Irenæus, does not accord with any one of the Synoptic Evangelists, but combines features from all the three.

they have not been fulfilled. These, he says, evidently refer to the reign of the just in a renewed earth, which shall be blessed with abundance.

As the elders relate, who saw John the disciple of the Lord, that they had heard from him how the Lord used to teach concerning those times, and to say, 'The days will come, in which vines shall grow, each having ten thousand shoots, and on each shoot ten thousand branches, and on each branch again ten thousand twigs, and on each twig ten thousand clusters, and on each cluster ten thousand grapes, and each grape when pressed shall yield five-and-twenty measures of wine. And when any of the saints shall have taken hold of one of their clusters, another shall cry, "I am a better cluster; take me, bless the Lord through me." Likewise also a grain of wheat shall produce ten thousand heads,' etc. These things Papias, who was a hearer of John and a companion of Polycarp, an ancient worthy, witnesseth in writing in the fourth of his books, for there are five books composed by him. And he added, saying, 'But these things are credible to them that believe.' And when Judas the traitor did not believe, and asked, 'How shall such growths be accomplished by the Lord?' he relates that the Lord said, 'They shall see, who shall come to these [times].'

I shall not stop to inquire whether there is any foundation of truth in this story, and, if so, how far it has been transmuted, as it passed through the hands of the elders and of Papias. It is sufficient for my purpose to remark that we here find just the three elements which the preface of Papias would lead us to expect: *first*, the saying or sayings of Christ recorded in the written Gospels: *secondly*, the interpretation of these sayings, which is characteristically millennial; *thirdly*, the illustrative story, derived from oral tradition, which relates 'what John said,' and to which the author 'gives a place along with his interpretation[1].'

---

[1] The view that Papias took *written* Gospels as the basis of his interpretations is maintained by no one more strongly than by Hilgenfeld in his recent works; *Papias von Hierapolis* (*Zeitschrift*, 1875) p. 238 sq; *Einleitung in das Neue Testament* (1875), pp. 53 sq, 454 sq. But it seems to me that he is not carrying out this view to its logical conclusion, when he still interprets βιβλία of Evangelical narratives, and talks of Papias as holding these written records in little esteem.

So far everything seems clear. But if this be so, what becomes of the disparagement of written Gospels, which is confidently asserted by our author and others? When the preface of Papias is thus correctly explained, the 'books' which he esteems so lightly assume quite a different aspect. They are no longer Evangelical records, but works commenting on such records. The contrast is no longer between oral and written Gospels, but between oral and written *aids to interpretation*. Papias judged rightly that any doctrinal statement of Andrew or Peter or John, or any anecdote of the Saviour which could be traced distinctly to their authority, would be far more valuable to elucidate his text than the capricious interpretations which he found in current books. If his critical judgment had corresponded to his intention, the work would have been highly important.

The leading object of Papias therefore was not to substitute a correct narrative for an imperfect and incorrect, but to counteract a false exegesis by a true. But where did he find this false exegesis? The opening passage of Irenæus supplies the answer. This father describes the Gnostic teachers as 'tampering with the oracles of the Lord (τὰ λόγια Κυρίου), showing themselves bad expositors of things well said' (ἐξηγηταὶ κακοὶ τῶν καλῶς εἰρημένων γινόμενοι)¹. Here we have the very title of Papias' work reproduced. Papias, like Irenæus after him, undertook, we may suppose, to stem the current of Gnosticism. If, while resisting the false and exaggerated spiritualism of the Gnostics, he fell into the opposite error, so that his Chiliastic doctrine was tainted by a somewhat gross materialism, he only offended in the same way as Irenæus, though probably to a greater degree. The Gnostic leaders were in some instances no mean thinkers; but they were almost

---

¹ *Hær.* Præf. 1; see also i. 3. 6: 'Not only do they attempt to make their demonstrations from the Evangelical and Apostolic [writings] by perverting the interpretations and falsifying the expositions (ἐξηγήσεις), but also from the law and the prophets; as . . . being able to wrest what is ambiguous into many [senses] by their exposition' (διὰ τῆς ἐξηγήσεως).

invariably bad exegetes. The Gnostic fragments in Irenæus and Hippolytus are crowded with false interpretations of Christ's sayings as recorded in the Gospels. Simonians, Ophites, Basilideans, Valentinians, Gnostics of all sects, are represented there, and all sin in the same way. These remains are only the accidental waifs and strays of a Gnostic literature which must have been enormous in extent. As by common consent the work of Papias was written in the later years of his life, a very appreciable portion of this literature must have been in existence when he wrote. More especially the elaborate work of Basilides on 'the Gospel,' in twenty-four books, must have been published some years. Basilides flourished, we are told, during the reign of Hadrian[1] (A.D. 117—138). Such a lengthy work would explain the sarcastic allusion in Papias to those 'who have so very much to say' (τοῖς τὰ πολλὰ λέγουσιν)[2], and who are afterwards described as 'teaching foreign commandments[3].' There are excellent reasons for believing this to be the very work from which the fragments quoted by Hippolytus, as from Basilides, are taken[4]. These fragments contain false interpretations of passages from St Luke and St John, as well as from several Epistles of St Paul. But, however this may be, the general character of the work appears from the fact that Clement of Alexandria quotes it under the title of 'Exegetics[5].' It is quite possible too, that the writings of Valentinus were in circulation before Papias wrote, and exegesis was a highly important instrument with him and his school. If we once recognize the fact that Papias wrote when Gnosticism was rampant, the drift of his language becomes clear and consistent.

---

[1] Clem. Alex. *Strom.* vii. 17, p. 898.

[2] Compare also the language of Hippolytus respecting the books of the Naassenes; *Hær.* v. 7, 'These are the heads of very numerous discourses (πολλῶν πάνυ λόγων), which they say that James,' etc.

[3] This same epithet 'foreign' (ἀλλότριος) is applied several times in the Ignatian Epistles to the Gnostic teaching which the writer is combating; *Rom.* inscr., *Trall.* 6, *Philad.* 3.

[4] Reasons are given by Dr Westcott in the fourth edition of his *History of the Canon* p. 288.

[5] *Strom.* iv. 12, p. 599.

This account of the 'books' which Papias disparages seems to follow from the grammatical interpretation of the earlier part of the sentence. And it alone is free from difficulties. It is quite plain for instance, that Eusebius did not understand our Gospels to be meant thereby; for otherwise he would hardly have quoted this low estimate without expostulation or comment. And again, the hypothesis which identifies these 'books' with written Evangelical records used by Papias charges him with the most stupid perversity. It makes him prefer the second-hand report of what Matthew had said about the Lord's discourses to the account of these discourses which Matthew himself had deliberately set down in writing[1]. Such a report might have the highest value outside the written record; but no sane man could prefer a conversation repeated by another to the immediate and direct account of the same events by the person himself. Nor again, is it consistent with the language which Papias himself uses of the one Evangelical document about which (in his extant fragments) he does express an opinion. Of St Mark's record he says that the author 'made no mistake,' and that it was his one anxiety 'not to omit anything that he had heard, or to set down any false statement therein.'

[1] The following passage in *Supernatural Religion* is highly instructive, as showing the inconsistencies involved in the author's view (I. p. 485): 'It is not possible that he [Papias] could have found it better to inquire "what John or Matthew, or what any other of the disciples of the Lord . . . say," if he had known of Gospels such as ours,' ['and believed them to have been' inserted in the Complete Edition] 'actually written by them, deliberately telling him what they had to say. The work of Matthew which he mentions being, however, a mere collection of discourses of Jesus, he might naturally inquire what the Apostle himself said of the history of the Master.' Here the author practically concedes the point for which I am contending, and which elsewhere he resists; for he states that Papias as a sane man must, and as a matter of fact did, prefer *a book* to oral tradition. In other words, he allows that when Papias disparages books (meaning Evangelical records, such as the St Matthew of Papias was on *any* showing), he cannot intend all books of this class, but only such as our author himself arbitrarily determines that he shall mean. This point is not at all affected by the question whether the St Matthew of Papias did or did not contain doings, as well as sayings, of Christ. The only escape from these perplexities lies in supposing that a wholly different class of books is intended, as I have explained in the text.

Is this the language of one speaking of a book to which 'he attached little or no value¹'?

But, if Papias used written documents as the text for his 'expositions,' can we identify these? To this question his own language elsewhere supplies the answer at least in part. He mentions Evangelical narratives written by Mark and Matthew respectively; and it is therefore the obvious inference that our first two Gospels at all events were used for his work.

An obvious inference, but fiercely contested nevertheless. It has been maintained by many recent critics, that the St Mark of Papias was not our St Mark, nor the St Matthew of Papias our St Matthew; and as the author of *Supernatural Religion* has adopted this view, some words will be necessary in refutation of it.

The language then, which Papias uses to describe the document written by St Mark, is as follows:—

And the elder said this also: Mark, having become the interpreter of Peter, wrote down accurately everything that he remembered, without however recording in order what was either said or done by Christ. For neither did he hear the Lord, nor did he follow Him; but afterwards, as I said, [attended] Peter, who adapted his instructions to the needs [of his hearers] but had no design of giving a connected account of the Lord's oracles [*or* discourses] (ἀλλ' οὐχ ὥσπερ σύνταξιν τῶν κυριακῶν ποιούμενος λογίων *or* λόγων). So then Mark made no mistake, while he thus wrote down some things as he remembered them; for he made it his one care not to omit anything that he heard, or to set down any false statement therein.

Eusebius introduces this passage by a statement that it 'refers to Mark, the writer of the Gospel;' and the authority

---

¹ *S. R.* I. p. 445. It is not likely that our author would appreciate the bearing of these references to St Mark, because, as I pointed out in my first article [see above, p. 8], he mistranslated οὐδὲν ἥμαρτε 'did no wrong,' instead of 'made no mistake,' thus obscuring the testimony of Papias to the perfect accuracy of the result of St Mark's conscientious labours. The translation is altered in the last edition, but the new rendering, 'committed no error in thus writing,' is ambiguous, though not incorrect.

whom Papias here quotes is apparently the Presbyter John, who has been mentioned immediately before.

Now it will be plain, I think, to any reader of common sense, that Papias is giving an account of the circumstances under which the Evangelical narrative in question was composed. There were two phenomena in it which seemed to him to call for explanation. In the first place, it is not a *complete* narrative. In the second place, the events are not recorded in *strict chronological order*. These two phenomena are explained by St Mark's position and opportunities, which were necessarily limited. His work was composed from reminiscences of St Peter's preaching; and, as this preaching was necessarily fragmentary and adapted to the immediate requirements of his hearers (the preacher having no intention of giving a continuous narrative), the writer could not possess either the materials for a complete account or the knowledge for an accurate chronological arrangement. Papias obviously has before him some other Gospel narrative or narratives, which contained sayings or doings of Christ not recorded by St Mark, and moreover related those which he did record in a different order. For this discrepancy he desires to account. The motive and the treatment have an exact parallel, as I shall show hereafter, in the account of the Gospels given by the author of the Muratorian Canon.

This is the plain and simple inference from the passage; and we have only to ask whether this description corresponds with the phenomena of our St Mark. That it does so correspond, I think, can hardly be denied. As regards *completeness*, it is sufficient to call attention to the fact that any one of our Canonical Gospels records many doings, and above all, many sayings, which are omitted in St Mark. As regards *order* again, it may, I believe, safely be said that no writer of a 'Life of Christ' finds himself able to preserve the sequence of events exactly as it stands in St Mark. His account does not profess to be strictly chronological. There are indeed chronological links in the narrative here and there; but throughout considerable parts of our Lord's ministry the successive incidents are quite unconnected by notices of time. In short, the Gospel is just what we should expect, if the author had derived his information in the way reported by the Presbyter. But our author objects, that it 'does not depart in any important degree from the order of the other two Synoptics,' and that it 'throughout has the most evident character of orderly arrangement[1].' Persons may differ as to what is important or unimportant; but if the reader will refer to any one of the common harmonies, those of Anger and Tischendorf for instance, he will see that constant transpositions are necessary in one or other of the Synoptic Gospels to bring them into accordance, and will be able to judge for himself how far this statement is true. 'Orderly arrangement' of some sort, no doubt, there is; but it is just such as lay within the reach of a person obtaining his knowledge at second-hand in this way. Our author himself describes it lower down as 'artistic and orderly arrangement.' I shall not quarrel with the phrase, though somewhat exaggerated. Any amount of 'artistic arrangement' is compatible with the notice of Papias, which refers only to historical sequence. 'Artistic arrangement' does not require the direct knowledge of an eye-witness. It will be observed however, that our author speaks of a comparison with 'the order of the other two Synoptics.' But what, if the comparison which Papias had in view was wholly different? What, if he adduced this testimony of the Presbyter to explain how St Mark's Gospel differed not from another Synoptic narrative, but *from St John*? I shall return to this question at a later point in these investigations.

Our author is no stranger to the use of strong words: 'If our present Gospel,' he writes, 'cannot be proved to be the very work referred to by the Presbyter John, as most certainly it cannot, the evidence of Papias becomes fatal to the claims of the second Canonical Gospel[2].' The novelty of the logic in this sentence rivals the boldness of the assumption.

[1] I. p. 456.
[2] I. p. 460. [So too ed. 6; but struck out in the Complete Edition.]

Yet so entirely satisfied is he with the result of his arguments, that he does not consider it 'necessary to account for the manner in which the work to which the Presbyter John referred disappeared, and the present Gospel according to Mark became substituted for it[1].' But others are of a more inquiring turn of mind. They will be haunted with this difficulty, and will not be able thus to shelve the question. They will venture to ask how it is that not any, even the faintest, indication of the existence of this other Mark can be traced in all the remains of Christian antiquity. They will observe too, that if the date which our author himself adopts be correct, Irenæus was already grown up to manhood when Papias wrote his work. They will remember that Irenæus received his earliest Christian education from a friend of Papias, and that his great authorities in everything which relates to Christian tradition are the associates and fellow-countrymen of Papias. They will remark that, having the work of Papias in his hands and holding it in high esteem, he nevertheless is so impressed with the conviction that our present four Gospels, and these only, had formed the title-deeds of the Church from the beginning, that he ransacks heaven and earth for analogies to this sacred number. They will perhaps carry their investigations further, and discover that Irenæus not only possessed our St Mark's Gospel, but possessed it also with its present ending, which, though undoubtedly very early, can hardly have been part of the original work. They will then pass on to the Muratorian author, who probably wrote some years before Irenæus, and, remembering that Irenæus represents the combined testimony of Asia Minor and Gaul, they will see that they have here the representative of a different branch of the Church, probably the Roman. Yet the Muratorian writer agrees with Irenæus in representing our four Gospels, and these only, as the traditional inheritance of the Church; for though the fragment is mutilated at the beginning, so that the names of the first two Evangelists have disappeared,

[1] I. p. 459.

the identity cannot be seriously questioned. They will then extend their horizon to Clement in Alexandria and Tertullian in Africa; and they will find these fathers also possessed by the same belief. Impressed with this convergency of testimony from so many different quarters, they will be utterly at a loss to account for the unanimity of these early witnesses—all sharing in the same delusion, all ignorant that a false Mark has been silently substituted for the true Mark during their own lifetime, and consequently assuming as an indisputable fact that the false Mark was received by the Church from the beginning. And they will end in a revolt against the attempt of our author to impose upon them with his favourite commonplace about the 'thoroughly uncritical character of the fathers.'

Indeed, they will begin altogether to suspect this wholesale denunciation; for they will observe that our author is convicted out of his own context. They will remark how he repels an inconvenient question of Tischendorf by a scornful reference to 'the frivolous character of the *only* criticism in which they [Eusebius and the other Christian Fathers] *ever* indulged[1].' Yet they will remember at the same time to have read in this very chapter on Papias a highly intelligent criticism of Eusebius, with which this father confronts a statement of Irenæus, and which our author himself adopts as conclusive[2]. They will recall also, in this same context, a reference to a passage in Dionysius of Alexandria, where this 'great Bishop' anticipates by nearly sixteen centuries the criticisms of our own age concerning the differences of style between the Fourth Gospel and the Apocalypse[3].

From St Mark we pass to St Matthew. Papias has something to tell us of this Gospel also; but here again we are asked to believe that we have a case of mistaken identity.

After the notice relating to St Mark, Eusebius continues:—

But concerning Matthew, the following statement is made [by

---

[1] I. p. 460. [So also ed. 6; the word 'ever' disappears in the Complete Edition.]

[2] I. p. 447. This criticism is given above, p. 143 sq.

[3] I. p. 447.

Papias]: 'So then Matthew (Ματθαῖος μὲν οὖν) composed the Oracles in the Hebrew language, and each one interpreted them as he could.'

The assumption that this statement, like the former, was made on the authority of the Presbyter, depends solely on the close proximity in which the two extracts stand in Eusebius. It must therefore be regarded as highly precarious. In Papias' own work the two extracts may have been wide apart. Indeed the opening particles in the second passage prove conclusively that it cannot have followed immediately on the first. Just as the ὡς ἔφην in the extract relating to St Mark showed that it was a fragment torn from its context, so we have the similar evidence of a violent severance here in the words μὲν οὖν. The ragged edge is apparent in both cases[1]. This fact must be borne in mind in any criticisms which the passages suggest.

In this extract then Papias speaks of a state of things in which each man interpreted the original Hebrew for himself. There can have been no authoritative Greek Gospel of St Matthew at that time, if his account be correct. So far his meaning is clear. But it is equally clear that the time which he is here contemplating is not the time when he writes his book, but some earlier epoch. He says not 'interprets,' but 'interpreted.' This past tense 'interpreted,' be it observed, is not the tense of Eusebius reporting Papias, but of Papias himself. Everything depends on this distinction; yet our author deliberately ignores it. He does indeed state the grammatical argument correctly, as given by others:—

Some consider that Papias or the Presbyter use the verb in the

---

[1] The manner in which Eusebius will tear a part of a passage from its context is well illustrated by his quotation from Irenæus, ii. 22. 5:—'A quadragesimo autem et quinquagesimo anno declinat jam in aetatem seniorem, quam habens Dominus noster docebat, sicut Evangelium [et omnes seniores testantur, qui in Asiâ apud Joannem discipulum Domini convenerunt] id ipsum [tradidisse eis Joannem. Permansit autem cum eis usque ad Trajani tempora]. Quidam autem eorum non solum Joannem, sed et alios Apostolos viderunt, et haec eadem ab ipsis audierunt et testantur de hujusmodi relatione.' Eusebius gives only the part which I have enclosed in brackets: *H. E.* iii. 23.

past tense, ἡρμήνευσε, as contrasting the time when it was necessary for each to interpret as best he could with the period when, from the existence of a recognized translation, it was no longer necessary for them to do so[1].

Yet a few lines after, when he comes to comment upon it, he can write as follows:—

The statement [of Papias] is perfectly simple and direct, and it is at least quite clear that it conveys the fact that translation was requisite: and, as each one translated 'as he was able,' that no recognized translation existed to which all might have recourse. There is absolutely not a syllable which warrants the conclusion that Papias was acquainted with an authentic Greek version, although it is possible that he may have known of the existence of some Greek translations of no authority. The words used, however, imply that, if he did, he had no respect for any of them[2].

Our author has here imposed upon himself by a grammatical trick. Hard pressed by the argument, he has covered his retreat under an ambiguous use of tenses. The words 'each one translated as he was able' are perfectly clear in the direct language of Papias; but adopted without alteration into the oblique statement of our author, they are altogether obscure. 'Translation *was* requisite.' Yes, but at what time? The fact is that no careful reader can avoid asking why Papias writes 'interpreted,' and not 'interprets.' The natural answer is that the necessity of which he speaks had already passed away. In other words, it implies the existence of a recognized Greek translation, *when Papias wrote*. Whence our author got his information that Papias 'had no respect for' any such translation, it is difficult to say. Certainly not from 'the words used'; for Papias says nothing about it, and we only infer its existence from the suppressed contrast implied in the past tense.

But, if a Greek St Matthew existed in the time of Papias, we are forbidden by all considerations of historical probability to suppose that it was any other than our St Matthew. As in

[1] I. p. 474.
[2] [I. p. 475. So also ed. 6; modified in the Complete Edition.]

the case of St Mark, so here the contrary hypothesis is weighted with an accumulation of improbabilities. The argument used there might be repeated *totidem verbis* here. It was enough that we were asked to accept the theory of a mistaken identity once; but the same demand is renewed again. And the improbability of this double mistake is very far greater than the sum of the improbabilities in the two several cases, great as this sum would be.

The testimony of Papias therefore may be accepted as valid so far as regards the recognition of our St Matthew in his own age. But it does not follow that his account of the origin was correct. It may or may not have been. This is just what we cannot decide, because we do not know exactly what he said. It cannot be inferred with any certainty from this fragmentary excerpt of Eusebius, what Papias supposed to be the exact relation of the Greek Gospel of St Matthew which he had before him to the Hebrew document of which he speaks. Our author indeed says that our First Gospel bears all the marks of an original, and cannot have been translated from the Hebrew at all. This, I venture to think, is far more than the facts will sustain. If he had said that it is not a homogeneous Greek version of a homogeneous Hebrew original, this would have been nearer to the truth. But we do not know that Papias said this. He may have expressed himself in language quite consistent with the phenomena. Or on the other hand he may, as Hilgenfeld supposes, have made the mistake which some later fathers made, of thinking that the Gospel according to the Hebrews was the original of our St Matthew. In the absence of adequate data it is quite vain to conjecture. But meanwhile we are not warranted in drawing any conclusion unfavourable either to the accuracy of Papias or to the identity of the document itself.

Our author however maintains that the Hebrew St Matthew of which Papias speaks was not a Gospel at all—*i.e.* not a narrative of our Lord's life and ministry—but a mere collection of discourses or sayings. It is urged that the expression,

'Matthew compiled the oracles' (ξυνεγράψατο τὰ λόγια), requires this interpretation. If this explanation were correct, the notice would suggest that Papias looked upon the Greek Gospel as not merely a translation, but an enlargement, of the original document. In this case it would be vain to speculate how or when or by whom he supposed it to be made; for either he did not give this information, or (if he did) Eusebius has withheld it. This hypothesis was first started, I believe, by Schleiermacher, and has found favour with not a few critics of opposite schools. Attempts have been made from time to time to restore this supposed document by disengaging those portions of our First Gospel, which would correspond to this idea, from their historical setting. The theory is not without its attractions: it promises a solution of some difficulties; but hitherto it has not yielded any results which would justify its acceptance.

Our author speaks of those critics who reject it as 'in very many cases largely influenced by the desire to see in these λόγια our actual Gospel according to St. Matthew[1].' This is true in the same sense in which it is true that those who take opposite views are largely influenced in very many cases by the opposite desire. But such language is only calculated to mislead. By no one is the theory of a collection of discourses more strongly denounced than by Bleek[2], who apparently considers that Papias did not here refer to a Greek Gospel at all. 'There is nothing,' he writes, 'in the manner in which Papias expresses himself to justify this supposition; he would certainly have expressed himself as he does, if he meant an historical work like our New Testament Gospels, if he were referring to a writing whose contents were those of our Greek Gospel according to Matthew.' Equally decided too is the language of Hilgenfeld[3], who certainly would not be swayed by any bias in this direction.

[1] I. p. 465.
[2] *Introduction to the New Testament*, I. p. 109 sq (Eng. Transl.), where there is more to the same effect.
[3] *Einleitung in das Neue Testament*, p. 456 sq. 'An eine blosse Aufzeich-

Indeed this theory is encumbered with the most serious difficulties. In the first place, there is no notice or trace elsewhere of any such 'collection of discourses.' In the next place, all other early writers from Pantænus and Irenæus onwards, who allude to the subject, speak of St Matthew as writing a Gospel, not a mere collection of sayings, in Hebrew. If they derived their information in every case from Papias, it is clear that they found no difficulty in interpreting his language so as to include a narrative: if they did not (as seems more probable, and as our author himself holds[1]), then their testimony is all the more important, as of independent witnesses to the existence of a Hebrew St Matthew, which was a narrative, and not a mere collection of discourses.

Nor indeed does the expression itself drive us to any such hypothesis. Hilgenfeld, while applying it to our First Gospel, explains it on grounds which at all events are perfectly tenable. He supposes that Papias mentions only the *sayings* of Christ, not because St Matthew recorded nothing else, but because he himself was concerned only with these, and St Matthew's Gospel, as distinguished from St Mark's, was the great storehouse of materials for his purpose[2]. I do not however think that this is the right explanation. It supposes that only λόγοι ('discourses' or 'sayings') could be called λόγια ('oracles'); but usage does not warrant this restriction. Thus we are expressly told that the Scriptures recognized by Ephraem, Patriarch of Antioch (about A.D. 525—545), consisted of 'the Old Testament and the Oracles of the Lord (τὰ κυριακὰ λόγια) and the Preachings of the Apostles[3].' Here we have the very same expression which occurs in Papias; and it is obviously employed as a synonyme for the Gospels. Our author does not mention this

---

nung der Reden Jesu hat er nicht einmal gedacht... Nicht eine blosse Redensammlung, sondern ein vollständiges Evangelium lässt schon Papias den Matthäus hebräisch geschrieben haben.' See also pp. 54 sq, 454 sq.

[1] I. p. 470 sq, 'That Irenæus did not derive his information solely from Papias may be inferred,' etc. ... 'The evidence furnished by Pantænus is certainly independent of Papias.'

[2] *Einleitung* pp. 54 sq, 456 sq.

[3] Photius *Bibl.* 228.

close parallel, but he alleges that 'however much the signification [of the expression 'the oracles,' τὰ λόγια] became afterwards extended, it was not then at all applied to doings as well as sayings'; and again, that 'there is no linguistic precedent for straining the expression, used at that period, to mean anything beyond a collection of sayings of Jesus which were oracular or divine[1].' This objection, if it has any force, must involve one or both of these two assumptions; *first*, that books which were regarded as Scripture could not at this early date be called oracles, unless they were occupied entirely with divine sayings; *secondly*, that the Gospel of St Matthew in particular could not at this time be regarded as Scripture. Both assumptions alike are contradicted by facts.

The first is refuted by a large number of examples. St Paul, for instance, describes it as the special privilege of the Jews, that they had the keeping of the 'oracles of God' (Rom. iii. 2). Can we suppose that he meant anything else but the Old Testament Scriptures by this expression? Is it possible that he would exclude the books of Genesis, of Joshua, of Samuel and Kings, or only include such fragments of them as professed to give the direct sayings of God? Would he, or would he not, comprise under the term the account of the creation and fall (1 Cor. xi. 8 sq), of the wanderings in the wilderness (1 Cor. x. 1 sq), of Sarah and Hagar (Gal. iv. 21 sq)? Does not the main part of his argument in the very next chapter (Rom. iv.) depend much more on the narrative of God's dealings than of His words? Again, when the author of the Epistle to the Hebrews refers to 'the first principles of the oracles of God' (v. 12), his meaning is explained by his practice; for he elicits the divine teaching quite as much from the history as from the direct precepts of the Old Testament. But, if the language of the New Testament writers leaves any loophole for doubt, this is not the case with their contemporary Philo. In one place he speaks of the words in Deut. x. 9, 'The Lord God

---

[1] I. p. 464. [And so all later editions.]

is his inheritance,' as an 'oracle' (λόγιον); in another he quotes as an 'oracle' (λόγιον) the *narrative* in Gen. iv. 15, 'The Lord God set a mark upon Cain, lest any one finding him should kill him[1].' From this and other passages it is clear that with Philo an 'oracle' is a synonyme for a 'scripture'. Similarly Clement of Rome writes, 'Ye know well the sacred Scriptures, and have studied the oracles of God[2],' and immediately he recalls to their mind the account in Deut. ix. 12 sq, Exod. xxxii. 7 sq, of which the point is not any divine precept or prediction, but *the example of Moses*. A few years later Polycarp speaks in condemnation of those who 'pervert the oracles of the Lord[3].' How much he included under this expression, we cannot say, but it must be observed that he does not write τὰ κυριακὰ λόγια 'the Dominical oracles,' or τὰ λόγια 'the oracles' simply—the two expressions which occur in Papias—but τὰ λόγια τοῦ Κυρίου, 'the oracles of the Lord,' which form of words would more directly suggest the Lord as the speaker. Again Irenæus, denouncing the interpretations of the Scriptures current among the Gnostics, uses the very expression of Papias, τὰ κυριακὰ λόγια[4]; and though he does not define his exact meaning, yet as the 'oracles of God' are mentioned immediately afterwards, and as the first instance of such false interpretation which he gives is not a saying, but an incident in the Gospels—the healing of the ruler's daughter—we may infer that he had no idea of restricting the term to sayings of Christ. Again when we turn to Clement of Alexandria, we find that the Scriptures in one passage are called 'the oracles of truth,' while in another among the good deeds attributed to Ezra is the 'discovery and restoration of the inspired oracles[5].' Similarly Origen

---

[1] *De Conj. erud. grat.* 24 (p. 538); *de Profug.* 11 (p. 555). Elsewhere he says that all things which are written in the sacred books (of Moses) are oracles (χρησμοί) pronounced (χρησθέντες) through him; and he proceeds to distinguish different kinds of λόγια (*Vit. Moys.* iii. 23, p. 163).

[2] Clem. Rom. 53 ἐγκεκύφατε εἰς τὰ λόγια τοῦ [Θεοῦ]. Elsewhere (§ 45) he uses the expression ἐγκύπτειν εἰς τὰς γραφάς.

[3] Polyc. *Phil.* 7.

[4] Iren. *Hær.* i. 8. 1.

[5] Clem. Alex. *Coh. ad Gent.* p. 84 (ed. Potter), *Strom.* i. p. 392.

speaks of the teachings of the Scripture as 'the oracles,' 'the oracles of God¹.' In the context of the latter of the two passages to which I refer, he has clearly stated that he is contemplating the histories, the law, and the prophets alike. So too St Basil uses 'sacred' (or divine) 'oracles,' 'oracles of the Spirit²,' as synonymes for the Scriptures. And this catena of passages might be largely extended.

This wide sense of the word 'oracles' therefore in itself is fully substantiated by examples both before and after the time of Papias. But our author objects that it is not consistent with the usage of Papias himself elsewhere. The examples alleged however fail to prove this. If Papias entitled his work 'Exposition of Oracles of the Lord,' or rather 'of Dominical Oracles,' there is nothing to show that he did not include narrative portions of the Gospels, as well as discourses; though from the nature of the case the latter would occupy the chief place. On the contrary, it is certain from the extant notices that he dealt largely with incidents. And this he would naturally do. By false allegory and in other ways Gnostic teachers misinterpreted the facts, not less than the sayings, of the Gospels; and Papias would be anxious to supply the corrective in the one case as in the other. The second example of its use in Papias certainly does not favour our author's view. This father, as we have seen³, describes St Mark as not writing down 'in order the things said or done by Christ' (οὐ μέντοι τάξει τὰ ὑπὸ τοῦ Χριστοῦ ἢ λεχθέντα ἢ πραχθέντα). This, he states, was not within the Evangelist's power, because he was not a personal disciple of our Lord, but obtained his information from the preaching of Peter, who consulted the immediate needs of his hearers and had 'no intention of giving a consecutive record of the Dominical oracles' (οὐχ ὥσπερ σύνταξιν τῶν κυριακῶν ποιούμενος λογίων). Here the obvious inference is that τὰ κυριακὰ λόγια in the second clause is equivalent to τὰ ὑπὸ τοῦ

---

[1] *De Princ.* iv. 11 (I. p. 168, Delarue), *in Matth.* x. § 6 (III. p. 447).

[2] *Hom.* xi. 5 (II. p. 96); *ib.* xii. 1 (p. 97).

[3] See p. 163.

Χριστοῦ ἢ λεχθέντα ἢ πραχθέντα in the first, just as the σύνταξιν in the second clause corresponds to the τάξει in the first. Our author however, following the lead of those who adopt the same interpretation of 'the oracles,' explains it differently[1].

There is an evident contrast made. Mark wrote ἢ λεχθέντα ἢ πραχθέντα, because he had not the means of writing discourses, but Matthew composed the λόγια. Papias clearly distinguishes the work of Mark, who had written reminiscences of what Jesus had said and done, from that of Matthew, who had made a collection of his discourses[2].

This interpretation depends altogether on the assumption that the extracts relating to St Mark and St Matthew belonged to the same context; but this is only an assumption. Moreover it introduces into the extract relating to St Mark a contrast which is not only not suggested by the language, but is opposed to the order of the words. The leading idea in this extract is the absence of strict historical sequence in St Mark's narrative. Accordingly the emphatic word in the clause in question is σύνταξιν, which picks up the previous τάξει, and itself occupies the prominent position in its own clause. If our author's interpretation were correct, the main idea would be a contrast between a work relating deeds as well as sayings, and a work relating sayings only; and λογίων, as bringing out this idea, would demand the most emphatic place (οὐχ ὥσπερ τῶν λογίων σύνταξιν ποιούμενος); whereas in its present position it is entirely subordinated to other words in the clause.

The examples quoted above show that 'the oracles' (τὰ λόγια) can be used as co-extensive with 'the Scriptures' (αἱ γραφαί) in the time of Papias. Hence it follows that 'the Dominical Oracles' (τὰ κυριακὰ λόγια) can have as wide a meaning as 'the Dominical Scriptures' (*Dominicae Scripturae, αἱ κυριακαὶ γρα-*

---

[1] I. p. 466.
[2] Our author has not mentioned the various reading λόγων for λογίων here, though Hilgenfeld speaks of it as the reading of the 'best editions.' If it were correct, it would upset his argument; but the most recent critical editor, Laemmer, has adopted λογίων.

φαί)—an expression occurring in Irenæus and in Dionysius of Corinth[1]—or, in other words, that the Gospels may be so called. If any difficulty therefore remains, it must lie in the *second* of the two assumptions which I mentioned above—namely, that no Evangelical record could at this early date be invested with the authority implied by the use of this term, or (in other words) could be regarded as Scripture. This assumption again is contradicted by facts. The Gospel of St Matthew is twice quoted in the Epistle of Barnabas, and in the first passage the quotation is introduced by the common formula of Scriptural reference—'as it is written[2].' To what contortions our author puts his argument, when dealing with that epistle, in the vain attempt to escape the grip of hard fact, I shall have occasion to show when the proper time comes[3]. At present it is sufficient to say that the only ground for refusing to accept St Matthew as the source of these two quotations, which are found there, is the assumption that St Matthew could not at this early date be regarded as 'Scripture.' In other words, it is a *petitio principii*. But the Epistle ascribed to Barnabas, on any showing, was written before the date which our author himself assigns to the Exposition of Papias. Some place it as early as A.D. 70, or thereabouts; some as late as A.D. 120; the majority incline to the later years of the first, or the very beginning of the second century. If therefore this Gospel could be quoted as Scripture in Barnabas, it could *à fortiori* be described as 'oracles' when Papias wrote.

[1] Iren. *Hær.* v. 20. 2; Dion. Cor. in Euseb. *H. E.* iv. 23.

[2] *Ep. Barn.* 4, 5. The bearing of this fact on the testimony of Papias is pointed out in an able and scholarly article on *Supernatural Religion* in the April [1875] number of the *Dublin Review*, p. 403.

[3] [The Essay on the Epistle of Barnabas was never written; see the Preface to this Reprint.]

VI.—PAPIAS OF HIERAPOLIS.

Continued.

[OCTOBER, 1875.]

IT has been seen that, in the meagre fragments of his work which alone survive, Papias mentions by name the Evangelical records of St Matthew and St Mark. With the Third and Fourth Gospels the case is different. Eusebius has not recorded any reference to them by Papias, and our author therefore concludes that they were unknown to this early writer. I have shown in a previous paper on the 'Silence of Eusebius[1],' that this inference is altogether unwarrantable. I have pointed out that the assumption on which it rests is not justified by the principles which Eusebius lays down for himself as his rule of procedure[2], while it is directly refuted by almost every instance in which he quotes a writing now extant, and in which therefore it is possible to apply a test. I have proved that, as regards the four Gospels, Eusebius only pledges himself to give, and (as a matter of fact) only does give, traditions of interest respecting them. I have proved also that it is not consistent either with his principles or with his practice to refer to mere quotations, however numerous, even though they are given by name. Papias therefore might have quoted the Third Gospel any number of times as written by Luke the companion of Paul, and the Fourth Gospel not less frequently as written by John the Apostle; and Eusebius would not have cared to record the fact.

All this I have proved, and the author of *Supernatural*

[1] See above, p. 34 sq.   [2] [See above, pp. 36 sq, 46 sq.]

Religion is unable to disprove it. In the preface to his last edition[1] he does indeed devote several pages to my argument; but I confess that I am quite at a loss to understand how any writer can treat the subject as it is there treated by him. Does he or does he not realize the distinction which underlies the whole of my argument—the distinction between *traditions about* the Gospels on the one hand, and *quotations from* the Gospels on the other?

At times it appears as if this distinction were clearly before him. He quotes a passage from my article, in which it is directly stated[2], and even argues upon it. I gave a large number of instances where ancient authors whose writings are extant do quote our Canonical Scriptures, sometimes directly, sometimes indirectly, sometimes anonymously, sometimes by name, and where nevertheless Eusebius does not mention the circumstance. This is his mode of dealing with such facts—

That he omitted to mention a reference to the Epistle to the Corinthians in the Epistle of Clement of Rome, or the reference by Theophilus to the Gospel of John, and other supposed quotations, might be set down as much to oversight as intention[3].

Does it not occur to him that he is here cutting the throat of his own argument? The reference to the First Epistle to the Corinthians is the single direct reference by name to the Canonical Scriptures of the New Testament in Clement; the reference to the Gospel of St John again is the single direct reference by name in the extant work of Theophilus. What would be said of a traveller who paid a visit to the Gorner-Grat for the express purpose of observing and recording the appearance of the Alps from this commanding position, and returned from his survey without having noticed either the Matterhorn or Monte Rosa? If Eusebius could have overlooked these most obvious notices, he could have overlooked

---

[1] [Preface to *S. R.* ed. 6, pp. xi—xxiii.]

[2] [The passage quoted occurs above, p. 38 'Eusebius therefore proposes—however precise.']

[3] Preface to *S. R.* ed. 6, p. xv.

anything. His gross and habitual carelessness would then cover any omission. Nor again, I venture to think, will our author deceive any fairly intelligent person, who has read my article with moderate care, by his convenient because cloudy expression, 'other supposed quotations.' I need only remind my readers that among these 'other supposed quotations' are included (to take only one instance) numerous and direct references by name to the Acts of the Apostles and to eleven Epistles of St Paul in Irenæus[1], of which Eusebius says not a word, and they will judge for themselves by this example what dependence can be placed on the author's use of language.

But our author speaks of the 'ability' of my article, as a reason for discrediting its results. I am much obliged to him for the compliment, but I must altogether decline it. It is the ability of facts which he finds so inconvenient. I brought to the task nothing more than ordinary sense. I found our author declaring, as others had declared before him, that under certain circumstances Eusebius would be sure to act in a particular way. I turned to Eusebius himself, and I found that, whenever we are able to test his action under the supposed circumstances, he acts in precisely the opposite way. I discovered that he not only sometimes, but systematically, ignores mere quotations from the four Gospels and the Acts and the thirteen Epistles of St Paul, however numerous and however precise. I cannot indeed recollect a single instance where he adduces a quotation for the mere purpose of authenticating any one of these books.

But our author asks[2],

Is it either possible or permissible to suppose that, had Papias known anything of the other two Gospels [the third and fourth], he would not have inquired about them from the presbyters and recorded their information? And is it either possible or permissible to suppose that if Papias had recorded any similar information regarding the composition of the third and fourth Gospels, Eusebius would have omitted to quote it?

To the first question I answer that it is both possible and

[1] [See above, p. 44 sq.]   [2] Preface to ed. 6, p. xxi.

permissible to make this supposition. I go beyond this, and say that it is not only possible and permissible, but quite as probable as the opposite alternative. In the absence of all definite knowledge respecting the motive of Papias, I do not see that we are justified in giving any preference to either hypothesis over the other. There is no reason for supposing that Papias made these statements respecting St Mark and St Matthew in his preface rather than in the body of his work, or that they were connected and continuous, or that he had any intention of giving an exhaustive account of all the documents with which he was acquainted. On the contrary, these notices bear every mark of being incidental. If we take the passage relating to St Mark for instance, the natural inference is that Papias in the course of his expositions stumbled on a passage where this Evangelist omitted something which was recorded by another authority, or gave some incident in an order different from that which he found elsewhere, and that in consequence he inserted the notice of the presbyter respecting the composition of this Gospel, to explain the divergence. He might, or might not, have had opportunities of inquiring from the presbyters respecting the Gospel of St Luke. They might, or might not, have been able to communicate information respecting it, beyond the fact which every one knew, and which therefore no one cared to repeat, that it was written by a companion of St Paul. He might, or might not, have found himself confronted with a difficulty which led him to repeat his information, assuming he had received any from them.

As regards the second question, I agree with our author. I am indeed surprised that after ascribing such incredible carelessness to Eusebius as he has done a few pages before, he should consider it impossible and impermissible to suppose him guilty of any laches here. But I myself have a much higher opinion of the care manifested by Eusebius in this matter. So far as I can see, it would depend very much on the nature of the information, whether he would care to repeat it. If Papias had reported any 'similar' information respecting the two last Gospels, I should certainly expect Eusebius to record it. But if (to give an illustration) Papias had merely said of the fourth Evangelist that 'John the disciple of the Lord wished by the publication of the Gospel to root out that error which had been disseminated among men by Cerinthus, and long before by those who are called Nicolaitans,' or language to that effect, it would be no surprise to me if Eusebius did not reproduce it; because Irenæus uses these very words of the fourth Gospel[1], and Eusebius does not allude to the fact.

But our author argues that, 'if there was a Fourth Gospel in his knowledge, he [Papias] must have had something to tell about it[2].' Perhaps so, but it does not follow either that he should have cared to tell this something gratuitously, or that any occasion should have arisen which led him to tell it. Indeed, this mode of arguing altogether ignores the relations in which the immediate circle addressed by Papias stood to St John. It would have been idle for Papias to have said, as Irenæus says, 'John the disciple of the Lord, who also lay upon His breast, published his Gospel, while living in Ephesus of Asia[3].' It would have been as idle as if a writer in this Review were to vouchsafe the information that 'Napoleon I was a great ruler of the French who made war against England.' On the hypothesis of the genuineness of the Fourth Gospel, such information would have been altogether superfluous. Papias might incidentally, when quoting the Gospel, have introduced his quotation in words from which a later generation could gather these facts; but he is not at all likely to have communicated them in the form of a direct statement. And, if he did not, there is no reason to think that Eusebius would have quoted the passage.

So far however, our author seems to recognize the distinction which I drew between stories about, and quotations from,

[1] Iren. *Hær.* iii. 11. 1.
[2] Preface to ed. 6, p. xxi. So again he says (II. p. 323): 'It is scarcely probable that when Papias collected from the presbyter the facts concerning Matthew and Mark he would not also have inquired about the Gospel of John, if he had known it, and recorded what he had heard,' etc.
[3] Iren. *Hær.* iii. 1. 1.

VI. PAPIAS OF HIERAPOLIS. 183

the Gospels. But elsewhere, when the practical consequences become inconvenient, he boldly ignores it. Take, for instance, the following passage:—

The only inference which I care to draw from the silence of Eusebius is precisely that which Dr Lightfoot admits that, both from his promise and his practice, I am entitled to deduce. When any ancient writer 'has something to *tell about*' the Gospels, 'any *anecdote* of interest respecting them,' Eusebius will record it. This is the only information of the slightest value to this work which could be looked for in these writers[1].

What? does our author seriously maintain that, supposing Papias to have quoted the Fourth Gospel several times by name as the work of John the Apostle, this fact would not be of 'the slightest value' in its bearing on the question at issue between us—the antiquity and genuineness of that Gospel—because, forsooth, he did not give any anecdote respecting its composition?

So again a few pages later, he writes—

Eusebius fulfils his pledge, and states what disputed works were used by Hegesippus and what he said about them, and one of these was the Gospel according to the Hebrews. He does not, however, record a remark of any kind regarding our Gospels, and the legitimate inference, and it is the only one I care to draw, is that Hegesippus did not say anything about them[2].

Yes; 'did not say anything *about* them,' in the sense of not recording any traditions respecting them, though he may have quoted them scores of times and by name. If this is the only inference which our author cares to draw, I cannot object. But it is not the inference which his words would suggest to the incautious reader; and it is not the inference which will assist his argument at all. Moreover this passage ignores another distinction, which I showed to be required by the profession and practice alike of Eusebius. Eusebius relates of Hegesippus that he 'sets down some things from the Gospel according to the Hebrews[3];' but, as our author correctly says, he does not

---

[1] Preface to ed. 6, p. xvi.
[2] Preface to ed. 6, p. xix.
[3] Euseb. *H. E.* iv. 22.

directly mention his using our four Canonical Gospels. This is entirely in accordance with his procedure elsewhere. I showed that he makes it his business to note every single quotation from an apocryphal source, whereas he deliberately ignores any number of quotations from the Canonical Gospels, the Acts, and the Pauline Epistles. How else (to take a single instance) can we explain the fact that, in dealing with Irenæus, he singles out the one anonymous quotation from the Shepherd of Hermas[1], and is silent about the two hundred quotations (a very considerable number of them by name) from the Pauline Epistles?

But the passage which I have just given is not the only one in which the unwary reader will be entirely misled by this juggle between two meanings of the preposition 'about'. Thus our author has in several instances[2] tacitly altered the form of expression in his last edition; but the alteration is made in such a way as, while satisfying the letter of my distinction, to conceal its true significance. Thus he writes of Dionysius[3]—

Earlier Editions.	Last Edition[4].
It is certain that, had Dionysius *mentioned* books of the New Testament, Eusebius would, as usual, have stated the fact.	It is certain that had Dionysius *said anything about* books of the New Testament, Eusebius would, as usual, have stated the fact.

And again of Papias[5]—

Earlier Editions.	Last Edition.
Eusebius, who never fails to *enumerate the works of the New Testament to which the Fathers refer*, does not pretend that Papias knew either the Third or Fourth Gospels.	Eusebius, who never fails to *state what the Fathers say about the works of* the New Testament, does not mention that Papias knew either the Third or Fourth Gospels.

These alterations tell their own tale. One meaning of the expression, 'say about,' is suggested to the reader by the context

---

[1] [See above, p. 44 sq.]
[2] [Attention has been drawn to these passages above, p. 35 sq.]
[3] II. p. 166.
[4] [The Sixth Edition.]
[5] I. p. 483.

and required by the author's argument, while another is alone consistent with the facts.

Elsewhere however the distinction is not juggled away, but boldly ignored. Thus he still writes—

The presumption therefore naturally is that, as Eusebius did not mention the fact, he did not find any reference to the Fourth Gospel in the work of Papias[1].

I have shown that there is not any presumption—even the slightest—on this side.

Elsewhere he affirms still more boldly of Hegesippus—

It is certain that had he mentioned our Gospels, and we may say particularly the Fourth, the fact would have been recorded by Eusebius[2].

I have proved that, so far from this being certain, the probability is all the other way.

I confess that I cannot understand this treatment of the subject. It may indeed serve an immediate purpose. It may take in an unwary reader, or even a stray reviewer. I must suppose that it has even deceived the writer himself. But *magna est veritas*. My paper on the Silence of Eusebius was founded on an induction of facts; and therefore I feel confident that, unwelcome as these results are to the author of *Supernatural Religion*, and unexpected as they may be to many others, they must be ultimately accepted in the main.

The absence therefore of any direct mention by Eusebius respecting the use of the Third and Fourth Gospels by Papias affords no presumption one way or the other; and we must look elsewhere for light on the subject.

Unfortunately the fragments and notices of the work of Papias which have been preserved are very scanty. They might easily be compressed into less than two ordinary octavo pages, though the work itself extended to five books. It must therefore be regarded as a mere accident, whether we find in these meagre reliques the indications which we seek.

---

[1] II. p. 323. [See above, p. 35.]   [2] II. p. 320. [See above, p. 35.]

As regards St Luke, these indications are precarious and inadequate. They may afford a presumption that Papias used this Gospel, but they will not do more. Independent writers indeed, like Credner and Hilgenfeld, are satisfied, from certain coincidences of expression in the preface of Papias, that he was acquainted with this Evangelist's record, though he did not attach any value to it; but I agree with the author of *Supernatural Religion* in thinking that the inference is not warranted by the expressions themselves. It seems to me much more to the purpose that an extant fragment of Papias, in which he speaks of the overthrow of Satan and his angels, and their fall to the earth, appears to have been taken from an exposition of Luke x. 18[1]. At least there is no other passage in the Gospels to which it can so conveniently be referred. But obviously no great stress can be laid on this fact. It must indeed seem highly improbable that Papias should have been unacquainted with a Gospel which Marcion, a contemporary and a native of Asia Minor, thought fit to adapt to his heretical teaching, and which at this time is shown by the state of the text to have been no recent document[2]. But this is a consideration external to the evidence derivable from Papias himself.

The case with the Fourth Gospel however is quite different. Here we have a combination of circumstantial evidence, which is greater than we had any right to expect beforehand, and which amounts in the aggregate to a very high degree of probability.

.1. In the first place, Eusebius informs us that Papias 'has employed testimonies from the first (former) Epistle of John, and likewise from that of Peter.' The knowledge of the First Epistle almost necessarily carries with it the knowledge of the Gospel. The identity of authorship in the two

[1] The passage is given below, p. 200 sq.

[2] In justification of this statement, I must content myself for the present with referring to an able and (as it seems to me) unanswerable article on Marcion's Gospel by Mr Sanday, in the June [1875] number of the *Fortnightly Review*, in reply to the author of *Supernatural Religion*.

books, though not undisputed, is accepted with such a degree of unanimity that it may be placed in the category of acknowledged facts.

But, if I mistake not, their relation is much closer than this. There is not only an identity of authorship, but also an organic connection between the two. The first Epistle has sometimes been regarded as a preface to the Gospel. It should rather be described, I think, as a commendatory postscript. This connection will make itself felt, if the two books are read continuously. The Gospel seems to have been written or (more properly speaking) dictated for an immediate circle of disciples. This fact appears from special notices of time and circumstance, inserted here and there, evidently for the purpose of correcting the misapprehensions and solving the difficulties of the Evangelist's hearers. It is made still more clear by the sudden transition to the second person, when the narrator breaks off, and looking up (as it were), addresses his hearers—'He that saw it hath borne record...that *ye* might believe.' 'These things are written that *ye* might believe[1].' There were gathered about the Apostle, we may suppose, certain older members of the Church, like Aristion and the Presbyter John, who, as eyewitnesses of Christ's earthly life, could guarantee the correctness of the narrative. The twenty-fourth verse of the last chapter is, as it were, the endorsement of these elders—'This is the disciple which testifieth of these things, and wrote these things, and *we know* that his testimony is true.' After the narrative is thus ended, comes the hortatory postscript which we call the First Epistle, and which was intended (we may suppose) to be circulated with the narrative. It has no opening salutation, like the two Epistles proper—the second and third—which bear the same Apostle's name. It begins at once with a reference to the Gospel narrative which (on this hypothesis) has preceded—'That which was from the beginning, which we have heard, which we have seen with our eyes, which we beheld and our hands handled, of the Word of Life...that which we have

---

[1] John xix. 35; xx. 31.

seen and heard declare we unto you.' The use of the plural here links on the opening of the Epistle with the close of the Gospel. The Apostle begins by associating with himself the elders, who have certified to the authorship and authenticity of the narrative. Having done this, he changes to the singular, and speaks in his own name—'I write.' The opening phrase of the Epistle, 'That which was from the beginning,' is explained by the opening phrase of the Gospel, 'In the beginning was the Word.' The whole Epistle is a devotional and moral application of the main ideas which are evolved historically in the sayings and doings of Christ recorded in the Gospel. The most perplexing saying in the Epistle, 'He that came by water and by blood,' illustrates and itself is illustrated by the most perplexing incident in the Gospel, 'There came forth water and blood.' We understand at length, why in the Gospel so much stress is laid on the veracity of the eye-witness just at this point, when we see from the Epistle what significance the writer would attach to the incident, as symbolizing Christ's healing power.

This view of the composition of the Gospel and its connection with the Epistle has been suggested by internal considerations; but it is strongly confirmed by the earliest tradition which has been preserved. The Muratorian fragment[1] on the Canon must have been written about A.D. 170. As I shall have occasion to refer to this document more than once before I have done, I will here give an account of the passage relating to the Gospels, that it may serve for reference afterwards.

The fragment is mutilated at the beginning, so that the passage describing the First Gospel is altogether wanting. The text begins

[1] This fragment may be conveniently consulted in the edition of Tregelles (Oxford, 1867), or in Westcott's *History of the Canon* p. 514 sq (ed. 4). It must be remembered, *first*, that this document is an unskilful Latin translation from a lost Greek original; and, *secondly*, that the extant copy of this translation has been written by an extremely careless scribe, and is full of clerical errors. These facts however do not affect the question with which I am concerned, since on all the points at issue the bearing of the document is clear.

with the closing sentence in the description of the Second Gospel—obviously St Mark—which runs thus: 'At which however he was present, and so he set them down.'

'The Third Book of the Gospel' is designated 'according to Luke.' The writer relates that this Luke was a physician, who after the Ascension of Christ became a follower of St Paul, and that he compiled the Gospel in his own name. 'Yet,' he adds, 'neither did *he* (nec ipse) see the Lord in the flesh, and he too set down incidents as he was able to ascertain them¹. So he began his narrative from the birth of John.' Then he continues—

'The Fourth Gospel is (the work) of John, one of the (personal) disciples² (of Christ). Being exhorted by his fellow-disciples and bishops, he said, "Fast with me to-day for three days, and let us relate to one another what shall have been revealed to each." The same night it was revealed to Andrew, one of the Apostles, that John should write down everything in his own name, and all should certify (ut recognoscentibus cunctis Johannes suo nomine cuncta describeret). And therefore, although various elements (principia) are taught in the several books of the Gospels, yet it makes no difference to the faith of the believer, since all things in all of them are declared by one Supreme Spirit, concerning the nativity, the passion, the resurrection, His intercourse with His disciples, and His two advents, the first in despised lowliness, which is already past, the second with the magnificence of kingly power, which is yet to come. What wonder then, if John so boldly puts forward each statement in his Epistle (ταῖς ἐπιστολαῖς)³ also saying of himself,

---

¹ I venture to offer a conjectural emendation of the text, which is obviously corrupt or defective. It runs— 'et idē prout assequi potuit ita et ad nativitate Johannis incipet dicere.' I propose to insert 'posuit ita' after 'potuit ita,' supposing that the words have dropped out owing to the homœoteleuton. The text will then stand, 'et idem, prout assequi potuit, ita posuit. Ita et ab nativitate,' etc. (καὶ αὐτός, καθὼς ἠδύνατο παρακολουθεῖν, οὕτως ἔθηκε, κ.τ.λ.), 'And he too [like Mark] set down events according as he had opportunity of following them' (see Luke i. 3). But the general meaning of the passage is quite independent of any textual conjectures.

² 'Johannis ex discipulis' *i.e.* τοῦ ἐκ τῶν μαθητῶν, where μαθητής, 'a disciple,' is applied, as in Papias and Irenæus, in conformity with the language of the Gospels, to those who had been taught directly by Christ.

³ The plural appears to be used here, as not uncommonly, of a single letter. See above, p. 114. The sentence runs in the Latin (when some obvious errors of transcription are corrected):— 'Quid ergo mirum si Johannes singula etiam in epistulis suis proferat dicens in semet ipsum, *Quae vidimus*,' etc.; and so I have translated it. But I cannot help suspecting that the order in

"What we have seen with our eyes and heard with our ears, and our hands have handled, these things we have written unto you?" For so he avows himself to be not only an eye-witness and a hearer, but also a recorder, of all the wonderful things of the Lord in order.'

After speaking of the Acts and Epistles of St Paul, this anonymous writer arrives at the Catholic Epistles; and here he mentions *two* Epistles of St John as received in the Church.

I shall have something to say presently about the coincidences with Papias in this passage. For the moment I wish to call attention to the account which the writer gives of the origin of St John's Gospel[1]. There may be some legendary matter mixed up with this account; the interposition of Andrew and the dream of John may or may not have been historical facts; but its general tenor agrees remarkably with the results yielded by an examination of the Gospel itself. Yet it must be regarded as altogether independent. To suppose otherwise would be to ascribe to the writer in the second century an amount of critical insight and investigation which would do no dishonour to the nineteenth. But there is also another point of importance to my immediate subject. The writer detaches the First Epistle of St John from the Second and Third, and connects it with the Gospel. Either he himself, or some earlier authority whom he copied, would appear to have used a manuscript in which it occupied this position.

But our author attempts to invalidate the testimony of Eusebius respecting the use of the First Epistle by Papias. He wrote in his earlier editions:—

the original was, ἕκαστα προφέρει, καὶ ἐν ταῖς ἐπιστολαῖς αὐτοῦ λέγων εἰς ἑαυτόν, κ.τ.λ., 'puts forward each statement (*i.e.* in the Gospel), as he says in his epistle also respecting himself,' etc.; and that the translator has wrongly attached the words καὶ ἐν ταῖς ἐπιστολαῖς κ.τ.λ. to the former part of the sentence.

Arnold recognises the great importance of this tradition in the Muratorian Fragment (*Contemporary Review*, May, 1875, p. 977). Though I take a somewhat different view of its bearing, it has always seemed to me to contain in itself a substantially accurate account of the circumstances under which this Gospel was composed.

[1] I am glad to find that Mr Matthew

VI. PAPIAS OF HIERAPOLIS.

As Eusebius however does not quote the passages from Papias, we must remain in doubt whether he did not, as elsewhere, assume from some similarity of wording that the passages were quotations from these Epistles, whilst in reality they might not be. Eusebius made a similar statement with regard to a supposed quotation in the so-called Epistle of Polycarp[5] upon very insufficient grounds[1].

In my article on the Silence of Eusebius[2], I challenged him to produce any justification of his assertion 'as elsewhere.' I stated, and I emphasized the statement, that '*Eusebius in no instance which we can test gives a doubtful testimony.*' I warned him that, if I were not proved to be wrong in this statement, I should use the fact hereafter. In the preface to his new edition he has devoted twelve pages to my article on Eusebius; and he is silent on this point.

Of his silence I have no right to complain. If he had nothing to say, he has acted wisely. But there is another point in the paragraph quoted above, which demands more serious consideration. In my article[3] I offered the conjecture that our author had been guilty of a confusion here. I called attention to his note [5] which runs, 'Ad Phil. vii.; Euseb. *H. E.* iv. 14,' and I wrote:—

> The passage of Eusebius to which our author refers in this note relates how Polycarp 'has employed certain testimonies from the First (former) Epistle of Peter.' The chapter of Polycarp, to which he refers, contains a reference to the First Epistle *of St John*, which has been alleged by modern writers, but *is not alleged by Eusebius*. This same chapter, it is true, contains the words 'Watch unto prayer,' which presents a coincidence with 1 Pet. iv. 7. But no one would lay any stress on this one expression: the strong and unquestionable coincidences are elsewhere. Moreover our author speaks of a single 'supposed quotation,' whereas the quotations from 1 Peter in Polycarp are numerous.

I then pointed out ten other coincidences with the First Epistle of St Peter, scattered through Polycarp's Epistle. Some

---

[1] I. p. 483. He uses similar language in another passage also, II. p. 323.

[2] See above, p. 49.

[3] [See above, p. 49 sq.]

of these are verbal; almost all of them are much more striking and cogent than the resemblance in c. vii. Our author will not allow the error, but replies in his preface:—

I regret very much that some ambiguity in my language (*S. R.* I. p. 483) should have misled, and given Dr Lightfoot much trouble. I used the word 'quotation' in the sense of a use of the Epistle of Peter, and not in reference to any one sentence in Polycarp. I trust that in this edition I have made my meaning clear[1].

Accordingly, in the text, he substitutes for the latter sentence the words:—

Eusebius made a similar statement with regard to the use of the Epistle of Peter in the so-called Epistle of Polycarp, upon no more definite grounds than an apparent resemblance of expressions[2].

But the former part of the sentence is unaltered; the assertion 'as elsewhere' still remains unsubstantiated; and what is more important, he leaves the note exactly as it stood before, with the single reference to c. vii. Thus he has entirely misled his readers. He has deliberately ignored more than nine-tenths of the evidence in point of amount, and very far more than this proportion in point of cogency. The note was quite appropriate, supposing that the First Epistle of St John were meant, as I assumed; it is a flagrant *suppressio veri*, if it refers to the First Epistle of St Peter, as our author asserts that it does. The charge which I brought against him was only one of carelessness, which no one need have been ashamed to confess. The charge which his own explanation raises against him is of a far graver kind. Though he regrets the trouble he has given me, I do not regret it. It has enabled me to bring out the important fact that Eusebius may always be trusted in these notices relating to the use made of the Canonical Scriptures by early writers.

2. But this is not the only reason which the fragments in Eusebius supply for believing that Papias was acquainted with the Fourth Gospel. The extract from the preface suggests

---

[1] Preface to ed. 6, p. xv.
[2] [*S. R.* I. p. 483 (ed. 6); the whole passage including the note is omitted in the Complete Edition.]

points of coincidence, which are all the more important because they are incidental. In the words, 'What was said by Andrew, or by Peter, or by Philip, or by Thomas or James, or by John or Matthew,' the first four names appear in the same order in which they are introduced on the scene by this Evangelist. As this order, which places Andrew before Peter, is anything but the natural order, the coincidence has a real significance. Moreover, three of these four hold a prominent place in the Fourth Gospel, which they do not hold in the others—Philip and Thomas being never once named by the Synoptic Evangelists, except in their lists of the Twelve. It has been said indeed that the position assigned to the name of John by Papias in his enumeration is inconsistent with the supposition that this Apostle wrote a Gospel, or even that he resided and taught in Asia Minor, because so important a personage must necessarily have been named earlier. But this argument proves nothing, because it proves too much. No rational account can be given of the sequence, supposing that the names are arranged 'in order of merit.' Peter, as the chief Apostle, must have stood first; and John, as a pillar Apostle, would have been named next, or (if the James here mentioned is the Lord's brother) at all events next but one. This would have been the obvious order in any case; but, if Papias had any Judaic sympathies, as he is supposed to have had, no other is imaginable. This objection therefore is untenable. On the other hand, it is a remarkable fact that the two names, which are kept to the last and associated together, are just those two members of the Twelve to whom alone the Church attributes written Gospels. As Evangelists, the name of John and Matthew would naturally be connected. On any other hypothesis, it is difficult to account for this juxtaposition.

Again, it should be noticed that when Papias speaks of incidents in our Lord's life which are related by an eye-witness without any intermediation between Christ and the reporter, he describes them as 'coming from the Truth's self'[1] (ἀπ' αὐτῆς

---

[1] [The passage is quoted above, p. 143.]

τῆς ἀληθείας). This personification of Christ as 'the Truth' is confined to the Fourth Gospel.

3. When we turn from Eusebius to Irenæus, we meet with other evidence pointing to the same result. I refer to a passage with which the readers of these articles will be familiar, for I have had occasion to refer to it more than once[1]; but I have not yet investigated its connection with Papias. Irenæus writes[2]:—

As the elders say, then also shall they which have been deemed worthy of the abode in heaven go thither, while others shall enjoy the delight of paradise, and others again shall possess the brightness of the city; for in every place the Saviour shall be seen, according as they shall be worthy who see him. [They say] moreover that this is the distinction between the habitation of them that bring forth a hundred-fold, and them that bring forth sixty-fold, and them that bring forth thirty-fold; of whom the first shall be taken up into the heavens, and the second shall dwell in paradise, and the third shall inhabit the city; and that therefore our Lord has said, 'In my Father's abode are many mansions' (ἐν τοῖς τοῦ πατρός μου μονὰς εἶναι πολλάς); for all things are of God, who giveth to all their appropriate dwelling, according as His Word saith that allotment is made unto all by the Father, according as each man is, or shall be, worthy. And this is the banqueting-table at which those shall recline who are called to the marriage and take part in the feast. The presbyters, the disciples of the Apostles, say that this is the arrangement and disposal of them that are saved, and that they advance by such steps, and ascend through the Spirit to the Son, and through the Son to the Father, the Son at length yielding His work to the Father, as it is said also by the Apostle, 'for He must reign until He putteth all enemies under his feet,' etc.[3]

---

[1] Iren. *Hær.* v. 36. 1, 2.

[2] [See above, pp. 3 sq, 52 sq, 124 sq.]

[3] After two successive alterations, our author has at length, in his last [sixth] edition, translated the oblique infinitives correctly, though from his reluctance to insert the words 'they say,' or 'they teach,' the English requires, his meaning is somewhat obscure. But he has still left two strange errors, within four lines of each other, in his translation of this passage, II. p. 328. (1) He renders ἐν τοῖς τοῦ πατρός μου, 'In the (heavens) of my Father,' thus making τοῖς masculine, and understanding οὐρανοῖς from οὐρανοὺς which occurs a few lines before. He seems not to be aware that τὰ τοῦ πατρός μου means 'my Father's *house*'

VI. PAPIAS OF HIERAPOLIS. 195

I am glad to be saved all further trouble about the grammar of this passage. Our author now allows that the sentence with which we are mainly concerned is oblique, and that the words containing a reference to our Lord's saying in St John's Gospel are attributed to the elders who are mentioned before and after. He still maintains however, that 'it is unreasonable to claim' the reference 'as an allusion to the work of Papias.' He urges in one place that there is 'a wide choice of presbyters, including even evangelists, to whom the reference of Irenæus may with equal right be ascribed[1];' in another, that 'the source of the quotation is quite indefinite, and may simply be the exegesis of his own day[2].' To the one hypothesis it is sufficient to reply that no such explanation is found in the only four Evangelists whom Irenæus recognized; to the other, that when Irenæus wrote there were no 'disciples of the Apostles' living, so that he could have used the present tense in speaking of them.

This reference to the tense leads to a distinction of real importance. Critics have remarked that these reports of the

(see Lobeck *Phryn.* p. 100; Wetstein on Luke ii. 49). Thus he has made the elders contradict themselves; for of the 'many mansions' which are mentioned only the first is 'in the heavens,' the second being in paradise, and the third on earth. [In the Complete Edition the passage runs 'In the ...(plural) of my Father.'] (2) He has translated 'Omnia enim Dei sunt, qui omnibus aptam habitationem praestat, quemadmodum verbum ejus ait, omnibus *divisum esse* a Patre,' etc., 'For all things are of God, who prepares for all the fitting habitation as His Word says, *to be allotted*' ['that distribution is made,' Compl. Ed.] 'to all by the Father,' etc. He can hardly plead that this is 'a paraphrase,' for indeed it is too literal.

A few pages before (II. pp. 325, 326), I find '*Mag sie aber daher stammen*,' translated 'Whether *they are* derived from thence,' ['whether this be its origin or not,' Compl. Ed. II. p. 323]. A few pages after (p. 332), I find the work of Irenæus, *de Ogdoade*, cited instead of the *Epistle to Florinus*, for the relations between Irenæus and Polycarp. [This error is likewise tacitly corrected in the Compl. Ed. II. p. 330.] It might have been supposed that any one who had looked into the subject at all must have been aware that this *locus classicus* was in the *Epistle to Florinus*. But Eusebius happens to quote the treatise *de Ogdoade* in the same chapter; and hence the mistake. Such errors survive, though these pages have undergone at least two special revisions, and though this 'sixth' edition is declared on the title page to be 'carefully revised.'

[1] *S. R.* II. p. 333 (334).
[2] *S. R.* II. p. 329 (330).

opinions of the presbyters in Irenæus must be accepted with reserve; that the reporter may unconsciously have infused his own thoughts and illustrations into the account; and that therefore we cannot adduce with entire confidence the quotations from the canonical writings which they contain. This caution is not superfluous, but it must not be accepted without limitation. The reports in Irenæus are of two kinds. In some cases he repeats the *conversations* of his predecessors; in others he derives his information from *published records*. The hesitation, which is prudent in the one case, would be quite misplaced in the other. We shall generally find no difficulty in drawing the line between the two. Though there may be one or two doubtful instances, the language of Irenæus is most commonly decisive on this point. Thus, when he quotes the opinions of the elder on the Two Testaments, he is obviously repeating oral teaching; for he writes, 'The presbyter used to say,' 'The presbyter would entertain us with his discourse,' 'The old man, the disciple of the Apostles, used to dispute[1].' On the other hand, when in the passage before us he employs the present tense, 'As the elders say,' 'The presbyters, the disciples of the Apostles, say,' he is clearly referring to some *document*. No one would write, 'Coleridge maintains,' or 'Pitt declares,' unless he had in view some work or speech or biographical notice of the person thus quoted.

We may therefore safely conclude that in the passage before us Irenæus is citing from some *book*. So far as regards the main question at issue, the antiquity of the Fourth Gospel, it matters little whether this book was the exegetical work of Papias or not. Indeed the supposition that it was a different

[1] Iren. *Hær.* iv. 27. 1 sq; iv. 30. 1; iv. 31. 1; iv. 32. 1. Even in this case there remains the possibility that we have a report of lectures taken down at the time. The early work of Hippolytus on Heresies was drawn up from a synopsis which he had made of the lectures of Irenæus (Photius *Bibl.* 121). Galen again speaks of his pupils taking down his lectures as he delivered them (*Op.* xix. p. 11, ed. Kühn). The discourses which Irenæus reports from the lips of this anonymous elder (perhaps Melito or Pothinus) are so long and elaborate, that the hypothesis of lecture notes seems almost to be required to account for them.

work is slightly more favourable to my position, because it yields additional and independent testimony of the same date and character as that of Papias. But the following reasons combined make out a very strong case for assigning the passage to Papias. (1) It entirely accords with the *method* of Papias, as he himself describes it in his preface[1]. Scriptural passages are interpreted, and the sayings of the elders are interwoven with the interpretations. It accords equally well with the *subject* of his Expositions; for we know that he had a great fondness for eschatological topics, and that he viewed them in this light. (2) The possibilities are limited by the language, which confines our search to written documents. So far as we know there was, prior to the time of Irenæus, no Christian work which would treat the same subject in the same way, and would at the same time satisfy the conditions implied in the words, 'The elders, the disciples of the Apostles, say.' (3) The connection with a previous passage is highly important in its bearing on this question. In the thirty-third chapter of his fifth and last book Irenæus gives the direct reference to Papias which has been considered already[2]; in the thirty-sixth and final chapter occurs the passage with which we are now concerned. Is there reason to believe that the authority in these two passages is the same or different? Several considerations aid us in answering this question, and they all tend in the same direction. (i) The subject of the two passages is the same. They both treat of the future kingdom of Christ, and both regard it from the same point of view as a visible and external kingdom. (ii) In the next place the authorities in the two passages are described in similar terms. In the first passage they are designated at the outset 'the elders who saw John, the disciple of the Lord,' while at the close we are told that 'Papias records these things in writing in his fourth book.' It is not clear whether these elders are the authorities whom Papias quotes, or the class to whom Papias himself belongs,

---

[1] See above, p. 143. [2] See above, p. 158 sq.

and whom therefore he represents. Since Irenæus regards Papias as a direct hearer of St John, this latter alternative is quite tenable, though perhaps not as probable as the other. But this twofold possibility does not affect the question at issue. In the second passage the authorities are described in the opening as 'the elders' simply, and at the close as 'the elders, the disciples of the Apostles.' Thus the two accord. Moreover, in the second passage 'the elders' are introduced without any further description, as if they were already known, and we therefore naturally refer back to the persons who have been mentioned and described shortly before. (iii) The subject is continuous from the one passage to the other, though it extends over four somewhat long chapters (c. 33—36). The discussion starts, as we have seen, from Christ's saying about drinking the fruit of the vine in His kingdom[1]. The authority of the elders, recorded in the work of Papias, is quoted to support a literal interpretation of these words, as implying a material recompense of the believers. Irenæus then cites those prophecies of Isaiah which foretell the reign of peace on God's Holy Mountain (xi. 6 sq, lxv. 25 sq). This leads him to the predictions which announce the future triumphs of Israel and the glories of the New Jerusalem, all of which are interpreted literally as referring to a reign of Christ on earth. Creation thus renovated, he argues, will last for ever, as may be inferred from the promise of the new heavens and the new earth (Isaiah lxvi. 22). Then follows the passage in question, which contains the interpretation, given by the elders, of Christ's saying concerning the many mansions in His Father's house. A few lines lower down Irenæus refers again to the words respecting the fruit of the vine from which he had started; and after two or three sentences more the book ends.

These seem to be very substantial reasons for assigning the words to Papias. And probably the two passages which I have been considering do not stand alone. In an earlier part of this same fifth book Irenæus writes[2]:—

[1] See above, p. 158.   [2] Iren. *Hær.* v. 5. 1.

Where then was the first man placed? In paradise plainly, as it is written 'And God planted a paradise ....;' and he was cast out thence into this world, owing to his disobedience. Wherefore also the elders, disciples of the Apostles, say that those who were translated were translated thither (for paradise was prepared for righteous and inspired men, whither also the Apostle Paul was carried ....) and that they who are translated remain there till the end of all things (ἕως συντελείας), preluding immortality.

On this passage our author remarks:—

It seems highly probable that these 'presbyters the disciples of the Apostles' who are quoted on paradise are the same 'presbyters the disciples of the Apostles' referred to on the same subject (v. 36. §§ 1, 2), whom we are discussing[1].

With this opinion I entirely agree. 'But,' he adds, 'there is nothing whatever to connect them with Papias.' Here I am obliged to join issue. It seems to me that there are several things. In the first place, there is the description of the authorities, 'the elders, the disciples of the Apostles,' which exactly accords with the statement in Papias' own preface[2]. Next there is the subject and its treatment. This latter point, if I mistake not, presents some considerations which strongly confirm my view of the source of these references in Irenæus. The elders here quoted maintain that the paradise of Genesis is not a terrestrial paradise; it is some region beyond the limits of this world, to which Enoch and Elijah were translated; it is the abode, as Irenæus says, of the righteous and the spiritual (πνευματικοί), of whom these two respectively are types; their translation preludes the immortality of the faithful in Christ. In the second passage where paradise is mentioned by these elders, it is declared to be one of the 'many mansions' in the Father's house. But it is clear from this latter passage that the work from which these sayings of the elders are quoted must have contained much more about paradise. The inter-

[1] *S. R.* II. p. 333. [2] See above, p. 143.

mediate position there assigned to it between the celestial and the terrestrial kingdom does not explain itself, and must have required some previous discussion. Is there any reason to think that Papias did directly occupy himself with this subject?

The work of Papias was in the hands of Anastasius of Sinai, who (as we have seen) set a very high value on it[1]. He tells us in his 'Hexaemeron[2]' that 'the more ancient interpreters... contemplated the sayings about paradise *spiritually*, and referred them to the Church of Christ.' They 'said that there was a certain *spiritual* paradise[3].' Among these 'more ancient interpreters,' of whom he gives a list, he names 'the great Papias of Hierapolis, the scholar of John the Evangelist, and Irenæus of Lyons.' Here the two are associated together as dealing with this same subject in the same way. How much of the exegesis which Anastasius gives in the context, and attributes to these ancient interpreters, may be due to Papias in particular, it is impossible to say. But it may be observed that the expression 'the delight of the paradise,' in the saying of the elders reported by Irenæus, is taken from the Septuagint of Ezekiel xxviii. 13, where the Prince of Tyre is addressed, 'Thou wast in the delight of the paradise of God;' and that Anastasius represents 'the interpreters' (among whom he had previously mentioned Papias) as 'especially confirming their views of a spiritual paradise' by appealing to this very passage, 'where God seems to reveal to us enigmatically the fall of the devil from heaven,' the Prince of Tyre being interpreted as Satan, and the 'stones of fire' the hosts of intelligent beings; and he immediately afterwards quotes in illustration our Lord's words in Luke x. 18, 'I beheld Satan as lightning fall from

---

[1] [See above, p. 154.]

[2] *Patrol. Græc.* lxxxix. p. 962 (ed. Migne).

[3] Under this 'spiritual' interpretation, Anastasius includes views as wide apart as those of Philo, who interprets paradise as a philosophical allegory, and Irenæus, who regards it as a supramundane abode; for both are named. But they have this in common, that they are both opposed to a terrestrial region; and this is obviously the main point which he has in view.

heaven¹.' 'See,' he concludes, 'we have heard plainly that he was cast down to the earth from some paradise of delight high above, and from the cherubic coals of fire. (Ezek. xxviii. 16.)'

From the Hexaemeron of Anastasius I turn to the Catena on the Apocalypse, bearing the names of Œcumenius and Arethas, which was published by Cramer², and here I find fresh confirmation. On Rev. xii. 9, the compiler of this commentary quotes the same passage of St Luke to which Anastasius refers. He then goes on to explain that there was a twofold fall of Satan—the one at the time of the creation of man, the other at the Incarnation; and he proceeds—

Seeing then that Michael, the chief captain [of the heavenly hosts], could not tolerate the pride of the devil, and had long ago cast him out from his own abode by warlike might, according as Ezekiel says, that 'he was cast out by the cherubim from the midst of the stones of fire,' that is to say, the angelic ranks, because 'iniquities were found in him' (xxviii. 15, 16); again at the coming of Christ, as has been said ... he hath fallen more completely. This is confirmed by the tradition of the fathers, especially of Papias (καὶ πατέρων παράδοσις καὶ Παπίου), a successor of the Evangelist John who wrote this very Apocalypse with which we are concerned. Indeed Papias speaks thus concerning the war in these express words: 'It so befell that their array,' that is, their warlike enterprise, 'came to nought; for the great dragon, the old serpent, who is also called Satan and the devil, was cast down, yea, and was cast down to the earth, he and his angels³.'

I turn again to Anastasius; and I read in him that 'the above-mentioned interpreters' gave these explanations of paradise to counteract the teaching of divers heretics, among

---

¹ *Patrol. Græc.* lxxxix. p. 964 sq.
² Cramer *Catena* p. 358 sq.
³ Routh (*Rel. Sacr.* I. p. 41) would end the quotation from Papias at 'their array came to nought;' but the concluding sentence seems to be required as part of the quotation, which otherwise would be very meaningless. Papias, adopting the words of the Apocalypse, emphasizes the fact that Satan was cast down to the earth, because this shows that paradise was a supramundane region. As I have said before (p. 186), the only saying of our Lord to which we can conveniently assign this exposition is Luke x. 18. St Luke is also the only Evangelist who mentions paradise (xxiii. 43).

whom he especially mentions the Ophites who 'offered the greatest thanksgivings to the serpent, on the ground that by his counsels, and by the transgression committed by the woman, the whole race of mankind had been born[1].' This notice again confirms the view which I adopted, that it was the design of Papias to supply an antidote to the false exegesis of the Gnostics. Thus everything hangs together, and we seem to have restored a lost piece of ancient exegesis. If this restoration is uncertain in its details, it has at least materially strengthened my position, that the two sayings of the elders respecting paradise, quoted by Irenæus, must be attributed to the same authority, Papias, whom Irenæus cites by name in the intermediate passage relating to the millennial kingdom. I must add my belief also that very considerable parts of the fifth book of Irenæus, which consists mainly of exegesis, are borrowed from the exegetical work of Papias. It is the unpardonable sin of Papias in the eyes of Eusebius, that he has misled subsequent writers, more especially Irenæus, on these eschatological subjects. This is speaking testimony to the debt of Irenæus. Literary property was not an idea recognized by early Christian writers. They were too much absorbed in their subject to concern themselves with their obligations to others, or with the obligations of others to them. Plagiarism was not a crime, where they had all literary things in common. Hippolytus, in his chief work, tacitly borrows whole paragraphs, and even chapters, almost word for word, from Irenæus. He mentions his name only twice, and does not acknowledge his obligations more than once[2]. The liberties, which Hippolytus takes with his master Irenæus, might well have been taken by Irenæus himself with his predecessor Papias.

I have adduced three distinct reasons for believing that Papias was acquainted with the Gospel of St John; and their combined force is all the greater, because each is independent of the other. I will now add some other considerations pointing in the same direction.

---

[1] Anastasius *Hex.* p. 963.   [2] Hippolytus *Ref. Hær.* vi. 42, 55.

4. Eusebius tells us that Papias 'relates also another story concerning a woman accused of many sins before the Lord,' and he adds that it is 'contained in the Gospel according to the Hebrews.'

The story in question is allowed to be the narrative of the woman taken in adultery, which appears in the common texts of the Fourth Gospel, vii. 53—viii. 11. In the oldest Greek MS which contains this pericope, the *Codex Bezae*, the words 'taken in adultery' are read 'taken in sin.' In the *Apostolic Constitutions*[1], where this incident is briefly related, the woman is described as 'having sinned.' And again Rufinus, who would possibly be acquainted with Jerome's translation of the Gospel according to the Hebrews, boldly substitutes 'a woman, an adulteress,' for 'a woman accused of many sins,' in his version of Eusebius.

But it is equally certain that this pericope is an interpolation where it stands. All considerations of external evidence are against it. It is wanting in all Greek MSS before the sixth century; it was originally absent in all the oldest versions—Latin, Syriac, Egyptian, Gothic; it is not referred to, as part of St John's Gospel, before the latter half of the fourth century. Nor is the internal evidence less fatal. It is expressed in language quite foreign to St John's style, and it interrupts the tenor of his narrative. The Evangelist is here relating Christ's discourses on 'the last day, that great day, of the feast' of Tabernacles. Our Lord seizes on the two most prominent features in the ceremonial—the pouring out of the water from Siloam upon the altar, and the illumination of the city by flaming torches, lighted in the Temple area. Each in succession furnishes Him with imagery illustrating His own person and work. In the uninterrupted narrative, the one topic follows directly upon the other. He states first, that the streams of *living water* flow from Him (vii. 37 sq). He speaks 'again' (πάλιν), and declares that He is the *light of*

---

[1] *Apost. Const.* ii. 24.

the world (viii. 12 sq). But the intervention of this story dislocates the whole narrative, introducing a change of time, of scene, of subject.

On the other hand, it will be felt that the incident, though misplaced here, must be authentic in itself. Its ethical pitch is far above anything which could have been invented for Him by His disciples and followers, 'whose character and idiosyncrasies,' as Mr Mill says, 'were of a totally different sort[1].' They had neither the capacity to imagine nor the will to invent an incident, which, while embodying the loftiest of all moral teaching, would seem to them dangerously lax in its moral tendencies.

But, if so, how came it to find a place in the copies of St John's Gospel? Ewald incidentally throws out a suggestion[2] that it was originally written on the margin of some ancient manuscript, to illustrate the words of Christ in John viii. 15, 'Ye judge after the flesh; I judge no man.' This hint he has not followed up, but it seems to me to be highly valuable. The pericope in question occurs, in most authorities which contain it, after vii. 52; in one MS however it stands after vii. 36; and in several it is placed at the end of the Gospel. This is just what might have been expected if it was written, in the first instance, on the margin of a MS containing two or three columns on a page. When transferred from the margin to the text, it would find a place somewhere in the neighbourhood, where it least interfered with the narrative, or, if no suitable place appeared, it would be relegated to the end of the book. It should be added, that some good cursives give it at the end of the twenty-first chapter of St Luke—the most appropriate position, historically, that could be found for it. Whether this was an independent insertion in St Luke, or a transference from St John made on critical grounds, it is not easy to say.

But if this was the motive of the insertion, what was its source? Have we not here one of those illustrative anecdotes

---

[1] J. S. Mill *Three Essays* p. 254.
[2] Ewald *Die Johanneischen Schriften* p. 271.

which Papias derived from the report of the elders, and to which he 'did not scruple to give a place along with his interpretations' of our Lord's sayings? Its introduction as an illustration of the words in John viii. 15 would thus be an exact parallel to the treatment of the saying in Matthew xxvi. 29, as described in the first part of this paper[1]. A reader or transcriber of St John, familiar with Papias, would copy it down in his margin, either from Papias himself or from the Gospel of the Hebrews; and hence it would gain currency. The *Codex Bezæ*, the oldest Greek manuscript by two or three centuries which contains this narrative, is remarkable for its additions. May we not suspect that others besides this pericope (I would name especially our Lord's saying to the man whom He found working on the sabbath) were derived from this exegetical work of Papias? At all events Eusebius speaks of it as containing 'some strange parables and teachings of the Saviour, and some other matters more or less fabulous ($\mu\nu\theta\iota\kappa\acute{\omega}\tau\epsilon\rho\alpha$),' which Papias derived from oral tradition.

5. I have already suggested[2] that the notice relating to St Mark in Papias might have been given to explain some peculiarities in the Second Gospel, *as compared with St John*. This conjecture, standing alone, appears to have a very slight value, but it assumes a higher importance when we find that a writer who was a younger contemporary of Papias speaks of St Mark's Gospel in this same way and with this same motive.

The extract from the Muratorian fragment relating to the Gospels has been given above[3]. The writer is obviously desirous of accounting for the differences in the four Evangelists. As the fragment is mutilated at the beginning, we cannot say what he wrote about the First Gospel. But the half sentence which alone survives of his account of the Second Gospel tells its own tale; 'Quibus interfuit et ita tamen posuit.' It is evident that he, like Papias, describes St Mark as dependent on

---

[1] See above, p. 158 sq.
[2] [See above, p. 165.]
[3] See above, p. 188 sq.

the oral preaching of St Peter for his information respecting Christ's life. He 'set down' such facts as he knew from having been 'present' when the Apostle related them to his hearers. If the words themselves had left any room for doubt, it would be cleared up by his account of the Third Gospel, which follows immediately. St Luke, he tells us, was a follower of St Paul, and so wrote his Gospel; 'but *neither* did *he* (ἀλλ' οὐδ' αὐτὸς) see the Lord in the flesh,' and so he gave such information as came within his reach. On the other hand, he declares that the Fourth Gospel was written by John, a personal *disciple* of Christ, at the instance and with the sanction of other personal disciples like himself. Hence, he argues, though there must necessarily be differences in detail, yet this does not affect the faith of believers, since there is perfect accordance on the main points, and all the Gospels alike are inspired by the same Spirit. At the same time, the authority of the Fourth Gospel is paramount, as the record of an immediate eye-witness; and this claim John asserts for himself in the opening of his Epistle, when he declares that he has written what he himself had seen and heard.

Probably, if the notice of St Mark had not been mutilated, the coincidence would have been found to be still greater. Even as it stands, this account throws great light on the notice of Papias. The Muratorian writer lays stress on the secondary character of St Mark's account; so does Papias. The Muratorian writer quotes from the First Epistle of St John in evidence; so did Papias. We are not told with what object Papias adduced this testimony from the Epistle; but it is at least a plausible hypothesis that he had the same end in view as the Muratorian writer. It should be observed also that Eusebius mentions Papias as quoting not only the First Epistle of St John, but also the First Epistle of St Peter. May not the two have been connected together in the context of Papias, as they are in the notice of Eusebius? It is quite clear that Papias had already said something of the relations existing between St Peter and St Mark previously to the extract which gives an account of the Second Gospel; for he there refers back to a preceding notice, 'But afterwards, *as I said*, he followed Peter.' Would he not naturally have quoted, as illustrating these relations, the reference to the Evangelist in the Apostle's own letter, 'Marcus my son saluteth you' (1 Pet. v. 13)? If the whole of the Muratorian writer's notice of the Second Gospel had been preserved, we should not improbably have found a parallelism here also. But, however this may be, the resemblance is enough to suggest that the Muratorian writer was acquainted with the work of Papias, and that he borrowed his contrast between the secondary evidence of St Mark and the primary evidence of St John from this earlier writer.

And such a contrast offers a highly natural explanation of Papias' motive. The testimony of the elder respecting the composition of St Mark's Gospel was introduced by him, as we saw, to explain its phenomena. Though strictly accurate in its relation of facts, as far as it went, this Gospel had, he tells us, two drawbacks, which it owed to its secondary character. The account could not be taken as *complete*, and the order could not be assumed to be strictly *chronological*. In other words, compared with other evangelical narratives which Papias had in view, it showed *omissions* and *transpositions*. A comparison with St John's narrative would yield many instances of both. We have ample evidence that within a very few years after Papias wrote, the differences between St John and the Synoptic Gospels had already begun to attract attention. The Muratorian writer is a competent witness to this, nor does he stand alone. Claudius Apollinaris, who succeeded Papias in the see of Hierapolis, perhaps immediately, certainly within a very few years, mentions that on the showing of some persons 'the Gospels seem to be at variance with one another[1].' He is referring especially to the account of the Crucifixion in St Matthew and St John respectively.

It is much to be regretted that the Muratorian writer's account of St Matthew also has not been preserved; for here

[1] Routh *Rel. Sacr.* i. p. 160.

again we should expect much light to be thrown on the corresponding account in Papias. Why did Papias introduce this notice of the Hebrew original of St Matthew? We may suspect that the same motive which induced him to dwell on the secondary character of St Mark's knowledge led him also to call attention to the fact that St Matthew's Gospel was not an original, but a translation. I turn to an exegetical work of Eusebius, and I find this father dealing with the different accounts of two Evangelists in this very way. He undertakes to solve the question, why St Matthew (xxviii. 1) says that the resurrection was revealed to Mary Magdalene on the evening of (or 'late on') the sabbath (ὀψὲ σαββάτων), whereas St John (xx. 1) places this same incident on the first day of the week (τῇ μιᾷ τῶν σαββάτων); and among other explanations which he offers is the following:—

The expression 'on the evening of the sabbath' is due to the translator of the Scripture; for the Evangelist Matthew published (παρέδωκε) his Gospel in the Hebrew tongue; but the person who rendered it into the Greek language changed it, and called the hour dawning on the Lord's day ὀψὲ σαββάτων[1].

He adds, that each Evangelist corrects any misapprehension which might arise—St Matthew by adding 'as it began to dawn towards the first day of the week,' St John by a similar qualifying expression 'when it was yet dark.' Being acquainted with the work of Papias, Eusebius might have borrowed this mode of explanation, if not this very explanation, from him.

But it may be urged that on this hypothesis the motive of Papias must have appeared in the context, and that, if it had so appeared, Eusebius must have quoted it. The reply is simple. Papias must in any case have had some object or other in

[1] Euseb. *Quæst. ad Marin.* 2, iv. p. 941 (ed. Migne). Jerome, who seems to have had Eusebius before him, says more plainly (Epist. 120, *ad Hedib.* i. p. 826):—'Mihi videtur evangelista Matthaeus qui evangelium Hebraeo sermone conscripsit, non tam *vespere* dixisse quam *sero*, et eum qui interpretatus est, verbi ambiguitate deceptum, non *sero* interpretatum esse sed *vespere*.'

VI. PAPIAS OF HIERAPOLIS.

citing this testimony of the presbyter, and none is given. But I would answer further, that under the supposed circumstances Eusebius was not likely to quote the context. As a matter of fact, he has not done so in a very similar case, where he tears out a fragment from a passage in Irenæus which intimately affects the relations of the Evangelists to one another[1]. He commences in the middle of a sentence, and extracts just as much as serves his immediate purpose, leaving out everything else. On this point, I am glad that I can reckon beforehand on the assent of the author of *Supernatural Religion* himself. Speaking of this extract from Irenæus, he says, 'Nothing could be further from the desire or intention of Eusebius than to represent any discordance between the Gospels[2].' I do not indeed join in the vulgar outcry against the dishonesty of Eusebius. Wherever I have been able to investigate the charge, I have found it baseless. We have ample evidence that Eusebius was prepared to face the difficulties in harmonizing the Gospels, when the subject came properly before him. But here he might fairly excuse himself from entering upon a topic which had no bearing on his immediate purpose, and which once started would require a lengthy discussion to do justice to it. Moreover it is obvious that he is very impatient with Papias. He tells us twice over that he has confined his extracts to the very narrowest limits which bare justice to his subject would allow[3]; he warns his readers that there are a great many traditions in Papias which he has passed over; and he refers them to the book itself for further information. Though exceptionally long in itself compared with his notices of other early Christian writers, his account of Papias is, we may infer, exceptionally brief in proportion to the amount of material which this father afforded for such extracts.

6. I have said nothing yet about the direct testimony of a

---

[1] Iren. ii. 22. 5; Euseb. *H. E.* iii. 23. φιλομαθεῖς ἀναπέμψαντες ἀναγκαίως νῦν προσθήσομεν, κ.τ.λ., and again, ταῦτα δ' ἡμῖν ἀναγκαίως πρὸς τοῖς ἐκτεθεῖσιν ἐπιτετηρήσθω.

[2] Preface to ed. 6, p. xvii.

[3] Euseb. *H. E.* iii. 39 ἐφ' ἃς τοὺς

late anonymous writer, which (if it could be accepted as trustworthy) would be decisive on the point at issue.

In an argument prefixed to this Gospel in a Vatican MS, which is assigned to the ninth century, we read as follows:—

The Gospel of John was made known (manifestatum), and given to the Churches by John while he yet remained in the body (adhuc in corpore constituto); as (one) Papias by name, of Hierapolis, a beloved disciple of John, has related in his exoteric, that is, in his last five books (in extericis, id est, in extremis quinque libris); but he wrote down the Gospel at the dictation of John, correctly (descripsit vero evangelium dictante Johanne recte). But Marcion the heretic, when he had been censured (improbatus) by him, because he held heretical opinions (eo quod contraria sentiebat), was cast off by John. Now he had brought writings or letters to him from the brethren that were in Pontus[1].

No stress can be laid on testimony derived from a passage which contains such obvious anachronisms and other inaccuracies; but the mention of Papias here courts inquiry, and time will not be ill spent in the endeavour to account for it. It will be worth while, at all events, to dispose of an erroneous explanation which has found some favour. When attention was first called to this passage by Aberle and Tischendorf, Overbeck met them with the hypothesis that the notice was taken from a spurious work ascribed to Papias. He supposed that some one had forged five additional books in the name of this father, in which he had gathered together a mass of fabulous matter, and had entitled them 'Exoterica,' attaching them to the genuine five books. To this work he assigned also the notice respecting the four Maries which bears the name of Papias[2]. This explanation might have been left to itself if it had remained as a mere hypothesis of Overbeck's,

---

[1] This argument to St John's Gospel was published long ago by Cardinal Thomasius (*Op.* I. p. 344); but it lay neglected until attention was called to it by Aberle *Theolog. Quartalschr.* xlvi. p. 7 sq (1864), and by Tischendorf *Wann wurden etc.*

[2] Overbeck's article is in Hilgenfeld's *Zeitschr. f. Wissensch. Theol.* x. p. 68 sq (1867). The notice relating to the four Maries will be found in Routh *Rel. Sacr.* I. p. 16.

but it has been recently accepted by Hilgenfeld. He speaks of these five 'exoteric' books, as attached to 'the five esoteric or genuine books;' and to this source he attributes not only the account of the four Maries, but also a notice relating to the death of St John which is given by Georgius Hamartolos on the authority of Papias[1].

This however seems to be altogether a mistake. We find no notice or trace elsewhere of any such spurious work attributed to Papias. Moreover these titles are quite unintelligible. There is no reason why the five genuine books should be called 'esoteric,' or the five spurious books 'exoteric.' About the notice of the four Maries again Hilgenfeld is in error. It is not taken from any forged book fathered upon the bishop of Hierapolis, but from a genuine work of another Papias, a Latin lexicographer of the eleventh century. This is not a mere hypothesis, as Hilgenfeld assumes, but an indisputable fact, as any one can test who will refer to the work itself, of which MSS exist in some libraries, and which was printed four times in the fifteenth century[2]. Nor again does the passage in Georgius Hamartolos give any countenance to this theory. This writer, after saying that St John survived the rest of the twelve and then suffered as a martyr ($\mu\alpha\rho\tau\upsilon\rho\iota\text{ov}\ \kappa\alpha\tau\eta\xi\iota\text{-}\omega\tau\alpha\iota$), continues:—

For Papias, the bishop of Hierapolis, having been an eye-witness of him, says in the second book ($\lambda\delta\gamma\psi$) of the 'Oracles of the Lord' ($\tau\hat{\omega}\nu\ \kappa\upsilon\rho\iota\alpha\kappa\hat{\omega}\nu\ \lambda o\gamma\iota\omega\nu$) that he was slain by the Jews, having, as is clear, with his brother James, fulfilled the prediction of Christ......' Ye shall drink my cup,' etc.[3]

Here we have an obvious error. The fate which really

---

[1] *Einleitung* p. 63 (1875); comp. *Zeitschr. f. Wissensch. Theol.* xviii. p. 269 (1875).

[2] I verified this for myself ten years ago, and published the result in the first edition of my *Galatians*, p. 459 sq (1865). About the same time Dr Westcott ascertained the fact from a friend, and announced it in the second edition of his *History of the Canon*.

[3] This fragment was first published by Nolte *Theolog. Quartalschr.* xliv. p. 466 (1862). It will be found in the collection of fragments of Papias given by Hilgenfeld *Zeitschr. f. Wissensch. Theol.* (1875), p. 258.

befell James is attributed to John. Georgius Hamartolos therefore cannot be quoting directly from Papias, for Papias cannot have reported the *martyrdom* of John. But, on the other hand, Papias seems plainly to have been the ultimate source of his information. The work is precisely and correctly quoted. The general tenor accords with the main object of Papias' book—the exposition of a saying of Christ, and the illustration of it by a story derived from tradition. This being so, the error is most easily explained by a lacuna. In the intermediate authority from whom Georgius got the reference, some words must have dropped out; a line or two may have been omitted in his copy; and the sentence may have run in the original somewhat in this way; Παπίας...φάσκει ὅτι Ἰωάννης [μὲν ὑπὸ τοῦ Ῥωμαίων βασιλέως κατεδικάσθη μαρτυρῶν εἰς Πάτμον, Ἰάκωβος δὲ] ὑπὸ Ἰουδαίων ἀνηρέθη, 'Papias says that John [was condemned by the Roman emperor (and sent) to Patmos for bearing witness (to the truth) while James] was slain by the Jews[1].'

The hypothesis of a spurious Papias therefore is wholly unsupported; and we must seek some other explanation of the statement in the Vatican MS. This passage seems to be made up of notices gathered from different sources. The account of Marcion, with which it closes, involves an anachronism (to say nothing else), and seems to have arisen from a confusion of the interview between St John and Cerinthus and that between Polycarp and Marcion, which are related by Irenæus in the

---

[1] This solution of the difficulty by means of a lacuna was suggested to me by a friend. In following up the suggestion, I have inserted the missing words from the parallel passage in Origen, to which Georgius Hamartolos refers in this very context: *in Matth.* tom. xvi. 6 (III. p. 719 sq, Delarue), πεπώκασι δὲ ποτήριον καὶ τὸ βάπτισμα ἐβαπτίσθησαν οἱ τοῦ Ζεβεδαίου υἱοί, ἐπείπερ Ἡρώδης μὲν ἀπέκτεινεν Ἰάκωβον τὸν Ἰωάννου μαχαίρᾳ, ὁ δὲ Ῥωμαίων βασιλεύς, ὡς ἡ παράδοσις διδάσκει, κατεδίκασε τὸν Ἰωάννην μαρτυροῦντα διὰ τὸν τῆς ἀληθείας λόγον εἰς Πάτμον τὴν νῆσον. It must be noticed that Georgius refers to this passage of Origen as testimony that *St John suffered martyrdom*, thus mistaking the sense of μαρτυροῦντα. This is exactly the error which I suggested as an explanation of the blundering notice of John Malalas respecting the death of Ignatius (see above p. 79).

same context[1]. The earlier part, referring to Papias, is best explained in another way—by clerical errors and mistranslation rather than by historical confusion. The word 'exotericis' ought plainly to be read 'exegeticis[2].' In some handwritings of the seventh or eighth century, where the letters have a round form, the substitution of OT for EG would be far from difficult[3]. In this case *extremis*, which should perhaps be read *externis*, is the Latin interpretation of the false reading *exotericis*. Thus purged of errors, the reference to Papias presents no difficulties. We may suppose that Papias, having reported some saying of St John on the authority of the elders, went on somewhat as follows: 'And this accords with what we find in his own Gospel, which he gave to the Churches when he was still in the body' (ἔτι ἐν τῷ σώματι καθεστῶτος). In this contrast between the story repeated after his death and the Gospel taken down from his lips during his lifetime, we should have an explanation of the words *adhuc in corpore constituto*, which otherwise seem altogether out of place. The word *constituto* shows clearly, I think, that the passage must have been translated from the Greek. If St John's authorship of the Gospel had been mentioned in this incidental way, Eusebius would not have repeated it, unless he departed from his usual practice. On the other hand, the statement that Papias was the amanuensis of the Evangelist can hardly be correct, though it occurs elsewhere[4]. Whether it was derived from a misunderstanding of Papias, or of some one else, it would be impossible to say. But I venture

[1] See Lipsius *Die Quellen der Aeltesten Ketzergeschichte* p. 237 (1875). Though the notice in Clem. Alex. *Strom.* vii. 17 (p. 898) makes Marcion a contemporary of the Apostles, there is obviously some error in the text. All other evidence, which is trustworthy, assigns him to a later date. The subject is fully discussed by Lipsius in the context of the passage to which I have given a reference. See also Zahn in *Zeitschr. f. Hist. Theol.* 1875 p. 62.

[2] Aberle suggested 'exegeseos,' for which Hilgenfeld rightly substituted 'exegeticis.' This was before he adopted Overbeck's suggestion of the spurious Papias.

[3] The photographs, Nos. 3, 7, 10, 20, in the series published by the Palæographical Society, will show fairly what I mean.

[4] In the *Catena Patr. Græc. in S. Joann.* Procœm. (ed. Corder), αἱρέσεων διαφυεισῶν δεινῶν ὑπαγόρευσε τὸ εὐαγγέλιον τῷ ἑαυτοῦ μαθητῇ Παπίᾳ εὐβιώτῳ (sic) τῷ Ἱεραπολίτῃ, κ. τ. λ.

to suggest a solution. Papias may have quoted the Gospel 'delivered by John to the Churches, which *they* wrote down from his lips' (ὃ ἀπέγραφον ἀπὸ τοῦ στόματος αὐτοῦ); and some later writer, mistaking the ambiguous ἀπέγραφον, interpreted it, '*I* wrote down,' thus making Papias himself the amanuensis[1]. The *dictation* of St John's Gospel is suggested, as I have said already[2], by internal evidence also. Here again, so far as we can judge from his practice elsewhere, Eusebius would be more likely than not to omit such a statement, if it was made thus casually. This seems to me the most probable explanation of the whole passage. But obviously no weight can be attached to such evidence. Like the statement of John Malalas respecting Ignatius, which I considered in a former paper[3], it is discredited by its companionship with an anachronism, though the anachronism is not so flagrant as those of John Malalas, and the statement itself does not, like his, contradict the unanimous testimony of all the preceding centuries.

But the author of *Supernatural Religion* closes with an argument which he seems to think a formidable obstacle to the belief that Papias recognized the Fourth Gospel as the work of St John:—

Andrew of Cæsarea, in the preface to his commentary on the Apocalypse, mentions that Papias maintained 'the credibility' (τὸ ἀξιόπιστον) of that book, or in other words, its Apostolic origin... Now, he must, therefore, have recognized the book as the work of the Apostle John, and we shall hereafter show that it is impossible that the author of the Apocalypse is the author of the Gospel; therefore, in this way also, Papias is a witness against the Apostolic origin of the Fourth Gospel[4].

[1] Or, the confusion may have been between ἀπέγραψα (ἀπέγραψαν), and ἀπέγραψα.

[2] [See above, p. 187.]

[3] [See above, p. 79 sq.]

[4] The passage of Andreas of Cæsarea will be found in Routh *Rel. Sacr.* I. p. 15. It is not there said that Papias ascribed the Apocalypse to St John the Apostle, or even that he quoted it by name. Our author's argument therefore breaks down from lack of evidence. It seems probable however, that he would ascribe it to St John, even though he may not have said so distinctly. Suspicion is thrown on the testimony of Andreas by the fact that Eusebius does not directly mention its

This argument however is an anachronism. Many very considerable critics of the nineteenth century, it is true, maintain that the two works cannot have come from the same author. I do not stop now to ask whether they are right or wrong; but the nineteenth century is not the second. In the second century there is not the slightest evidence that a single writer felt any difficulty on this score, or attempted to separate the authorship of the two books. It is true that Eusebius mentions one or two authors, whose works unfortunately are lost, as using the Apocalypse, while he does not mention their using the Gospel; and this negative fact has obviously misled many. But here again the inference arises from a fundamental misconception of his purpose. I have shown[1] that his principles required him to notice quotations from and references to the Apocalypse in every early writer, because the authorship and canonicity of the work had been questioned by Church writers before his time; whereas it would lead him to ignore all such in the case of the Fourth Gospel, because no question had ever been entertained within the Church respecting it. This indeed is precisely what he does with Theophilus; he refers to this father's use of the Apocalypse, and he ignores his direct quotations from the Gospel. The inference therefore must be set aside as a fallacy. Beyond this, all the direct evidence points the other way. There was indeed a small sect or section of men outside the pale of the Church, before the close of the second century, who rejected the Gospel, but they rejected the Apocalypse also. Moreover they ascribed both *to a single author*, and (what is more important still) this author was Cerinthus, *a contemporary of St John*[2]. Thus the very oppo-

use by Papias, as his practice elsewhere would demand. But I suppose that Eusebius omitted any express mention of this use, because he had meant his words to be understood of the Apocalypse, when, speaking of the Chiliastic doctrine of Papias higher up, he said that this father 'had mistaken the Apostolic statements,' and 'had not comprehended what was said by them mystically and in figurative language' (ἐν ὑποδείγμασι).

[1] [See above, pp. 36 sq, 46.]

[2] These persons are discussed at great length by Epiphanius (*Hær.* li.), who calls them *Alogi*. They are mentioned also, with special reference to the Gospel, by Irenæus (iii. 11. 9).

nents of the Gospel in the second century are witnesses not only to the very early date of the two writings, but also to the identity of authorship. On the other hand, every Church writer without exception during this century (so far as our knowledge goes) who accepted the one accepted the other also. The most doubtful case is Justin Martyr, who refers by name to the Apocalypse; but even Hilgenfeld says that it is difficult to deny the use of the Gospel of St John in his case[1]. Melito again commented on the Apocalypse; and there is ample evidence (as I trust to show hereafter) that he recognized the Fourth Gospel also. Both books alike are used in the Letter of the Gallican Churches (A.D. 177). Both alike are accepted by Theophilus of Antioch, by the Muratorian writer, by Irenæus, and by Clement. It is the same during the first half of the third century. Tertullian and Cyprian, Hippolytus and Origen, place them on an equal footing, and attribute them to the same Apostle. The first distinct trace of an attempt to separate the authorship of the two books appears in Dionysius of Alexandria[2], who wrote about the middle or early in the second half of the third century. Even he argues entirely upon considerations of internal criticism, and does not pretend to any traditional evidence. He accepts both works as canonical; and he questions the Apostolic authorship, not of the Gospel, but of the Apocalypse.

Hippolytus wrote a work 'In defence of the Gospel and Apocalypse of John,' which was apparently directed against them. It may be suspected that Epiphanius is largely indebted to this work for his refutation of them.

[1] *Einleitung* p. 67; comp. p. 733 sq.

[2] Euseb. *H. E.* vii. 25. Gaius the Roman Presbyter, who wrote about A.D. 220, is often cited as an earlier instance. I gave reasons some years ago for suspecting that the Dialogue bearing this name was really written by Hippolytus (*Journal of Philology*, I. p. 98, 1868); and I have not seen any cause since to change this opinion. But whether this be so or not, the words of Gaius reported by Eusebius (*H. E.* iii. 28) seem to be wrongly interpreted as referring to the Apocalypse. [The important discovery of Prof. Gwynn (*Hermathena* vol. VI. p. 397 sq, 1888), showing as it does that there was a Gaius different from Hippolytus, does not allow me to speak now as I spoke in 1875 about the identity of Gaius the Roman Presbyter and Hippolytus.]

VII. THE LATER SCHOOL OF ST JOHN.

[FEBRUARY, 1876.]

IT has been stated in a former paper that at the fall of Jerusalem a remnant of the Apostolic company, together with other primitive disciples, sought a new home in Asia Minor[1]. Of this colony Ephesus was the head-quarters, and St John the leader. Here he is reported to have lived and laboured for more than a quarter of a century, surviving the accession of Trajan, who ascended the imperial throne A.D. 98[2]. In this respect his position is unique among the earliest preachers of Christianity. While St Peter and St Paul converted disciples and organized congregations, St John alone was the founder of a school. The prolongation of his life after the Church was firmly rooted, and his fixed residence in the midst of a compact Christian society, combined to give a certain definiteness to his personal influence, which would be wanting to the labours of these more strictly missionary preachers. Hence the traditions of St John are more direct, more consistent, and more trustworthy, than those which relate to the other Apostles.

Thus we may, without any great impropriety, speak of the 'school of St John.' The existence of such a body of disciples gathered about the veteran teacher is indicated by notices in various writers. The author of the Muratorian fragment, for instance, speaks of this Apostle as writing his Gospel at the request not only of his fellow-disciples, but also of his

[1] See above, p. 89 sq.   [2] Iren. ii. 22. 5; iii. 3. 4.

'bishops[1].' Clement of Alexandria again, among whose teachers was one from this very district, and probably of this very school[2], represents him as going about from place to place in the neighbourhood of Ephesus, appointing bishops and providing in other ways for the government of the Churches[3]. More especially Irenæus, who had received his earliest lessons in Christianity from an immediate disciple of St John, appeals again and again to such a body as preserving and handing down the correct tradition of the Apostolic doctrine and practice. He describes these persons in one place as 'the elders who in Asia associated with John the disciple of the Lord[4];' in another as 'all the Churches which are in Asia,' specifying more particularly the 'Church in Ephesus...the true witness of the Apostolic tradition[5];' in a third as 'those who saw John face to face[6],' or 'the elders who saw John the disciple of the Lord[7];' in a fourth as 'the elders who were before us, and who also were pupils of the Apostles[8];' in a fifth 'as the elders who have their succession from the Apostles[9];' in a sixth as 'the elders, disciples of the Apostles[10],' with similar expressions elsewhere. The prominent members of this school in the first age were Polycarp of Smyrna and Papias of Hierapolis, of whom the former survived beyond the middle of the century, and the latter probably died not many years before. In the next generation the most famous names are Melito of Sardis and Apollinaris of Hierapolis, who flourished in the third quarter of the century. They again are succeeded by other writers, of whom the most celebrated was Polycrates of Ephesus, already an old man, when in the last decade of the century a controversial question obliged him to take up his pen in defence of the traditions of his Church.

---

[1] See above, p. 189.
[2] Clem. Alex. *Strom.* i. 1 (p. 322) ὁ μὲν ἐπὶ τῆς Ἑλλάδος, ὁ Ἰωνικός.
[3] Clem. Alex. *Quis div. salv.* 42, p. 959.
[4] Iren. ii. 22. 5.
[5] Iren. iii. 3. 4.
[6] Iren. v. 30. 1.
[7] Iren. v. 33. 3.
[8] *Ep. ad Flor.* in Euseb. *H. E.* v. 20. See above, p. 96.
[9] Iren. iv. 26. 2.
[10] Iren. v. 5. 1.

VII. THE LATER SCHOOL OF ST JOHN.

Asia Minor appears to have been far in advance of the other Churches of Christendom in literary activity, during the second century. This pre-eminence was due mainly, we may suppose, to the fact already mentioned, that it had become the second home of the Apostles and primitive teachers of Christianity. But the productiveness of the Asiatic Christians in this respect was doubtless stimulated by the pressure of opposition. This region was the hot-bed of heresies and the arena of controversy. Nor is it unimportant to observe that the main subjects of discussion were of such a kind as must necessarily have involved questions intimately connected with the Canon. Montanism, with its doctrine of the Paraclete and its visions of the New Jerusalem, would challenge some expression of opinion respecting the Gospel and the Apocalypse of St John, if these writings were disputed. The Paschal controversy courted investigation into the relations between the narratives of the Synoptists and the Fourth Evangelist. Marcionism, resting as it did on the paramount and sole authority of St Paul's Epistles and of the Pauline Gospel, would not suffer friend or foe to preserve silence on this fundamental question. And so again, though in a less degree, the disputes with Cerinthians, with Ophites, with Basilideans, with Valentinians, with all the various sects of Gnostics, could not have been conducted, as we see plainly from the treatises of Irenæus and Hippolytus, without constant appeals to the testimony of written documents—thus indicating, at all events roughly, the amount of authority which the writers accorded to the more prominent books of our New Testament Canon. To men like Irenæus or Eusebius, who had this extensive literature in their hands, the teaching of this Church generally, as well as of the more prominent individual writers belonging to it, could not have been open to question. Their approval of its orthodoxy therefore, either by silent assent or by studied panegyric, is a fact of real moment.

Over and above this relation to the books of the New Testament generally, the two points to which modern controversy directs attention, and which therefore deserve special consideration in any review of the writers belonging to the school of St John, are—*first*, what indications the extant fragments and notices contain, that they recognized or rejected the Fourth Gospel; and *secondly*, what can be learnt from these same sources as to the degree of authority which they accorded to the Apostle of the Gentiles.

Polycarp and Papias have been discussed in my earlier articles[1]. In the case of both these fathers, a recognition of the Fourth Gospel has been inferred from the use made of the First Epistle; in the case of the latter, from other indications also. As regards St Paul the testimony of Polycarp is as full and explicit as it well could be; while, on the other hand, the meagre fragments of Papias do not in themselves warrant any inference on this point.

The next extant document in chronological order is the account of Polycarp's martyrdom, written immediately after the occurrence (A.D. 155), and addressed to the Churches of the neighbouring province of Pontus, more especially to the Christians of Philomelium. In this letter the brethren of Smyrna draw a parallel between the sufferings of their martyred friend and the Passion of our Lord, which is suggested by some remarkable coincidences. 'Nearly all the incidents,' we are told at the outset, 'which preceded (his death) came to pass that the Lord might exhibit anew to us a martyrdom after the pattern of the Gospel; for Polycarp remained that he might be betrayed, as did also the Lord[2]." This account is thus the earliest instance of a favourite type of hagiology, which sees the sufferings of Christ visibly reflected and imaged in detail in the servants of Christ, and of which ancient and mediæval biography furnishes numerous examples. This idea of literal conformity to the life and Passion of Christ runs through the document. Some of the coincidences are really striking; but in other cases the parallelism is highly artificial. The name of the convicting magistrate is Herod, and special stress is

---

[1] See above, pp. 89 sq, 142 sq. [2] *Martyr. Polyc.* § 1.

VII. THE LATER SCHOOL OF ST JOHN.

naturally laid on this fact[1]. The time of the martyrdom is the passover—'the great sabbath,' as it is here called[2]. Polycarp's place of refuge is ascertained from information elicited by torture from a youth, apparently a slave in his employ. This poor boy, much more sinned against than sinning, is cruelly compared to Judas; and we are told accordingly that Polycarp, like our Lord, was 'betrayed by them of his own household[3].' When apprehended, he is put upon an ass, and thus taken back to the city[4]; and this is of course intended as a parallel to the triumphal entry into Jerusalem. His pursuers come on horseback and in arms, 'as against a robber[5].' When he is apprehended, he prays, 'The will of God be done[6];' and so forth. These parallels, at the same time that they show the idea dominant in the mind of the narrators, are a valuable testimony to the truth of the narrative itself, where so much violent treatment is necessary to produce the desired effect[7].

Most of the incidents have their counterparts in the circumstances of the Passion, as recorded by the Synoptic Evangelists alone or in common with St John. This is natural; for they refer to external events, in which the Synoptic narrative is rich. But there are exceptions, where the writers obviously have the account of the Fourth Evangelist in their mind. Thus we are told that at the crisis of Polycarp's fate a voice came from heaven, saying, 'Be strong, and play the man, Polycarp[8].' 'And the speaker,' it is added, 'no man saw; but the voice those of our company that were present heard.' This corresponds to the voice which St John records as

---

[1] *ib.* § 6 ὁ κεκληρωμένος τὸ αὐτὸ ὄνομα, Ἡρώδης ἐπιλεγόμενος, where κεκληρωμένος (not καὶ κληρονόμος) is the right reading, 'who chanced to have the same name,' *i.e.*, with the tyrant of the Gospels.

[2] *ib.* § 8. It is right to add however, that the meaning of the expression 'great sabbath' here has been questioned.

[3] *ib.* § 6 οἱ προδιδόντες αὐτὸν οἰκεῖοι ὑπῆρχον.

[4] *ib.* § 8.

[5] *ib.* § 7 ὡς ἐπὶ λῃστήν; comp. Matt. xxvi. 55; Mark xiv. 48; Luke xxii. 52.

[6] *ib.* § 7; comp. Matt. xxvi. 42; Acts xxi. 14.

[7] The objections which have been urged against this narrative are not serious. See above, p. 108.

[8] *Martyr. Polyc.* § 9: see Deut. xxxi. 7, 23.

addressing our Lord from heaven, and as imperfectly apprehended by the bystanders[1]. Again, Polycarp, in consequence of a vision, predicts that he shall be burnt alive[2], though at the time the intention obviously is to throw him to the wild beasts, as the games are going on. A fortuitous circumstance frustrates this intention, and brings about a fulfilment of his prophecy as to the manner of his death[3]. Just in the same way in the Fourth Gospel Jesus is represented as 'signifying by what death He should die[4].' Death by crucifixion seemed altogether unlikely at the time, for His enemies were the Jews, and this was not a Jewish mode of punishment; but by an accidental turn of circumstances He was transferred from the Jews to Pilate, and so His prediction was fulfilled[5]. Again, it is related that when the fire would not consume the body of the saint, his persecutors 'ordered an executioner to go up to him and thrust a small sword into him. When he had done this,' we are told, 'there came forth [a dove and] a quantity of blood[6].' The parallel to the incident recorded in St John's account of the crucifixion is obvious[7]; and just as the Evangelist lays stress on his own presence as an eye-witness of the scene, so also do these hagiologers, when relating a strange occurrence at his martyrdom. 'We saw a great marvel,' they say, 'we to whom it was given to see; and we have been saved that we might relate to the rest what happened[8].' And lastly, as St John emphasizes the fact that everything was accomplished in the death of Jesus[9], so also they declare of Polycarp, that 'every

---

[1] John xii. 28.

[2] *Martyr. Polyc.* § 5.

[3] *ib.* § 12 ἔδει γὰρ τὸ τῆς ... ὀπτασίας πληρωθῆναι ὅτε ... εἶπεν, κ.τ.λ.

[4] John xii. 33.

[5] John xviii. 32 ἵνα ὁ λόγος τοῦ Ἰησοῦ πληρωθῇ, ὃν εἶπεν σημαίνων κ. τ. λ. The coincidence extends to the language used when the change is brought about. In Polycarp's case Philippus the Asiarch says (§ 12), μὴ εἶναι ἐξὸν αὐτῷ, κ. τ. λ.; in our Lord's case, the language of the Jews is (xviii. 31), ἡμῖν οὐκ ἔξεστιν ἀποκτεῖναι οὐδένα.

[6] *Martyr. Polyc.* § 16 ἐξῆλθε [περιστερὰ καὶ] πλῆθος αἵματος. It is unnecessary for my purpose to inquire whether the words περιστερὰ καὶ should be altered into περὶ στύρακα according to Bishop Wordsworth's ingenious emendation, or omitted altogether as in the text of Eusebius.

[7] John xix. 34 sq.

[8] *Martyr. Polyc.* § 15.

[9] John xix. 28, 30.

word which he uttered out of his mouth hath been and shall be accomplished[1].' To these facts it should be added that the dying prayer of Polycarp contains two coincidences with the phraseology of the Fourth Gospel—'the resurrection of life,' 'the true God[2].'

MELITO, bishop of Sardis, flourished soon after the middle of the second century. This fact appears from two of his works, to which we are able to assign an approximate date. His treatise 'On the Paschal Festival,' he himself tells us, was written while Sergius Paulus was proconsul of Asia[3]; and the recent investigations of M. Waddington into the fasti of this province have led to the result that this proconsulate should probably be dated about A.D. 164—166[4]. Again we are informed that he addressed his 'Apology' to M. Antoninus (A.D. 161—180)[5]. It appears however from an extant fragment, that L. Verus, the colleague of M. Antoninus, was no longer living; for Melito speaks of prayer on behalf of the emperor's son (Commodus), without mentioning his brother and co-emperor (Verus). Now Verus died in the very beginning of the year 169. On the other hand ancient authorities assign the Apology to the year 169 or 170; and, as there is no reason for rejecting their statement, we may suppose that it was written soon after the death of Verus. Probably its date was ascertainable within a year or two from internal evidence. This Apology however is regarded by Eusebius as the latest of Melito's writings[6]; and, as the catalogue of his works comprises some twenty treatises at least, his literary activity must have extended over a considerable period of time, so that we shall probably not be far wrong if we place the commencement of his career as an author

---

[1] *Martyr. Polyc.* § 16.

[2] *ib.* § 14; comp. John v. 29, xvii. 3.

[3] Quoted in Euseb. *H. E.* iv. 26.

[4] *Fastes des Provinces Asiatiques* p. 731, in Le Bas and Waddington's *Voyage Archéologique* etc. Borghesi (*Œuvres* viii. p. 507) had placed it between A.D. 163—168.

[5] Euseb. *l. c.* See Otto *Corp. Apol. Christ.* ix. p. 377 sq.

[6] He writes—ἐπὶ πᾶσι καὶ τὸ πρὸς Ἀντωνῖνον βιβλίδιον. The meaning assigned in the text to ἐπὶ πᾶσι is generally accepted, but cannot be considered quite certain.

about the middle of the century. He appears to have died soon after the Apology was written. In the last decade of the century Polycrates mentions him among other worthies of the past who had gone to their rest[1]. He was buried at Sardis. From the context it may be inferred that he did not suffer martyrdom, like so many of his famous contemporaries, but died a natural death.

These chronological notices suggest that Melito was born in the early part of the second century, within a very few years after the death of St John. During the greater part of his life at all events, he must have been a contemporary of St John's disciple Polycarp, who was martyred at an advanced age in the year 155 or 156; and likewise of Papias, who had conversed with personal disciples of Christ, and seems also to have survived till towards the middle of the century. As the communications between Sardis on the one hand, and Smyrna and Hierapolis on the other, were easy, a prominent man like Melito, whose religious zeal led him on one occasion to undertake a distant journey to Palestine, would be sure to cultivate the acquaintance of these older teachers, even if circumstances did not throw him directly in their way.

Thus Melito is a significant link of connection with the past. At the same time he holds an equally important position with respect to the succeeding age. It can hardly be doubted that among the Asiatic elders, whose authority Irenæus invokes so constantly, Melito must have held a prominent place. It may be suspected that he was the very Ionian whom Clement of Alexandria mentions among his earlier teachers[2]. It is quite certain that his writings were widely known and appreciated in the generations next succeeding his own. He is quoted or referred to by Polycrates at Ephesus, by Clement and Origen at Alexandria, by Tertullian at Carthage, by Hippolytus at Rome.

I have already mentioned that he was a very voluminous writer. Eusebius gives a catalogue of his works, which how-

---

[1] Quoted by Euseb. *H. E.* v. 24. [2] See above, p. 218.

ever he does not profess to be complete. The historian's knowledge was obviously limited by the contents of the library which his friend Pamphilus had gathered together at Cæsarea. The titles of these works are as follows:— *On the Paschal Festival* (two treatises)[1], *On the Life of the Prophets, On the Church. On the Lord's Day, On the Nature of Man, On Creation, On the Obedience of Faith and on the Senses, On the Soul and Body [and Mind], On Baptism, On Truth, On the Creation and Generation of Christ, On Prophecy, On Hospitality, The Key, On the Devil and on the Apocalypse of John, On a Corporeal Deity, An Apology to Antoninus, Selections from the Law and the Prophets*[2]. Besides these works here enumerated, other writings of Melito are quoted elsewhere under the titles, *On the Incarnation of Christ, On the Passion, On the Cross, On the Faith*[3], though some of these may perhaps represent the same works to which Eusebius refers under other names. Comprising this wide range of subjects, doctrinal, exegetical, practical, and controversial, the works of Melito must have furnished the next succeeding generations with ample data for determining his exact theological position. To them it must have been clear, for instance, whether he did or did not accept the Gospel of St John or the Epistles of St Paul. It was hardly possible for him to write on the Paschal question without indicating his views on the Fourth Gospel. It is almost inconceivable that he should have composed a controversial treatise against Marcion without declaring himself respecting the Apostle of the Gentiles. The few meagre fragments which have come down to us supply only incidental notices and resemblances,

---

[1] περὶ τοῦ πάσχα. The author of *Supernatural Religion*, speaks of it as 'Melito's work on the *Passion*' (II. p. 180). This error survives to the sixth edition [but is tacitly corrected in the Complete Edition].

[2] Euseb. *H. E.* iv. 26. This reference serves for all the facts relating to Melito, which are derived from Eusebius, unless otherwise stated. There is a little difficulty respecting the exact titles of the works in one or two cases owing to various readings; but the differences are not important enough to be considered here.

[3] These titles are taken from Anastasius of Sinai, and from the Syriac fragments.

from which we are left to draw our own inferences; but where we grope in the twilight, they were walking in the broad noonday.

Eusebius has happily preserved Melito's preface to his *Selections*, which is of considerable interest. The work itself comprised passages from the Law and the Prophets relating to the Saviour and to the Christian faith generally ($\pi\epsilon\rho\grave{\iota}$ $\tau o\hat{v}$ $\Sigma\omega\tau\hat{\eta}\rho o\varsigma$ $\kappa a\grave{\iota}$ $\pi\acute{a}\sigma\eta\varsigma$ $\tau\hat{\eta}\varsigma$ $\pi\acute{\iota}\sigma\tau\epsilon\omega\varsigma$ $\dot{\eta}\mu\hat{\omega}\nu$), arranged in six books. It seems to have been accompanied with explanatory comments bringing out the prophetical import of the several passages, as Melito understood them. In the preface, addressed to his friend Onesimus, at whose instance the work had been undertaken, he relates that having made a journey to the East and visited the actual scenes of the Gospel history, he informed himself respecting the books of the Old Testament, of which he appends a list. The language which he uses is significant from its emphasis. He writes that his friend had 'desired to be accurately informed about the *old* books' ($\mu a\theta\epsilon\hat{\iota}\nu$ $\tau\grave{\eta}\nu$ $\tau\hat{\omega}\nu$ $\pi a\lambda a\iota\hat{\omega}\nu$ $\beta\iota\beta\lambda\acute{\iota}\omega\nu$ $\dot{\epsilon}\beta ov\lambda\acute{\eta}\theta\eta\varsigma$ $\dot{a}\kappa\rho\acute{\iota}\beta\epsilon\iota a\nu$). He adds that he himself during his Eastern tour had 'obtained accurate information respecting the books of the *Old* Testament ($\dot{a}\kappa\rho\iota\beta\hat{\omega}\varsigma$ $\mu a\theta\grave{\omega}\nu$ $\tau\grave{a}$ $\tau\hat{\eta}\varsigma$ $\pi a\lambda a\iota\hat{a}\varsigma$ $\delta\iota a\theta\acute{\eta}\kappa\eta\varsigma$ $\beta\iota\beta\lambda\acute{\iota}a$).' From these expressions Dr Westcott argues that Melito must have been acquainted with a corresponding Christian literature, which he regarded as the books of the New Testament. To any such inference the author of *Supernatural Religion* demurs[1], and he devotes several pages to proving (what nobody denies) that the expressions 'Old Testament,' 'New Testament,' did not originally refer to a written literature at all, and need not so refer here. All this is beside the purpose, and betrays an entire misunderstanding of the writer whom he ventures to criticize. The contention is not that the expression 'Old Testament' here in itself signifies a collection of books, and therefore implies another collection called the 'New Testament,' but that the

---

[1] *S. R.* II. p. 174 sq.

VII. THE LATER SCHOOL OF ST JOHN.

emphatic and reiterated mention of an *old* Biblical *literature* points naturally to the existence of a *new*. To any one who is accustomed to weigh the force of Greek sentences, as determined by the order of the words, this implied contrast must, I think, make itself felt. It is impossible to read the clauses, having regard to the genius of the language, without throwing a strong emphasis on the recurrent word *old*, which I have therefore italicized, as the only way of reproducing the same effect for the English reader. Dr Westcott therefore is perfectly justified in maintaining that the expression naturally implies a recognized New Testament literature.

And if this reference is suggested by strict principles of exegesis, it alone is consonant with historical probability. It is a fact that half a century, or even more, before Melito wrote, the author of the epistle bearing the name of Barnabas quotes as 'Scripture' a passage found in St Matthew's Gospel, and not known to have existed elsewhere[1]. It is a fact that about that same time, or earlier, Polycarp wrote a letter which is saturated with the thoughts and language of the Apostolic Epistles[2]. It is a fact that some twenty or thirty years before Melito, Justin Martyr speaks of certain Gospels (whether our Canonical Gospels or not, it is unnecessary for my present purpose to inquire) as being read together with the writings of the prophets at the religious services of the Christians on Sundays, and taken afterwards as the subject of exhortation and comment by the preacher[3]. It is a fact that about the same time when Justin records this as the habitual practice of the Church, the heretic Marcion, himself a native of Asia Minor, constructed a Canon for himself by selecting from and mutilating the Apostolic and Evangelical writings which he found in circulation. It is a fact that Dionysius of Corinth, a contemporary of Melito, speaks of certain writings as 'the Scriptures of the Lord,' or

---

[1] See above, p. 177.
[2] See above, p. 104 sq, where the arguments of our author against the genuineness of the Epistle are refuted.
[3] Justin Martyr *Apol.* i. 67 τὰ ἀπομνημονεύματα τῶν ἀποστόλων ἢ τὰ συγγράμματα τῶν προφητῶν ἀναγινώσκεται κ.τ.λ., compared with *ib.* 66 οἱ ἀπόστολοι ἐν τοῖς γενομένοις ὑπ' αὐτῶν ἀπομνημονεύμασιν ἃ καλεῖται εὐαγγέλια.

'the Dominical Scriptures,' and denounces those who tamper with them[1]. It is a fact that Irenæus, who had received his early education in Asia Minor, writing within some ten or twenty years after the death of Melito, quotes the Four Gospels, the Acts of the Apostles, the great majority of the Apostolic Epistles, and the Apocalypse, as Scripture, declaring more especially of the Four Gospels, that they had been received by the Churches from the beginning, and treating all these writings alike with the same deference which they have received from subsequent generations of Christians ever since. The inference from these facts (and they do not stand alone) is obvious. If Melito knew nothing about books of the New Testament, he must have been the only bishop of the Church from the banks of the Euphrates to the pillars of Hercules, who remained in this state of dense ignorance—Melito, who could refer to the Hebrew and the Syriac while interpreting a passage of Genesis, and who made careful inquiries respecting the Canon of the Old Testament Scriptures in the very land where those Scriptures had their birth.

The extant fragments attributed to Melito are meagre and scattered[2]; but, supposing them to be genuine, they afford ample evidence of the theological views of this father, while indirectly they indicate his general relation to the Canon in a way which can hardly be mistaken. The genuineness of many of these fragments however has been seriously questioned. In one or two instances the grounds of hesitation deserve every consideration; but in the majority of cases the objections must be set aside as groundless. Thus it is sought to throw discredit on all those writings which are not named by Eusebius. The author of *Supernatural Religion*, for instance, says that 'Eusebius gives what he evidently considers a complete list of the works of Melito[3].' On the contrary, Eusebius carefully guards himself against any such interpretation of his words. He

---

[1] Quoted by Euseb. *H. E.* iv. 23.
[2] The only complete collection of the fragments of Melito is in Otto
Corp. Apol. Christ. ix. p. 374 sq.
[3] *S. R.* ii. p. 180.

merely professes to give a list of 'those works which have come to his own knowledge.' Obviously he either suspects or knows that there are other writings of Melito in circulation, of which he can give no account. Again, other fragments have been discredited, because they contain false sentiments or foolish interpretations, which are considered unworthy of a father in the second century. I cannot think that this is any argument at all; and I may confidently assume that the author of *Supernatural Religion* will agree with me here. There is much that is foolish in Papias, in Justin Martyr, in Irenæus, in Tertullian, even in Clement of Alexandria, and Origen. Only it is frequently mixed up with the highest wisdom, which more than redeems it. Again others (and among these our author) would throw doubt on the genuineness of the Greek and Syriac fragments which were certainly in circulation some six centuries before, because some mediæval Latin writers attach the name of Melito to forgeries or to anonymous writings, such as the *Clavis*, the *Passing away of the Blessed Virgin Mary*, and the *Passion of St John*[1]. A moment's reflection will show that the two classes of writings must be considered quite apart. When these groundless objections are set aside, the great majority of the Greek and Syriac fragments remain untouched. Otto, the most recent editor of Melito, takes a sensible view on the whole. I do not agree with him on some minor points, but I am quite content to take the fragments which he accepts, as representing the genuine Melito; and I refer those of my readers, who are really desirous to know what this ancient father taught and how he wrote, to this editor's collection.

We have fortunately the evidence of two writers, who lived in the next age to Melito, and therefore before any spurious works could have been in circulation—the one to his style, the other to his theology. On the former point our authority is Tertullian, who in a work now lost spoke of the 'elegans et declamatorium ingenium' of Melito[2]; on the latter, a writer

---

[1] For an account of these writings see Otto, p. 390 sq, p. 402 sq.

[2] Quoted by Jerome *Vir. Ill.* 24.

quoted anonymously by Eusebius but now identified with Hippolytus, who exclaims, 'Who is ignorant of the books of Irenæus and Melito and the rest, which declare Christ to be God and man[1].' The fragments, and more especially the Syriac fragments, accord fully with both these descriptions. They are highly rhetorical, and their superior elegance of language (compared with other Christian writings of the same age) is apparent even through the medium of a Syriac version. They also emphasize the two natures of Christ in many a pointed antithesis.

Of the Greek fragments, not mentioned by Eusebius, the following quoted by Anastasius of Sinai as from the third book on the Incarnation of Christ[2] is important in its bearing on our subject:—

The things done by Christ after the baptism, and especially the miracles (signs), showed his Godhead concealed in the flesh, and assured the world of it. For being perfect God, and perfect man at the same time, He assured us of His two essences (οὐσίας)—of His Godhead by miracles in the three years after His baptism, and of His manhood in the thirty seasons (χρόνοις) before His baptism, during which, owing to his immaturity as regards the flesh (διὰ τὸ ἀτελὲς τὸ κατὰ σάρκα), He concealed the signs of His Godhead, although He was true God from eternity (καίπερ Θεὸς ἀληθὴς προαιώνιος ὑπάρχων).

The genuineness of this fragment has been impugned, partly on the general considerations which have been already discussed, partly on special grounds. It has been said, for instance, that Anastasius must here be reproducing the general substance, and not the exact words, of Melito's statement; but he at all events gives it as a direct quotation. It has been urged again, that linguistic reasons condemn this fragment, since the use of 'seasons' or 'times' for 'years' betrays a later age; but abundant instances of the use are found in earlier writers, even if so very natural a device for avoiding the repetition of the

---

[1] Euseb. *H. E.* v. 28.
[2] Migne's *Patrol. Græc.* xxxix. p. 228 sq.

VII. THE LATER SCHOOL OF ST JOHN. 231

same word (ἔτος) needed any support at all. It has been suggested that there may possibly be some confusion between Melito and Meletius. But the work from which this passage comes is distinctly stated by Anastasius to have been written against Marcion, who by his docetism attacked the true humanity of Christ. Now Melito lived in the very thick of the Marcionite controversy, and must have taken his part in it. On the other hand, Meletius, who held the see of Antioch in the latter part of the fourth century, was one of the principal figures in the Arian controversy and, as such, far too intimately involved in the questions of his own day to think of writing an elaborate work on a subject so comparatively dead as the docetism of Marcion. Moreover, there is no instance in any Greek writer, so far as I have observed, of a confusion between the names Melito and Meletius. Again it is suggested that the Christological views of the writer are too definite for the age of Melito, and point to a later date; but to this the distinct statement of Hippolytus respecting Melito's opinions, which has been already quoted, is a complete answer; and indeed the Ignatian Epistles, which (even if their genuineness should not be accepted) cannot reasonably be placed later than the age of Melito, are equally precise in their doctrinal statements.

But if this be a genuine fragment, the inference is obvious. The author of *Supernatural Religion* will no doubt be ready here, as elsewhere, to postulate any number of unknown apocryphal Gospels which shall supply the facts thus assumed by Melito. The convenience of drawing unlimited cheques on the bank of the unknown is obvious. But most readers will find themselves unable to resist the inference, that for the thirty years of our Lord's silence this father is indebted to a familiar passage in St Luke[1], while, in fixing three years as the duration of His ministry, he is thinking of the three Passovers mentioned by St John.

Of the other fragments ascribed to Melito one deserves to be

[1] St Luke iii. 23.

quoted, not only because the author has made it the subject of some criticisms, but because it exhibits in a concentrated form Melito's views of evangelical history and doctrine[1].

We have made collections from the Law and the Prophets relating to those things which are declared concerning our Lord Jesus Christ, that we might prove to your love that He is the perfect Reason, the Word of God: who was begotten before the light, who was Creator together with the Father, who was the fashioner of man, who was all things in all, who among the patriarchs was Patriarch, who in the law was Law, among the priests Chiefpriest, among the kings Governor, among the prophets Prophet, among the angels Archangel, and among voices[2] the Word, among spirits the Spirit, in the Father the Son, in God God, the King for ever and ever. For this is He who was pilot to Noah, who conducted Abraham, who was bound with Isaac, who was in exile with Jacob, who was sold with Joseph, who was captain with Moses, who was divider of the inheritance with Joshua the son of Nun, who foretold His own sufferings in David and the prophets, who was incarnate in the Virgin, who was born at Bethlehem, who was wrapped in swaddling clothes in the manger, who was seen of the shepherds, who was glorified of the Angels, who was worshipped by the Magi, who was pointed out by John, who gathered together the Apostles, who preached the Kingdom, who healed the maimed, who gave light to the blind, who raised the dead, who appeared in the temple, who was not believed on by the people, who was betrayed by Judas, who was laid hold on by the priests, who was condemned by Pilate, who was transfixed in the flesh, who was hanged on the tree, who was buried in the earth, who rose from the dead, who appeared to the Apostles, who ascended into heaven, who sitteth on the right hand of the Father, who is the rest of those that are departed, the

---

[1] Given in Pitra's *Spicil. Solesm.* II. p. lix. sq, and in Cureton's *Spicil. Syr.* p. 53 sq. See also Otto, p. 420.

[2] The translators hitherto (Renan, Cureton, Sachau) have rendered this expression by the singular '*in voce*, in the voice.' But this makes no sense; and I can hardly doubt that it should be translated as I have given it, though the *ribui*, the sign of the plural, seems to have disappeared in the existing Syriac text. We have here the distinction between φωνή and λόγος, on which writers of the second and third centuries delighted to dwell. It occurs as early as Ignatius *Rom.* 2 (the correct reading). They discovered this distinction in John i. 1, 14, 23, where the Baptist is called φωνὴ βοῶντος, while Christ is ὁ Λόγος.

VII. THE LATER SCHOOL OF ST JOHN. 233

recoverer of those that are lost, the light of those that are in darkness, the deliverer of those that are captives, the guide of those that have gone astray, the refuge of the afflicted, the Bridegroom of the Church, the Charioteer of the Cherubim, the Captain of the Angels, God who is of God, the Son who is of the Father, Jesus Christ, the King for ever and ever. Amen.

This fragment is not in any way exceptional. The references to evangelical history, the modes of expression, the statements of doctrine, all have close parallels scattered through the other fragments ascribed to Melito. Indeed it is the remarkable resemblance of these fragments to each other in thought and diction (with one or two exceptions), though gathered together from writers of various ages, in Greek and in Syriac, which is a strong argument for their genuineness. But the special value of this particular passage is that it gathers into a focus the facts of the evangelical history, on which the faith of Melito rested.

And I do not think it can be reasonably doubted whence these facts are derived. The author of *Supernatural Religion* of course suggests some unknown apocryphal Gospel. But this summary will strike most readers as wonderfully like what a writer might be expected to make who recognized our four canonical Gospels as the sources of evangelical truth. And, when they remember that within a very few years (some twenty at most) Irenæus, who was then a man past middle life, who had intimate relations with the region in which Melito lived, and who appeals again and again to the Asiatic Elders as his chief authorities for the traditional doctrine and practice, declares in perfect good faith that the Church had received these four, and these only, from the beginning, it will probably seem to them irrational to look elsewhere, when the solution is so very obvious.

But the author of *Supernatural Religion* writes that this fragment taken from a treatise *On Faith*, together with another which purports to be a work on the *Soul and Body*, though these two works 'are mentioned by Eusebius,' must nevertheless 'for every reason be pronounced spurious[1].' Let us see what these reasons are.

1. He writes first:

They have in fact no attestation whatever except that of the Syriac translation, which is unknown, and which therefore is worthless.

The fact is that in a very vast number of literary remains, classical and ecclesiastical, whether excerpts or entire works, we are entirely dependent on the scribe for their authentication. Human experience has shown that such authentication is generally trustworthy, and hence it is accepted. In forty-nine cases out of fifty, or probably more, it is found to be satisfactory, and *à priori* probabilities are very strongly against the assumption that any particular case is this fiftieth exception. If there is substantial ground for suspicion, the suspicion has its weight, but not otherwise. A man who would act on any other principle is as unreasonable as a visitor to London, who refuses to believe or trust any one there, because the place is known to harbour thieves and liars.

2. We come therefore to the positive grounds of our author's suspicions, and here he tells us that—

The whole style and thought of the fragments are unlike anything else of Melito's time, and clearly indicate a later stage of theological development.

It is to be regretted that he has not explained himself more fully on this point. I have already pointed out that the theology and the style of these fragments generally are exactly what the notices of Hippolytus and Tertullian would lead us to expect in Melito. And this is especially true of the passage under consideration. What the 'later stage of theological development' indicated may be, I am unable to say. On the

---

[1] *S. R.* II. p. 184. Our author has stated just before: 'It is well known that there were many writers' ['other writers' Compl. Ed.] 'in the early Church bearing the names of Melito and Miletius or Meletius, which were frequently confounded.' It is dangerous always to state a sweeping negative; but I am not aware of any other writer in the early Church bearing the name of Melito.

contrary, the leading conception of this passage, which sees all theology through the medium of the Logos, and therefore identifies all the theophanies in the Old Testament with the Person of Christ, though it lingers on through the succeeding ages, is essentially characteristic of the second century. The apologists generally exhibit this phenomenon; but in none is it more persistent than in Justin Martyr, who wrote a quarter of a century before Melito. Even the manner in which the conception is worked out by Melito has striking parallels in Justin. Thus Justin states that this Divine Power, who was begotten by God before all creation, is called sometimes 'the glory of the Lord, sometimes Son, sometimes Wisdom, sometimes God, sometimes Lord and Word, while sometimes He calls Himself Chief-captain ($ἀρχιστράτηγος$), appearing in the form of man to Joshua the son of Nun ($τῷ\ τοῦ\ Ναυῆ\ \text{'}Ιησοῦ$)[1].' Elsewhere he states that Christ is 'King and Priest and God and Lord and Angel and Man and Chief-captain and Stone,' etc., and he undertakes to show this 'from all the Scriptures[2].' And again, in a third passage he says that the same Person, who is called Son of God in the memoirs of the Apostles, 'went forth from the Father before all created things through His power and counsel,' being designated ' Wisdom and Day and Orient and Sword and Stone and Staff and Jacob and Israel, now in one way, and now in another, in the sayings of the prophets,' and that 'He became man through the Virgin[3].' Nor do these passages stand alone. This same conception pervades the whole of Justin's *Dialogue*, and through it all the phenomena of the Old Testament are explained.

Only on one point has our author thought fit to make a definite statement. 'It is worthy of remark,' he writes, 'that the Virgin is introduced into all these fragments [the five Syriac fragments which he has mentioned just before] in a manner quite foreign to the period at which Melito lived.' What can this mean? In the passage before us the only allusion to the

---

[1] Justin Martyr *Dial.* § 61 (p. 284).   [2] Justin Martyr *Dial.* § 100 (p. 327).
[3] Justin Martyr *Dial.* § 34 (p. 251).

subject is in the words 'incarnate in the Virgin' (or 'a virgin'); and the references in the other fragments are of the same kind. It is difficult to see how any one, recognizing the statements of the Synoptic Gospels, could pass over the mention of the Virgin more lightly. Here again, if he will turn to Justin Martyr, he will find a far fuller and more emphatic reference[1].

3. But our author states also:

> In the Mechitarist Library at Venice there is a shorter version of the same passage in a Syriac MS, and an Armenian version of the extract as given above, in both of which the passage is distinctly ascribed to Irenæus.

This is a fact of some importance, to which he has rightly directed attention. It would have been well if he had been a little more accurate in his statement. The extract in the Armenian version (of which the shorter Syriac form is obviously an abridgment), though mainly the same as our passage, begins in quite a different way. While Melito commences, 'We have made collections from the Law and the Prophets relating to those things which are declared concerning our Lord Jesus Christ,' etc., as quoted above, the Armenian extract, ascribed to Irenæus, runs thus: 'The Law and the Prophets and the Evangelists have declared that Christ was born of a virgin and suffered on the cross, and that He was raised from the dead, and ascended into heaven, and was glorified and reigneth for ever. The same is called the perfect Reason, the Word of God,' etc.[2]. Now it is obvious from a comparison of these two openings, that in the former, ascribed to Melito, we have the passage in its original setting, whereas in the latter, ascribed to Irenæus, it has been altered to suit some other context or to explain itself independently. The reference to the author and the occasion of writing is omitted, while the 'Evangelists' are introduced by the side of 'the Law and the Prophets' for the sake of completeness. Melito, as we happen to know, did make

---

[1] Justin Martyr *Dial.* § 100 (p. 327). Syriac abridgment commences in the
[2] See *Spicil. Solesm.* i. p. 4. The same way. See *ib.* p. 3.

such a collection of extracts from the Law and the Prophets as is here mentioned, and for the very purpose which is here stated; and the correspondence of language in this opening passage with the dedication of his collection to Onesimus, referred to above, is sufficiently striking. To Melito therefore evidence, internal and external alike, requires us to ascribe the passage. But, if so, how came the name of Irenæus to be attached to it? Was this mere accident? I think not. Nothing would be more natural than that Irenæus should introduce a passage of Melito, as a famous Asiatic elder, either anonymously or otherwise, into one of his own writings. I have already had occasion to refer to the free use which the early fathers made of their predecessors, frequently without any acknowledgement[1]. In this particular case, Irenæus may or may not have acknowledged his obligation. I venture to think that this solution of the double ascription will appear not only plausible, but probable, when I mention another fact. In a second Armenian extract I find a passage headed, 'The saying of Irenæus[2].' I turn to the passage, and I find that it contains not the words of Irenæus himself, but of Papias quoted by Irenæus. In the Armenian extract the name of the original author has entirely disappeared, though in this case Irenæus directly mentions Papias as his authority.

The attitude of Melito towards the Apostle of the Gentiles appears clearly enough from the title of one of his works, 'On the Obedience of Faith,' which is a characteristic expression of St Paul[3], and also from occasional coincidences of language, such as 'putting on the form of a servant[4].'

CLAUDIUS APOLLINARIS, bishop of Hierapolis, was a contemporary of Melito, but apparently a younger man, though only by a very few years. His date is fixed approximately by the extant notices. He addressed an Apology to the Emperor M. Aurelius, who reigned from A.D. 161—180; and as in this work he mentioned the incident of the so-called Thundering

[1] See above, p. 202.
[2] *Spicil. Solesm.* I. p. 1.
[3] Rom. i. 5, xvi. 26.
[4] Phil. ii. 7.

Legion, which happened between A.D. 172—174, it cannot have been written before that date[1]. At the same time there are some reasons, though not conclusive, for thinking that it should not be placed much later[2]. On the other hand, when Serapion writes towards the close of the century, he speaks of Apollinaris as no longer living; and judging from the language used, we may infer that his death had not been very recent[3].

Like Melito, he was a voluminous writer. Eusebius indeed only gives the titles of four works by this father, the *Apology* (already mentioned), *Against the Greeks* (five treatises or books), *On Truth* (two books), *Against the Jews* (two books), besides referring to certain writings *Against the Montanists* (κατὰ τῆς Φρυγῶν αἱρέσεως), which he places later than the others. But he is careful to say that his list comprises only those works which he had seen, and that many others were extant in different quarters[4]. Photius mentions reading three works only by this father, of which one, the treatise *On Godliness*, is not in Eusebius' list; but he too adds, 'Other writings of this author also are said to be notable, but I have not hitherto met with them[5].' Besides these, the author of the Paschal Chronicle quotes from a treatise of Apollinaris *On the Paschal Festival*[6], and Theodoret speaks of his writing against the Severians or Encratites[7]. As in the case of Melito, the character and variety of his works, so long as they were extant, must have afforded ample material for a judgment on his theological views. More especially his writings against the Montanists and on the Paschal Festival would indicate his relations to the Canonical books of the New Testament. His orthodoxy is attested by Serapion, by Eusebius, by Jerome, by

---

[1] Euseb. *H. E.* iv. 27. This is the reference for all the facts relating to Apollinaris given by Eusebius, unless otherwise mentioned.

[2] See Otto *Corp. Apol. Christ.* ix. p. 480 sq.

[3] Quoted by Eusebius, *H. E.* v. 19.

[4] Euseb. *H. E.* iv. 27 πολλῶν παρὰ πολλοῖς σωζομένων, τὰ εἰς ἡμᾶς ἐλθόντα ἐστὶ τάδε.

[5] Photius *Bibl.* 14 λέγεται δὲ αὐτοῦ καὶ ἕτερα συγγράμματα ἀξιομνημόνευτα εἶναι, οἷς οὔπω ἡμεῖς ἐνετύχομεν.

[6] *Chron. Pasch.* p. 13 (ed. Dind.).

[7] Theodoret, *H. F.* i. 21.

VII. THE LATER SCHOOL OF ST JOHN.

Theodoret, by Socrates, and by Photius[1], from different points of view.

Besides a reference in Eusebius to his Apology, which hardly deserves the name of a quotation, only two short extracts remain of these voluminous writings. They are taken from the work on the Paschal Festival, and are preserved, as I have already stated, in the *Paschal Chronicle*.

The first runs as follows:—

There are persons who from ignorance dispute about these questions, acting in a way that is pardonable; for ignorance is no proper subject for blame, but needs instruction. And they say that on the fourteenth the Lord ate the lamb (τὸ πρόβατον) with His disciples, but Himself suffered on the great day of unleavened bread, and they affirm that Matthew represents it so, as they interpret him. Thus their interpretation is out of harmony with the law (ἀσύμφωνος νόμῳ), and on their showing the Gospels seem to be at variance with one another (στασιάζειν δοκεῖ κατ' αὐτοὺς τὰ εὐαγγέλια).

The second fragment is taken from the same book, and apparently from the same context.

The fourteenth was the true passover of the Lord, the great sacrifice, the Son of God substituted for the lamb, the same that was bound and Himself bound the strong man, that was judged being judge of the quick and dead, and that was delivered into the hands of sinners to be crucified; the same that was lifted on the horns of the unicorn, and that was pierced in His holy side; the same that poured forth again the two purifying elements, water and blood, word and spirit, and that was buried on the day of the passover, the stone being laid against His sepulchre.

If the publication of this work was suggested by Melito's treatise on the same subject, as seems probable, it must have been written about A.D. 164—166, or soon after. The references to the Gospels are obvious. In the first extract Apollinaris has in view the difficulty of reconciling the chronology

---

[1] Serapion, *l. c.*; Eusebius, *H. E.* iv. 21; Jerome, *Ep.* 70 (1. p. 428); Theodoret, *H. F.* iii. 2; Socrates, *H. E.* iii. 7; Photius, *l. c.*

of the Paschal week as given by St John with the narratives of the Synoptic Evangelists; and he asserts that the date fixed for the Passion by some persons (the 15th instead of 14th) can only be maintained at the expense of a discrepancy between the two accounts; whereas, if the 14th be taken, the two accounts are reconcilable. At the same time he urges that their view is not in harmony with the law, since the paschal lamb, the type, was slain on the 14th, and therefore it follows that Christ, the antitype, must have been crucified on the same day. I am not concerned here with the question whether Apollinaris or his opponents were right. The point to be noticed is that he speaks of 'the Gospels' (under which term he includes at least St Matthew and St John) as any one would speak of received documents to which the ultimate appeal lies. His language in this respect is such as might be used by a writer in the fourth century, or in the nineteenth, who was led by circumstances to notice a difficulty in harmonizing the accounts of the Evangelists. The second extract bears out the impression left by the first. The incident of the water and the blood is taken from the Fourth Gospel; but a theological interpretation is forced upon it which cannot have been intended by the Evangelist. Some time must have elapsed before the narrative could well be made the subject of a speculative comment like this. Thus both extracts alike suggest that the Fourth Gospel was already a time-honoured book when they were written.

But the author of *Supernatural Religion* meets the inference by denying the genuineness of the extracts. I hardly think, however, that he can have seen what havoc he was making in his own ranks by this movement. He elsewhere asserts very decidedly (without however giving reasons) that the Quartodeciman controversy turned on the point whether the 14th Nisan was the day of the Last Supper or the day of the Crucifixion, the Quartodecimans maintaining the former[1]. In other words, he believes that it was the anniversary, not of the Passion, but of the Last Supper, which the Quartodecimans

[1] [See above, p. 17].

VII. THE LATER SCHOOL OF ST JOHN.

kept so scrupulously on the 14th, and that therefore, as they pleaded the authority of St John for their practice, the Fourth Gospel cannot have been written by this Apostle, since it represents the Passion as taking place on the 14th. As I have before intimated, this view of the Paschal dispute seems to me to be altogether opposed to the general tenor of the evidence. But it depends, for such force or plausibility as it has, almost solely on these fragments from ancient writers quoted in the *Paschal Chronicle*, of which the extracts from Apollinaris are the most important. If therefore he refuses to accept the testimony of the *Paschal Chronicle* to their authorship, he undermines the very foundation on which his theory rests.

On this inconsistency however I need not dwell. The authorship of these extracts was indeed questioned by some earlier writers[1], but on entirely mistaken grounds; and at the

---

[1] Our author says (II. p. 190): 'The two fragments have by many been conjecturally ascribed to Pierius of Alexandria, a writer of the third century, who composed a work on Easter;' and in his note he gives references to four persons, Tillemont, Lardner, Donaldson, and Routh, apparently as supporting this view. Routh however mentions it only to reject it, and distinctly ascribes the fragments to Apollinaris (*Rel. Sacr.* I. p. 167). Neither have I yet found any passage in Tillemont, where he assigns them to Pierius. Lardner indeed states this of Tillemont; but in the only reference which he gives (T. ii. P. iii. p. 91, ed. Bruxelles), nothing of the kind is said. Tillemont there refers in the margin to 'S. Pierre d'Alex.,' because this *Peter* of Alexandria is likewise quoted in the preface of the *Chronicon Paschale*, and the question of the genuineness of the fragments ascribed to Apollinaris is reserved to be discussed afterwards in connection with this Peter (*ib.* p. 268 sq). But he does not ascribe them to Peter, and he does not mention Pierius there at all, so far as I have observed. It should be added that the title of Pierius' work was 'A Discourse relating to the Passover and Hosea' (ὁ εἰς τὸ πάσχα καὶ Ὡσηὲ λόγος); see Photius *Bibl.* cxix. So far as we can judge from the description of Photius, it seems to have been wholly different in subject and treatment from the works of Melito and Apollinaris. It was perhaps an exposition of Hosea ii. 6—17. [In the Complete Edition Tillemont and Routh are tacitly omitted from the note, and 'some' substituted for 'many' in the text.]

Our author also by way of discrediting the *Chronicon Paschale* as a witness, rejects (II. p. 190) a passage of Melito quoted on the same authority (p. 482, ed. Dind.); but he gives no reasons. The passage bears every mark of genuineness. It is essentially characteristic of an Apologist in the second century, and indeed is obviously taken from the Apology of Melito, as the chronicler intimates. Otto accepts it without hesitation.

present time the consensus among critics of the most opposite schools is all but universal. 'On the genuineness of these fragments, which Neander questioned, there is now no more dispute,' writes Scholten[1]. Our author however is far too persistent to let them pass. Their veracity has once been questioned, and therefore they shall never again be suffered to enter the witness-box.

It may be presumed that he has alleged those arguments against their genuineness which seemed to him to be the strongest, and I will therefore consider his objections. They are twofold.

1. He urges that the external testimony to their authorship is defective. His reasoning is as follows[2]:—

Eusebius was acquainted with the work of Melito on the Passion, and quotes it, which must have referred to his contemporary and antagonist, Apollinaris, had he written such a work as this fragment denotes. Not only, however, does Eusebius know nothing of his having composed such a work, but neither do Theodoret, Jerome, Photius, nor other writers, who enumerate other of his works; nor is he mentioned in any way by Clement of Alexandria, Irenæus, nor by any of those who took part in the great controversy.

Here is a tissue of fallacies and assumptions. In the first place, it is a *petitio principii*, as will be seen presently, that Apollinaris was an antagonist of Melito. Even, if this were so, there is not the smallest evidence, nor any probability, that Apollinaris would have written before Melito, so that the latter could have quoted him. How, again, has our author learnt that Eusebius 'knows nothing of his having composed such a work'? It is certain, indeed, that Eusebius had not seen the work when he composed his list of the writings of Apollinaris; but it nowhere appears that he was unaware of its existence. The very language in which he disclaims any pretension of giving a complete list seems to imply that he had observed other books quoted in other writers, which he had not

---

[1] *Die ält. Zeugn.* p. 105, quoted by Otto.

[2] *S. R.* II. p. 189. [This paragraph is rewritten in the Complete Edition.]

VII. THE LATER SCHOOL OF ST JOHN. 243

read or seen himself. Theodoret does not 'enumerate other of his works,' as the looseness of the English would suggest to the reader. He only mentions incidentally, when describing the sects of the Severians and Montanists respectively, that Apollinaris had written against them[1]. There is not the smallest reason why he should have gone out of his way in either passage to speak of the work on the Paschal Festival, supposing him to have known of it. And if not, where else does our author find in Theodoret any notice which can be made to yield the inference that he was unacquainted with this treatise? Nor again does Jerome, in the passage to which our author refers in his note[2], allude to a single work by this writer, but simply mentions him by name among those versed in profane as well as sacred literature. Elsewhere indeed he does give a catalogue of Apollinaris' writings[3], but there he simply copies Eusebius. With regard to Photius again, the statement, though not so directly inaccurate, is altogether misleading. Photius simply mentions three works of Apollinaris, which he read during his embassy, but he does not profess to give a list; and he says distinctly that there were other famous works by the same author which he had not seen. Who the 'other writers' may be, who 'enumerate other of his works,' I am altogether at a loss to imagine. But the last sentence, 'Nor is he mentioned in any way by Clement of Alexandria, Irenæus, etc.,' is the most calculated to mislead the reader. Of the treatise of Clement on the Paschal Festival only two short fragments are preserved. He does not mention any person in these, nor could he have done so without going out of his way. For the rest, Clement is reported by Eusebius to have stated in his work that he was prompted to write it by Melito's treatise on the same subject[4]. Eusebius is there discussing Melito, and any mention of Apollinaris would have been quite out of place. What ground is there then for the assumption

[1] Theodoret *H. F.* i. 21; iii. 2.
[2] 'Epist. ad Magnum Ep. p. 83.'
[3] Jerome *Vir. Ill.* 26.
[4] Euseb. *H. E.* iv. 26.

that Clement did not mention Apollinaris, because Eusebius has not recorded the fact? When at a later point Eusebius comes to speak of Clement, he says of this father that in the treatise of which we are speaking he 'mentions Melito and Irenæus and *certain others,* whose explanations also he has given[1].' Why may not Apollinaris have been included among these 'certain others' whom Clement quoted? The same fallacy underlies our author's reference to Irenæus. The work of Irenæus is lost. Eusebius, it is true, preserves some very meagre fragments[2]; but in these not a single writer on either side in the Quartodeciman controversy is mentioned, not even Melito. Irenæus may have quoted Apollinaris by name in this lost treatise, just as he quotes Papias by name in his extant work on heresies, where nevertheless Eusebius does not care to record the fact. All this assumed silence of writers whose works are lost is absolutely valueless against the direct and explicit testimony of the *Paschal Chronicle.*

2. But secondly; our author considers that the contents of these fragments are inconsistent with their attribution to Apollinaris. His argument is instructive[3].

It is stated that all the Churches of Asia, including some of the most distinguished members of the Church, such as Polycarp, and his own contemporary Melito, celebrated the Christian festival on the 14th Nisan, the practice almost universal, therefore, in the country in which Claudius Apollinaris is supposed to write this fragment. How is it possible, therefore, that this isolated convert to the views of Victor and the Roman Church could write of so vast and distinguished a majority as 'some who through ignorance raised contentions' on this point, when notably all the Asiatic Churches at that time were agreed to keep the fourteenth of Nisan, and in doing so raised no new contention at all, but, as Polycrates represented, followed the tradition handed down to them from their fathers, and authorized by the practice of the Apostle John himself?

with more to the same effect.

---

[1] Euseb. *H. E.* vi. 13.
[2] Euseb. *H. E.* v. 24.
[3] *S. R.* II. p. 189. [Rewritten in the Complete Edition.]

VII. THE LATER SCHOOL OF ST JOHN. 245

I will hand over this difficulty to those who share our author's views on the point at issue in the Quartodeciman controversy. Certainly I cannot suggest any satisfactory mode of escape from the dilemma which is here put. But what, if the writer of these fragments was not an 'isolated convert to the views of Victor,' but a Quartodeciman himself? What, if the Quartodecimans kept the 14th, not as the commemoration of the Last Supper, but of the Passion, so that Melito himself would have heartily assented to the criticisms in these fragments[1]? This is the obvious view suggested by the account of the controversy in Eusebius, and in Irenæus as quoted by Eusebius; and it gains confirmation from these fragments of Apollinaris. It seems to me highly improbable that Apollinaris should have been an exception to the practice of the Asiatic Churches. So far I agree with our author. But this is a reason for questioning the soundness of his own views on the Quartodeciman controversy, rather than for disputing the genuineness of the fragments attributed to Apollinaris.

After this account of Melito and Apollinaris, the two chief representatives of the later school of St John, it will be worth while to call attention to a statement of Irenæus in which he professes to record the opinion of the Asiatic elders on a point intimately affecting the credibility of the Fourth Gospel, the chronology of our Lord's life and ministry[2].

The Valentinians, against whom this father is arguing, sought for analogies to the thirty æons of their pleroma, or supra-sensual world, in the Gospel history. Among other examples they alleged the thirty years' duration of our Lord's life. This computation of the Gospel chronology they derived

---

[1] Our author himself says elsewhere (II. p. 472): 'A violent discussion arose as to the day upon which 'the true Passover of the Lord' should be celebrated, the Church in Asia Minor maintaining that it should be observed on the 14th Nisan, etc.' This is exactly what Apollinaris does. By incidentally quoting the words of Apollinaris ($\tau\grave{o}$ $\dot{a}\lambda\eta\theta\iota\nu\grave{o}\nu$ $\tau o\hat{u}$ $K\nu\rho\acute{\iota}o\nu$ $\pi\acute{a}\sigma\chi a$), he has unconsciously borne testimony to the true interpretation of the passage, though himself taking the opposite view.

[2] Iren. *Hær.* ii. 22.

from the notices in St Luke as interpreted by themselves. At the commencement of His ministry, so they maintained, He had completed His twenty ninth and was entering upon His thirtieth year, and His ministry itself did not extend beyond a twelve-month, 'the acceptable *year* of the Lord' foretold by the prophet. Irenæus expresses his astonishment that persons professing to understand the deep things of God should have overlooked the commonest facts of the evangelical narrative, and points to the three passovers recorded in St John's Gospel during the term of our Lord's ministry. Independently of the chronology of the Fourth Gospel, Irenæus has an *à priori* reason of his own, why the Saviour must have lived more than thirty years. He came to sanctify every period of life— infancy, childhood, youth, declining age. It was therefore necessary that He should have passed the turn of middle life. From thirty to forty, he argues, a man is still reckoned young (*juvenis*).

But from his fortieth and fiftieth year he is already declining into older age, which was the case with our Lord when He taught, as the Gospel and all the elders who associated with John the disciple of the Lord in Asia testify that John delivered this account. For he remained with them till the times of Trajan. But some of them saw not only John, but other Apostles also, and heard these same things from their lips, and bear testimony to such an account.

Irenæus then goes on to argue that the same may be inferred from the language of our Lord's Jewish opponents, who asked: 'Thou art not yet fifty years old, and hast thou seen Abraham?' This, he maintains, could not properly be said of one who was only thirty years of age, and must imply that the person so addressed had passed his fortieth year at least, and probably that he was not far off his fiftieth.

On this passage it must be remarked that the Valentinian chronology was derived from a *prima facie* interpretation of the Synoptic narrative; whereas the Asiatic reckoning, which Irenæus maintains, was, or might well have been, founded on the Fourth Gospel, but could not possibly have been elicited from the first three Gospels independently of the fourth.

On this question generally I have spoken already in a former paper[1]. Though it seems probable that our Lord's ministry was confined to three years, yet there is not a single notice in any of the four Gospels inconsistent with the hypothesis that it extended over a much longer period, and that He was some forty years old at all events at the time of the Passion. The Synoptic narratives say absolutely nothing about the interval which elapsed between the Baptism and the Passion. St John mentions three passovers, but he nowhere intimates that he has given an exhaustive list of these festivals. The account of Irenæus therefore is not so unreasonable after all; and we need not have hesitated to accept it, if there had been any definite grounds for doing so.

It will be seen however, that Irenæus, while maintaining that our Lord was forty years old, grounds his opinion mainly on a false inference from John viii. 57. At the same time he adduces the testimony of the Gospel and 'all the elders,' not for this particular view of our Lord's age, but for the more general statement that He was past middle life; and this vagueness of language suggests that, though their testimony was distinctly on his side as against the Valentinians, it did not go beyond this. It is very far from improbable indeed, that he borrowed this very interpretation of John viii. 57 from one of these Asiatic elders, just as we have seen him[2] elsewhere borrowing an interpretation of another passage of this Gospel (xiv. 2) from the same source. But, as he has here forced the testimony of the Fourth Gospel to say more than it really does say, so also he may have strained the testimony of 'all the elders' in the same direction. Yet the broad fact remains that he confidently appeals to them in support of a chronology suggested by the Fourth Gospel, but certainly not deducible from the Synoptic narratives.

And the extant remains of this school support the appeal so

[1] See above, p. 131.   [2] [See above, p. 4 sq.]

qualified. We have seen that its two most famous authors, Melito and Apollinaris, distinctly follow the chronology of the Fourth Evangelist, the one in the duration of the Lord's ministry, the other in the events of the Paschal week[1].

Of the special references to these fathers of the Asiatic Church, which appear elsewhere in Irenæus, it is sufficient to say that in one instance an elder is represented as quoting a saying of our Lord contained only in the Gospel of St John[2] while the words ascribed to another are most probably suggested by the language of the same Evangelist[3]. This latter elder, whose speculations are given at great length, also introduces two direct quotations from St Paul's Epistles, and treats the Apostle's authority throughout as beyond dispute[4].

The last father of the Asiatic school, whom it will be necessary to mention, is POLYCRATES, bishop of Ephesus. When Victor of Rome in the closing years of the second century attempted to force the Western usage with respect to Easter on the Asiatic Christians, Polycrates wrote to remonstrate. The letter is unhappily lost, but a valuable extract is preserved by Eusebius[5]. In this the writer claims to speak authoritatively on the subject of dispute, owing to the special opportunities which he had enjoyed. He states that he had received the observance of the 14th by tradition from his relations, of whom seven had been bishops; he says that he had conferred with the brethren from all parts of the world; and he adds that he had 'gone through every holy scripture.' When we remember the question at issue, and recall the language of Apollinaris respecting the Gospels, in writing on the same subject, we see what is implied in this last sentence. The

---

[1] I observe also that Melito, while commenting on the sacrifice of Isaac, lays stress on the fact that our Lord was τέλειος, not νέος, at the time of the Passion, as if he too had some adversary in view; *Fragm.* 12 (p. 418). This is an incidental confirmation of the statement of Irenæus respecting the Asiatic elders.

[2] See above, p. 194. Reasons are there given for identifying this elder with Papias.

[3] Iren. *Hær.* iv. 31. 1. See John viii. 56.

[4] Iren. *Hær.* iv. 27 sq.

[5] Euseb. *H. E.* v. 24.

VII. THE LATER SCHOOL OF ST JOHN. 249

extract, which is short, contains only two references to the writings of the New Testament. The one is to the Fourth Gospel; St John is described in the very words of this Gospel, as 'he that leaned on the bosom of the Lord' (ὁ ἐπὶ τὸ στῆθος τοῦ Κυρίου ἀναπεσών)[1]. The other is to a book of the Pauline cycle, the Acts of the Apostles; 'They that are greater than I,' writes Polycrates, 'have said, *We must obey God rather than men*[2].'

We have now reached the close of the second century, and it is not necessary to pursue the history of the School of St John in their Asiatic home beyond this point. But in the meantime a large and flourishing colony had been established in the cities of southern Gaul, and no account of the traditions of the school would be adequate which failed to take notice of this colony. This part of the subject however must be left for a subsequent paper. Meanwhile the inferences from the notices passed under review cannot, I think, be doubtful. Out of a very extensive literature, by which this school was once represented, the extant remains are miserably few and fragmentary; but the evidence yielded by these meagre relics is decidedly greater, in proportion to their extent, than we had any right to expect. As regards the Fourth Gospel, this is especially the case. If the same amount of written matter—occupying a very few pages in all—were extracted accidentally from the current theological literature of our own day, the chances, unless I am mistaken, would be strongly against our finding so many indications of the use of this Gospel. In every one of the writers, from Polycarp and Papias to Polycrates, we have observed phenomena which bear witness directly or indirectly, and with different degrees of distinctness, to its recognition. It is quite possible for critical ingenuity to find a reason for discrediting each instance in turn. An objector may urge in one case, that the writing itself is a forgery; in a second, that the particular passage is an interpolation; in a

---

[1] John xxi. 20; comp. xiii. 25.   [2] Acts v. 29.

third, that the supposed quotation is the original and the language of the Evangelist the copy; in a fourth, that the incident or saying was not deduced from this Gospel but from some apocryphal work, containing a parallel narrative. By a sufficient number of assumptions, which lie beyond the range of verification, the evidence may be set aside. But the early existence and recognition of the Fourth Gospel is the one simple postulate which explains all the facts. The law of gravitation accounts for the various phenomena of motion, the falling of a stone, the jet of a fountain, the orbits of the planets, and so forth. It is quite possible for any one, who is so disposed, to reject this explanation of nature. Provided that he is allowed to postulate a new force for every new fact with which he is confronted, he has nothing to fear. He will then

> "gird the sphere
> With centric and eccentric scribbled o'er,
> Cycle and epicycle, orb in orb,"

happy in his immunity. But the other theory will prevail nevertheless by reason of its simplicity.

VIII. The Churches of Gaul.

[August, 1876.]

IN the preceding papers I have investigated the testimony borne by the Churches of Asia Minor to the Canonical Gospels, and more especially to the Fourth Evangelist. The peculiar value of this testimony is due to the close personal relations of these communities with the latest surviving Apostles, more particularly with St John. At the same time I took occasion incidentally to remark on their attitude towards St Paul and his writings, because an assumed antagonism between the Apostle of the Gentiles and the Twelve has been adopted by a modern school of critics as the basis for a reconstruction of early Christian history. I purpose in the present paper extending this investigation to the Churches of Gaul. The Christianity of Gaul was in some sense the daughter of the Christianity of Asia Minor.

Of the history of the Gallican Churches before the middle of the second century we have no certain information. It seems fairly probable indeed that, when we read in the Apostolic age of a mission of Crescens to 'Galatia' or 'Gaul',[1] the western country is meant rather than the Asiatic settlement which bore the same name; and, if so, this points to some relations with St Paul himself. But, even though this explanation should be accepted, the notice stands quite alone. Later tradition indeed supplements it with legendary matter,

[1] 2 Tim. iv. 10. Gaul was almost universally called 'Galatia' in Greek at this time and for many generations afterwards.

but it is impossible to say what substratum of fact, if any, underlies these comparatively recent stories.

The connection between the southern parts of Gaul and the western districts of Asia Minor had been intimate from very remote times. Gaul was indebted for her earliest civilization to her Greek settlements like Marseilles, which had been colonized from Asia Minor some six centuries before the Christian era; and close relations appear to have been maintained even to the latest times. During the Roman period the people of Marseilles still spoke the Greek language familiarly along with the vernacular Celtic of the native population and the official Latin of the dominant power[1]. When therefore Christianity had established her head-quarters in Asia Minor, it was not unnatural that the Gospel should flow in the same channels which had already conducted the civilization and the commerce of the Asiatic Greeks westward.

At all events, whatever we may think of the antecedent probabilities, the fact itself can hardly be disputed. In the year A.D. 177, under Marcus Aurelius, a severe persecution broke out on the banks of the Rhone in the cities of Vienne and Lyons—a persecution which by its extent and character bears a noble testimony to the vitality of the Churches in these places. To this incident we owe the earliest extant historical notice of Christianity in Gaul. A contemporary record of the martyrdoms on this occasion is preserved in the form of a letter from the persecuted Churches, addressed to 'the brethren that are in Asia and Phrygia[2].' The communities thus addressed, it will be observed, belong to the district in which St John's influence was predominant, and which produced all the writers of his school who have been discussed in the preceding papers—Polycarp, Papias, Melito, Apollinaris, Polycrates. Of the references to the Canonical Scriptures in this letter I shall speak presently. For the moment it is sufficient to say that

[1] They are called 'trilingues,' Varro in Isid. *Etym.* xv. 1.

[2] It is preserved in great part by Eusebius, *H. E.* v. 1, and may be read conveniently in Routh *Rel. Sacr.* i. p. 295 sq.

the very fact of their addressing the communication to these distant Churches shows the closeness of the ties which connected the Christians in Gaul with their Asiatic brethren. Moreover, in the body of the letter it is incidentally stated of two of the sufferers, that they came from Asia Minor—Attalus a Pergamene by birth, and Alexander a physician from Phrygia who 'had lived many years in the provinces of Gaul;' while nearly all of them bear Greek names. Among these martyrs the most conspicuous was Pothinus, the aged bishop of Lyons, who was more than ninety years old when he suffered. A later tradition makes him a native of Asia Minor[1]; and this would be a highly probable supposition, even if unsupported by any sort of evidence. Indeed it is far from unlikely that the fact was stated in the letter itself, for Eusebius has not preserved the whole of it. But whether an Asiatic Greek or not, he must have been a growing boy when St John died; and through him the Churches of Southern Gaul, when they first appear in the full light of history, are linked directly with the Apostolic age.

Immediately after this persecution the intimate alliance between these distant parts of Christendom was manifested in another way. The Montanist controversy was raging in the Church of Phrygia, and the brethren of Gaul communicated to them their views on the controverted points[2]. To this communication they appended various letters of the martyrs, 'which they penned, while yet in bonds, to the brethren in Asia and Phrygia.' About the same time the martyrs sent Irenæus, then a presbyter, as their delegate with letters of recommendation to Eleutherus, bishop of Rome, for the sake of conferring with him on this same subject[3].

Some twenty years later, as the century was drawing to a close, another controversy broke out, relating to the observance of Easter, in which again the Asiatic Churches were mainly concerned; and here too we find the Christians of Gaul interposing with their counsels. When Victor of Rome issued his

[1] See the references in Tillemont *Mémoires* II. p. 343.
[2] Euseb. *H. E.* v. 3.
[3] Euseb. *H. E.* v. 4.

edict of excommunication against the Churches of Asia Minor, Irenæus wrote to remonstrate. The letter sent on this occasion however did not merely represent his own private views, for we are especially told that he wrote 'in the name of the brethren in Gaul over whom he presided.' Nor did he appeal to the Roman bishop alone, but he exchanged letters also with 'very many divers rulers of the Churches concerning the question which had been stirred[1].'

Bearing these facts in mind, and inferring from them, as we have a right to infer, that the Churches of Gaul for the most part inherited the traditions of the Asiatic school of St John, we look with special interest to the documents emanating from these communities.

The Epistle of the brotherhoods in Vienne and Lyons, already mentioned, is the earliest of these. The main business of the letter is a narrative of contemporary facts, and any allusions therefore to the Canonical writings are incidental.

But, though incidental, they are unequivocal. Of the references to St Paul, for instance, there can be no doubt. Thus the martyrs and confessors are mentioned as 'showing in very truth that *the sufferings of this present time are not worthy to be compared with the glory which shall be revealed in us*,' where a sentence containing fourteen words in the Greek is given *verbatim* as it stands in Rom. viii. 18. Thus again, they are described as 'imitators of Christ, *who being in the form of God thought it not robbery to be equal with God*,' where in like manner a sentence of twelve words stands *verbatim* as we find it Phil. ii. 6. No one, I venture to think, will question the source of these passages, though they are given anonymously and without any signs of quotation. Nor can there be any reasonable doubt that when Attalus the martyr is called 'the pillar and ground' ($\sigma\tau\hat{\upsilon}\lambda o\nu$ $\kappa\alpha\hat{\iota}$ $\hat{\epsilon}\delta\rho\alpha\hat{\iota}\omega\mu\alpha$) of the Christians at Lyons, the expression is taken from 1 Tim. iii. 15; or that when Alcibiades, who had hitherto lived on bread and water,

[1] Euseb. *H. E.* v. 24.

received a revelation rebuking him for 'not using *the creatures of God*,' in obedience to which he 'partook of all things freely and *gave thanks* to God,' there is a reference to 1 Tim. iv. 3, 4. These passages show the attitude of the author or authors of this letter towards St Paul; but I have cited them also as exhibiting the manner of quotation which prevails in this letter, and thus indicating what we are to expect in other cases.

From the third and fourth Gospels then we find quotations analogous to these.

Of Vettius Epagathus, one of the sufferers, we are told, that though young he 'rivalled the testimony borne to the elder Zacharias (συνεξισοῦσθαι τῇ τοῦ πρεσβυτέρου Ζαχαρίου μαρτυρίᾳ), for verily (γοῦν) he had *walked in all the commandments and ordinances of the Lord blameless.*' Here we have the same words and in the same order, which are used of Zacharias and Elisabeth in St Luke (i. 6). Moreover, it is stated lower down of this same martyr, that he was 'called the paraclete (or advocate) of the Christians, having the Paraclete in himself, the Spirit more abundantly than Zacharias.' This may be compared with Luke i. 67, 'And Zacharias his father was filled with the Holy Ghost.'

The meaning of the expression 'the testimony of Zacharias' (τῇ τοῦ Ζαχαρίου μαρτυρίᾳ) has been questioned. It might signify either 'the testimony borne to Zacharias,' *i.e.* his recorded character, or 'the testimony borne by Zacharias,' *i.e.* his martyrdom. I cannot doubt that the former explanation is correct; for the connecting particle (γοῦν) shows that the assertion is intended to find its justification in words which immediately follow, '*he walked in all the commandments,*' etc. I need not however dwell on this point, for the author of *Supernatural Religion* himself adopts this rendering[1]. Yet with an inconsis-

---

[1] S. R. II. p. 201. In earlier editions the words are translated 'the testimony of the elder Zacharias;' but in the sixth I find substituted 'the testimony borne to the elder Zacharias.' The adoption of this interpretation therefore is deliberate. [In the Complete Edition (II. p. 199 sq) the rendering 'borne by the elder Zacharias' is substituted for the above, and defended at some length.]

tency, of which his book furnishes not a few examples, though he not only adopts this rendering himself, but silently ignores the alternative, he proceeds at once to maintain a hypothesis which is expressly built upon the interpretation thus tacitly rejected.

An early tradition or conjecture identified the Zacharias, who is mentioned in the Gospels as having been slain between the temple and the altar (Matt. xxiii. 35), with this Zacharias the father of the Baptist. And in the extravagant romance called the Protevangelium, which is occupied mainly with the birth, infancy, and childhood of our Lord, the Baptist's father is represented as slain by Herod 'at the vestibule of the temple of the Lord[1].' Our author therefore supposes that these Christians of Gaul are quoting not from St Luke, but from some apocryphal Gospel which gave a similar account of the martyrdom of Zacharias.

Whether this identification which I have mentioned is true or false it is unnecessary for my purpose to inquire. Nor again do I care to discuss the question whether or not the authors of this letter accepted it, and so believed the Baptist's father to have fallen a martyr. I am disposed on the whole to think that they did. This supposition, which however must remain uncertain, would give more point to the parallelism with Vettius Epagathus. But it is a matter of little or no moment as regards the point at issue. The quotation found in St Luke's Gospel has (according to the interpretation which our author rightly receives) no reference whatever to the martyrdom; and therefore affords no ground for the assumption that the document from which it is taken contained any account of or any reference to the death of the Baptist's father.

But, granting that the writers of this letter assumed the identification (and this assumption, whether true or false, was very natural), our Third Gospel itself does furnish such a reference; and they would thus find within the limits of this

---

[1] *Protev.* 23. See Tischendorf *Evang. Apocr.* p. 44.

Gospel everything which they required relating to Zacharias. The author of *Supernatural Religion* indeed represents the matter otherwise; but then he has overlooked an important passage. With a forgetfulness of the contents of the Gospels which ought surely to suggest some reflections to a critic who cannot understand how the Fathers, 'utterly uncritical' though they were, should ever quote any writing otherwise than with the most literal accuracy, he says, 'There can be no doubt that the reference to Zacharias in Matthew, in the Protevangelium, and in this Epistle of Vienne and Lyons, is not based upon Luke, *in which there is no mention of his death*[1].' Here and throughout this criticism he appears to have forgotten Luke xi. 51, 'the blood of Zacharias which perished between the altar and the temple.' If the death of the Baptist's father is mentioned in St Matthew, it is mentioned in St Luke also.

But, if our author disposes of the coincidences with the Third Gospel in this way, what will he say to those with the Acts? In this same letter of the Gallican Churches we are told that the sufferers prayed for their persecutors 'like Stephen the perfect martyr, *Lord, lay not this sin to their charge.*' Will he boldly maintain that the writers had before them another

---

[1] *S. R.* II. p. 203. So previously (p. 202), 'his martyrdom, *which Luke does not mention.*' I have already had occasion to point out instances where our author's forgetfulness of the contents of the New Testament leads him into error; see above, p. 125. Yet he argues throughout on the assumption that the memory of early Christian writers was perfect. [The whole section is struck out in the Complete Edition.]

The *Protevangelium* bears all the characteristics of a romance founded partly on notices in the Canonical Gospels. Some passages certainly are borrowed from St Luke, from which the very words are occasionally taken (*e.g.* §§ 11, 12); and the account of the martyrdom of Zacharias is most easily explained as a fiction founded on the notice in Luke xi. 51, the writer assuming the identity of this Zacharias with the Baptist's father. I have some doubts about the very early date sometimes assigned to the *Protevangelium* (though it may have been written somewhere about the middle of the second century); but, the greater its antiquity, the more important is its testimony to the Canonical Gospels. At the end of § 19 the writer obviously borrows the language of St Thomas in John xx. 25. This, as it so happens, is the part of the *Protevangelium* to which Clement of Alexandria (*Strom.* vii. p. 889) refers, and therefore we have better evidence for the antiquity of this, than of any other portion of the work.

Acts containing words identical with our Acts, just as he supposes them to have had another Gospel containing words identical with our Third Gospel? Or will he allow this account to have been taken from Acts vii. 60, with which it coincides? But in this latter case, if they had the second treatise which bears the name of St Luke in their hands, why should they not have had the first also?

Our author however does not stop here. He maintains that these same writers quoted not only from a double of St Luke, but from a double of St John also[1]. 'That was fulfilled,' they write, 'which was spoken by the Lord, saying, *There shall come a time in which whosoever killeth you will think that he doeth God service,*' where the words of St John (xvi. 2) are exactly reproduced, with the exception that for 'There cometh an hour when' (ἔρχεται ὥρα ἵνα) they substitute 'There shall come a time in which' (ἐλεύσεται καιρὸς ἐν ᾧ). This substitution, which was highly natural in a quotation from memory, is magnified by our author into 'very decided variations from the Fourth Gospel.' He would therefore assign the quotation to some apocryphal gospel which has perished. No such gospel however is known to have existed. Moreover this passage occurs in a characteristic discourse of the Fourth Gospel, and the expression itself is remarkable—far more remarkable than it appears in the English version (λατρείαν προσφέρειν τῷ Θεῷ, not 'to do God service,' but 'to offer a religious service to God'). I may add also that the mention of the Spirit as the Paraclete, already quoted, points to the use of this Gospel by the writers, and that the letter presents at least one other coincidence with St John. Our author certainly deserves credit for courage. Here, as elsewhere, he imagines that, so long as he does not advance anything which is demonstrably impossible, he may pile one improbability upon another without endangering the stability of his edifice.

But even if his account of these evangelical quotations

[1] *S. R.* II. p. 381.

could survive this accumulation of improbabilities, it will appear absolutely untenable in the light of contemporary fact. Irenæus was the most prominent and learned member of the Church from which this letter emanated, at the very time when it was written. According to some modern critics he was the actual composer of the letter; but for this there is no evidence of any kind. According to our author himself he was the bearer of it[1]; but this statement again is not borne out by facts. There can be no doubt however, that Irenæus was intimately mixed up with all the incidents, and he cannot have been ignorant of the contents of the letter. Now this letter was written A.D. 177 or, as our author prefers, A.D. 178, while Irenæus published his third book before A.D. 190 at all events, and possibly some years earlier. Irenæus in this book assumes that the Church from the beginning has recognized our four Canonical Gospels, and these only. The author of *Supernatural Religion* maintains on the other hand that only twelve years before, at the outside, the very Church to which Irenæus belonged, in a public document with which he was acquainted, betrays no knowledge of our Canonical Gospels, but quotes from one or more Apocryphal Gospels instead. He maintains this though the quotations in question are actually found in our Canonical Gospels.

[1] *S. R.* II. p. 200; 'The two communities [of Vienne and Lyons] some time after addressed an Epistle to their brethren in Asia and Phrygia, and also to Eleutherus, Bishop of Rome, relating the events which had occurred...This Epistle has in great part been preserved by Eusebius;' and again, II. p. 210; 'We know that he [Irenæus] was deputed by the Church of Lyons to bear to Eleutherus, then Bishop of Rome, the Epistle of that Christian community describing their sufferings during the persecution,' etc. [So also in the Complete Edition.] Accordingly in the index, pp. 501, 511, Irenæus is made the bearer of the Epistle.

This is a confusion of two wholly distinct letters — the letter to the Churches of Phrygia and Asia, containing an account of the persecution, which is in great part preserved by Eusebius, but of which Irenæus was certainly not the bearer; and the letter to Eleutherus, of which Irenæus was the bearer, but which had reference to the Montanist controversy, and of which Eusebius has preserved only a single sentence recommending Irenæus to the Roman Bishop. This latter contained references to the persecutions, but was a distinct composition: Euseb. *H. E.* v. 3, 4.

Here then the inference cannot be doubtful. But what must be the fate of a writer who can thus ride roughshod over plain facts, when he comes to deal with questions which demand a nice critical insight and a careful weighing of probabilities?

From this letter relating to the martyrdoms in Vienne and Lyons, we are led to speak directly of the illustrious Gallican father, whose name has already been mentioned several times, and who is the most important of all witnesses to the Canonical writings of the New Testament.

The great work of Irenæus is entitled *Refutation and Overthrow of Knowledge falsely so called*, and consists of five books. The third book was published during the episcopate of Eleutherus, who was Bishop of Rome from about A.D. 175 to A.D. 190; for he is mentioned in it as still living[1]. It must therefore have been written before A.D. 190. On the other hand it contains a mention of Theodotion's version of the LXX[2]; and Theodotion's version is stated not to have been published till the reign of Commodus (A.D. 182—190). Unfortunately Epiphanius, the authority mainly relied on by our author and others for this statement, contradicts himself in this same passage, which is full of the grossest chronological and historical blunders[3]. No stress therefore can be laid on his

---

[1] Iren. iii. 3. 3.

[2] Iren. iii. 21. 1.

[3] *De Pond. et Mens.* 16, 17. Epiphanius states that Antoninus Pius was succeeded by Caracalla, who also bore the names of Geta and M. Aurelius Verus, and who reigned seven years; that L. Aurelius Commodus likewise reigned these same seven years; that Pertinax succeeded next, and was followed by Severus; that in the time of Severus Symmachus translated the LXX; that 'immediately after him, that is, in the reign of the second Commodus, who reigned for thirteen years after the before-mentioned L. Aurelius Commodus,' Theodotion published his translation; with more of the same kind. The *Chronicon Paschale* also assigns this version to the reign of Commodus, and even names the year A.D. 184; but the compiler's testimony is invalidated by the fact that he repeats the words of Epiphanius, from whom he has obviously borrowed.

I should be sorry to say (without thoroughly sifting the matter), that even in this mass of confusion there may not be an element of truth; but it is strange to see how our author's habitual scepticism deserts him just where it would be most in place.

statement; nor indeed can we regard its truth or falsehood as of any real moment for our purpose. It is immaterial whether the third book dates from the earlier or later years of Eleutherus. As the several books were composed and published separately, the author of *Supernatural Religion* has a right to suppose, though he cannot prove, that the fourth and fifth were written during the episcopate of Victor (A.D. 190—198 or 199). But in his partiality for late dates he forgets that the weapon which he wields is double-edged. If the fourth and fifth books 'must,' as he confidently asserts, have been written some years after the third, it follows by parity of reasoning, that the first and second must have been written some years before it. Yet, with a strange inconsistency, he assumes in the very same sentence that the two first books cannot have been written till the latest years of Eleutherus, because on his showing the third must date from that epoch[1].

With the respective dates of the several books however we need not concern ourselves; for they all exhibit the same phenomena, so far as regards the attitude of the author towards the Canonical writings of the New Testament. On this point, it is sufficient to say that the authority which Irenæus attributes to the Four Gospels, the Acts of the Apostles, the Epistles of St Paul, several of the Catholic Epistles, and the Apocalypse, falls short in no respect of the estimate of the Church Catholic in the fourth or the ninth or the nineteenth century. He treats them as on a level with the Canonical books of the Old Testament; he cites them as Scripture in the same way; he attributes them to the respective authors whose names they bear; he regards them as writings handed down in the several Churches from the beginning; he fills his pages with quotations from them; he has not only a very thorough knowledge of their

---

[1] *S. R.* II. p. 213, 'We are therefore brought towards the end of the episcopate of Eleutherus as the earliest date at which the *first three books* of his work against Heresies can well have been written, and the rest *must* be assigned to a later period under the episcopate of Victor († 198–199.)' [So also in the Complete Edition.] The italics are my own.

contents himself, but he assumes an acquaintance with and a recognition of them in his readers[1].

In the third book especially he undertakes to refute the opinions of his Valentinian opponents directly from the Scriptures. This leads him to be still more explicit. He relates briefly the circumstances under which our Four Gospels were written. He points out that the writings of the Evangelists arose directly from the oral Gospel of the Apostles. He shows that the traditional teaching of the Apostles has been preserved by a direct succession of elders which in the principal Churches can be traced man by man, and he asserts that this teaching accords entirely with the Evangelical and Apostolic writings. He maintains on the other hand, that the doctrine of the heretics was of comparatively recent growth. He assumes throughout, not only that our four Canonical Gospels alone were acknowledged in the Church in his own time, but that this had been so from the beginning. His Valentinian antagonists indeed accepted these same Gospels, paying especial deference to the Fourth Evangelist; and accordingly he argues

---

[1] Our author sums up thus (II. p. 203 sq); 'The state of the case, then, is as follows: We find a coincidence in a few words in connection with Zacharias between the Epistle [of the Churches of Vienne and Lyons] and our Third Gospel; but so far from the Gospel being in any way indicated as their source, the words in question are, on the contrary, in association with' ['connected with' Compl. Ed.] 'a reference to events unknown to our Gospel, but which were indubitably chronicled elsewhere. It follows clearly, and *few venture to doubt the fact*, that the allusion in the Epistle is to a Gospel different from ours, and not to our third Synoptic at all.' Of 'the events unknown to our Gospel' I have disposed in the text. But the statement which I have italicized is still more extraordinary. I am altogether unable to put any interpretation upon the words which is not directly contradictory to the facts, and must therefore suppose that we have here again one of those extraordinary misprints, which our author has pleaded on former occasions. As a matter of fact, the references to the Third and Fourth Gospels in this letter are all but universally allowed, even by critics the least conservative. They are expressly affirmed, for instance, by Hilgenfeld (*Einleitung* p. 73) and by Scholten (*Die ältesten Zeugnisse* p. 110 sq). [In the Complete Edition the last sentence is considerably modified and runs as follows; 'As part of the passage in the Epistle, therefore, could not have been derived from our third Synoptic, the natural inference is that the whole emanates from a Gospel, different from ours, which likewise contained that part.']

with them on this basis. But they also superadded other writings, to which they appealed, while heretics of a different type, as Marcion for instance, adopted some one Gospel to the exclusion of all others. He therefore urges not only that four Gospels alone have been handed down from the beginning, but that in the nature of things there could not be more nor less than four. There are four regions of the world, and four principal winds; and the Church therefore, as destined to be conterminous with the world, must be supported by four Gospels, as four pillars. The Word again is represented as seated on the Cherubim, who are described by Ezekiel as four living creatures, each different from the other. These symbolize the four Evangelists, with their several characteristics. The predominance of the number four again appears in another way. There are four general covenants, of Noah, of Abraham, of Moses, of Christ. It is therefore an act of audacious folly to increase or diminish the number of the Gospels. As there is fitness and order in all the other works of God, so also we may expect to find it in the case of the Gospel.

What is the historical significance of this phenomenon? Can we imagine that the documents which Irenæus regards in this light had been produced during his own lifetime? that they had sprung up suddenly full-armed from the earth, no one could say how? and that they had taken their position at once by the side of the Law and the Psalmist and the Prophets, as the very voice of God?

The author of *Supernatural Religion* seems to think that no explanation is needed. 'The reasons,' he writes, 'which he [Irenæus] gives for the existence of precisely that number [four Gospels] in the Canon of the Church illustrate the thoroughly uncritical character of the Fathers, and the slight dependence which can be placed upon their judgments[1].' Accordingly he does not even discuss the testimony of Irenæus, but treats it as if it were not. He does not see that there is all the difference in the world between the value of the same man's evidence as

[1] *S. R.* II. p. 474.

to matters of fact, and his opinions as to the causes and bearings of his facts. He does not observe that these fanciful arguments and shadowy analogies are *pro tanto* an evidence of the firm hold which this quadruple Gospel, as a fact, had already obtained when he wrote. Above all, I must suppose from his silence that he regards this testimony of Irenæus as the isolated opinion of an individual writer, and is unconscious of the historical background which it implies. It is this last consideration which led me to speak of Irenæus as the most important witness to the early date and authorship of the Gospels, and to which I wish to direct attention.

The birth of Irenæus has been placed as early as A.D. 97 by Dodwell, and as late as A.D. 140 by our author and some others, while other writers again have adopted intermediate positions. I must frankly say that the very early date seems to me quite untenable. On the other hand, those who have placed it as late as A.D. 140 have chosen this date on the ground of the relation of Irenæus to Polycarp in his old age[1], and on the supposition that Polycarp was martyred about A.D. 167. Since however it has recently been shown that Polycarp suffered A.D. 155 or 156[2], it may be presumed that these critics would now throw the date of his pupil's birth some ten or twelve years farther back, *i.e.* to about A.D. 128 or 130. But there is no reason why it should not have been some few years earlier. If the suggestion which I have thrown out in a previous paper deserves atten-

---

[1] Iren. iii. 3. 4, 'Whom we also saw in early life (ἐν τῇ πρώτῃ ἡμῶν ἡλικίᾳ); for he survived long (ἐπιπολὺ γὰρ παρέμεινε), and departed this life at a very great age (πάνυ γηραλέος) by a glorious and most notable martyrdom.' This passage suggests the inference that, if Polycarp had not had a long life, Irenæus could not have been his hearer; but it cannot be pressed to mean that Polycarp was already in very advanced years when Irenæus saw him, since the words πάνυ γηραλέος refer, not to the period of their intercourse, but to the time of his martyrdom. A comparison with a parallel expression relating to St John in ii. 22. 5, παρέμεινε γὰρ αὐτοῖς μέχρι κ.τ.λ., will show that the inference, even when thus limited, is precarious, and that the γὰρ does not necessarily imply as much. Extreme views with respect to the bearing of this passage are taken on the one hand by Ziegler *Irenæus der Bischof von Lyon* p. 15 sq, and on the other by Leimbach *Wann ist Irenäus geboren* p. 622 sq (in *Stud. u. Krit.* 1873), in answer to Ziegler.

[2] See above, p. 103 sq.

tion[1], he was probably born about A.D. 120. But the exact date of his birth is a matter of comparatively little moment. The really important fact is, that he was connected directly with the Apostles and the Apostolic age by two distinct personal links, if not more.

Of his connection with POLYCARP I have already spoken[2]. Polycarp was the disciple of St John; and, as he was at least eighty-six years old when he suffered martyrdom (A.D. 155), he must have been close upon thirty when the Apostle died. Irenæus was young when he received instruction from Polycarp. He speaks of himself in one passage as 'still a boy,' in another as 'in early life.' If we reckon his age as from fifteen to eighteen, we shall probably not be far wrong, though the expressions themselves would admit some latitude on either side. At all events, he says that he had a vivid recollection of his master's conversations; he recalled not only the substance of his discourses, but his very expressions and manner; more especially he states that he remembers distinctly his descriptions of his intercourse with John and other personal disciples of Christ together with their account of the Lord's life and teaching; and he adds that these were 'altogether in accordance with the Scriptures[3].'

But Irenæus was linked with the Apostolic age by another companionship also. He was the leading presbyter in the Church of Lyons, of which POTHINUS was bishop, and succeeded to this see on the martyrdom of the latter in A.D. 177 or 178. With Pothinus therefore he must have had almost daily intercourse. But Pothinus lived to be more than ninety years old, and must have been a boy of ten at least, when the Apostle St John died. Moreover there is every reason to believe, as we have already seen[4], that like Irenæus himself Pothinus came originally from Asia Minor. Under any circumstances, his long life and influential position would give a special value to his testimony re-

---

[1] See above, p. 98, note 1.
[2] See above, p. 96 sq.
[3] See the last reference, where the passage is given in full.
[4] See above, p. 253.

specting the past history of the Church; and, whether he was uncritical or not (of which we are ignorant), he must have known whether certain writings attributed to the Evangelists and Apostles had been in circulation as long as he could remember, or whether they came to his knowledge only the other day, when he was already advanced in life.

In one passage in his extant work, Irenæus gives an account of elaborate discourses which he had heard from an elder who had himself 'listened to those who had seen the Apostles and to those who had been disciples,' *i.e.* personal followers of Christ[1]. It seems most natural to identify this anonymous elder with Pothinus. In this case the 'disciples' whom he had heard would be such persons as Aristion and John the presbyter, who are mentioned in this same way by Papias; while under the designation of 'those who had seen the Apostles' Polycarp more especially might be intended. But, if he were not Pothinus, then he forms a third direct link of connection between Irenæus and the Apostolic age. Whoever he was, it is clear that the intercourse of Irenæus with him was frequent and intimate. 'The elder,' writes Irenæus, 'used to say,' 'The elder used to refresh us with such accounts of the ancient worthies,' 'The elder used to discuss.' Indeed the elaborate character of these discourses suggests, as I have stated in a former paper[2], that Irenæus is here reproducing notes of lectures which he had heard from this person. With the references direct or indirect to the Canonical writings in this anonymous teacher I am not concerned here; nor indeed is it necessary to add anything to what has been said in a previous paper[3]. I wish now merely to call attention to these discourses as showing, that through his intercourse with this elder Irenæus could not fail to have ascertained the mind of the earlier Church with regard to the Evangelical and Apostolic writings.

Nor were these the only exceptional advantages which Irenæus enjoyed. When he speaks of the recognition of the

---

[1] Iren. iv. 27. 1 sq.
[2] See above, p. 196, note.
[3] See above, p. 247 sq.

VIII. THE CHURCHES OF GAUL. 267

Canonical writings his testimony must be regarded as directly representing three Churches at least. In youth he was brought up, as we saw, in Asia Minor. In middle life he stayed for some time in Rome, having gone there on an important public mission[1]. Before and after this epoch he for many years held a prominent position in the Church of Gaul. He was moreover actively engaged from the beginning to the end of his public career in all the most important controversies of the day. He gave lectures as we happen to know; for Hippolytus attended a course on 'All the Heresies,' delivered perhaps during one of his sojourns at Rome[2]. He was a diligent letter-writer, interesting himself in the difficulties and dissensions of distant Churches, and more than one notice of such letters is preserved. He composed several treatises more or less elaborate, whose general character may be estimated from his extant work. The subjects moreover, with which he had to deal, must have forced him to an examination of the points with which we are immediately concerned. He took a chief part in the Montanist controversy; and the Montanist doctrine of the Paraclete, as I have before had occasion to remark[3], directly suggested an investigation of the promise in the Fourth Gospel. He was equally prominent in the Paschal dispute, and here again the relation between the narratives of St John and the Synoptists

---

[1] See above, p. 253. The author of *Supernatural Religion* himself (II. p. 211) writes: 'It is not known how long Irenæus remained in Rome, but there is every probability that he must have made a somewhat protracted stay, for the purpose of making himself acquainted with the various tenets of Gnostic and other heretics,' etc.

There is reason to think that this was not his first visit to Rome. The notice at the end of the Moscow MS of the *Martyrium Polycarpi*, recently collated by Gebhardt (see *Zeitschr. f. Hist. Theol.* 1875, p. 362 sq), states that Irenæus, 'being in Rome at the time of the martyrdom of Polycarp, taught many,' and that it was recorded in his writings how at the precise time of his master's death he heard a voice announcing the occurrence. This story is not unlikely to have had some foundation in fact.

[2] Photius *Bibl.* 121; see above, p. 196. It is not stated where these lectures were delivered; but inasmuch as we know Hippolytus only as the Bishop of Portus and as dwelling in Rome and the neighbourhood, the metropolis is the most likely place, in the absence of direct evidence.

[3] [See above, p. 219.]

must have entered largely into the discussion. He was contending all his life with Gnostics, or reactionists against Gnosticism, and how large a part the authority and contents of the Gospels and Epistles must have played in these controversies generally we see plainly from his surviving work against the Valentinians.

Thus Irenæus does not present himself before us as an isolated witness, but is backed by a whole phalanx of past and contemporaneous authority. All this our author ignores. He forecloses all investigation by denouncing, as usual, the uncritical character of the fathers; and Irenæus is not even allowed to enter the witness-box.

The truth is that, speaking generally, the fathers are neither more nor less uncritical on questions which involve the historical sense, than other writers of their age. Now and then we meet with an exceptional blunderer; but for the most part Christian writers will compare not unfavourably with their heathen contemporaries. If Clement of Rome believes in the story of the phœnix, so do several classical writers of repute. If Justin Martyr affirms that Simon Magus received divine honours at Rome, heathen historians and controversialists make statements equally false and quite as ridiculous with reference to the religion and history of the Jews[1]. Even the credulity of

---

[1] It is only necessary to refer to the account of Jews given by an intelligent author like Tacitus (*Hist.* v. 1 sq). It is related, he says, that the Jews migrated to Libya from Ida in Crete, about the time when Saturn was expelled from his kingdom by Jupiter, and were thence called *Iudæi*, i.e. *Idæi*. Some persons, he adds, say that Egypt being over-populated in the reign of Isis, a multitude, led by their chieftains Hierosolymus and Judas, settled in the neighbouring lands. He states it, moreover, as an account in which 'plurimi auctores consentiunt,' that the Jews consecrated an image of an ass in their temple, because a herd of these animals had disclosed to them copious springs of water in their wanderings; these wanderings lasted six days continuously; on the seventh they obtained possession of the land, where they built their city and temple; with more to the same effect. All this he writes, though at the time the Jews in Rome counted by tens of thousands, any one of whom would have set him right. The comparatively venial error of Justin, who mistook the Sabine deity *Semo Sancus* for *Simo Sanctus*, cannot be judged harshly in the face of these facts.

a Papias may be more than matched by the credulity of an Apion or an Ælian. The work of the sceptical Pliny himself abounds in impossible stories. On the other hand individual writers may be singled out among the Christian fathers, whom it would be difficult to match in their several excellences from their own or contiguous generations. No heathen contemporary shows such a power of memory or so wide an acquaintance with the classical literature of Greece in all its branches as Clement of Alexandria. No heathen contemporary deserves to be named in the same day with Origen for patience and accuracy in textual criticism, to say nothing of other intellectual capacities, which, notwithstanding all his faults, distinguish him as the foremost writer of his age. And again, the investigations of Theophilus of Antioch, the contemporary of Irenæus, in comparative chronology are far in advance of anything which emanates from heathen writers of his time, however inadequate they may appear in this nineteenth century, which has discovered so many monuments of primeval history. There are in fact as many gradations among the Christian fathers as in any other order of men; and here, as elsewhere, each writer must be considered on his own merits. It is a gross injustice to class the authors whom I have named with such hopeless blunderers as Epiphanius and John Malalas, for whom nothing can be said, but in whom nevertheless our author places the most implicit confidence, when their statements serve his purpose.

Now Irenæus is not one whose testimony can be lightly set aside. He possessed, as we have seen, exceptional opportunities of forming an opinion on the point at issue. His honesty is, I think, beyond the reach of suspicion. He is a man of culture and intelligence. He possesses a considerable knowledge of classical literature, though he makes no parade of it. He argues against his opponents with much patience. His work is systematic, and occasionally shows great acuteness. His traditions, no doubt, require sifting, like other men's, and sometimes dissolve in the light of criticism. He has his weak points also, whether in his interpretations or in his views of things. But what then? Who refuses to listen to the heathen rhetorician Aristides or the apostate Emperor Julian on matters of fact, because they are both highly superstitious—the one paying a childish deference to dreams, the other showing himself a profound believer in magic? In short, Irenæus betrays no incapacity which affects his competency as a witness to a broad and comprehensive fact, such as that with which alone we are concerned.

And his testimony is confirmed by evidence from all sides. The recognition of these four Gospels from a very early date is the one fact which explains the fragmentary notices and references occurring in previous writers. Moreover his contemporaries in every quarter of the Church repeat the same story independently. The old Latin version, already existing when Irenæus published his work and representing the Canon of the African Christians, included these four Gospels, and these only. The author of the Muratorian fragment, writing a few years before him, and apparently representing the Church of Rome, recognizes these, and these alone. Clement, writing a few years later, as a member of the Alexandrian Church, who had also travelled far and wide, and sat at the feet of divers teachers, in Greece, in Asia Minor, in Palestine, in Italy, doubts the authenticity of a story told in an apocryphal writing, on the ground that it was not related in any of the four Gospels handed down by the Church[1]. What is the meaning of all this coincidence of view? It must be borne in mind that the Canon of the New Testament was not made the subject of any conciliar decree till the latter half of the fourth century. When therefore we find this agreement on all sides in the closing years of the second, without any formal enactment, we can only explain it as the convergence of independent testimony showing that, though individual writers might allow themselves the use of other documents, yet the general sense of the Church had for some time past singled out these four Gospels by tacit consent, and placed them in a position of exceptional authority.

[1] Clem. Alex. *Strom.* iii. 13, p. 553.

VIII. THE CHURCHES OF GAUL. 271

One other remark on the testimony of Irenæus suggests itself before closing. Irenæus is the first extant writer in whom, from the nature of his work, we have a right to expect explicit information on the subject of the Canon. Earlier writings, which have been preserved entire, are either epistolary, like the letters of the Apostolic Fathers, where any references to the Canonical books must necessarily be precarious and incidental (to say nothing of the continuance of the oral tradition at this early date as a disturbing element); or devotional, like the Shepherd of Hermas, which is equally devoid of quotations from the Old Testament and from the New; or historical, like the account of the martyrdoms at Vienne and Lyons, where any such allusion is gratuitous; or apologetic, like the great mass of the extant Christian writings of the second century, where the reserve of the writer naturally leads him to be silent about authorities which would carry no weight with the Jewish or heathen readers whom he addressed. But the work of Irenæus is the first controversial treatise addressed to Christians on questions of Christian doctrine, where the appeal lies to Christian documents. And here the testimony to our four Gospels is full and clear and precise.

If any reader is really in earnest on this matter, I will ask him to read Irenæus and judge for himself. He will find many things for which perhaps he is not prepared, and which will jar with his preconceived ideas; but on the one point at issue I have no fear that I shall be accused of exaggeration. Indeed it is impossible to convey in a few paragraphs the whole force of an impression which is deepened by each successive page of a long and elaborate work.

IX. Tatian's Diatessaron[1].

[May, 1877.]

ALL that is known of the life of Tatian can be soon told. He was an Assyrian by birth, as he himself distinctly states. If other writers call him a Syrian, the discrepancy may be explained by the common confusion between the two nationalities; or possibly it should be accounted for by his place of residence during the later years of his life. As a heathen he exercised the profession of a sophist, and in this capacity travelled far and wide. His mind was first turned towards Christianity by reading the Scriptures, which impressed him greatly. As a Christian he became the hearer—in some sense the disciple—of Justin Martyr, doubtless at Rome; and when Crescens, the cynic, succeeded in bringing about his master's death, Tatian's life also was imperilled by the plots of this machinator. While he remained in the metropolis he had among his disciples Rhodon, who in later years undertook to refute one of his heretical works. Subsequently he left Rome, and seems to have spent the remainder of his life in the East, more especially in Syria and the neighbouring countries.

After the death of Justin Martyr—how soon after we do not know—his opinions underwent a change. Hitherto he had been regarded as strictly orthodox; but now he separated himself from the Church, and espoused views closely allied to those of the Encratites. A leading tenet of his new ascetic creed was the rejection of marriage as an abomination. But he is stated also to have adopted opinions from Gnostic teachers,

[1] [See the note at the close of this Essay.]

more especially the doctrine of Æons, which he derived from the Valentinian school[1]. The author of *Supernatural Religion* further says that, 'although Tatian may have been acquainted with some of his (St Paul's) Epistles, it is certain that he did not hold the Apostle in any honour, and permitted himself the liberty of altering his phraseology[2].' Where did he learn this 'certain' piece of information that Tatian thought lightly of St Paul? Assuredly not from any ancient writer. It is quite true that Tatian is stated to have mutilated some of St Paul's Epistles and rejected others. But so did Marcion, who held the Apostle in extravagant honour. And the motive was the same in both cases. The Apostle's actual language did not square with their favourite tenets in all respects, and therefore they assumed that his text must have been corrupted or interpolated. So far from its being at all doubtful, as our author seems to suggest, whether Tatian was acquainted with any of St Paul's Epistles, we have positive evidence that he did receive some[3]; and moreover one or two coincidences in his extant work point to an acquaintance with the Apostle's writings. His leanings, like those of Marcion and Valentinus, were generally in the opposite direction to Judaism. His tendency would be not to underrate but to overrate St Paul. At the same time such passages as 1 Tim. iv. 3, where the prohibition of marriage is denounced as a heresy, were a stumbling-block. They must therefore be excised as interpolations, or the Epistles containing them must be rejected as spurious.

[1] The principal ancient authorities for the life of Tatian are the following:—Tatian *Orat. ad Græc.* 19, 29, 35, 42; Irenæus i. 28. 1; Rhodon, in Euseb. *H. E.* v. 13; Clement of Alexandria *Strom.* iii. 12, p. 547; *Exc. Theod.* 38, p. 999; Eusebius *H. E.* iv. 16, 28, 29; Epiphanius *Hær.* xlvi.; Theodoret *Hær. Fab.* i. 20. The statements in the text are justified by one or other of these references.

[2] All the references to *Supernatural Religion* in this article will be found in II. pp. 148 sq, 374 sq.

[3] *e.g.* Clement of Alexandria (*l.c.* p. 547) gives Tatian's comment on 1 Cor. vii. 5; and Jerome writes (*Præf. ad. Tit.* vii. p. 686), 'Tatianus, Encratitarum patriarches, qui et ipse nonnullas Pauli epistolas repudiavit, hanc vel maxime, hoc est, ad Titum, apostoli pronuntiandam credidit.'

The date of Tatian is a matter of some uncertainty. He was a hearer, as we have seen, of Justin Martyr in Rome; and if the chronology of this father had been established beyond the reach of doubt, we should be treading on firm ground. On this point however there has been much variety of opinion. The prevailing view is, or was, in favour of placing Justin's death as late as A.D. 163—165, on the authority of Eusebius; but the most careful investigations of recent criticism have tended towards a much earlier date[1]. The literary activity of Tatian seems to have begun about the time of Justin Martyr's death; and after this we have to allow for his own career, first as an orthodox Christian, and then as a heretic. When Irenæus wrote his first book, Tatian was no longer living, as may be inferred from the language of this father[2]: and this book must have been written before A.D. 190, and may have been written as early as A.D. 178[3]. Again, if we may assume that the 'Assyrian,' whom the Alexandrian Clement mentions among his teachers[4], was Tatian, as seems highly probable, we have another indication of date. The first book of the *Stromateis*, in which this fact is recorded, was itself written about A.D. 194 or 195; and Clement there speaks of the Assyrian as one of his earlier masters, whom he had met with in the East, before he settled down under the tuition of Pantænus at Alexandria. In like manner Tatian's connection with Rhodon would point roughly to the same conclusion. On the whole, we shall perhaps not be far wrong if we place the literary activity of Tatian at about A.D. 155—170. It may have begun some few years earlier, or it may have extended some few years later.

Tatian was a voluminous writer; but of several writings mentioned by the ancients only one has come down to us, his *Apology* or *Address to the Greeks*. It was written after the death of Justin, but apparently not very long after. At all

---

[1] Hort (*Journal of Philology*, iii. p. 155 sq, *On the date of Justin Martyr*) places it as early as A.D. 148.

[2] Iren. i. 28. 1.

[3] See above, p. 260 sq.

[4] Clem. Alex. *Strom.* i. 1 (p. 322).

events it would seem to have been composed before he had separated from the Church and set himself up as a heretical teacher. Its date therefore is dependent on the uncertain chronology of Justin. The author of *Supernatural Religion* speaks of it as 'generally dated between A.D. 170—175,' and seems himself to acquiesce in this view. Though I think this date probably several years too late, the point is not worth contending for.

As a rule, the early Apologies abstain from quotations, whether from the Old Testament or from the New. The writers are dealing with Gentiles, who have no acquaintance with and attribute no authority to their sacred books, and therefore they make little or no use of them[1]. Thus the *Apologeticus* of Tertullian does not contain a single passage from the New Testament, though his writings addressed to Christians teem with quotations from our Canonical books. Hence it is not in this extant work that we should expect to obtain information as to Tatian's Canon of the Scriptures. Any allusion to them will be purely incidental. As regards our Synoptical Gospels, the indications in Tatian's Apology are not such that we can lay much stress on them. But the evidence that he knew and accepted the Fourth Gospel is beyond the reach of any reasonable doubt.

The passages are here placed side by side :—

TATIAN.	ST JOHN.
'God is a Spirit' (πνεῦμα ὁ Θεός), § 4.	'God is a Spirit' (πνεῦμα ὁ Θεός), iv. 24.
'And this then is the saying (τὸ εἰρημένον); The darkness comprehendeth not the light' (ἡ σκοτία τὸ φῶς οὐ καταλαμβάνει), § 13.	'And the light shineth in the darkness, and the darkness comprehended it not' (καὶ ἡ σκοτία αὐτὸ οὐ κατέλαβεν), i. 5.

---

[1] See Westcott *History of Canon* p. 116 sq, where this point is brought out. Many erroneous deductions have been drawn from the reserve of the Apologists by writers who have overlooked it.

'Follow ye the only God. All things have been made by Him, and apart from Him hath been made no one thing' (πάντα ὑπ' αὐτοῦ καὶ χωρὶς αὐτοῦ γέγονεν οὐδὲ ἕν), § 19.	'All things were made through Him, and apart from Him was made no one thing' (πάντα δι' αὐτοῦ ἐγένετο καὶ χωρὶς αὐτοῦ ἐγένετο οὐδὲ ἕν), i. 3.

In the last passage from St John I have stopped at the words οὐδὲ ἕν, because the earliest Christian writers universally punctuated in this way, taking ὃ γέγονεν κ.τ.λ. with the following sentence, 'That which hath been made was life in Him.'

Besides these passages there are other coincidences of exposition, with which however I need not trouble the reader, as they may fairly be disputed.

It is difficult to see how any one can resist coincidences like these; and yet the author of *Supernatural Religion* does resist them.

The first passage our author has apparently overlooked, for he says nothing about it. If it had stood alone I should certainly not have regarded it as decisive. But the epigrammatic form is remarkable, and it is a characteristic passage of the Fourth Gospel.

Of the second passage it should be noticed that Tatian introduces it with the expression (τὸ εἰρημένον) which is used in the New Testament in quoting the Scriptures (Luke ii. 24, Acts ii. 16, xiii. 40, Rom. iv. 18); that in the context he explains 'the Word' (Logos) to be 'the light of God,' and 'the darkness' to be 'the unintelligent soul;' that this use of καταλαμβάνειν is very peculiar, and has caused perplexity to interpreters of St John, being translated variously 'comprehended' or 'surprised' or 'overcame;' that the passage in the Fourth Gospel here again is highly characteristic, and occurs in its most characteristic part; and lastly, that the changes made by Tatian are just such as a writer would make when desiring to divest the saying of its context and present it in the briefest form. On the other hand, the author of *Supernatural Religion* has nothing to allege

IX. TATIAN'S DIATESSARON. 277

against this coincidence; he can produce nothing like it elsewhere; but he falls back on 'the constant use of the same similitude of light and darkness,' and other arguments of the kind, which are valueless because they do not touch the point of the resemblance.

On the third passage he remarks that, unlike the author of the Fourth Gospel, 'Tatian here speaks of God, and not of the Logos.' Just so; but then he varies the preposition accordingly, substituting ὑπὸ for the Evangelist's διὰ to suit his adaptation. Our author also refers to 'the first chapters of Genesis;' but where is there any language in the first chapters of Genesis which presents anything like the same degree of parallelism? Here again, he is unable to impugn the coincidence, which is all the more remarkable because the words are extremely simple in themselves, and it is their order and adaptation which gives a character of uniqueness to the expression.

So much for the individual coincidences. But neither here nor elsewhere does our author betray any consciousness of the value of cumulative evidence. It is only necessary to point to the enormous improbability that any two writers should exhibit accidentally three such resemblances as in the passages quoted; and the inference will be plain.

It is not however in this testimony which his extant work bears to the Fourth Gospel, however decisive this may be, that the chief importance of Tatian consists. Ancient writers speak of him as the author of a Harmony or Digest of the four Gospels, to which accordingly he gave the name of *Diatessaron*. This statement however has been called in question by some recent critics, among whom the author of *Supernatural Religion* is, as usual, the most uncompromising. It is necessary therefore to examine the witnesses:—

1. In the first place then, Eusebius states definitely[1]—'Tatian composed a sort of connection and compilation, I know not how, of the Gospels, and called it the *Diatessaron* (συνάφειάν τινα καὶ συναγωγὴν οὐκ οἶδ' ὅπως τῶν εὐαγγελίων συνθεὶς τὸ διὰ

[1] Euseb. *H.E.* iv. 29.

278   ON SUPERNATURAL RELIGION.

τεσσάρων τοῦτο προσωνόμασεν). This work is current in some quarters (with some persons) even to the present day.'

This statement is explicit; yet our author endeavours to set it aside on the ground that 'not only is it based upon mere hearsay, but it is altogether indefinite as to the character of the contents, and the writer admits his own ignorance (οὐκ οἶδ᾽ ὅπως) regarding them[1].'

His inference however from the expression 'I know not how' is altogether unwarranted. So far from implying that Eusebius had no personal knowledge of the work, it is constantly used by writers in speaking of books where they are perfectly acquainted with the contents, but do not understand the principles or do not approve the method. In idiomatic English it signifies 'I cannot think what he was about,' and is equivalent to 'unaccountably,' 'absurdly,' so that, if anything, it implies knowledge rather than ignorance of the contents. I have noticed at least twenty-six examples of its use in the treatise of Origen against Celsus alone[2], where it commonly refers to Celsus' work which he had before him, and very often to passages which he himself quotes in the context. It is not ignorance of the contents, but disparagement of the plan of Tatian's work, which the expression of Eusebius implies. The *Diatessaron* was commonly current, as we shall see presently, in the neighbouring districts: and it would be somewhat strange if Eusebius, who took a special interest in apocryphal literature, should have remained unacquainted with it.

2. Our next witness is overlooked by the author of *Supernatural Religion*. Yet the testimony is not unimportant. In the *Doctrine of Addai*, an apocryphal Syriac work, which professes to give an account of the foundation and earliest history of Christianity at Edessa, the new converts are represented as meeting together to hear read, along with the Old Testament, 'the New (Testament) of the *Diatessaron*[3].' It seems clear

---

[1] [This sentence is omitted in the Complete Edition, where see I. p. 150.]

[2] The references are: Pref. 1; i. 14, 38, 42, 49, 50, 58; ii. 15, 44, 48, 49; iii. 35; iv. 14, 68, 86, 98; v. 8, 58; vi. 65, 81; vii. 8, 56; viii. 42, 45, 48, 59.

[3] This work first appeared in a mutilated form in Cureton's posthu-

from this notice that, at the time when the writer composed this fiction, the form in which the Evangelical narratives were commonly read in the churches with which he was best acquainted was a *Diatessaron*, or *Harmony of Four Gospels*. From internal evidence however it is clear that the work emanated from Edessa or its neighbourhood. The date of the fiction is less certain; but it is obviously an early writing. The St Petersburgh MS containing it is assigned to the sixth century, and the British Museum MSS to the fifth or sixth century[1]; while there exists an Armenian version said to have been made as early as the fifth century. The work itself therefore must have been written much earlier than this. There is indeed no good reason for doubting that it is the very Syriac document to which Eusebius refers as containing the correspondence of our Lord with Abgarus, and preserved among the archives of Edessa, and which therefore cannot have been very recent when he wrote, about A.D. 325[2]. At the same time it contains gross anachronisms and misstatements respecting earlier Christian history, which hardly allow us to place it much earlier than the middle of the third century[3]. Whatever may be its date, the fact is important that the writer uses *Diatessaron*, adopted from the Greek into the Syriac, as the familiar name for the Gospel narrative which was read in public. Of the authorship

mous volume, *Ancient Syriac Documents* p. 6 sq (London, 1864), from MSS in the British Museum, and has recently been published entire by Dr Phillips, *The Doctrine of Addai* (London 1876), from a St Petersburgh MS. In the British Museum MS which contains this part, the word is corrupted into *Ditornon* which has no meaning; but Cureton conjectured that the reading was *Diatessaron* (see pp. 15, 158), and his conjecture is confirmed by the St Petersburgh MS, which distinctly so reads (see Phillips, p. 94). In the Armenian version (*Lettre d'Abgare*, Venise, 1868, p. 41), a mention of the *Trinity* is substituted. This would seem to be a still further corruption; and, if so, it presents a parallel to the *Diapente* in the text of Victor of Capua, mentioned below.

[1] Wright's *Catalogue* pp. 1082, 1083.

[2] Euseb. *H. E.* i. 13.

[3] See a valuable article by Zahn in the *Götting. Gelehrte Anzeigen*, February 6, 1877, p. 161 sq. On this document I am unable to accept the conclusion of Cureton and of Dr Phillips, that the work itself is a much earlier and authentic document, and that the passages containing these anachronisms are interpolations.

of this work however he says nothing. This information we have to seek from other sources. Nor is it far to seek.

3. We are told that the most famous of the native Syrian fathers, Ephraem, the deacon of Edessa (who died A.D. 373[1]), wrote a commentary on the *Diatessaron* of Tatian. Our informant is Dionysius Bar-Salibi, who flourished in the last years of the twelfth century, and died A.D. 1207. In his own Commentary on the Gospels, he writes as follows[2]:—

Tatian, the disciple of Justin, the philosopher and martyr, selected and patched together from the Four Gospels and constructed a Gospel, which he called *Diatessaron*, that is *Miscellanies*. On this work Mar Ephraem wrote an exposition; and its commencement was—*In the beginning was the Word*. Elias of Salamia, who is also called Aphthonius, constructed a Gospel after the likeness of the *Diatessaron* of Ammonius, mentioned by Eusebius in his prologue to the Canons which he made for the Gospel. Elias sought for that Diatessaron and could not find it, and in consequence constructed this after its likeness. And the said Elias finds fault with several things in the Canons of Eusebius, and points out errors in them, and rightly. But this copy (work) which Elias composed is not often met with.

This statement is explicit and careful. The writer distinguishes two older works, bearing the name of *Diatessaron*, composed respectively by Tatian and Ammonius. In addition he mentions a third, composed at a later date by this Elias. Of the work of Ammonius of Alexandria (about A.D. 220) Eusebius, as Bar-Salibi correctly states, gives an account in his *Letter to Carpianus*, prefixed to his Canons. It was quite different in its character from the *Diatessaron* of Tatian. The *Diatessaron* of Tatian was a patchwork of the Four Gospels, commencing with the preface of St John. The work of Ammonius took the Gospel of St Matthew as its standard, preserving its continuity,

---

[1] The exact date of his death is given in a Syriac MS in the British Museum (Wright's *Catalogue* p. 947) as 'Ann. Græc. 684.'

[2] Assem. *Bibl. Orient.* ii. p. 159 sq. The English reader should be warned that Assemani's translations are loose and often misleading. More correct renderings are given here.

IX. TATIAN'S DIATESSARON.

and placed side by side with it the parallel passages from the other Gospels[1]. The principle of the one work was *amalgamation*; of the other, *comparison*. No one who had seen the two works could confuse them, though they bore the same name, *Diatessaron*. Eusebius keeps them quite distinct. So does Bar-Salibi. Later on in his commentary, we are told, he quotes both works in the same place[2]. When therefore he relates that Ephraem wrote a commentary on the *Diatessaron* of Tatian, he is worthy of all credit. From the last witness we have learnt that the *Diatessaron* was commonly read in the churches of Edessa; and it was therefore most natural that this famous Edessan father should choose it for commenting upon.

It is quite true that other Syrian writers have confused these two *Diatessarons*[3]. But this fact is only valid to show

---

[1] Euseb. *Op*. iv. p. 1276 (ed. Migne) Ἀμμώνιος μὲν ὁ Ἀλεξανδρεὺς......τὸ διὰ τεσσάρων ἡμῖν καταλέλοιπεν εὐαγγέλιον, τῷ κατὰ Ματθαῖον τὰς ὁμοφώνους τῶν λοιπῶν εὐαγγελιστῶν περικοπὰς παραθείς, ὡς ἐξ ἀνάγκης συμβῆναι τὸν τῆς ἀκολουθίας εἱρμὸν τῶν τριῶν διαφθαρῆναι, ὅσον ἐπὶ τῷ ὕφει ἀναγνώσεως—i.e. 'He placed side by side with the Gospel according to Matthew the corresponding passages of the other Evangelists, so that as a necessary result the connection of sequence in the three was destroyed, so far as regards the order (texture) of reading.'

[2] Assem. *Bibl. Orient*. ii. p. 158. See Hilgenfeld *Einleitung* p. 77.

[3] The confusion of later Syrian writers may be explained without difficulty:—

(i) Bar-Hebræus in the latter half of the thirteenth century (Assem. *Bibl. Orient*. i. p. 57 sq) writes: 'Eusebius of Cæsarea, seeing the corruptions which Ammonius of Alexandria introduced into the Gospel of the *Diatessaron*, that is *Miscellanies*, which commenced, *In the beginning was the Word*, and which Mar Ephraem expounded, kept the Four Gospels in their integrity, etc.' It is tolerably plain, I think, from the language of this writer, that he had before him the passage of Bar-Salibi (or some corresponding passage), and that he misunderstood him, as if he were speaking of the same work throughout. From the coincidence in the strange interpretation of Diatessaron, it is clear that the two passages are not independent. Assemani has omitted this interpretation in his translation in both cases, and has thus obliterated the resemblance.

(ii) To the same source also we may refer the error of Ebed-Jesu in the beginning of the fourteenth century, who not only confuses the books but the men. He writes (Assem. *Bibl. Orient*. iii. p. 12): 'A Gospel which was compiled by a man of Alexandria, Ammonius, who is also Tatian; and he called it *Diatessaron*.' He too supposed the two independent sentences of Bar-Salibi to refer to the same thing. In the preface to his collection of canons however, he gives a description of Tatian's work which is substantially correct: 'Tatianus quidam philosophus cum evangelistarum

that confusion was possible; it is powerless to impugn the testimony of this particular author, who shows himself in this passage altogether trustworthy. Who would think of throwing discredit on Lord Macaulay or Mr Freeman, because Robertson or Hume may be inaccurate?

4. Our next witness is more important than any. The famous Greek father Theodoret became bishop of Cyrus or Cyrrhus, near the Euphrates, in the year 420 or 423 according to different computations, and held this see till his death, which occurred A.D. 457 or 458. In the year 453 he wrote his treatise on *Heresies*, in which he makes the following statement:—

He (Tatian) composed the Gospel which is called *Diatessaron*, cutting out the genealogies[1] and such other passages as show the Lord to have been born of the seed of David after the flesh. This work was in use not only among persons belonging to his sect, but also among those who follow the apostolic doctrine, as they did not perceive the mischief of the composition, but used the book in all

loquentium sensum suo intellectu cepisset, et scopum scriptionis illorum divinae in monte sua fixisset, unum ex quatuor illis admirabile collegit evangelium, quod et Diatessaron nominavit, in quo cum cautissime seriem rectam eorum, quae a Salvatore dicta ac gesta fuere, servasset, ne unam quidem dictionem e suo addidit' (Mai *Script. Vet. Nov. Coll.* x. pp. 23, 191).

(iii) In Bar-Bahlul's Syriac Lexicon, *s. v.* (see Payne Smith *Thes. Syr.* p. 870), *Diatessaron* is defined as 'the compiled Gospel (made) from the four Evangelists,' and it is added : 'This was composed in Alexandria, and was written by Tatian the Bishop.' The mention of Alexandria suggests that here also there is some confusion with Ammonius, though neither Ammonius nor Tatian was a bishop. Bar-Bahlul flourished in the latter half of the tenth century; and if this notice were really his, we should have an example (doubtful however) of this confusion, earlier than Bar-Salibi. But these Syrian Lexicons have grown by accretion; the MSS, I am informed, vary considerably; and we can never be sure that any word or statement emanated from the original compiler.

Since writing the above, I am able to say, through the kindness of Dr Hoffmann, that in the oldest known MS of Bar-Bahlul, dated A.H. 611, *i.e.*, A.D. 1214, this additional sentence about Tatian is wanting, as it is also in another MS of which he sends me an account through Professor Wright. It is no part therefore of the original Bar-Bahlul. Thus all the instances of confusion in Syriac writers are later than Bar-Salibi, and can be traced to a misunderstanding of his language.

[1] *H. F.* i. 20. The Syrian lexicographer Bar Ali also, who flourished about the end of the ninth century, mentions that Tatian omitted both the genealogies : see Payne Smith's *Thes. Syr. s. v.* p. 869 sq.

simplicity on account of its brevity. And I myself found more than two hundred such copies held in respect in the churches in our parts (ταῖς παρ' ἡμῖν ἐκκλησίαις). All these I collected and put away, and I replaced them by the Gospels of the Four Evangelists.

The churches to which he refers were doubtless those belonging to his diocese of Cyrrhestice, which contained eight hundred parishes[1]. The proportion of copies will give some idea of the extent of its circulation in these parts.

It is vain, in the teeth of these facts, to allege the uncritical character of the father as discrediting the evidence. The materials before Theodoret were ample; the man himself was competent to form a judgment; and the judgment is explicit. Neither can there be any reasonable doubt, considering the locality, that the *Diatessaron* here mentioned is the same which is named in the *Doctrine of Addai*, and the same which was commented on by Ephraem Syrus. When the author of *Supernatural Religion* argues that Theodoret does not here regard this *Diatessaron* as patched together from the four canonical Gospels, it is unnecessary to follow him. This point may be safely left to the intelligence of the reader.

Here then we have the testimony of four distinct witnesses, all tending to the same result. Throughout large districts of Syria there was in common circulation from the third century down to the middle of the fifth a *Diatessaron* bearing the name of Tatian[2]. It was a compilation of our Four Gospels, which recommended itself by its concise and convenient form, and so superseded the reading of the Evangelists themselves in some churches. It commenced, as it naturally could commence, with the opening words of the Fourth Gospel—a gospel which, as we have seen, Tatian quotes in his extant work. It was probably in

---

[1] Theodoret *Epist.* 113 (iv. p. 1190, ed. Schulze).

[2] Zahn (*Gött. Gel. Anz.* p. 184) points out that Aphraates also, a somewhat older Syrian father than Ephraem, appears to have used this *Diatessaron*. In his first Homily (p. 13, ed. Wright) he says, 'And Christ is also the Word and the Speech of the Lord, as it is written in the beginning of the Gospel of our Saviour—*In the beginning was the Word.*' The date of this Homily is A.D. 337.

the main a fairly adequate digest of the evangelical narratives, for otherwise it would not have maintained its grounds; but passages which offended Tatian's Encratic and Gnostic views, such as the genealogies, were excised; and this might easily be done without attracting notice under cover of his general plan. All this is consistent and probable in itself. Moreover the range of circulation attributed to it is just what might have been expected; for Syria and Mesopotamia are especially mentioned as the scene of Tatian's labours[1].

In this general convergence of testimony however, there are two seemingly discordant voices, of which the author of *Supernatural Religion* makes much use. Let us see what they really mean.

1. Epiphanius was bishop of Constantia, in Cyprus, in the latter half of the fourth century. In his book on *Heresies*, which he commenced A.D. 374, he writes of Tatian, 'The *Diatessaron* Gospel is said to have been composed by him; it is called by some *according to the Hebrews*[2].'

Here then our author supposes that he has discerned the truth. This *Diatessaron* was not a digest of our four Gospels, but a distinct evangelical narrative, the *Gospel according to the Hebrews*. Of this Gospel according to the Hebrews he says that 'at one time it was exclusively used by the fathers.' I challenge him to prove this assertion in the case of one single father, Greek or Latin or Syrian. But this by the way. If indeed this Hebrew Gospel had been in its contents anything like what our author imagines it, it would have borne some resemblance at all events to the *Diatessaron*; for, wherever he meets with any evangelical passage in any early writer, which is found literally or substantially in any one of our four Gospels (whether characteristic of St Matthew, or of St Luke, or of St John, it matters not) he assigns it without misgiving to this Hebrew Gospel. But his Hebrew Gospel is a pure effort of the imagination. The only 'Gospel according to the Hebrews' known to antiquity was a very different document. It was not

---

[1] Epiphan. *Hær.* xlvi. 1. [2] See the reference in the last note.

co-extensive with our four Gospels; but was constructed on the lines of the first alone. Indeed so closely did it resemble the canonical St Matthew—though with variations, omissions, and additions—that Jerome, who translated it, supposed it to be the Hebrew original[1], of which Papias speaks. Such a Gospel does not answer in any single particular, unless it be the omission of the genealogy (which however does not appear to have been absent from all copies of this Gospel), to the notices of Tatian's *Diatessaron*. More especially the omission of all reference to the Davidic descent of Christ would be directly opposed to the fundamental principle of this Gospel, which, addressing itself to the Jews, laid special stress on His Messianic claims.

How then can we explain the statement of Epiphanius? It is a simple blunder, not more egregious than scores of other blunders which deface his pages. He had not seen the *Diatessaron*: this our author himself says. But he had heard that it was in circulation in certain parts of Syria; and he knew also that the Gospel of the Hebrews was current in these same regions, there or thereabouts. Hence he jumped at the identification. To a writer who can go astray so incredibly about the broadest facts of history, as we have seen him do in the succession of the Roman Emperors[2], such an error would be the easiest thing in the world. Yet it was perfectly consistent on the part of our author, who in another instance prefers John Malalas to the concurrent testimony of all the preceding centuries[3], to set aside the direct evidence of a Theodoret, and to accept without hesitation the hearsay of an Epiphanius.

2. 'Tatian's Gospel,' writes the author of *Supernatural Religion*, 'was not only called *Diatessaron*, but according to Victor of Capua, it was also called *Diapente* (διὰ πέντε) "by five," a complication which shows the incorrectness of the ecclesiastical theory of its composition.'

---

[1] All the remains of the Hebrew Gospel, and the passages of Jerome relating to it, will be found in Westcott's *Introduction to the Gospels* p. 462 sq.

[2] See above, p. 260, where this specimen of his blundering is given.

[3] See above, p. 79 sq.

This is not a very accurate statement. If our author had referred to the actual passage in Victor of Capua, he would have found that Victor does not himself call it *Diapente*, but says that Eusebius called it *Diapente*. This makes all the difference.

Victor, who flourished about A.D. 545, happened to stumble upon an anonymous Harmony or Digest of the Gospels[1], and began in consequence to investigate the authorship. He found two notices in Eusebius of such Harmonies; one in the *Epistle to Carpianus* prefixed to the Canons, relating to the work of Ammonius; another in the *Ecclesiastical History*, relating to that of Tatian. Assuming that the work which he had discovered must be one or other, he decides in favour of the latter, because it does not give St Matthew continuously and append the passages of the other evangelists, as Eusebius states Ammonius to have done. All this Victor tells us in the preface to this anonymous Harmony, which he publishes in a Latin dress.

There can be no doubt that Victor was mistaken about the authorship; for, though the work is constructed on the same general plan as Tatian's, it does not begin with John i. 1, but with Luke i. 1, and it does contain the genealogies. It belongs therefore, at least in its present form, neither to Tatian nor to Ammonius.

But we are concerned only with the passage relating to Tatian, which commences as follows:—

Ex historia quoque ejus (*i.e.* Eusebii) comperi quod Tatianus vir eruditissimus et orator illius temporis clarus unum ex quatuor compaginaverit Evangelium cui titulum *Diapente* imposuit.

Thus Victor gets his information directly from Eusebius, whom he repeats. He knows nothing about Tatian's *Diatessaron*, except what Eusebius tells him. But we ourselves have this

---

[1] *Patrol. Lat.* lxviii. p. 253 (ed. Migne). An old Frankish translation of this Harmony is also extant. It has been published more than once; *e.g.* by Schmeller (Vienna, 1841).

same passage of Eusebius before us, and find that Eusebius does not call it *Diapente* but *Diatessaron*. This is not only the reading of all the Greek MSS without exception, but likewise of the Syriac Version[1], which was probably contemporary with Eusebius and of which there is an extant MS belonging to the sixth century, as also of the Latin Version which was made by Rufinus a century and a half before Victor wrote. About the text of Eusebius therefore there can be no doubt. Moreover Victor himself, who knew Greek, says *ex quatuor*, which requires *Diatessaron*, and the work which he identifies with Tatian's Harmony is made up of passages from our Four Gospels alone. Therefore he can hardly have written *Diapente* himself; and the curious reading is probably due to the blundering or the officiousness of some later scribe[2].

Thus we may safely acquiesce in the universal tradition, or as our author, οὐκ οἶδ' ὅπως, prefers to call it, the 'ecclesiastical theory,' respecting the character and composition of Tatian's Diatessaron[3].

[1] The Syriac version is not yet published, but I have ascertained this by inquiry.

[2] This seems to be Hilgenfeld's opinion also (*Einleitung* p. 79); and curious as the result is, I do not see how any other explanation is consistent with the facts.

[3] [An important monograph on Tatian's *Diatessaron* by Zahn has been published since this Article was written (Erlangen, 1881).]

[The actual *Diatessaron* of Tatian has since been discovered, though not in the original language, so that no doubt can now remain on the subject. The history of this discovery has been given in the careful and scholarly work of Prof. Hemphill of Dublin (*The Diatessaron of Tatian* 1888), where (see esp. p. xx sq) full information will be found. Ephraem's Commentary exists in an Armenian translation of some works of this Syrian father, which had been published in Venice as early as 1836. I had for some years possessed a copy of this work in four volumes, and the thought had more than once crossed my mind that possibly it might throw light on Ephraem's mode of dealing with the Gospels, as I knew that it contained notes on St Paul's epistles or some portion of them. I did not however then possess sufficient knowledge of Armenian to sift its contents, but I hoped to investigate the matter when I had mastered enough of the language. Meanwhile a Latin translation was published by Moesinger under the title of *Evangelii concordantis expositio facta a Sancto Ephraemo doctore Syro* Venet. 1876, just about the time when I wrote the above article; but it was not known in England till some years after. Later still an Arabic translation of the *Diatessaron* itself has been discovered and published in Rome by Ciasca (*Tatiani Evangeliorum Harmoniae Arabice nunc primum etc.*, 1888). On the relation of Victor's *Diatessaron*, which seems to be shown after all not to be independent of Tatian, and for the quotations in Aphraates, etc., see Hemphill's *Diatessaron*. Thus the 'ecclesiastical theory'—the only theory which was supported by any sound continuous tradition—is shown to be unquestionably true, and its nineteenth century critical rivals must all be abandoned.]

APPENDIX.

The following paper has no reference to the work entitled 'Supernatural Religion'; but, as it is kindred in subject and appeared in the same Review, I have given it a place here.

Discoveries illustrating the Acts of the Apostles.

[May, 1878.]

IN a former volume M. Renan declared his opinion that 'the author of the Third Gospel and the Acts was verily and indeed (*bien réellement*) Luke, a disciple of St Paul[1].' In the last instalment of his work he condemns as untenable the view that the first person plural of the later chapters is derived from some earlier document inserted by the author, on the ground that these portions are identical in style with the rest of the work[2]. Such an expression of opinion, proceeding from a not too conservative critic, is significant; and this view of the authorship, I cannot doubt, will be the final verdict of the future, as it has been the unbroken tradition of the past. But at a time when attacks on the genuineness of the work have been renewed, it may not be out of place to call attention to some illustrations of the narrative which recent discoveries have brought to light. No ancient work affords so many tests of veracity; for no other has such numerous points of contact in all directions with contemporary history, politics, and topography, whether Jewish or Greek or Roman. In the publications of the year 1877 Cyprus and Ephesus have made important contributions to the large mass of evidence already existing.

1. The government of the Roman provinces at this time was peculiarly dangerous ground for the romance-writer to venture upon. When Augustus assumed the supreme power

[1] *Les Apôtres* p. xviii.   [2] *Les Evangiles* p. 436.

he divided the provinces under the Roman dominion with the Senate. From that time forward there were two sets of provincial governors. The ruler of a senatorial province was styled a proconsul (ἀνθύπατος), while the officer to whom an imperatorial province was entrusted bore the name of proprætor (ἀντιστράτηγος) or legate (πρεσβευτής). Thus the use of the terms 'proconsul' and 'proprætor' was changed; for, whereas in republican times they signified that the provincial governors bearing them had previously held the offices of consul and prætor respectively at home, they were now employed to distinguish the superior power under which the provinces were administered without regard to the previous rank of the governors administering them. Moreover, the original subdivision of the provinces between the Emperor and Senate underwent constant modifications. If disturbances broke out in a senatorial province and military rule was necessary to restore order, it would be transferred to the Emperor as the head of the army, and the Senate would receive an imperatorial province in exchange. Hence at any given time it would be impossible to say without contemporary, or at least very exact historical knowledge, whether a particular province was governed by a proconsul or a proprætor. The province of Achaia is a familiar illustration of this point. A very few years before St Paul's visit to Corinth, and some years later, Achaia was governed by a proprætor. Just at this time, however, it was in the hands of the Senate, and its ruler therefore was a proconsul, as represented by St Luke.

Cyprus is a less familiar, but not less instructive, example of the same accuracy. Older critics, even when writing on the apologetic side, had charged St Luke with an incorrect use of terms; and the origin of their mistake is a significant comment on the perplexities in which a later forger would find himself entangled in dealing with these official designations. They fell upon a passage in Strabo[1] where this writer, after mentioning the division of the provinces between the Emperor and the

[1] xvii. p. 840.

APPENDIX.

Senate, states that the Senate sent consuls to the two provinces of Asia and Africa but prætors to the rest on their list,— among which he mentions Cyprus; and they jumped at the conclusion—very natural in itself—that the governor of Cyprus would be called a proprætor. Accordingly Baronio[1] suggested that Cyprus, though a prætorian province, was often handed over *honoris causa* to be administered by the proconsul of Cilicia, and he assumed therefore that Sergius Paulus held this latter office; while Grotius found a solution in the hypothesis that proconsul was a title bestowed by flatterers on an official whose proper designation was proprætor. The error illustrates the danger of a little learning, not the less dangerous when it is in the hands of really learned men. Asia and Africa, the two great prizes of the profession, exhausted the normal two consuls of the preceding year; and the Senate therefore were obliged to send ex-prætors and other magistrates to govern the remaining provinces under their jurisdiction. But it is now an unquestioned and unquestionable fact that all the provincial governors who represented the Senate in imperial times, whatever magistracy they might have held previously, were styled officially proconsuls[2].

The circumstances indeed, so far as regards Cyprus, are distinctly stated by Dion Cassius. At the original distribution of the provinces (B.C. 27) this island had fallen to the Emperor's share; but the historian, while describing the assignment of the several countries in the first instance, adds that the Emperor subsequently gave back Cyprus and Gallia Narbonensis to the Senate, himself taking Dalmatia in exchange[3]; and at a later point, when he arrives at the time in question (B.C. 22), he repeats the information respecting the transfer. 'And so,' he adds, 'proconsuls began to be sent to those nations

---

[1] Sub ann. 46.

[2] See Becker u. Marquardt *Röm. Alterth.* III. i. p. 294 sq. Even De Wette has not escaped the pitfall, for he states that 'according to Strabo Cyprus was governed by proprætors,' and he therefore supposes that Strabo and Dion Cassius are at variance. De Wette's error stands uncorrected by his editor, Overbeck.

[3] Dion Cassius liii. 12.

also[1].' Of the continuance of Cyprus under the jurisdiction of the Senate, about the time to which St Luke's narrative refers, we have ample evidence. Contemporary records bear testimony to the existence of proconsuls in Cyprus not only before and after but during the reign of Claudius. The inscriptions mention by name two proconsuls who governed the province in this Emperor's time (A.D. 51, 52)[2]; while a third, and perhaps a fourth, are recorded on the coins[3]. At a later date, under Hadrian, we come across a propraetor of Cyprus[4]. The change would probably be owing to the disturbed state of the province consequent on the insurrection of the Jews. But at the close of the same century (A.D. 198)—under Severus—it is again governed by a proconsul[5]; and this was its normal condition.

Thus the accuracy of St Luke's designation is abundantly established; but hitherto no record had been found of the particular proconsul mentioned by him. This defect is supplied by one of General Cesnola's inscriptions. It is somewhat mutilated indeed, so that the meaning of parts is doubtful; but for our purpose it is adequate. A date is given as ΕΠΙ·ΠΑΥΛΟΥ·[ΑΝΘ]ΥΠΑΤΟΥ, 'in the proconsulship of Paulus.' On this Cesnola remarks: 'The proconsul Paulus may be the Sergius Paulus of the Acts of the Apostles (chap. xiii), as instances of the suppression of one of two names are not rare[6].' An example of the suppression in this very name Sergius Paulus will be given presently, thus justifying the identification of the proconsul of the Acts with the proconsul of this inscription.

Of this Sergius Paulus, the proconsul of Cyprus, Dean Alford says that 'nothing more is known.' But is it certain that he is not mentioned elsewhere? In the index of contents and authorities which forms the first book of Pliny's *Natural History*, this

---

[1] Dion Cassius liv. 4.

[2] Q. Julius Cordus and L. Annius Bassus in Boeckh *Corp. Inscr. Graec.* 2631, 2632.

[3] Cominius Proclus, and perhaps Quadratus: see Akerman's *Numismatic Illustrations of the New Testament* p. 39.

[4] *Corp. Inscr. Lat.* iii. 6072, an Ephesian inscription discovered by Mr Wood.

[5] *Corp. Inscr. Lat.* iii. 218.

[6] Cesnola's *Cyprus* p. 425.

writer twice names one Sergius Paulus among the Latin authors to whom he was indebted. May not this have been the same person? The name is not common. So far as I have observed, only one other person bearing it[1]—probably a descendant of this Cyprian proconsul—is mentioned, of whom I shall have something to say hereafter; and he flourished more than a century later. Only one test of identity suggests itself. The Sergius Paulus of Pliny is named as an authority for the second and eighteenth books of that writer. Now on the hypothesis that the proconsul of Cyprus is meant, it would be a natural supposition that, like Sir J. Emerson Tennent or Sir Rutherford Alcock, this Sergius Paulus would avail himself of the opportunities afforded by his official residence in the East to tell his Roman fellow-countrymen something about the region in which he had resided. We therefore look with interest to see whether these two books of Pliny contain any notices respecting Cyprus, which might reasonably be explained in this way; and our curiosity is not disappointed. In the second book, besides two other brief notices (cc. 90, 112) relating to the situation of Cyprus, Pliny mentions (c. 97) an area in the temple of Venus at Paphos on which the rain never falls. In the eighteenth book again, besides an incidental mention of this island (c. 57), he gives some curious information (c. 12) with respect to the Cyprian corn, and the bread made therefrom. It should be added that for the second book, in which the references to Cyprus come late, Sergius Paulus is the last-mentioned Latin authority; whereas for the eighteenth, where they are early, he occupies an earlier, though not very early, place in the list.

---

[1] Dean Alford indeed (on Acts xiii. 7), following some previous writers, mentions a Sergius Paulus, intermediate in date between the two others—the authority of Pliny and the friend of Galen—whom he describes as 'one of the consules suffecti in A.D. 94.' This however is a mistake. A certain inscription, mentioning L. Sergius Paullus as consul, is placed by Muratori (p. cccxiv. 3) and others under the year 94; but there is good reason to believe that it refers to the friend of Galen, and must be assigned to the year when he was consul for the first time, as suffectus, *i.e.* about A.D. 150. See Marini *Atti e Monumenti de' Fratelli Arvali* p. 198; Waddington *Fastes des Provinces Asiatiques* p. 731.

These facts may be taken for what they are worth. In a work, which contains such a multiplicity of details as Pliny's *Natural History*, we should not be justified in laying too much stress on coincidences of this kind.

From the Sergius Paulus of Luke the physician we turn to the Sergius Paulus of Galen the physician. Soon after the accession of M. Aurelius (A.D. 161) Galen paid his first visit to Rome, where he stayed for three or four years. Among other persons whom he met there was L. Sergius Paulus, who had been already consul suffectus about A.D. 150, and was hereafter to be consul for the second time in A.D. 168 (on this latter occasion as the regular consul of the year), after which time he held the Prefecture of the City[1]. He is probably also the same person who is mentioned elsewhere as proconsul of Asia in connection with a Christian martyrdom[2]. This later Sergius Paulus reproduces many features of his earlier namesake. Both alike are public men; both alike are proconsuls; both alike show an inquisitive and acquisitive disposition. The Sergius Paulus of the Acts, dissatisfied (as we may suppose) alike with the coarse mythology of popular religion and with the lifeless precepts of abstract philosophies, has recourse first to the magic of the sorcerer Elymas, and then to the theology of the Apostles

---

[1] This person is twice mentioned by Galen *de Anat. Admin.* i. 1 (*Op.* ii. p. 218, ed. Kühn): τοῦδε τοῦ νῦν ἐπάρχου τῆς Ῥωμαίων πόλεως, ἀνδρὸς τὰ πάντα πρωτεύοντος ἔργοις τε καὶ λόγοις τοῖς ἐν φιλοσοφίᾳ, Σεργίου Παύλου ὑπάτου: de *Praenot.* 2 (*Op.* ii. p. 612), ἀφίκοντο Σέργιός τε ὁ καὶ Παῦλος, ὃς οὐ μετὰ πολὺν χρόνον ὕπαρχος (l. ἔπαρχος) ἐγένετο τῆς πόλεως, καὶ Φλάβιος, ὑπατικὸς μὲν ὢν ἤδη καὶ αὐτός, ἐσπευκὼς δὲ περὶ τὴν Ἀριστοτέλους φιλοσοφίαν, ὥσπερ καὶ ὁ Παῦλος, οἷς διηγησάμενος κ. τ. λ. In this latter passage the words stand Σέργιός τε καὶ ὁ Παῦλος in Kühn and other earlier printed editions which I have consulted, but they are quoted Σέργιός τε ὁ καὶ Παῦλος by Wetstein and others.

I do not know on what authority this latter reading rests, but the change in order is absolutely necessary for the sense; for (1) in this passage nothing more is said about Sergius as distinct from Paulus, whereas Paulus is again and again mentioned, so that plainly one person alone is intended. (2) In the parallel passage Sergius Paulus is mentioned, and the same description is given of him as of Paulus here. The alternative would be to omit καὶ ὁ altogether, as the passage is tacitly quoted in Borghesi *Œuvres* viii. p. 504.

[2] Melito in Euseb. *H. E.* iv. 26: see Waddington *Fastes des Provinces Asiatiques* p. 731. [See above, p. 223.]

Barnabas and Saul, for satisfaction. The Sergius Paulus of Galen is described as 'holding the foremost place in practical life as well as in philosophical studies;' he is especially mentioned as a student of the Aristotelian philosophy; and he takes a very keen interest in medical and anatomical learning. Moreover, if we may trust the reading, there is another striking coincidence between the two accounts. The same expression, 'who is also Paul' (ὁ καὶ Παῦλος), is used to describe Saul of Tarsus in the context of the Acts, and L. Sergius in the account of Galen. Not the wildest venture of criticism could so trample on chronology as to maintain that the author of the Acts borrowed from these treatises of Galen; and conversely I have no desire to suggest that Galen borrowed from St Luke. But if so, the facts are a warning against certain methods of criticism which find favour in this age. To sober critics, the coincidence will merely furnish an additional illustration of the permanence of type which forms so striking a feature in the great Roman families. One other remark is suggested by Galen's notices of his friend. Having introduced him to us as 'Sergius who is also Paulus,' he drops the former name altogether in the subsequent narrative, and speaks of him again and again as Paulus simply. This illustrates the newly-published Cyprian inscription, in which the proconsul of that province is designated by the one name Paulus only.

2. The transition from General Cesnola's *Cyprus* to Mr Wood's *Ephesus* carries us forward from the first to the third missionary journey of St Paul. Here, again, we have illustrative matter of some importance. The main feature in the narrative of the Acts is the manner in which the cultus of the Ephesian Artemis dominates the incidents of the Apostle's sojourn in that city. As an illustration of this feature, it would hardly be possible to surpass one of the inscriptions in the existing collection[1]. We seem to be reading a running commentary on

---

[1] Boeckh *Corp. Inscr. Græc.* 2954. The first sentence which I have quoted is slightly mutilated; but the sense is clear. The document bears only too close a resemblance to the utterances of Lourdes in our own day.

the excited appeal of Demetrius the silversmith, when we are informed that 'not only in this city but everywhere temples are dedicated to the goddess, and statues erected and altars consecrated to her, on account of the manifest epiphanies which she vouchsafes' (τὰς ὑπ' αὐτῆς γεινομένας ἐναργεῖς ἐπιφανείας); that 'the greatest proof of the reverence paid to her is the fact that a month bears her name, being called Artemision among ourselves, and Artemisius among the Macedonians and the other nations of Greece and their respective cities;' that during this month 'solemn assemblies and religious festivals are held, and more especially in this our city, which is the nurse of its own Ephesian goddess' (τῇ τροφῷ τῆς ἰδίας θεοῦ τῆς Ἐφεσίας); and that therefore 'the people of the Ephesians, considering it meet that the whole of this month which bears the divine name (τὸν ἐπώνυμον τοῦ θείου ὀνόματος) should be kept holy, and dedicated to the goddess,' has decreed accordingly. 'For so,' concludes this remarkable document, 'the cultus being set on a better footing, our city will continue to grow in glory and to be prosperous to all time.' The sense of special proprietorship in this goddess of world-wide fame, which pervades the narrative in the Acts, could not be better illustrated than by this decree. But still the newly-published inscriptions greatly enhance the effect. The patron deity not only appears in these as 'the great goddess Artemis,' as in the Acts, but sometimes she is styled 'the supremely great goddess (ἡ μεγίστη θεός) Artemis.' To her favour all men are indebted for all their choicest possessions. She has not only her priestesses, but her temple-curators, her essenes, her divines (θεολόγοι), her choristers (ὑμνῳδοί), her vergers (σκηπτοῦχοι), her tire-women or dressers (κοσμητεῖραι), and even her 'acrobats,' whatever may be meant by some of these terms. Fines are allocated to provide adornments for her; endowments are given for the cleaning and custody of her images; decrees are issued for the public exhibition of her treasures. Her birthday is again and again mentioned. She is seen and heard everywhere. She is hardly more at home in her own sanctuary than in the Great Theatre. This last-mentioned place—the scene of the tumult in the Acts—is brought vividly before our eyes in Mr Wood's inscriptions. The theatre appears as the recognized place of public assembly. Here edicts are proclaimed, and decrees recorded, and benefactors crowned. When the mob, under the leadership of Demetrius, gathered here for their demonstration against St Paul and his companions, they would find themselves surrounded by memorials which might stimulate their zeal for the goddess. If the 'town-clerk' had desired to make good his assertion, 'What man is there that knoweth not that the city of the Ephesians is sacristan of the great goddess Artemis?' he had only to point to the inscriptions which lined the theatre for confirmation. The very stones would have cried out from the walls in response to his appeal.

Nor is the illustration of the magistracies which are named by St Luke less complete. Three distinct officers are mentioned in the narrative—the Roman proconsul ($\dot{a}\nu\theta\acute{u}\pi a\tau o\varsigma$), the governor of the province and supreme administrator of the law, translated 'deputy' in our version; the recorder ($\gamma\rho a\mu\mu a\tau\epsilon\acute{u}\varsigma$) or chief magistrate of the city itself, translated 'town-clerk;' and the Asiarchs ('$A\sigma\iota a\rho\chi a\acute{\iota}$), or presidents of the games and of other religious ceremonials, translated 'the chief of Asia.' All these appear again and again in the newly-discovered inscriptions. Sometimes two of the three magistracies will be mentioned on the same stone. Sometimes the same person will unite in himself the two offices of recorder and Asiarch, either simultaneously or not. The mention of the recorder is especially frequent. His name is employed to authenticate every decree and to fix every date.

But besides these more general illustrations of the account in the Acts, the newly-discovered inscriptions throw light on some special points in the narrative. Thus where the chief magistrate pronounces St Paul and his companions to be 'neither sacrilegious ($\iota\epsilon\rho o\sigma\acute{u}\lambda o\upsilon\varsigma$) nor blasphemers of our goddess[1],' we discover a special emphasis in the term on finding from these inscriptions that certain offences (owing to

---

[1] Acts xix. 37 where ἱεροσύλους is oddly translated 'robbers of churches.'

the mutilation of the stone, we are unable to determine the special offences) were treated as constructive sacrilege against the goddess. 'Let it be regarded as sacrilege and impiety' (ἔστω ἱεροσυλία καὶ ἀσέβεια), says an inscription found in this very theatre[1], though not yet set up at the time when the 'town-clerk' spoke. So again, where the same speaker describes the city of Ephesus as the 'neocoros,' the 'temple sweeper,' or 'sacristan of the great goddess Artemis,' we find in these inscriptions for the first time a direct example of this term so applied. Though the term 'neocoros' in itself is capable of general application, yet as a matter of fact, when used of Ephesus on coins and inscriptions (as commonly in the case of other Asiatic cities), it has reference to the cultus not of the patron deity, but of the Roman emperors. In this sense Ephesus is described as 'twice' or 'thrice sacristan,' as the case may be, the term being used absolutely. There was indeed every probability that the same term would be employed also to describe the relation of the city to Artemis. By a plausible but highly precarious conjecture it had been introduced into the lacuna of a mutilated inscription[2]. By a highly probable but not certain interpretation it had been elicited from the legend on a coin[3]. There were analogies too which supported it. Thus the Magnesians are styled on the coins 'sacristans of Artemis[4];' and at Ephesus itself an individual priest is designated by the same term 'sacristan of Artemis[5].' Nor did it seem unlikely that a city which styled itself 'the nurse of Artemis' should also claim the less audacious title of 'sacristan' to this same goddess. Still probability is not certainty; and (so far as I am aware) no direct example was forthcoming. Mr Wood's inscriptions supply this defect. On one of these 'the city of the Ephesians' is described as 'twice sacristan of the

[1] *Inscr.* vi. 1, p. 14.

[2] Boeckh *Corp. Inscr.* 2972, τ[οῖς νεωκόρων τῶν Σεβαστῶν, μόνω]ν ἀπα-[σῶν] δὲ τῆς Ἀρτέμιδος.

[3] Eckhel *Doctr. Num.* ii. p. 520. The legend is—ΕΦΕΣΙΩΝ · ΤΡΙΣ ·

ΝΕΩΚΟΡΩΝ · ΚΑΙ · ΤΗΣ · ΑΡΤΕΜΙ-ΔΟΣ.

[4] Mionnet, iii. p. 153, *Suppl.* vi. pp. 245, 247, 250, 253.

[5] Xen. *Anab.* v. 3, 6.

Augusti according to the decrees of the Senate and sacristan of Artemis¹.'

One other special coincidence deserves notice. The recorder, desirous of pacifying the tumult, appeals to the recognized forms of law. 'If Demetrius and his fellow-craftsmen,' he says, 'have a matter against any one, assizes are held, and there are proconsuls². Let them indict one another. But if you have any further question (*i.e.*, one which does not fall within the province of the courts of justice), it shall be settled in the lawful (regular) assembly.' By a 'lawful (regular) assembly' (ἔννομος ἐκκλησία) he means one of those which were held on stated days already predetermined by the law, as opposed to those which were called together on special emergencies out of the ordinary course, though in another sense these latter might be equally 'lawful.' An inscription, found in this very theatre in which the words were uttered, illustrates this technical sense of 'lawful.' It provides that a certain silver image of Athene shall be brought and 'set at every lawful (regular) assembly (κατὰ πᾶσαν νόμιμον ἐκκλησίαν) above the bench where the boys sit³.'

With these facts in view, we are justified in saying that ancient literature has preserved no picture of the Ephesus of imperial times—the Ephesus which has been unearthed by the sagacity and perseverance of Mr Wood—comparable for its life-like truthfulness to the narrative of St Paul's sojourn there in the Acts.

I am tempted to add one other illustration of an ancient Christian writer, which these inscriptions furnish. Ignatius, writing to the Ephesians from Smyrna in the early years of the

---

¹ *Inscr.* vi. 6, p. 50.

² Acts xix. 38, ἀγόραιοι [sc. ἡμέραι] ἄγονται καὶ ἀνθύπατοί εἰσιν, translated 'the law is open, and there are deputies,' in the Authorised Version, but the margin, 'the court days are kept,' gives the right sense of the first clause. In the second clause 'proconsuls' is a rhetorical plural, just as *e.g.* in Euripides (*Iph. Taur.* 1359) Orestes and Pylades are upbraided for 'stealing from the land its images and priestesses' (κλέπτοντες ἐκ γῆς ξόανα καὶ θυηπολούς), though there was only one image and one priestess.

³ *Inscr.* vi. 1, p. 38.

second century, borrows an image from the sacred pageant of some heathen deity, where the statues, sacred vessels, and other treasures, of the temple are borne in solemn procession. He tells his Christian readers that they all are marching in festive pomp along the Via Sacra—the way of love—which leads to God; they all are bearers of treasures committed to them,—for they carry their God, their Christ, their shrine, their sacred things, in their heart[1]. The image was not new. It is found in Stoic writers. It underlies the surname Theophorus, the 'God-bearer,' which Ignatius himself adopted. But he had in his company several Ephesian delegates when he wrote; and the newly discovered inscriptions inform us that the practice which supplies the metaphor had received a fresh impulse at Ephesus shortly before this letter was written. The most important inscriptions in Mr Wood's collection relate to a gift of numerous valuable statues, images, and other treasures to the temple of Artemis, by one C. Vibius Salutaris, with an endowment for their custody. In one of these (dated A.D. 104) it is ordained that the treasures so given shall be carried in solemn procession from the temple to the theatre and back ' at every meeting of the assembly, and at the gymnastic contests, and on any other days that may be directed by the Council and the People.' Orders are given respecting the persons forming the procession, as well as respecting its route. It must pass through the length of the city, entering by the Magnesian Gate and leaving by the Coressian[2].

[1] Ign. *Ephes.* 9.   [2] *Inscr.* vi. 1, p. 42.

INDICES.

I. *INDEX OF SUBJECTS.*

II. *INDEX OF PASSAGES.*

INDEX OF SUBJECTS.

Aberle, 210, 213 n
Abgarus, 279
Achaia, vicissitudes as a Roman province, 292
Acts of Peter, 37
Acts of the Apostles; Eusebius' method with regard to, 46; used by Polycarp, 95; by Polycrates, 249; ascribed by Irenæus to St Luke, 44; quoted in the *Letter of the Gallican Churches*, 257; Renan on its authorship, 291; recent discoveries illustrating, 291 sq
Addai; see *Doctrine of Addai*
Ælian, credulity of, 269
Æsop, Hitzig's derivation of the name, 25 n
African martyrs, 76, 83
Agathonice, 148
Alcibiades, 254
Alexander, 253
Alford, 9, 294, 295 n
Alogi, 215 n
Ambrosius, the friend of Origen, 7
Ammonius of Alexandria; his date, 280; his Harmony of the Gospels, 280; Eusebius' account of it, 280; its scope distinct from Tatian's *Diatessaron*, 280 sq; but confused with it by Syrian writers, 281 sq
Anastasius of Sinai; his high estimate of Papias, 154, 157, 200 sq; quotes Melito, 225 n, 230 sq
Andreas of Cæsarea, mentions Papias, 34 n, 214

Andrew (St), at Ephesus, 91, 143, 145, 146, 160, 189, 193
Anger, 165
Anicetus, 99, 100, 101, 102
Anthropomorphism, 139 n
Antinomianism, 119 sq
Antioch; Trajan at, 79; Antoninus Pius at, 98 n; earthquake at, 79 sq
Antoninus Pius; proconsul of Asia as T. Aurelius Fulvus, 98 n; his movements as emperor, 98 n
Aphraates, his acquaintance with Tatian's *Diatessaron*, 283 n, [288]
Aphthonius, 280
Apion, as a critic, 269
Apocalypse; its date, 14 n, 132; its differences from the Fourth Gospel, 15, 131 sq, 214 sq; the term Logos in, 15, 123; supposed allusions to St Paul in, 13 sq; the form of Gnosticism denounced in, 14 n; its position in the Canon of Eusebius, 47; Eusebius' treatment of patristic notices of, 37 n, 39, 43, 47, 215 sq; Papias on its authorship, 34 n, 214; Justin Martyr, 43, 216; Irenæus, 45, 47, 216; Eusebius, 144; the Johannine authorship admitted by the early fathers, 214 sq; notices in Justin Martyr, 43, 47, 216; in Melito, 47; his commentary on it, 216; in the Muratorian Canon, 216; in Theophilus, 44, 47, 52, 216; in Apollonius, 47
Apocalypse of Peter, 37, 47

Apollinaris, Claudius, of Hierapolis; a contemporary of Melito, 237; his date, 237 sq; his literary activity, 32, 102, 207, 238; his orthodoxy, 238 sq; his writings, 238, 242 sq; Eusebius' list of them incomplete, 238, 242 sq; his *Apology*, 237; his work against the Montanists, 238, 243; against the Severians, 243; on the Paschal Festival, 238 sq, 242 sq; the assumed silence of the fathers on this work considered, 242 sq; not an antagonist of Melito, 242, 244, 245; but a Quartodeciman, 244 sq; genuineness of the extant fragments of, 239 sq; references to the Gospels in them, 239, 240; to the Fourth Gospel, 240; follows the chronology of the Fourth Gospel, 248; mentions the miracle of the Thundering Legion, 237; his prominence in the School of St John, 218

Apollonius; notice of the Apocalypse in, 47; extracts in Eusebius from, 91 n

Apologies, absence of scriptural quotations in Christian, 33, 271, 275

Arethas, 201

Arianism, and the Ignatian controversy, 60, 62, 69

Aristides, the rhetorician, 98 n, 104, 270

Aristion, and Papias, 91, 143, 144 sq, 149, 150 n, 187, 266

Arnold, Matthew, 24, 190 n

Artemis, cultus of the Ephesian, 297 sq

Asia Minor; imperial visits to, 98; the proconsulate of, 293; the proconsular fasti of, 103 sq, 115, 121, 223, 295 n; its connexion with Southern Gaul, 105, 252

Asia Minor, the Churches of; importance of, 91 sq, 217 sq; Apostles resident in, 91, 217; episcopacy in, 84, 218; solidarity of, 102; the arena of controversy, 84, 219; literary activity of, 219, 249; testimony to the Fourth Gospel from, 249; the Church of Southern Gaul a colony of, 249; intimate relations between them, 105, 252 sq; Polycarp's Epistle publicly read in, 105 n

Asiarchs, 222 n, 299

Askar and Sychar, 17 n, 133 sq

Assemani, 280 n, 281 n

Athanasius, quotes the Ignatian Epistles, 80

Attalus, the Pergamene martyr, 253, 254

Aubertin, 66, 67

Augustus, the division of Roman provinces by, 291 sq

Balaam, as a type of St Paul, 13

Bar-Ali, the lexicographer; his date, 282 n; mentions Tatian, 282 n

Bar-Bahlul; his date, 282 n; Ammonius and Tatian confused in late MSS of his lexicon, 282 n

Bar-Hebræus; his date, 281 n; confuses Ammonius and Tatian, 281 n

Bar-Salibi; his date, 280; his testimony to Tatian's *Diatessaron*, 280 sq

Barnabas, Epistle of; its date, 177; quotes St Matthew's Gospel as 'Scripture,' 177, 227; employed by Clement of Alexandria, 47; Chiliasm in, 151

Baronio, 293

Basil (St), 175

Basilides; his date, 85, 161; his work *On the Gospel*, 161; fragments preserved in Hippolytus, 161; his appeal to the Fourth Gospel, 52, 219; the Vossian Epistles silent on, 85; his allusion to Glaucias, 21, 123

Basnage, 66, 67

Bassus, L. Annius, proconsul of Cyprus, 294 n

Baumgarten-Crusius, 68, 69

Baur, 24, 61, 64, 70

Beausobre, 68, 69

Bethesda, the pool of, 9, 126

Bleek, 65, 66, 69, 171

Blondel, 66, 67

Bochart, 66, 67, 83

INDEX OF SUBJECTS. 307

Böhringer, 65
Borghesi, 296 n
Bunsen, 61, 63, 64, 65, 66

Calvin, and the Ignatian controversy, 65, 66
Carpus, 148
Capitolinus, 98 n
Casaubon, 66, 67
Celsus, 6 sq, 25 n
Cerinthus; encountered by St John, 101, 212; his separationism, 118; attacked in St John's First Epistle, 118; according to Irenæus, the Fourth Gospel aimed at, 48, 182; the Fourth Gospel and Apocalypse ascribed to, 215; the question of the Canon involved in the controversy with, 219; confused with Marcion, 210, 212
Cesnola's explorations in Cyprus, 294, 297
Chemnitz, 65, 66
Chiliasm; of Papias, 151 sq, 158 sq, 160, 197, 215 n; of the early Church generally, 151
Christian literature; compared with the classics as regards external evidence for documents, 82; plagiarisms in, 202
Christian martyrs; coincidence with the Passion of Christ in the sufferings of, 220; zeal for martyrdom exhibited by, 82 sq
Christian prisoners, the treatment of, 74 sq
Christology; of the Synoptists and Fourth Gospel, 15 sq; of Cerinthus, 118; of Ignatius, 42, 86 sq, 108, 231; of Polycarp, 106, 108; of Justin Martyr, 235; of Melito, 230, 231, 234 sq
Christ's ministry, the duration of, 16 sq, 48, 131, 245 sq
Chronicon Paschale; see *Paschal Chronicle*
Chrysostom, the panegyric on Ignatius of, 80
[Ciasca, 288]

Claudius Apollinaris; see *Apollinaris*
Clemens, Flavius, cousin of Domitian, 94 n
Clement of Alexandria; coincidence in the name, 94 n; a pupil of Pantænus, 274; perhaps of Melito, 218, 224; perhaps also of Tatian, 274; quotes from Tatian, 273 n; his wide learning, 269; compared with his heathen contemporaries, 269; his travels, 270; his testimony to the Four Gospels, 270; to St Mark, 167; to the Fourth Gospel, 52; to the labours of St John, 218; accepts the identity of authorship of the Fourth Gospel and Apocalypse, 216; employs the Epistle of Clement of Rome, 47; the Epistle of Barnabas, 47; the *Apocalypse of Peter*, 47; the *Gospel according to the Hebrews*, 152; quotes Basilides, 161; his treatise on the Paschal Festival, 243 sq; date of his *Stromateis*, 274; his use of the word 'oracles,' 174
Clement of Rome; his name, 94 n; probably a Hellenist Jew, 94; and a freedman, 94; his position compared with that of Polycarp, 89; scriptural quotations in his Epistle, 40, 105, 110; Eusebius' method tested on it, 40, 47, 179; its testimony to the Epistle of the Hebrews, 40, 47, 49; employed by Clement of Alexandria, 47; its date and that of the book of Judith, 25 n; his use of the Canon and that of Polycarp, 94, 105; his use of the word 'oracles,' 174; the story of the phœnix in, 268; his place in modern German theories, 24
Clementines; as a romance, 15; Gnostic fragments preserved in the, 40 n; quote and employ the narrative of the Fourth Gospel, 50, 52
Cook, 66, 67
Cordus, Q. Julius, proconsul of Cyprus, 294 n
Cramer's *Catena*, 201
Credner, 12, 19, 124 sq, 186

20—2

Crescens, the Cynic, 148, 272
Cureton, 61, 63, 65, 68, 70, 71 sq, 81 n, 86, 232 n, 278 n, 279 n
Curetonian Epistles, 61 sq; see also *Ignatian Epistles*
Cyprian; his correspondence, 76; accepts identity of authorship of the Fourth Gospel and Apocalypse, 216
Cyprus; its vicissitudes as a Roman province, 292 sq; the evidence of inscriptions on this, 294; source of Pliny's information regarding, 295; proconsuls and proprætors of, 294; recent excavations at, 291 sq
Cyrrhestice, 282, 283

Dallæus, 65, 114
De Wette, 9, 293 n
Decian persecution, 76
Delitzsch, 17, 133, 135, 136
Demetrius, the silversmith of Ephesus, 298, 299, 301
Denzinger, 63, 71
Diapente, 279 n, 285 sq
Diatessaron; see *Tatian*
Dion Cassius, 293
Dionysius of Alexandria; his critical insight, 167; assigns the Fourth Gospel to St John, 216; but separates the authorship of the Apocalypse, 167, 216
Dionysius of Corinth; his evidence to the Canon, 156, 177, 227; the silence of Eusebius respecting, 35 sq, 39, 184
Docetism, attacked in the Ignatian Epistles, 118 n
Doctrine of Addai; discovery of the document, 278 n; its subject, 278; its date, 279; its country, 279; noticed in Eusebius, 279; mentions Tatian's *Diatessaron*, 278; the Armenian version, 279
Dodwell, 98 n, 264
Dogma and morality, 27 sq
Donaldson, 241 n
Dressel, 80 n
Dutch school of criticism, 2, 9, 36

Ebionism; no trace in the Ignatian Epistles, 42; nor in Polycarp, 43, 102 sq, 153 sq; nor in Papias, 42, 43, 151 sq
Edessa, 278 sq
Elders; quoted by Papias, 4 sq, 143, 145, 159, 163, 168, 181, 194, 197 sq; by Irenæus, 4, 6, 48, 54, 58, 102, 145, 195 sq, 218, 233, 245, 247 sq; who both reports their conversations, and cites their works, 196 sq; identification of some of them, 194 sq, 196 n, 224, 248 n, 266
Eleutherus, Bishop of Rome, 99, 261; Irenæus sent as delegate to, 253, 259 n
Elias of Salamia; his *Diatessaron*, 280; his name Aphthonius, 280
Encratites; Apollinaris' treatises against the, 238, 243; Tatian's connexion with the, 272, 284
Ephesus; St John at, 91, 101, 142 sq, 217 sq; other Apostles at, 91; Wood's excavations at, 291, 294 n, 297 sq; cultus of Artemis at, 297 sq; the great theatre at, 298 sq; the designation of magistrates, 299; the title neocoros, 300; the lawful assemblies, 301; image-processions at, 301 sq; gates of, 302
Ephraem of Antioch, 172
Ephraem Syrus; date of his death, 280; his commentary on Tatian's *Diatessaron*, 280 sq; [an Armenian version discovered, 287]
Epiphanius; date of his work on *Heresies*, 284; his treatise against the Alogi, 215 n; his obligations to Hippolytus, 216 n; his historical blunders, 260, 269, 285; confuses Tatian's *Diatessaron* with the *Gospel according to the Hebrews*, 284
Episcopacy; in the time of St John, 218; in Asia Minor in the time of Ignatius, 84; stress laid upon it in the Ignatian Epistles, 107; especially in the Vossian Letters, 87; the Ignatian controversy centres round the question of, 61; not mentioned

INDEX OF SUBJECTS. 309

in the Epistle of Polycarp, 106, 107 sq, 122; prominent in the writings of Irenæus, 122

Ernesti, 68

Euodia and Syntyche, extravagant German theories respecting, 24 sq

Eusebius; sources of his history, 32 sq; his rule of procedure in dealing with the Canon, 36 sq, 46 sq, 178 sq, 190 sq, 215 sq; tested on extant literature, 40 sq; what his silence means, 32 sq; its value as a direct testimony, 51; his trustworthiness and moderation, 49 sq, 209; his habit of incomplete and combined quotations, 168, 209; on the Ignatian Epistles, 72 sq, 80, 82; on Papias, 142 sq, 147, 151 sq, 154, 167, 186, 190 sq; his estimate of Papias, 209; on John the Presbyter, 143 sq; his lists of the works of Melito not exhaustive, 224 sq, 228; nor those of the works of Apollinaris, 238, 242; dependent upon Pamphilus' library, 225; on the Paschal controversy, 17, 245; attempts to harmonize the Gospel narrative, 208, 209; for this purpose perhaps borrows from Papias, 208

Evagrius, 80

Ewald, 63, 65, 136, 204

ἐπὶ Τραϊανοῦ, 81

ἐπιστολαί, of a single letter, 114, 189

ἐξήγησις, 155 n, 156, 160 n, 175 sq; and διήγησις, 157 n

Fathers, early; compared in historical accuracy with classical writers, 268 sq; considered as critics, 167, 229, 263, 268; the dearth of scriptural quotations in their works accounted for, 33, 271; explanation of their literary plagiarisms, 202, 237

Felicitas, 83

Florinus; a pupil of Polycarp, 96 sq; Irenæus letter to, 96 sq, 195 n; date of his connexion with the royal court, 97 sq; his subsequent history, 98

Four Gospels; that number only recognized in the Muratorian Canon, 166, 270; in Irenæus, 45, 48, 166, 233, 263 sq; in Eusebius, 39

Fourth Gospel; its spirit, 13; its Hebraic character, 14; the minuteness of its details, 14 sq; the narrative of an eye-witness, 14 sq; compared with the Apocalypse, in diction, 15, 34 n, 131 sq, 214 sq; in Christology, 15 sq; the bearing of Montanism on this question, 219, 238, 267; compared with the Synoptists in chronology and narrative, 16, 48, 131, 240, 245 sq; the relation of the Paschal controversy to this question, 17, 219, 225, 239 sq, 267; historical and geographical allusions considered, 17 sq; the personality of its author, 18 sq; association of others with him in the work, 187; anecdotes with regard to its composition, 48, 52, 187, 189 sq, 210, 217; probably dictated, 187, 214; its wide acceptance among orthodox and heretics, 52 sq; testimony given by the growth of various readings and interpolations, 9 sq, 52; by the commentary of Heracleon, 52; the evidence of the Ignatian Epistles, 41; of Papias, 4 sq, 35, 54 sq, 186 sq; of the *Martyrdom of Polycarp*, 221 sq; of the elders in Irenæus, 48; of the Muratorian Canon, 52, 189 sq, 206 sq; of Claudius Apollinaris, 240; of the School of St John generally, 249 sq; of the *Letter of the Gallican Churches*, 258; of Tatian, 275 sq, 280 sq; of Origen, 216; of Gaius, 216 n; Irenæus on its purpose, 48, 182; quoted by Theophilus of Antioch, 44, 52, 179, 215, 216; significance of the silence of Eusebius, 33 sq, 51 sq; ascribed to Cerinthus, 215; its connexion with the First Epistle of St John, 186 sq, 190, 220

Gaius; on the authorship of the Epistle to the Hebrews, 47; of the Apocalypse and Fourth Gospel, 216 n; his date 216 n; his relation to Hippolytus considered, 91 n, 216 n

Galen, 83, 153, 196 n, 295 n, 296 sq

Gallican Churches; a colony from the Churches of Asia Minor, 249, 251 sq; intimate connexion between the two bodies, 105, 249, 252 sq; persecuted under M. Aurelius, 252 sq; their letter to the brethren in Asia and Phrygia, 146 n, 216, 252 sq, 259 n, 271; its date, 259; scriptural quotations in it, 254 sq; their letters on the Montanist controversy, 253; their letter to Victor on the Paschal controversy, 253 sq

Gaul, called Galatia, 251

Georgius Hamartolos, 211 sq

Gfrörer, 69

Glaucias, 21

Gnosticism; the development of antinomian, 119; the literature of, 160 sq; the exegesis of, 160 sq, 175, 202; the opponents of, 160 sq, 219, 268; the scene of the conflict with, 219; attacked in St Paul's Epistles, 119; in the Apocalypse, 14 n, 119; in the Epistle of Polycarp, 116 sq; not alluded to in the Ignatian Epistles, 85; an appeal to the Canon requisite in the conflict with, 219

Gobarus, 12

Gospel of Peter, 37

Gospel according to the Hebrews; see *Hebrews, Gospel according to the*

Gospels; see *Matthew's (St) Gospel, Mark's (St) Gospel, Luke's (St) Gospel, Fourth Gospel, Four Gospels*

Grabe, 98 n

Griesbach, 68, 69

[Gwynn's (Prof.) discovery of a Gaius distinct from Hippolytus, 216 n]

Hadrian, 98

Hagenbach, 68

Harless, 69

Hase, 70

Hebrews, Gospel according to the; employed by Hegesippus, 47, 183; by other fathers, 152; perhaps quoted by Ignatius, 41 sq, 153; Papias not proved to have employed, 152, 203 sq; translated by Jerome, 203, 285; statements of Jerome about it, 42, 152; confused with the Hebrew original of St Matthew, 170, 285; with Tatian's *Diatessaron*, 284; distinct scope of the last-named work, 285

Hebrews, Epistle to the; in the notices of Eusebius, 37, 46, 47, 49, 52; the testimony of Clement of Rome, 40, 47, 49; of Irenæus, 46, 47; of Gaius, 47

Hefelé, 63

Hegesippus; his lost ecclesiastical history, 32, 39; the silence of Eusebius respecting, 34 sq, 183, 185; his attitude towards St Paul, 12; towards tradition, 155; employs the *Gospel according to the Hebrews*, 47, 183

'Hellenic' and 'Hellenistic,' 132 n

[Hemphill, 287, 288]

Henke, 68

Heracleon's commentary on the Fourth Gospel, 52

Hermas, the *Shepherd* of; its devotional character, 271; hence does not quote Scripture, 271; the citations in Eusebius, 37, 38, 47 sq; quoted by Irenæus, 45, 47, 184

Herodes, the magistrate, 220, 221

Heumann, 68

Hierapolis, 91, 102, 142, 153, 207, 218, 224

Hilgenfeld, 64, 71, 104, 116, 122, 146 n, 158 n, 159 n, 170, 171, 172, 176 n, 186, 211, 216, 262 n, 287 n

Hippolytus; pupil of Irenæus, 102, 145, 196 n, 267; probably at Rome, 267 n; opposes Gnosticism, 216 n, 219; defends the Fourth Gospel against the Alogi, 216 n; plagiarisms of, 202; plagiarisms from, 216 n; Gnostic fragments preserved in, 40, 161; his relation to Gaius considered, 91 n, 216 n

Hitzig, 24 sq
Hoffmann, 282 n
Hort, on the date of Justin Martyr, 274 n

Ignatian Epistles; date, place of writing and subject, 59, 93; three forms: (1) Long Recension, 60; documents, 60; date of the forgery, 60; (2) Vossian Epistles, 60 sq; MSS and Versions, 61; history of their discovery, 61; (3) Curetonian Epistles, 61; their discovery, 61; questions raised (A) whether the Vossian or Curetonian Epistles are prior, 61; the view of *S. R.*, 63, 74; the real balance of modern authorities, 63 sq; arguments against the priority of the Curetonian Epistles from (i) the Armenian Version, 60; a translation from the Syriac Version of the Curetonian Epistles, 71, 86; (ii) the abruptness of the Curetonian Epistles, 77 n, 86; the counter-argument from the confessedly spurious letters answered, 60, 71, 72 sq; the argument from quotations considered, 73 sq; (B) whether any form is genuine, 61; denied by *S. R.*, 62, 74; (i) internal evidence considered, (*a*) Ignatius' treatment as a prisoner, 74 sq; (*b*) the journey to Rome, 79 sq; (*c*) Ignatius' zeal for martyrdom, 82; (*d*) supposed anachronisms, 83; (*e*) evidence of style, 84; (ii) external evidence, 82; result, 84, 88; relation of the Vossian Epistles, 84 sq; argument from silence, 84 sq; limit of their date, 85; arguments for their genuineness, 86 sq; result, 88, [59 n]; scriptural quotations in the, 41; Eusebius' method tested on the, 41; theological controversies which have centred round, 61 sq; Christology of, 42, 86 sq, 108, 231; a metaphor of image-processions illustrated, 302

Ignatius; the name Theophorus, 302; his letters (see *Ignatian Epistles*); his journey to Rome, 59; its probability considered, 63, 79 sq, 111; his route, 93, 113; his treatment as a prisoner, 74 sq; his intercourse with Polycarp, 92 sq, 106 sq, 113; the notice in the Epistle of Polycarp, 11, 82, 113 sq; his zeal for martyrdom, 82; not martyred at Antioch, 79 sq, 212 n, 214; date of his martyrdom, 59; days of commemoration of, 79; extant martyrologies of, 73 n, 80

Irenæus; date of his birth, 98 n, 264; a pupil of Polycarp, date, 89, 97 sq; his letter to Florinus, 96 sq, 195 n; represents three Churches, 267; his connexion with the *Letter of the Gallican Churches*, 259; sent as delegate to Rome, 253, 259 n, 267; at Rome more than once, 267 n; his lectures there, 267; his pupil Hippolytus, 102, 145, 196 n, 267; date of his episcopate, 97; his remonstrance addressed to Victor, 100; his literary activity, 267; date of his *Refutation*, 259, 260; the first great controversial treatise, 271; its importance as evidence to the Canon, 271; his profuse scriptural quotations, 44 sq, 180, 184, 228, 261; Eusebius' method illustrated, 45, 46, 184; importance of his testimony to the Canon, 53, 89, 99, 166, 264 sq; appeals to the elders (see *Elders*); his evidence to the Fourth Gospel, 3 sq, 52, 53, 54 sq; to the motive of the Fourth Gospel, 48, 182; to four Gospels, 45, 48, 166, 233, 263 sq; to the Ignatian Epistles, 80, 82; to the Epistle of Polycarp, 82, 101, 104 sq; his appeal to the Gospels against the Valentinians, 219, 245 sq, 262; his controversial treatises, 267; his conflict with Gnosticism, 160, 219; on the Paschal question, 242, 244 sq, 267; on the duration of Christ's ministry, 246; on His age at the time of the Passion, 246 sq; on the Apocalypse, 45, 47, 216; on the old age of St John, 48, 92, 101; on Polycarp, 96 sq, 115, 116; on Papias, 4 sq, 127, 142 sq, 154, 158 sq, 166, 194 sq, 248 n; on the Hebrew original of St Matthew, 172; his Chiliasm, 151, 197; his evidence for episcopacy, 122; his use of the word 'oracles,' 174; his literary obligations to Papias, 202; to Melito, 236 sq; considered as a critic, 268 sq

Jacobson, 63, 66, 67 n, 69, 103 n, 123 n

Jerome; on the Hebrew original of St Matthew, 208 n, 285; on the *Gospel according to the Hebrews*, 42, 152, 208, 285; on the public reading of Polycarp's Epistle, 105 n; on Tatian's treatment of St Paul's Epistles, 273 n; on Apollinaris, 242, 243

Jerusalem, results to the Christian Church from the fall of, 90 sq, 217

John (St); at Ephesus, 91, 101, 142 sq; his church organisation, 218; the founder of a school, 217 sq; the repositary of Apostolic doctrine and practice, 218; his encounter with Cerinthus, 101, 212; his connexion with Polycarp, 89, 92; with Papias, 142 sq, 160, 193, 198, 210 sq; with his namesake John the Presbyter, 143 sq, 187; his longevity, 48, 89, 91, 92, 101, 217, 246; a story of his martyrdom explained, 211 sq; traditions respecting him, 48, 187, 189 sq, 210, 217; see also *Fourth Gospel*

John (St), the Epistles of; their position in the Canon of Eusebius, 39, 46 sq; two mentioned in the Muratorian Canon, 190; the First Epistle employed by Polycarp, 49 sq, 118, 191 sq, 220; by Papias, 49, 154, 186, 190 sq, 206, 220; by Irenæus, 45; a postscript to the Fourth Gospel, 186 sq, 190, 220; the evidence of Papias, and of the Muratorian Canon, to this fact, 189, 206

John Malalas; represents Ignatius as martyred at Antioch, 79 sq, 212 n, 214; his historical blunders, 80 sq, 214, 269, 285; on a visit of Antoninus Pius to Asia Minor, 98 n

John the Baptist; his designation in the Fourth Gospel, 18 sq, 124 sq; his father Zacharias, 146 n, 256 sq; the $\phi\omega\nu\dot{\eta}$, 232 n

John the Presbyter; in Asia Minor, 91; his connexion with Papias, 143 sq, 149, 150 n, 164, 165 sq, 266; with Pothinus, 266; with the Apostle St John, 143 sq, 187

Judith, date of the book of, 25 n

Julian, the Emperor, 270

Justa, the Syrophœnician, 129

Justin Martyr; his pupil Tatian, 272, 274; his accuser Crescens, 148, 272; his martyrdom, 148, 274; the account in Eusebius, 150; his evangelical quotations, 43; looseness of his quotations from the O. T., 12, 43; his lost writings, 33; Eusebius' method tested upon his extant works, 43; his Chiliasm, 151; his error as to Simon Magus, 268; his Logos doctrine compared with Melito, 235; his references to the Virgin Mary, 236; his evidence to the authorship of the Apocalypse, 43; to the public use of the Gospels, 227

Kestner, 68, 69

Lampe, 68

Lardner, 40, 41 n, 42 n, 68, 69, 94 n, 109 n, 241 n

Lechler, 70

Leimbach, 158 n, 264 n

Linus, 45

Lipsius, 64, 65, 71, 80 n, 81 n, 85, 103 n, 104, 116, 213 n

Logos; the expression common to the Apocalypse and Fourth Gospel, 15; as distinct from $\phi\omega\nu\dot{\eta}$, 232 n; the doctrine in the Ignatian Epistles, 86 sq; in Justin Martyr, 235; in Valentinus, 86; in Melito, 232, 234 sq; in Marcellus of Ancyra, 87;

INDEX OF SUBJECTS. 313

its importance a characteristic of the second century, 235

Lucian; illustrates the Ignatian Epistles, 76 sq; the Epistle of Polycarp, 77 n

Luke's (St) Gospel; the source of Marcion's Gospel, 8, 186; Papias acquainted with, 178 sq, 186; the evidence of the Muratorian Canon, 189; quoted in the *Letter of the Gallican Churches*, 255 sq; Renan on its authorship, 291

Luthardt, 14, 132

Λεόπαρδος, 67, 83

Λόγια, 155 n, 160, 163, 171, 172 sq

Magdeburg Centuriators, 65, 66.

Malalas; see *John Malalas*

Manes, 81

Mansel, 28

Marcellus of Ancyra, the Logos doctrine of, 87

Marcion; his date, 81, 116, 213 n; confused with Cerinthus, 210, 212; his Gospel, 6 n, 8, 186; his Canon, 117, 227, 263, 273; Papias' acquaintance with it, 186; his attitude towards St Paul, 273; his high moral character, 119; his distinctive views, 117 sq; not alluded to in the Ignatian Epistles, 85; nor in Polycarp's Epistle, 101, 115, 212; a supposed allusion considered, 106, 115 sq; opposed by Justin Martyr, 33; by Melito, 231; scene of his heresy, 219, 227, 231; the question of the Canon raised by it, 219, 225; his views on the resurrection and judgment, 120

Maries, the four, in Papias the lexicographer, 210 sq

Mark's (St) Gospel; the account and criticism of Papias, 8, 10, 19, 162 sq, 175 sq, 181, 205 sq; the motive of Papias' allusion, 207; compared by Papias with the Fourth Gospel, 165, 205 sq; identification of Papias' St Mark, 2, 10, 20, 46, 163 sq; evidence of the Muratorian Canon to, 189, 205 sq

Marseilles, 252

Martyrdom of Polycarp; see *Polycarp, Martyrdom of*

Massuet, 98 n

Matthew (St), and Papias, 143, 193

Matthew's (St) Gospel; the account in Papias, 163, 167 sq, 181; his testimony to the Hebrew original, 168, 172; its character, 170 sq; a Greek St Matthew in existence in his day, 168 sq; identical with the extant Gospel, 169 sq; relation of the Hebrew to the Greek Gospel, 170; confused with the *Gospel according to the Hebrews*, by Jerome, 285; perhaps by Papias, 170; motive of Papias' allusion, 208; quoted in the Epistle of Barnabas as 'Scripture,' 227

Meletius, confused with Melito, 231

Melito; his date, 223, 224; a contemporary of Polycarp and Papias, 224; perhaps one of the elders quoted in Irenæus, 196 n, 224; perhaps a teacher of Clement of Alexandria, 218, 224; his travels, 224, 226; his learning, 228; his orthodoxy, 230; range of his literary works, 32, 102, 224; their popularity, 102, 224, 230; his lost works, 223, 225, 229; his *Apology*, 223, 241 n; the preface to his *Selections*, 226; (1) the extant Greek fragments, their genuineness 228 sq; supported by the evidence of Tertullian and Hippolytus to his style, 229 sq, 234; not the work of Meletius, 231; their direct evidence to the Gospels, 231; (2) the Syriac fragments, 232 sq; their theology, 234 sq; his doctrine of the Logos, 234; his references to the Virgin Mary, 235 sq; passages from his works incorporated into Irenæus, 236 sq; Armenian version of a fragment and its Syriac abridgment, 236 sq; a quotation in *Chronicon Paschale*, 241 n; his work on the Paschal controversy, 223, 225, 241 n, 242 sq; evidence to the Fourth

Gospel therefrom, 248; notice of the Apocalypse in, 47, 216; coincidences with St Paul's Epistles, 237; his treatise against Marcion, 231; date and manner of his death, 224

Merx, 64, 71

Mill (J. S.), 28 sq, 204

Milman, 65

Ministry, the duration of our Lord's, 16 sq, 48, 131, 245 sq

Miracles, 26 sq

[Moesinger, 288]

Montanism; its centre in Asia Minor, 219; correspondence between the Churches of Asia and Gaul relating to, 253; Irenæus' mission to Rome respecting, 253, 259 n; not referred to in the Ignatian Epistles, 85; nor in the Epistle of Polycarp, 106; opposed by Apollinaris, 238; by Irenæus, 267; the question of the Canon involved in the controversy with, 219, 238, 267

Morality and dogma, 27 sq

Mosheim, 68

Mozley, 28

Muratori, 295 n

Muratorian Canon; date, 188; original language, 188 n; English translation, 189 sq; emendations in the text, 189 n; represents the Church of Rome, 53, 270; its evidence to St Mark's Gospel, 189, 205 sq; to St Luke's Gospel, 189, 206; to the Fourth Gospel, 52 sq, 91, 189 sq, 206, 216; to four Gospels, 164, 188 sq, 205 sq, 270; its testimony compared with that of Papias, 205 sq; perhaps borrowed from him, 207; Matthew Arnold's estimate of, 190 n

Naassenes, 161 n

Nature; two meanings of the term, 29 sq; its relation to a Personal God, 28 sq

Neander, 68, 69, 120 n, 141, 242

Neocoros, 300

Neubauer, 17 n, 133, 135, 136

Nicolaitans, 48, 182

Niebuhr, 25

Nolte, 211 n

Œcumenius, 201

Onesimus, the friend of Melito, 226

Ophites, 52, 161, 202, 219

Origen; on Celsus, 7; on the authorship of the Fourth Gospel, 216; of the Apocalypse, 216; uses the *Gospel according to the Hebrews*, 152 n; quotes the Ignatian Epistles, 80, 82; his accuracy in textual criticism, 269; his use of the word 'oracles', 174

Otto, 223 n, 228 n, 229, 238 n, 241 n

Oudin, 67

Overbeck, 210, 213 n, 293 n

Owen, 67

οὐκ οἶδ' ὅπως, 277 sq

Pamphilus, 225

Pantænus, 145 n, 172, 274

Papias; his date, 142, 147 sq; his name and namesakes, 153, 211; of heathen origin, 153; a companion of Polycarp, 142, 150, 153, 218; perhaps not a hearer of St John, 142, 143 sq, 146, 193, 198, 210 sq; his *Expositions*, 32, 39, 142; its title, 155 n, 156, 171 sq, 175 sq; its date, 150; its nature, 11, 155; directed against Gnostic exegesis, 160 sq, 175, 202; as affecting his attitude towards the written Gospels, 156, 159 n, 160; the extant Gospels the text for his exegesis, 163 sq; his method illustrated, 143, 158 sq, 194, 197; his informants the 'elders', 4 sq, 143, 145, 159, 163, 168, 181, 197 sq; especially Aristion and John the Presbyter, 143 sq, 149, 150 n, 164 sq, 266; his Chiliasm, 151 sq, 158 sq, 160, 197 sq, 215 n; not an Ebionite, 151 sq; his attitude towards St Paul, 151 sq; his use of the *Gospel according to the Hebrews* considered, 152, 203 sq; his orthodoxy, 154; story of his martyrdom explained,

INDEX OF SUBJECTS. 315

147 sq, 211 sq; his mention of St Matthew's Gospel, 163, 167 sq, 181, 208; character of the original Hebrew, 170 sq, 207 sq; the Greek extant in his time, 168, 208; his mention of St Mark's Gospel, 8, 10, 19, 162 sq, 175 sq, 181, 205 sq; his acquaintance with St Luke's Gospel, 178 sq, 186; with the Fourth Gospel, 4 sq, 35, 54 sq, 178 sq; evidenced by his acquaintance with 1 John, 186 sq, 190 sq; by other indications, 192 sq, 203 sq; Eusebius' method illustrated upon, 34 sq, 151, 178 sq; his testimony to the Apocalypse, 34 n, 214; his testimony to the Canon supported by that of the Muratorian fragment, 205 sq; which perhaps borrowed from him, 207; obligations of Irenæus to, 202; of Eusebius, 208; not the amanuensis of the Fourth Gospel, 210 sq, 213 sq; nor author of exoteric books, 210 sq; confusion of the name, 148 sq, 211; quotations in Irenæus, 4 sq, 127, 194, 248 n; the pericope adulterae and other interpolations in the Gospels perhaps from his work, 203 sq; his position as an authority, 10, 218; his credulity considered, 269

Papias, the lexicographer, 211

Papylus, confused with Papias, 148 sq

Paraclete; the Montanist doctrine of the, 219, 267; in the *Letter of the Gallican Churches*, 255, 258

Parker, 66, 67

Paschal Chronicle; confuses Papias and Papylus, 148 sq; preserves quotations from Apollinaris, 238, 239 sq; from Melito, 241 n; sources of its information, 148 n, 260 n; on the date of Theodotion's version of the LXX, 260 n

Paschal controversy; silence of the Ignatian Epistles upon, 85; of the Epistle of Polycarp, 106; Asia Minor the scene of, 219; Polycarp's visit to Rome respecting, 99 sq, 121; the account in Eusebius, 17, 245; the treatise of Melito on, 223, 225, 241 n, 242 sq; of Apollinaris, 238 sq; of Clement of Alexandria, 243 sq; of Pierius of Alexandria, 241 n; of Irenæus, 242, 244 sq, 267; action of the Gallican Churches with respect to, 253 sq; the attitude of Victor upon, 100, 244, 245, 248, 253 sq; remonstrance of Irenæus, 100; of Polycrates, 248; the error of *S. R.* regarding its character, 17, 240 sq, 245; its relation to the Canon, 17, 219, 225, 239 sq, 267

Paul (St); in Cyprus, 294 sq; at Ephesus, 299 sq; his attack on Gnosticism, 119 sq; his treatment as a prisoner, 75, 78; his claim to work miracles, 125; his directions as to idol-sacrifices, 14; his connexion with Gaul, 251; not aimed at in the Apocalypse, 13 sq; attitude of Clement of Rome towards, 40; of the Ignatian Epistles, 41, 42; of Polycarp, 42 sq, 95 sq, 101 sq; of Hegesippus, 12; of Papias, 151 sq; of Marcion, 117, 219, 225, 273; of the elders in Irenæus, 248; of Melito, 237; of Tatian, 273; of the School of St John generally, 251; of the Churches in Gaul, 255; position of his writings in the Canon of Eusebius, 37, 38, 46 sq; see also *Tübingen School*

Paul, Acts of, 37

Pearson, in the Ignatian controversy, 83, 86

Pella, 90, 91

Peregrinus Proteus, 76 sq

Pergamum, 147, 148

Pericope Adulterae, an insertion from Papias, 203 sq

Perpetua, 76, 83

Petau, 66, 67

Peter, Acts of, 37

Peter, Apocalypse of, 37, 47

Peter, Gospel of, 37

Peter, Preaching of, 37

Peter (St), the Epistles of; their position in the Canon of Eusebius, 36 sq, 46; Eusebius' method tested on, 43, 45, 47, 49; the First Epistle largely quoted by Polycarp, 43, 49 sq, 95, 109, 191 sq; employed by Papias, 186, 206 sq; by Irenæus, 45

Peter of Alexandria, 241 n

Petermann, 63, 71, 86 sq

Philip (St), the Apostle; at Hierapolis, 91, 143, 149; his daughters, 91, 149, 153; his intercourse with Papias, 143, 146, 149, 193; his identity, 91 n

Philip, the Asiarch, 222 n

Philippi, the Church at; Ignatius' visit to, 93, 106; Polycarp's correspondence with, 93 sq, 101, 106 sq, 121 (see *Polycarp, Epistle of*); episcopacy at, 106, 108

Philippians, German theories as to the Pauline Epistle to the, 24 sq

Phillips, 279 n

Philo, 173 sq, 200 n

Photius, 196 n, 238, 239, 241 n, 242, 243, 267 n

Pierius of Alexandria, 241 n

Pliny; his credulity and that of the early fathers, 269; his informant Sergius Paulus, 294 sq

Polycarp of Smyrna; date of his birth, 90; born at a crisis, 90 sq; of Christian parents, 94; reared in the centre of Christianity, 91 sq; under the influence of St John, 89, 92; bishop of Smyrna, 92; entertains Ignatius, 92, 113; his age at this time, 121; his letter to the Philippians (see *Polycarp, Epistle of*); a companion of Papias, 142, 150, 153, 218; his old age, 96; his pupils Florinus and Irenæus, 96 sq, 264, 265; his journey to Rome, 99 sq, 121; preaches at Rome, 101; his encounter with Marcion, 101, 115, 212; his attitude in the Paschal controversy, 99 sq; date of his martyrdom, 90, 97, 103 sq, 147, 264; details of it, 77 n, 103, 220 sq; document preserving it (see *Polycarp, Martyrdom of*); his position and that of Clement of Rome, 89, 94; the depositary of Apostolic tradition, 89 sq, 96; the link with Irenæus, 89, 100 sq; the reverence inspired by, 121 n; characteristic expressions of, 97, 115 sq; his use of the word 'oracles', 174

Polycarp, Epistle of; date and circumstances of writing, 93 sq, 101, 106 sq, 121; incomplete in the Greek, 11; its genuineness, 104 sq; (1) external evidence for, 104; (2) internal evidence, 105 sq; from (i) its formula of evangelical quotations, 105, 109; (ii) its picture of Church order, 106, 107 sq, 122; (iii) its Christology, 106, 108; (iv) the argument from silence, 106; (v) its style and subject-matter compared with the Ignatian Epistles, 106 sq; Ritschl's theory of interpretations considered, 110 sq; further objections dealt with, (a) the martyr journey of Ignatius, 111; (b) alleged anachronisms, 11, 111 sq, 122; (c) the Ignatian Epistles appended, 113 sq; (d) the thirteenth chapter, 114; (e) a supposed reference to Marcion, 115 sq; (f) the age of the writer, 121; scriptural quotations in, 42 sq, 49 sq, 93 sq, 109, 118, 227; Eusebius' method tested on, 42 sq, 49; the quotations from 1 Peter, 43, 49 sq, 95, 109, 191 sq; coincidence with 1 John, 49; relation to the Pauline Epistles, 95 sq, 101 sq; its testimony to the Ignatian Epistles, 11, 82, 113 sq

Polycarp, Martyrdom of; the document, 103, 220; its date, 220; emphasizes the coincidences with the Passion, 220 sq; its evidence to the Fourth Gospel, 221 sq; employed by the *Paschal Chronicle*, 148 n

Polycrates of Ephesus; his place in the School of St John, 218; his work on the Paschal controversy, 244, 248 sq; scriptural quotations in his letter to Victor, 248, 249; quotes

INDEX OF SUBJECTS. 317

the Fourth Gospel, 249; his reference to Melito, 224
Pontius Pilate, date of the termination of the procuratorship of, 131 n
Pothinus; probably a native of Asia Minor, 253, 265; date of his martyrdom, 253, 265; perhaps one of the elders of Irenæus, 196 n, 266
Presbyter John; see *John the Presbyter*
Presbyters in Irenæus; see *Elders*
Proclus, Cominius, proconsul of Cyprus, 294 n
Proconsuls; the title in imperial times, 292 sq; the Greek equivalent, 292; of Cyprus, 294
Proprætors; the title in imperial times, 292; the Greek equivalent, 292
Protevangelium, 15, 256 sq

Quadratus, proconsul of Cyprus, 294 n
Quadratus, Statius, the Asiatic proconsulship of, 103 sq
Quartodeciman; see *Paschal controversy*

Renan, 104, 232 n, 291
Rhodon, 272, 273 n, 274
Ritschl, 63, 65, 110 sq
Rivetus, 66, 67
Roman Church, its influence in the time of Ignatius, 59
Roman prisoners, treatment of, 75 sq
Roman provinces; Augustus' division of, 291 sq; the titles of their governors, 292; interchange of imperial and senatorial provinces, 292; Asia and Africa the most sought after, 293
Rosenmüller, 68
Routh, 154 n, 201 n, 214 n, 241 n, 252 n
Rufinus, 203
Rufus, 111
Ruinart, 76 n, 80

Sachau, 232 n
Salutaris, C. Vibius, 302
Sanday; on the Fourth Gospel, 15; on Marcion's Gospel, 186 n
Saturus, 76

Saumaise, 66
Schleiermacher, 171
Schliemann, 70
Schmidt, 68
Scholten, 64, 119, 242, 262 n
Schroeckh, 68, 69
Schwegler, 24
Second century; its voluminous ecclesiastical literature, 32, 102; meagre literary remains of the first three quarters, 33, 53, 89, 102; small bearing on the Canon of the extant works, 33, 271; importance of Irenæus at the close of the century, 53, 89
Semler, 68
Serapion, 238
Sergius Paulus, proconsul of Cyprus; perhaps an informant of Pliny, 294 sq; Cyprian inscription mentioning him, 294, 297
Sergius Paulus, L.; the friend of Galen, 296; proconsul of Asia, 223, 296; his date, 223; his cursus honorum, 296; his resemblance in character to his namesake in the Acts, 296; his scientific studies, 297; identification of an unknown, 295 n
Severians, Apollinaris' treatise against the, 238, 243
Severus of Antioch, 87
Shechem and Sychar, 17, 133 sq
Silence, its place in the Gnostic Systems, 86 sq
Siloam, 18, 203
Simon Magus, 268
Simonians, 86, 161
Smyrnæans, *Letter of the*; see *Polycarp, Martyrdom of*
Socinus, 66, 67
Socrates, the historian, 239
Stephanus Gobarus, 12
Strabo, 292, 293 n
Supernatural Religion; criticisms on his grammar and scholarship, 3 sq, 53 sq, 126 sq; on his impartiality, 9 sq, 20 sq, 130 sq, 140 sq, 191 sq; on the plan of his book, 26, 138 sq;

his charges against opponents, 20 sq,
137 sq; his lists of references, 23,
65 sq; his theological position,
139 n; on the silence of Eusebius,
33 sq; on the Paschal controversy,
17, 240 sq, 245; clerical and other
errors, and ambiguities in, 124 sq,
182 sq, 257

Supernatural, meaning of the term,
29 sq

Sychar, identification of, 17 sq, 133
sq

Synoptists; their points of contrast
with the Fourth Gospel, 15 sq; recognized by the early fathers, 207
sq, 239; their chronology compared,
16, 48, 131, 239 sq, 245 sq; see also
Fourth Gospel

Tacitus, 25, 268 n

Tatian; an Assyrian, 272; a heathen
sophist, 272; his travels, 272; his
conversion, 272; a pupil of Justin
Martyr, 272, 274; his disciples at
Rome, 272, 274; removes to the
East, 272; his subsequent heretical
opinions, 272; his attitude towards
St Paul and the Pauline Epistles,
273, 284; his views anti-Judaic, 273;
date of his literary activity, 274;
his extant *Apology*, 274; its date,
275; quotes from the Fourth Gospel,
50, 275; his formula of quotation,
276; his *Diatessaron*, 277 sq; its
description in Eusebius, 277; who
knew but disparaged it, 278; the
evidence of the *Doctrine of Addai*,
278 sq; the commentary of Ephraem
Syrus, 280, 283; [discovery of an
Armenian Version, 288;] Bar-Salibi's
statements, 280 sq; Theodoret's
testimony to its circulation, 282 sq,
summary of evidence, 283 sq; coun-
ter-statement of Epiphanius, 284 sq;
of Victor of Capua, 285 sq; read in
the Churches of Edessa, 278 sq;
of Cyrrhestice, 282 sq; its opening
words, 280, 281 n, 283; its plan,
280 sq; other than that of Ammonius' *Diatessaron*, 280 sq, 283;
confusion of the two works, 281 n;
Aphraates' knowledge of it, 283 n,
[288]; the range of its circulation,
284; confused with the *Gospel according to the Hebrews*, 284 sq;
[recent discovery of an Arabic Version, 288]

Tertullian; gives evidence to the Fourth
Gospel, 52; his *Apologeticum*, 275;
on the episcopate of Polycarp, 92 n;
on the style of Melito, 229; Chiliasm
of, 151

Theodoret; date of his episcopate, 282;
his treatise on Heresies, 282; his
evidence for the Ignatian Epistles,
72; for Tatian's *Diatessaron*, 282 sq;
for Apollinaris, 238, 239, 242 sq

Theodotion's Version of the LXX, 260

Theophilus of Antioch; his works,
extant and lost, 44; quotes the
Fourth Gospel, 44, 52, 179, 215, 216;
Eusebius' method tested on his *Autolycus*, 44, 52, 215; his testimony
to the Apocalypse, 44, 47, 216; his
investigations in comparative chronology, 269

Thiersch, 68

Thomas (St), 143, 193

Thomasius, 210 n

Tillemont, 241 n, 253 n

Tischendorf; defended against *S. R.*'s
charges, 5 sq, 54 sq, 125 n, 127 n,
128 n, 138; other references to, 4,
129, 165, 167, 210

Tübingen School, criticised, 12, 24, 42,
64, 82, 89 sq, 95 sq, 101 sq, 110 sq,
151 sq, 251

Uhlhorn, 63, 71
Ussher, 60, 61

Valens, the Presbyter, 108
Valentinianism; its expressions antici-
pated in the Ignatian Epistles, 85,
86 sq; opposed by Irenæus, 98, 101,
219, 245 sq, 262; by Hippolytus,
161; its appeal to the Canon, 219,
262, 268; to the Fourth Gospel, 52;

INDEX OF SUBJECTS. 319

to uncanonical books, 263; its bearing on the chronology of our Lord's Life, 245 sq; its exegesis, 161

Vettius Epagathus, 255, 256

Victor of Capua; his date, 286; discovers an anonymous Harmony of the Gospel, 286; Frankish translation of this Harmony, 286 n; assigns it to Tatian, 286; [perhaps rightly, 288;] the word *Diapente* in his notice of Tatian, 279 n, 285 sq

Victor of .Rome; his date, 261; his attitude in the Paschal controversy, 100, 244, 245, 248, 253 sq

Vienne and Lyons, Churches of; see *Gallican Churches*

Virgin Mary, character of the allusions in Justin Martyr and Melito to the, 235 sq

Volkmar, 24 sq, 64, 71, 79 sq

Voss, 61

Vossian Epistles; see *Ignatian Epistles*

Waddington, 98 n, 103 sq, 115, 121, 223, 295 n, 296 n

Weiffenbach, 146 n, 158 n

Weismann, 68, 69

Weiss, 63, 65, 71

Westcott; defended against the attacks of *S.R.*, 4 sq, 12 sq, 21 sq, 53 sq, 123 sq, 128 n, 137 sq; other references to, 93, 130, 155, 161 n, 211 n, 226 sq, 275 n; his reply to *S.R.*, 79 n

Whiston, 69

Wisdom of Solomon, 46

Wood's discoveries at Ephesus, 294 n, 297 sq

Wordsworth, Bishop Charles, 222 n

Wright, 282 n

Zacharias, 146 n, 255 sq, 262 n

Zahn, 63, 71, 75 n, 77 n, 79 n, 81 n, 115 n, 213 n, 279 n, 283 n, [287]

Zeller, 64

Ziegler, 68, 264 n

Zosimus, 111

Zunz, 153 n

INDEX OF PASSAGES.

		PAGE			PAGE
Genesis	iv. 15	174	St Luke	i. 1	286
Exodus	xxxii. 7 sq	174		i. 3	189
Deuteronomy	ix. 12 sq	174		i. 5 sq	146
	x. 9	173		i. 6	255
	xxxi. 7, 23	221		i. 67	255
1 Kings	iv. 33	25		ii. 24	276
Psalms	iv. 4	94		iii. 23	231
Isaiah	xi. 6 sq	198		x. 18	186, 200, 201
	lxv. 25 sq	198		xi. 51	257
	lxvi. 22	55, 198		xiii. 30	125
Ezekiel	xxviii. 13	200		xiii. 32, 33	16
	xxviii. 15, 16	201		xiii. 34	16, 131
Hosea	ii. 6–17	241		xiv. 13, 14	158
Tobit	iv. 10	94		xviii. 30	158
	xii. 9	94		xxi. 38	204
St Matthew	v. 44	123		xxii. 52	221
	x. 16	41		xxiii. 43	201
	xi. 27 sq	16	St John	i. 1	44, 232, 280, 281, 283, 286
	xii. 33	41			
	xiii. 8	4		i. 3	276
	xix. 12	41		i. 5	275
	xix. 29	158		i. 18	52
	xix. 30	125		i. 44	91
	xx. 16	125		iii. 8	41
	xxiii. 35	256		iv. 5	17, 133
	xxiii. 37	16, 131		iv. 18	52
	xxvi. 29	158, 205		iv. 24	275
	xxvi. 42	221		iv. 35	136
	xxvi. 55	221		v. 3, 4	9, 52, 126
	xxviii. 1	208		v. 29	223
St Mark	x. 29, 30	158		vii. 36	204
	x. 31	125		vii. 37 sq	203
	xiv. 48	221		vii. 52	204

INDEX OF PASSAGES.

		PAGE			PAGE
St John	vii. 53—viii. 11	203	1 Corinthians xv. 12		120
	viii. 15	204, 205	2 Corinthians xii. 12		125
	viii. 12 sq	204	Galatians	ii. 9	14
	viii. 29	41		iv. 21 sq	173
	viii. 44	13	Ephesians	iv. 26	95
	viii. 56	248		v. 21	109
	viii. 57	246, 247		vi. 14	50
	ix. 7	18		vi. 18	123
	xii. 21 sq	91	Philippians	ii. 6	254
	xii. 28	222		ii. 7	237
	xii. 33	222		iii. 18	123
	xiii. 25	249		iv. 2	24
	xiv. 2	4, 54, 194, 247	1 Timothy	ii. 2	123
	xvi. 2	258		iii. 15	254
	xvii. 3	223		iv. 3	273
	xviii. 31, 32	222		iv. 3, 4	255
	xix. 28, 30	222		v. 1, 2, 17, 19	146
	xix. 34 sq	222		vi. 7	123
	xix. 35	187		vi. 10	122
	xx. 1	208	2 Timothy	ii. 18	120
	xx. 25	257		iv. 10	251
	xx. 31	187	Hebrews	v. 12	173
	xxi. 20	249		xi. 2	145
Acts	ii. 16	276	1 Peter	i. 1	92
	ii. 24	95		i. 8	50
	v. 29	249		i. 13	50
	vii. 60	257		i. 21	50
	xiii. 7	292, 294, 295		ii. 11, 12	50
	xiii. 40	276		ii. 17	50, 122
	xix. 24 sq	297		ii. 22, 24	50
	xix. 31	299		iii. 9	50
	xix. 35	299, 300		iv. 7	49, 191
	xix. 37, 38	299, 301		iv. 14	50
	xxi. 9	149		v. 5	50, 109
	xxi. 14	221		v. 13	207
Romans	i. 5	237	1 John	i. 1	97, 190
	iii. 2	173		iv. 2, 3	118
	iv. 1 sq	173	Revelation	i. 4	133
	iv. 18	276		ii. 2	14
	viii. 18	254		ii. 6, 14, 15, 20, 24	119
	xv. 19	125		ii. 14	13
	xvi. 26	237		xii. 9	201
1 Corinthians	vi. 12—18	119		xix. 13	15
	vii. 5	273			
	viii. 1 sq	119			
	x. 1 sq	173	Anastasius of Sinai		154, 200, 201, 202, 225, 230
	x. 7, 8, 14, 21	14			
	xi. 8 sq	173	Andreas of Cæsarea		214

	PAGE		PAGE
Aphraates		*Hist. Eccl.* iii. 37	40
Hom. i. p. 13 (ed. Wright)	283	iii. 39	91, 143, 150
Apost. Constit. ii. 24	203		152, 157, 193,
Aristides Op. I. p. 453 (ed. Dind.)	98		209
Barnabæ Ep. 4, 5	177	iv. 14	43, 49, 150, 191
15	151	iv. 15	77, 90, 121,
Basil (St) *Hom.* xi. 5	175		148, 150, 220 sq
Hom. xii. 1	175	iv. 16	273
Capitol. *Vit. Anton.* 7	98	iv. 18	43
Chronicon Pasch. p. 13 (ed. Dind.)	238	iv. 21	239
p. 481	148	iv. 22	152, 183
Claudius Apollinaris	207	iv. 23	156, 177, 228
Clemens Alexandrinus		iv. 24	44
Coh. ad Gent. p. 84 (ed. Potter)	174	iv. 26	32, 47, 223, 225, 243, 296
Exc. Theod. 38	273	iv. 27	32, 238
Strom. i. 1	218, 274	iv. 28	273
Strom. i. p. 392	174	iv. 29	273, 277
Strom. ii. 9	152	v. 1	146, 252
Strom. iii. 12	270	v. 3, 4	253, 259
Strom. iii. 13	152, 270	v. 6	45
Strom. iv. 12	161	v. 8	45, 145, 156
Strom. vii. p. 889	257	v. 13	273
Strom. vii. 17	21, 161, 213	v. 15	98
Quis Div. Salv. 42	91, 218	v. 18	47, 91
Clem. Rom. 5	40	v. 19	238
25	268	v. 20	97, 98, 116, 218, 265
45	174		
47	40	v. 24	91, 100, 224, 244, 248, 254
53	174		
Dion Cassius liii. 12	293	v. 26	46
liv. 4	294	v. 28	102, 230
Euripides *Iph. Taur.* l. 1359	301	vi. 13	47, 145, 244
Epiphanius		vi. 14	47, 145
De Pond. et Mens. 16, 17	260	vi. 20	47
Hær. xlvi. 1	273, 284	vii. 25	216
Hær. li. 1 sq	215	*Quæst. ad Marin.* 2, iv.	208
Eusebius		*Quæst. ad Steph.* 1	73
Chron. (Syr. epit.) p. 216 (ed. Schöne)	149	Op. IV. p. 1276 (ed. Migne)	281
		Galen *de Anat. Admin.* i. 1	296
Eccl. Theol. ii. 9	87	*de Prænot.* 2	296
Hist. Eccl. i. 13	279	Op. XIX. p. 11 (ed. Kühn)	196
iii. 3	37, 145	Hippolytus	
iii. 23	48, 168, 209	*Ref. Hær.* v. 7	161
iii. 24	39	*Ref. Hær.* vi. 42, 55	145, 202
iii. 25, 27	152	Ignatius *Ephes.* 1	42
iii. 30, 31	91	*Ephes.* 7	42
iii. 36	41, 43, 152	*Ephes.* 9	302

INDEX OF PASSAGES.

	PAGE
Ignatius *Ephes.* 12	41, 42
Ephes. 14	41
Ephes. 19	73
Magn. 8	41, 42, 86
Magn. 11	118
Magn. 13	109
Trall. 6	161
Trall. 9	118
Rom. inscr.	161
Rom. 2	232
Rom. 4	41, 42, 114
Rom. 5	73, 74, 78
Rom. 6	42, 85
Rom. 7	85
Philad. 3	161
Philad. 6	42
Philad. 7	41
Smyrn. 1	118
Smyrn. 6	41
Polyc. 1–4	93
Polyc. 2	41
Polyc. 3	42, 93
Polyc. 7	77, 93
Irenæus	
Hær. pref. i.	160
i. 3. 6	160
i. 8. 1	174
i. 26. 1	118
i. 27. 2	117
i. 27. 3	117, 120
i. 28. 1	273, 274
ii. 22. 5	48, 91, 92, 131, 168, 209, 217, 218, 245, 264
ii. 31. 2	120
iii. 1. 1	48, 182
iii. 3. 3	260
iii. 3. 4	92, 101, 115, 217, 218, 264
iii. 11. 1	48, 182
iii. 11. 9	215
iii. 12. 12	117
iii. 16. 8	118
iii. 21. 1	260
iii. 25. 2	120
iii. 25. 3	120
iv. 26. 2	218
iv. 27. 1 sq	145, 196, 248, 266

	PAGE
Hær. iv. 30. 1	145, 196
iv. 31. 1	145, 196, 248
iv. 32. 1	196
v. 5. 1	145, 198, 218
v. 20. 2	177
v. 30. 1	218
v. 31. 1 sq	151
v. 33. 1	158
v. 33. 3	145, 218
v. 33. 4	142
v. 36. 1, 2	3, 54, 126, 145, 194, 199
Jerome	
de Vir. Illust. 16	42
de Vir. Illust. 17	105
de Vir. Illust. 24	229
de Vir. Illust. 26	243
Ep. ad Magnum (p. 83)	243
Ep. 70 (I. p. 428)	239
Ep. 120 *ad Hedib.* (I. p. 826)	208
præf. ad Tit. vii.	273
John Malalas p. 276 (ed. Bonn.)	79
p. 280	98
Justin Martyr *Apol.* i. 26	268
Apol. i. 66, 67	43, 227
Dial. 34	235
Dial. 51 sq	151
Dial. 61	235
Dial. 80 sq	151
Dial. 100	235, 236
Lucian *de Morte Peregr.* 12	76
de Morte Peregr. 41	77
Martyr. Polyc. 1	220
5	222
6, 7, 8	221
9	90, 221
12	222
13	121
14	223
15	222
16	77, 222, 223
Origen *c. Cels.* pref. etc.	278
c. Cels. i. 8	7
c. Cels. viii. 76	7
de Princ. iv. 11	175
in Matth. x. 6	175
in Matth. xvi. 6	212
in Luc. Hom. i.	152

	PAGE		PAGE
Philo *de Conj. Erud. Grat.* 24	174	Socrates *Hist. Eccl.* III. 7	239
de Profug. 11	174	VII. 32	118
Vit. Moys. iii. 23	174	Tacitus *Hist.* v. 1 sq	268
Photius *Bibl.* 14	238, 239	Tatian *Orat. ad Græc.* 4, 13	275
Bibl. 119	241	*Orat. ad Græc.* 19	273, 276
Bibl. 121	196, 267	*Orat. ad Græc.* 29, 35, 42	273
Pliny *Nat. Hist.* ii. 90, 97, 112	295	Tertullian *adv. Marc.* iii. 24	151
Nat. Hist. xviii. 12, 57	295	*adv. Marc.* iv. 2	8
Polycarp *Phil.* 1	50, 95	*adv. Marc.* v. 10	120
Phil. 2	50	*de Præscr. Hær.* 32	92
Phil. 3	93, 96, 112, 114	*de Præscr. Hær.* 33	120
Phil. 4	122	*de Resurr. Carn.* 19	120
Phil. 5	50, 108	*de Resurr. Carn.* 24	151
Phil. 7	49, 93, 115, 116, 174, 191	Theodoret *Hær. Fab.* i. 20	273, 282
		Hær. Fab. i. 21	238, 243
Phil. 8	50	*Hær. Fab.* iii. 2	239, 243
Phil. 9	111, 112	*Ep.* 113	283
Phil. 10	50, 94	Theophilus *ad Autol.* ii. 22	44
Phil. 12	95, 112, 122	Victor Cap. *Præf. ad Anon. Harm.*	
Phil. 13	11, 93, 111, 114	*Evang.*	286
Protevangelium 11, 12	257	Xenophon *Anab.* v. 3, 6	300
23	256		

www.ingramcontent.com/pod-product-compliance
Lightning Source LLC
Chambersburg PA
CBHW021206230426
43667CB00006B/574